How to Read
the Financial Pages

Michael Brett

Fifth Edition

RANDOM HOUSE
BUSINESS BOOKS

RANDOM HOUSE

BUSINESS BOOKS

Copyright © Michael Brett 1987, 1989, 1991, 1995, 2000

Michael Brett has asserted his right under the Copyright, Designs and
Patents Act, 1988, to be identified as the author of his work

Published by Random House Business Books
Random House, 20 Vauxhall Bridge Road, London SW1V 2SA

Random House Australia (Pty) Limited
20 Alfred Street, Milsons Point, Sydney
New South Wales 2061, Australia

Random House New Zealand Limited
18 Poland Road, Glenfield
Auckland 10, New Zealand

Random House South Africa (Pty) Limited
PO Box 337, Bergvlei, South Africa
Random House UK Limited Reg. No. 954009

A CIP catalogue record for this book
is available from the British Library

Papers used by Random House UK Limited are natural, recyclable
products made from wood grown in sustainable forests.
The manufacturing processes conform to the environmental
regulations of the country of origin.

ISBN 0 7126 8077 2

Typeset in Times by Hart McLeod, Cambridge
Printed and bound in Great Britain by
Creative Print and Design (Wales)

Cartoon page 380: Nick Newman

Contents

Acknowledgements

This book could not have been written without a great deal of help and advice from City institutions as well as from colleagues in the financial press. A full list of those who have assisted would be impossibly long, but I would like to thank first the *Financial Times*, *The Independent* and the *Investors Chronicle* for permission to reproduce material from their respective publications and Datastream International for the use of its charts.

Detailed comments and advice on the text from John Plender and Danny O'Shea were invaluable and I am also very grateful to Liisa Springham for casting a fresh eye over the typescript. I had the benefit of information and advice on individual sections from, among others, Adrienne Gleeson, Andrew Goodrick-Clarke, Helen Fearnley and Peter Wilson-Smith and considerable help from Prudential Assurance, The Takeover Panel and the press offices of The London Stock Exchange and the Securities and Investments Board. I am also grateful to Hugh Partridge and Brian Roy for technical help with the second and third editions. Many of those already named helped again with the fourth edition and I also very much appreciate Susan Bevan's helpful comments.

For the fifth edition I would again like to thank many of those mentioned above, and particularly acknowledge the help given by Capital DATA Bondware and Capital DATA Loanware with the euromarkets chapter. And I am very grateful to Antonia Oprita for reading the print-out and picking up my more careless errors and omissions. The views expressed – and the mistakes that remain – are my own.

Preface

Money is not complicated. The principles behind financial transactions are simple enough. It is usually the detail that confuses by obscuring the principles.

The money world, like many others, develops its own practices and jargon, which are usually incomprehensible to the layman. Even an intelligent watcher of the financial scene is at a disadvantage. Sometimes the financial world likes to keep it that way, because an aura of mystique can enhance the value of its services.

The financial press, at its best, attempts to bridge this comprehension gap, but it is often forced to satisfy two different markets. It is writing both for those in the money business and for the outsiders who like to follow the financial and economic scene and who, in their personal or business lives, have to choose among many financial services and investment products. A first-time reader of the *Financial Times* or the business pages of the national dailies or Sunday papers may still feel he is faced with a foreign language.

The escalating popularity of the Internet – covered for the first time in this edition – may help. Many of its financial pages are targeted very clearly at the general public. But even here, a little understanding of the basic investment principles can be a great advantage.

This book sets out to explain the language of money. It does so by explaining the principles and practices behind the markets and financial institutions that deal with money and investments. Understand the principles, and the jargon falls quickly into place. The book consists of two main parts. The narrative chapters provide a guide to the workings of the financial system and its main components. This is suitable for the newcomer to the financial scene, though will also serve as an *aide-mémoire* for those with existing knowledge. At the end of the book comes a combined glossary and index, which either provides explanations of financial terms or points to where they are explained in the text. Since the financial community often risks taking itself too seriously, an antidote is provided between the two parts in the form of a light-hearted look at some of the more oblique terms and techniques that financial journalists use in putting their message across.

The approach is intended to be practical. The explanations of financial terms are not aimed at the professional economist or banker and should not be taken as legal definitions. They explain the sense in which these terms are most likely to be encountered in the financial press.

The book follows the pattern of financial press coverage. Much of what is written concerns companies and the stockmarket, which therefore require explanation in detail. The sections on company accounts help to explain the background to the main investment yardsticks in use – they can be skipped if you are familiar with the concepts. Other areas such as the euromarket warrant less space. Though far larger than the domestic stockmarket, the euromarket or international market impinges less on the general public in Britain and attracts less coverage in the national press.

One point of detail: tax rates can change rapidly and examples incorporating tax calculations therefore risk being outdated soon after they are written. The tax rates adopted in this edition are those applying in the 2000-01 financial year. Thus, the basic rate of income tax is 22 per cent, the higher rate is 40 per cent and the corporation tax rate is 30 per cent. The dividend tax is deemed to be 10 per cent, with a higher rate of 32.5 per cent.

A final word of warning: in times of boom, investment markets become infected by their own enthusiasm. The money men forget the existence of the word 'bust'.

Journalists who write about the City are not immune to this enthusiasm. It sometimes colours their judgement, as it colours that of the City's professionals. The way to read the financial pages during a stockmarket boom is with a modicum of caution. Booms do not go on for ever and some journalists, like brokers, are better at advising when to buy than when to sell.

Introduction

If you had to characterize in a single word the financial developments of the last five years of the second millennium, the word would be 'globalization'. Money is now truly international. And it is a global business not only for the banks and other financial institutions that have operated for a long time in an international marketplace. Globalization has now come down to the level of the individual investor who, with a home computer and an Internet connection, can track share prices in New York as easily as those in London.

The explosion in information technology goes way beyond providing information on markets and investment opportunities around the world. It provides new routes into these markets. At the turn of the millennium, Internet-based stockbrokers were less developed in Britain than in the United States. But already a fair number of firms offered facilities for investors to place their buy and sell orders on-line, and many more Internet-based brokerages were on the way. Internet-based banks, not necessarily domiciled in Britain, were already making a bid for the savings of the British public.

With the help of the **Internet**, consumers have far more opportunity than in the past to compare prices for products across a range of suppliers. This applies to financial products as to any other and is bad news for the rip-off merchants. In the long run it should help to even out unwarranted price differentials and reduce the scope for overcharging.

But the globalization of investment activity on the back of information technology brings its dangers as well as its benefits. Even as far back as 1987, the worldwide stockmarket crash demonstrated how rapidly a market panic could spread from one financial centre to the next (see Chapter 7b) as dealers' screens showed instantly what was happening in other parts of the world. And the numerous currency crises of the past decade demonstrate clearly that no national economy can insulate itself from the global forces. The international currency speculators, with many billions of dollars at their disposal, are constantly waiting to place their bets on the rise or fall of a currency when signs of strength or weakness hold out the opportunity of a profit.

As when Britain was forced to drop out of the Exchange Rate Mechanism of the European Monetary System in September 1992, the speculators did not cause the weakness of sterling. But by selling pounds in vast quantities they greatly exacerbated it. The same process was at work when the speculators turned their attention to the currencies of the former 'tiger economies' – the high-growth countries of the Pacific Rim – in 1997 and helped to bring them low. In Britain, much of the emotional debate on whether or not to join the **single European currency** had tended to suggest that the country had independence in its economic management as long as it remained outside. In practice, decisions on interest rates and currency levels in Britain were greatly constrained by what other countries were doing, even while sterling remained nominally 'independent'.

As well as these obvious effects of globalization, there are other risks in the information explosion. Not all of the information available is reliable or accurate. Nobody edits, censors or regulates the Internet and it is also often difficult to tell whether information on web pages is up to date. Organizations are keen to put the latest favourable information on their website. They are often less punctilious in removing outdated material. Always check to see if a document is dated. If not, be cautious in making use of it. Remember that organizations provide the information that they want to provide. Only too frequently this fails to include such items as the name of the organization providing the site, its physical address and other vital information needed to establish the *bona fides* of the site.

Websites are also a godsend to the public relations industry. An organization can project exactly the image it wants, displaying the flattering material and choosing not to display the less flattering items. The growth of websites has made it far easier for the public to access certain standardized types of information. Paradoxically, it may have made it more difficult to obtain answers to the more unusual one-off information requests. The growth of the web seems (with honourable exceptions) to have been accompanied by a very marked deterioration in the quality of more traditional information offices or press offices. If your query is not one that is covered by the standardized information on the website, it may be considerably more difficult nowadays to get hold of anyone who understands your question, let alone someone who is capable of giving the answer. This is the flip side of the mass information explosion.

There is also a more specific danger for investors to be found in **Internet chat rooms**, discussion groups and the like. The promoter of an overvalued or dud share may all too easily get his pals to post messages tipping the share as the greatest thing since sliced bread. It is worth remembering an old stock exchange adage 'where's there's a tip there's a tap'. In other words, those who tip shares frequently have a supply of them to offload.

Thus, there is some very valuable information for investors out there on the World Wide Web and there is also a lot of absolute rubbish. Moreover, the ability to trade shares via the Internet opens the way for practices such as 'day trading' – already established in the United States and seeking a foothold in Britain. This is the game of betting on short-term movements in share prices over the computer screen which – like any other form of gambling – may sometimes deliver big profits but is more likely to prove a recipe for disaster.

There is another risk posed by the information explosion that is more subtle and more insidious. In the profusion of information on the way share prices are moving, the way different indices are moving, the rates of return available on different forms of investment and so on, these figures take on a life of their own. Investment is thus reduced to a numbers game in which investors risk losing sight completely of the businesses on which these numbers are based. They rush to buy the latest self-styled technology stock because others are rushing to buy and thus the price is rising. But unless there is a viable business underlying the hype, this will eventually end in tears. That Internet-based bank may appear to offer a very competitive rate of interest. But who is behind it, what resources does it have, in what country is it regulated and what are the safeguards for depositors if something goes wrong?

The Internet may therefore have brought a revolution in the availability of information and in the methods of accessing the markets, but it has not changed the fundamental principles of investment or the questions that any sensible investor will ask. As in earlier editions, this book concentrates on explaining the principles and it explains them mainly in a British context. This is not to ignore the international aspect. The same principles are at work in markets across the globe, though practice will differ slightly in line with local conditions and traditions and it is not possible in a single book to cover every variation.

For the first time this book provides **Internet** sources of information and services that may be useful to the investor. This is not intended to be comprehensive, nor is there necessarily any judgement on the quality of a particular Internet site. Change is so rapid in the Internet world that judgements – particularly negative ones – could be quickly outdated. The sites referred to are among those that offer useful information for the investor and which may, indeed, have proved useful in updating this book for the new, fifth edition. The more important sites are shown both at the end of the chapter to which they are most relevant and as a list in Chapter 23 – Print and Internet: the financial pages – which also contains some additional websites. One particular point to note: in the past there was much information from government departments, financial institutions and companies that was available only to journalists or others with special access. Today, any member of the public with an Internet connection can access most of this information – press releases, background briefings, statistical information – from the relevant website. It is a valuable resource for anyone who wants to delve a little deeper into financial affairs and is one of the undoubted plus-points of the Internet revolution.

We have dealt with the Internet revolution first because it is the sexiest and the most dramatic development of recent years. But there have been other important changes since the previous edition of *How to read the financial pages* went to press in 1995.

At a domestic level, a New Labour government came into power in 1997 after a long period of Conservative rule. It inherited a healthy economy which it nurtured successfully at least into the new millennium, though the service sector fared considerably better than traditional manufacturing industry. In contrast to much of the postwar period, the strength rather than the weakness of **sterling** was an on-going worry, particularly for the manufacturing sector. One of the first acts of the new government had been to give independence to the **Bank of England** in the operation of **monetary policy**, which involved some careful balancing acts. By the turn of the century, a renewed house-price boom had erupted, at least in the south of the country. Higher interest rates may have been necessary to contain house-price inflation in the south. But since they would tend to support or increase the value of sterling, they were the last thing that manufacturing industry wanted.

The new government also made some important changes to the system of company taxation early in its period of office. Because these changes could be presented as technical in nature, they did not receive the degree of coverage or comment that they warranted. By phasing out the **Advance Corporation Tax** system, in effect the government increased the total burden of taxation on company profits by several billion pounds a year, mainly to the detriment of the pension funds. And by rescheduling and accelerating the payment of **Corporation Tax** by companies it also imposed a swingeing penalty on corporate cash flows.

Up to the new millennium, **inflation** in Britain remained under tight control, at least in contrast with the 1970s and 1980s. No longer did consumers expect large automatic price increases month by month, though experience varied between different categories of goods. Technological products, such as computers, were actually becoming cheaper by the month – not so much because prices were falling but because buyers were getting vastly more for the same money with each new model. Accompanying the lower inflation were much lower nominal interest rates than investors and consumers had been accustomed to in previous decades, though short-term rates – low by British standards – were still high compared with those applying in the euro zone. While this meant that borrowing costs were considerably lower than in the past in the UK, it also meant that savers earned a great deal less on their money. The much lower long-term interest rates meant that anyone buying a pension got a considerably smaller income than he would have got for the same money in the recent past.

Against this economic background, the UK stockmarket had put up a sparkling performance in the second half of the 1990s, only temporarily and modestly damaged towards the end of 1998 by problems in some of the emerging markets and particularly in Russia. Towards the end of the century it was pharmaceutical and technology stocks that were making the running and dragging the market indices ever higher. In consequence these indices did not always provide a rounded picture of the market as a whole. Towards the end of 1999 the **London Stock Exchange** introduced a new market-within-a-market for technology stocks. This **techMARK** came complete with its own indices for the technology sector. As the millennium approached, investors' appetite for Internet-related companies reached fever pitch and market newcomers that had never made a profit were valued at many millions of pounds and saw their shares soar above the (often pretty optimistic) launch prices. Like most booms that get out of hand, this one showed all the signs of leading to future trouble.

The London Stock Exchange had vastly increased its dealing in overseas stocks in the 1990s and it also introduced a new trading system for the shares of larger British companies in 1997 (see Chapter 6). Meantime, shares held by major investors had been largely 'dematerialized'.

Ownership was recorded in electronic form and trades were settled via the new **CREST** electronic system, thus cutting out much of the paperwork and the need for new share certificates whenever shares changed hands. Private investors could, however, stick with the old paper-based system if they wanted to. But even greater changes were to come. Early in the new millennium the London Stock Exchange announced plans for a full merger with its German counterpart, to form a new grouping – **iX** or **Integrated Exchanges** – which might form the core of a truly pan-European exchange.

The regulatory system for financial products and financial markets in Britain was also undergoing a transformation at the millennium. A new 'super regulator', the **Financial Services Authority**, had taken over not only the regulatory powers of its predecessor, the Securities and Investments Board. It had also assumed regulatory responsibility for banks, building societies and various other financial entities.

The long period of economic prosperity leading up to the millennium was presenting commentators with an interesting problem,

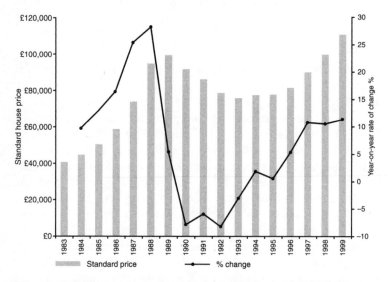

Figure Intro.1 Standard house prices in South-East England The 1990s were the decade that shattered the illusion that house prices could move in only one direction: upwards. The price boom of the late 1980s was followed by sharp falls in value in the first half of the 1990s, leaving many recent buyers with the problems of 'negative equity' (owing more on the house than it was worth). But in the second half of the decade prices were moving rapidly upwards again in the affluent South East and by the millennium official interest rates were being raised partly in an attempt to head off a runaway house price boom. Source: *Halifax plc.*

particularly in the United States – the powerhouse of world growth – but also in Britain. In the past, a period of economic growth had usually led to rising inflation and the need to damp down economic activity, giving rise the familiar '**stop–go**' economic cycle. This pattern seemed to have been broken in the 1990s when an unusually long period of growth appeared to have been achieved without seriously stoking the inflationary fires. Did this herald a new economic order, assisted by the productivity gains from the new technology, or had the inevitable downturn merely been deferred? In the United States the population as a whole had ceased to save, relying for its sense of prosperity on the value created by an ever-rising stockmarket. If the stockmarket fell, would this have a knock-on effect on the real economy by destroying the feel-good factor, discouraging spending and putting the brakes on economic growth? If so, the effects would be felt in Britain and across the rest of the world.

In Europe the old century culminated with the introduction of a new single currency – the **euro** – in eleven member states of the

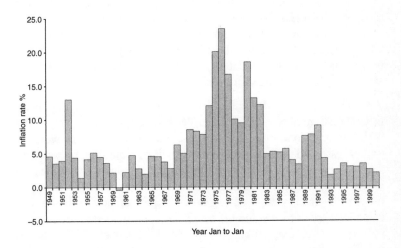

Figure Intro.2 Retail Prices Index – annual percentage rate of change Has low inflation come to stay? By the millennium the British had come to expect only modest price rises year on year and some technology goods such as computers were becoming cheaper all the time. But this was far from being typical of the post-war experience. Ignoring a blip caused by the Korean war in 1951–52, inflation began to take off in the 1970s and peaked around 25 per cent. The runaway boom of the late 1980s led to a resurgence of inflation at the turn of the decade, before Britain began to move into quieter waters. Source: *Office for National Statistics: Financial Statistics.*

European Union at the beginning of 1999. Britain stayed out of this 'euro zone', for the time being at least. The public debate on the merits and risks of joining the euro was conducted mainly at the usual 'yah, boo and sucks' level of British politics, disguising the fact that there were very real economic arguments for and against. In the foreign exchange markets the euro initially fared badly, losing over 16 per cent of its value against the dollar in its first year of trading. This weakness was cited by the anti-euro camp in Britain as a vindication of its stance. In reality, the economic cycle of the continental European countries was running behind that of the United States and Britain and the weakness of the currency was probably what European businesses needed in order to increase their competitiveness in world markets and assist the climb out of recession. The real tests for the euro were yet to come. But in one area the euro was highly successful from the outset. The international markets saw massive issues of bonds denominated in euros, reinforcing the argument that the new currency bloc would improve capital-raising efficiency for its members.

The end of the old century also saw a massive boom in **takeover** activity as businesses and industries regrouped, often across national borders, for the global marketplace. The world's biggest-ever takeover offer at the time, the £77 billion hostile bid from British mobile-phone group Vodafone AirTouch for German company Mannesmann, emerged shortly before 1999 drew to a close.

The process of **deregulation** in financial markets and financial institutions, already established in the last couple of decades of the 20th century, continued into the third millennium. Banks were no longer restricted to providing banking facilities, building societies no longer merely provided home loans and insurance companies no longer simply sold insurance. The old barriers between different types of business were breaking down or had already broken down. If banks were not yet selling frozen peas, supermarkets were already providing a range of banking services and the process had further to go. Telephone- or Internet-based banking and insurance services were challenging (or being developed to supplement) the traditional institutions. In Britain, one of the major casualties of the new financial free-for-all was the **building society** movement, which had provided many generations of Britons with the loans to buy their homes. Many of these previously mutual organizations took advantage of their new freedoms either to launch on the stockmarket in their own right or to sell out to an existing bank. The incentive was the free shares or 'windfall' cash payments that existing borrowers and savers would receive plus – dare one say it? – the far greater salaries and other financial benefits that the managers would collect as directors of public companies. Building societies that tried to retain their mutual status were fighting a rearguard action.

Greater competition among suppliers of financial products brought benefits for the consumer in the form of more competitive rates of interest and the like. But it was not all gain. At the millennium many thousands of savers who had been persuaded to opt out of perfectly good occupational **pension** schemes in favour of over-priced personal pension products were still awaiting compensation for the loss they had suffered from dishonest or incompetent advice. And the profusion of financial products on offer brought its own problems. Shoppers were already familiar with the marketing line of conventional retailers: 'find it cheaper elsewhere and we'll refund the difference'. In practice, the product in the other shop was always slightly different in weight, composition or content, thus precluding direct comparisons. How much more difficult to judge between competing financial products, each of which had its individual features and quirks. Many suppliers in the financial sector were, regrettably, only too ready to exploit the opportunities of 'confusion marketing'.

Alongside deregulation, the process of **'disintermediation'** – cutting out the middleman – was also strongly at work in the financial sphere. Larger businesses that might have gone to a bank for a loan in the past were now as likely to raise the money direct from investors by issuing securities in a market. And **banks** were trying to replace the business they were losing by generating fee income from organizing or underwriting these securities issues in the markets. They were also doing massive business in devising and selling **'derivative'** financial products. These are the products that businesses may use to protect themselves against movements in currencies and interest rates: in effect, often a sensible form of insurance. The other side of the coin is that these same products can be used speculatively to take massive bets on currency or interest rate movements. Britain's oldest merchant bank, **Barings**, went belly-up early in 1995 as a result of massive losses from unsuccessful speculation in these products in the Far-Eastern markets. The remaining years of the century saw further sporadic examples of multi-million losses from operations with derivatives, both at banks and at their corporate clients. The knock-on effects of these individual cases were generally small, though more widespread trouble for the financial system as a whole was still frequently predicted.

Private investors are less directly concerned with the banks' gambles in the financial markets and more directly concerned with the competing financial products and competing salesmen that daily scream for their attention. For them, the problem of finding sound, impartial advice grows ever more difficult. The pensions miss-selling scandal of ten years back was not, unfortunately, an isolated abuse. Until recently, many mortgage seekers were being persuaded into taking out endowment mortgages that were often wholly inappropriate to their circumstances but which, needless to say, paid juicy commissions to the vendors.

Lawyers, accountants, chartered surveyors and other professionals undergo many years of training before they are released on the public. Not so the myriad of financial salesmen and women whose commission-driven 'advice' may have even more serious repercussions on the wealth and comfort of their clients. In a sane world anyone putting the words 'Financial adviser' on a business card would be required to have at least a degree in financial management or a similar discipline. In practice, the words 'Financial adviser' should usually be translated simply as 'Salesman' or 'Saleswoman'.

Given the shortage of sound, impartial advice, individuals are thus thrown back on their own resources. A useful technique before buying a financial product or a share is to test the assumptions underlying the price. What rate of return would the vendor of the savings product have to earn on your money to deliver the benefits he promises? If he seems to be assuming much too low a rate, you may not be getting value for money – too much of the return will go to him rather than you. If he seems to be assuming abnormally high returns, his promises may be suspect. And when you read a tip for an Internet-related company whose share price is soaring into the stratosphere, just work out on the back of an envelope what profits that company would need to earn to justify its market value. It may help to bring you down to earth, even if it takes a little longer for the shares themselves to submit to the forces of gravity.

Chief among the resources available to individuals is the information that they can gather from the financial pages of the newspapers, from the broadcast media and, today, from the Internet. But the information itself is of limited help without sufficient knowledge of the background to be able to understand it and put it to use. That is where *How to read the financial pages* sets out to help.

1 First principles

Write about money, and you cannot entirely avoid technical terms. The simplest terms and concepts need to be dealt with at the outset. They will crop up time and again.

Fundamental to all financial markets is the idea of earning a **return** on money. Money has to work for its owner. Here – ignoring for the moment some of the tax complications that crop up in practice – are some of the ways it can do so:

- You deposit £1,000 with a bank which pays you, say, 5 per cent a year interest. In other words, your £1,000 of **capital** earns you £50 a year, which is the **return** on your money. When you want your £1,000 back you get £1,000, plus any accumulated interest, not more nor less. Provided your bank or building society does not go bust, your £1,000 of **capital** is not at risk, except from **inflation** which may reduce its **purchasing power** each year.

- You buy gold bullion to a value of £1,000 because you think the price of gold will rise. If, say, the price of gold has risen by 20 per cent after a year, you can sell your gold for £1,200. You have made a **profit** or a **capital gain** of £200 on your capital outlay of £1,000. In other words, you have a **return** of 20 per cent on your money. If the price of gold fails to move, you've earned nothing because commodities like gold do not pay interest.

- You use your £1,000 to buy **securities** that are traded on a stockmarket. Usually these will be **government bonds** (known as **gilt-edged securities** or **gilts** in the UK) or **ordinary shares** in a company. The first almost always provide an **income**; the second normally do. Traditional gilt-edged securities pay a fixed rate of interest. Ordinary shares in companies normally pay a **dividend** from the profits the company earns. If the company's profits rise, the dividend is likely to be increased. But there is no guarantee that there will be a dividend at all. If the company makes losses or runs short of cash, it may have to cease paying a dividend.

But when you buy securities that are traded on a stockmarket, the **return** on your £1,000 is not limited to the interest or dividends you receive. The prices of these securities in the stockmarket will also rise and fall, and your original £1,000 investment accordingly becomes worth more or less. So you are taking the risk of **capital gains** or **capital losses**.

Suppose you buy £1,000 worth of ordinary shares which pay you an annual dividend of £30 a year. You are getting a return, or **dividend yield,** of 3 per cent a year on your investment (£30 as a percentage of £1,000). If after a year the market value of your £1,000 of shares has risen to £1,070, you can sell them for a **capital gain** of £70 (or a 7 per cent profit on your original outlay). Thus your **overall return** over the year (before tax) consisted of the £30 income and the £70 capital gain: a total of £100, or a 10 per cent overall return on your original £1,000 investment.

Investors are generally prepared to accept much lower initial **yields** on shares than on fixed-interest stocks because they expect the income (and, in consequence, the **capital value** of the shares) to rise in the future. Most investors in ordinary shares are seeking capital gains at least as much as income. Note that if you are buying a security, you are taking the risk that the price may fall, whether it is a government bond or a share. But with the government bond the income is at least guaranteed by the government. With the share there is a second layer of risk: the company may not earn sufficient profits or have sufficient cash to pay a dividend.

- Finally, you can put the £1,000 directly to work in a business you run. Since this option does not initially involve the financial markets, we'll ignore it.

To summarize: money can be deposited to produce an income, it can be used to buy commodities or goods which are expected to rise in value but may not (including your own home), or it can be invested directly or indirectly in stockmarket securities which normally produce an income but show capital gains or losses as well. There are many variations on each of these themes. But keep the principles in mind and the variations fall into place.

Markets and interest rates

For each type of investment and for many of their derivatives there is a **market**. There is a market in money in London. It is not a physical marketplace: dealings take place over the telephone, and the price a borrower pays for the use of money is the interest rate. There is a market in **currencies**: the **foreign exchange** or **forex** market. There are markets in **commodities**. And there are markets in **government bonds** and company **shares**: the main domestic market here is the London Stock Exchange. Much of what you read in the financial press concerns these markets, their movements and the investments that are dealt on them.

The important point is that no market is entirely independent of the others. The linking factor is the **cost of money** (or the **return** an investor can get on money, which is the other side of the same coin). If interest rates rise or fall there is likely to be a ripple of movement through all the financial markets.

This is the most important single mechanism in the financial sphere and it lies behind a great deal of what is written in the financial press: from discussion of mortgage rates to reasons for movements in the gilt-edged securities market. Money will gravitate to where it earns the best return, commensurate with the risk the investor is prepared to take and the length of time for which he can tie up his money. As a general rule:

- The more money you have to invest, the higher the return you can expect.

- The longer you are prepared to tie your money up, the higher the return you can expect.

- The more risk you are prepared to take, the higher the return you can expect if all goes well.

Note, however, that the main factors influencing short-term interest rates are not always the same as those affecting long-term ones, though the two will interact (see below). Press comment should make it clear what type of interest rate it is primarily referring to.

Different returns on different investments

To match investors' different needs, there is a whole range of different **returns** available across the financial system. **Interest rates** can move rapidly, and any real cases we take can be quickly outdated. So we are safer sticking with hypothetical examples. At a particular time an investor might, say, be prepared to accept a return of 4 per cent or less on money he deposited with a bank for a short time and might need in a hurry. The low interest rate is the price of safety and convenience. At the same time he might expect to get 5 per cent if he were prepared to lock up his money by lending it for a year. And if he were prepared to take the chance of capital gain or loss by buying a gilt-edged security in the stockmarket, he might expect a return of, say, 6.5 per cent.

But these and other returns available to investors would rise and fall with changes in the cost of money in Britain and abroad. What causes these changes is a different matter. Sufficient for the moment to note that there are times when money is cheap (interest rates are low) and times when it is expensive (interest rates are high).

Suppose interest rates rise. The investor who was content with 4 per cent for money he could put his hands on quickly would expect a higher return to match the interest rates being offered elsewhere. So the rate for short-term deposits might rise to 5 per cent. Likewise, the investor who considers tucking his money away for a year would no longer be content with 5 per cent. He'll only be prepared to lend his money for a year if he's offered, say, 6 per cent. So anyone wanting to borrow money for a year has to offer the higher rate to lenders.

The precise rates are not important to the argument. The essential fact is that when one interest rate moves significantly, most other rates will usually move in the same direction. There will still be a differential between the rate the investor gets if he deposits his money for a few weeks and the rate he gets for locking it up for a year, though the size of the differential may change. But both rates will usually move up if interest rates generally are rising.

There is often, however, a difference in the behaviour of **short-term** and **long-term interest rates**. The government may manipulate short-term interest rates to achieve particular economic objectives. Rates might be forced up, for example, to damp down economic activity if the economy is overheating or to support the value of the currency if it shows signs of undesired weakness. Longer term interest rates – the yield on a bond with a ten-year life, say – are influenced more by investors' expectations of **inflation** in the long run. If investors consider inflation is on a long-term falling trend, you could have the situation where long-term bond yields are well below the interest rates for short-term money, which are being held deliberately high to prevent a runaway boom.

Opportunity cost of money

There is one other concept we need to introduce at this stage: the **opportunity cost of money**. Look at it like this. Suppose you could invest your money perfectly safely with a bank for a year at a fixed rate of interest of 5 per cent. The £100 you invest will have grown to £105 after a year with the interest added in (again, we are ignoring tax). If you decide to do something different with your money, you are losing the opportunity to earn this perfectly safe 5 per cent. Thus 5 per cent is your opportunity cost of money, and it makes sense to use your money in other ways only if you think you could earn a better return than 5 per cent. If you buy a painting for £100 as an investment with the hope of selling it at a profit after a year, it makes sense only if you reckon you can sell it for more than £105. If you think of investing in

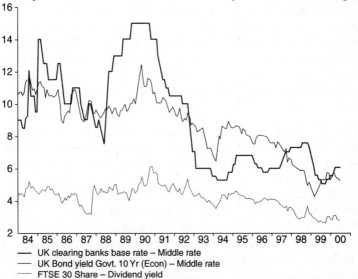

Figure 1.1 How yields compare How yields on different types of investment influence each other. The heavy line provides a measure of short-term interest rates, represented by UK clearing banks' base rate. The second line gives a measure of longer-term rates with the yield on 10-year government bonds. And the bottom line shows the dividend yield on the ordinary shares in the FT 30 Share Index. Sometimes short-term interest rates are higher and sometimes long-term rates are higher, depending on economic and political circumstances. But, overall, it is clear how returns on different investments affect each other and follow broadly similar trends. Source: *Datastream*.

a manufacturing process, you would need to be aiming for a return above (and in practice considerably above) 5 per cent. Changes in interest rates alter the opportunity cost of money and have profound effects on a vast range of investment decisions.

An allied concept is the **time value of money**. If you can earn 5 per cent interest, £1 today could be invested to grow to £1.05 in a year with the interest added in. That £1.05 could then be invested for a further year at 5 per cent interest and would grow to £1.103. And so on. Thus we could say that, at a **compound interest rate** (see glossary) of 5 per cent, £1.103 receivable in two years' time is worth the same as £1 today because £1 today would grow to £1.103 after two years. Another way of putting it is that, again at a 5 per cent interest rate, £1.103 is the **future value** after two years of £1 today. Or, looking at it the other way round, £1 is the **present value** of £1.103 that is receivable in two years.

In other words, even if we forget about inflation, money receivable in the future is worth less than the same amount of money today. At a 5 per cent rate of interest (or 5 per cent **discount rate**) the present value of £1 that is receivable in one year is £0.952, because £0.952 is the amount in today's money that would grow to £1 in a year's time at 5 per cent interest. At a 10 per cent discount rate, the present value of £1 that is receivable in one year is only £0.909. And so on.

Essentially, most investment is a matter of paying a lump sum today in return for the right to receive a sum or series of sums in the future. So, if somebody says that he will give you £1 in a year's time, what could you afford to pay for that right today? If you expect a 5 per cent return on your money you would discount at 5 per cent and find that you could afford to pay £0.952. If you expect a 10 per cent return, you would discount at 10 per cent and find you could only afford to pay £0.909. Calculations such as these – at a considerably more complex level and applied to a whole series of future receipts – lie at the root of much investment figuring. The important aspect, for our purposes, is that they illustrate the effect of interest rate movements on many types of investment. As interest rates rise and the returns that investors expect also rise, so (all else being equal) the price that they can afford to pay for a given investment will fall.

Interest rates and bond prices

We can see an aspect of this process at work in the bond markets. A change in interest rates has important implications for the stockmarket prices of bonds that pay a fixed rate of interest: **fixed-interest securities**, of which the traditional **gilt-edged securities** issued by the government are the most familiar, though companies also issue fixed-interest bonds. It works like this.

Gilt-edged securities, which are also known as government stocks or government bonds, are a form of **IOU** (I owe you) or **promissory note** issued by the government when it needs to borrow money. The government undertakes to pay so much a year in interest to the people who put up the money and who get the IOU in exchange. Normally the government agrees to repay (**redeem**) the stock at some date in the future, but to illustrate the interest rate mechanism it is easiest initially to take an **irredeemable** or **undated** stock which does not have to be repaid. The original investors who lend the money to the government by buying the IOUs do not, however, have to hold on to them indefinitely. They can sell them to other investors, who then become entitled to receive the interest from the government.

Suppose the government needs to borrow money at a time when investors would expect a 6.5 per cent yield on a gilt-edged security. The government has to offer £6.50 a year interest for every £100 it borrows. The investor is prepared to pay £100 for the right to receive £6.50 a year interest, because this represents a 6.5 per cent return on his outlay.

Then suppose that interest rates rise to the point where an investor would expect a 7 per cent return if he bought a gilt-edged security. He will no longer pay £100 for the right to £6.50 a year in income. He will only be prepared to pay a price that gives him a 7 per cent return on his outlay. The 'right' price in this case is around £93, because if he pays only £93 for the right to receive £6.50 a year in income, he is getting a 7 per cent return on his investment (6.50 as a percentage of 93). So, in the stockmarket the price of the irredeemable gilt-edged security that pays £6.50 a year interest would have to fall to around £93 before investors would be prepared to buy it. The original investor who paid £100 thus sees the value of his investment fall because of the rise in interest rates. Conversely, the value of his investment would have risen if interest rates had fallen.

This is one reason why there is so much comment in the financial press on the outlook for interest rates. Higher interest rates mean higher borrowing costs for companies and individuals. They also mean losses for existing investors in fixed-interest bonds.

Markets discount future events

In practice, the movement in stockmarket prices is slightly more complex than this would suggest and there is another vital principle to grasp. Stockmarkets always look ahead and **discount** future events, or what investors expect these events to be. Prices of stocks in the bond markets don't fall or rise simply in response to actual changes in interest rates. If investors think interest rates are going to rise in the near future, they will probably start selling fixed-interest stocks. So there will be more sellers than buyers and the market price will begin to fall before the adjustment in general interest rates actually takes place. Likewise, investors will begin buying fixed-interest stocks if they think interest rates are going to come down, so that they have a profit by the time the interest rate cut has taken place and market prices have adjusted upwards to reflect the new lower interest rates. Making profits in the stockmarkets is all about guessing better (or faster) than the next man or woman.

What is the market?

Reports in the press tend to say 'the market did this' or 'the market expected good news on the economic front', as if the **market** were a single living entity with a single conscious mind. This is not, of course, the case. To understand reports of market behaviour you have to bear in mind the way the market works.

A market is simply a mechanism which allows individuals or organizations to trade with each other. It may be a physical marketplace – a trading floor – where buyers and sellers or their representatives can meet and buy and sell face to face. Or it may simply be a network of buyers and sellers who deal with each other over the telephone or computer screen. The principle is much the same.

In either type of market, the buyers and sellers (or the **brokers** acting as their agents) may deal direct with each other or they may deal through a middleman known as a **marketmaker**. If they deal direct, each would-be buyer has to find a corresponding would-be seller. John Smith who wants to sell must locate Tom Jones who wants to buy. If there is a marketmaker, John Smith will sell instead to the marketmaker, who buys on his own account (acts as a **principal**) in the hope that he will later be able to find a Tom Jones to whom he can sell at a profit. Marketmakers **make a book** in shares or bonds. They are prepared to buy shares in the hope of finding somebody to sell to or sell shares (which they may not even have) in the expectation of finding somebody from whom they can buy to **balance their books**. Either way, they make their living on the difference between the prices at which they buy and sell. Marketmakers (in practice there will normally be a number of them competing with each other) lend **liquidity** – fluidity – to a market. A potential buyer can always buy without needing to wait until he can find a potential seller; securities can readily be turned into cash. The **London Stock Exchange** traditionally operated a trading system incorporating marketmakers. But the system is now in the process of change, at least for the shares of the largest companies.

The market price of a security (or anything else) reflects a balance between the views of all the possible buyers and sellers in the particular market. This is what commentators really mean when they say 'the market thought ...'. They are describing the dominant view among those operating in the market. An example helps to show how this operates on security prices.

How prices rise or fall

Suppose a security (it could be the government bond we looked at earlier) **stands in the market** at a price of £90. This is the last price at which it changed hands. Suppose there are only ten such securities in existence. But the price has been moving down, and even at £90 there are seven investors who think it is too expensive and would like to sell, and only three who would be prepared to buy. If £90 remained the price, only three sellers could find buyers and there would be an unsatisfied desire to sell.

Suppose the price is £89 instead. At this level one of the previous sellers decides the security is no longer expensive and he may as well hold on, while another investor decides it would be worth buying at this lower price. There are now only six sellers and four buyers. Still no balance.

Now suppose the price is £88. Another potential seller changes his mind if he can only get £88, while another investor reckons it is now attractive and emerges as a potential buyer at this lower price. There are now five sellers and five buyers so all would-be buyers can buy and all would-be sellers can sell. Thus at £88 the price has reached an **equilibrium** which holds good until something happens to persuade some of the investors to change their view again.

If there are marketmakers operating in the market, they will probably have moved their quoted price down from £90 to £88 – the price at which they can **balance their books** by matching buyers and sellers. Though their operations are in practice more complex (see Chapters 6 and 7a) and they also quote a **spread** between the price at which they are prepared to sell and the one at which they will buy, the principle holds good. Prices will move towards the point where there is equilibrium between buyers and sellers at a given time.

This principle operates in all markets, not just the markets in securities. In the **money markets,** banks will need to adjust the interest rates they offer and charge until they have the right balance between those who are prepared to lend to them and those who want to borrow. Building societies need to adjust the rates they pay to savers and charge to borrowers so that they keep a balance between the money coming in and the amount going out as mortgage loans. In the **foreign exchange markets** the value of the pound will need to find a level at which there is a balance between those who want to buy pounds and those who want to sell. Free markets in commodities, in gold bullion and in office accommodation in the City of London are affected by the same interaction of sellers and takers.

Primary and secondary markets

Fixed-interest securities and ordinary shares are the main stock-in-trade of the **securities markets** and the London Stock Exchange is the main domestic securities market. By buying one or the other, investors are helping – directly or indirectly – to provide the finance that government or industry needs. Why do we say 'directly or indirectly'? Because the stockmarket is two markets in one: a **primary market** and a **secondary market**.

A **primary market** is one in which the government, companies or other bodies can sell new securities to investors to raise cash. A **secondary market** is a market in which the investors can buy and sell these securities among each other, and one market serves both functions. The buying and selling in the secondary market does not directly affect the finances of government or companies. But if investors did not know they could buy and sell securities in the secondary market they might well be reluctant to put up cash for the government or companies by buying securities in the primary market when they were first issued. And the prices established by the buying and selling by investors in the secondary market help to determine the price that government and companies will receive next time they need to sell further securities for cash in the primary market. In this way secondary market prices determine the price a company has to pay to raise new money. A reasonably **liquid** secondary market is normally considered vital for a healthy primary market.

Interest rates and currencies

Another facet of interest rates: at a time of volatile **exchange rates** between different **currencies**, the interaction between interest rates and the value of currencies (or **parities**) dominates much financial comment. Investment is increasingly international, and in their search for the best returns investors look not simply at the different options available in their own country but at the relative attractiveness of different countries as a haven for funds.

If Britain offers higher interest rates than, say, the United States or Switzerland, international investors may be tempted to invest in Britain. This means they will need to exchange whatever currency they hold into pounds sterling in order to make deposits or buy securities in Britain. They will therefore be buying pounds on the foreign exchange market. If the buying of pounds exceeds any selling taking place, the **value of the pound** (the price of the pound in terms of other currencies) is likely to rise.

Interest rates are by no means the only factor affecting the value of a currency. And the **overall return** a foreign investor receives when he invests in Britain depends not only on the yield his money can earn but on the movement in the pound itself. If the pound rises against his own currency he makes a profit on the movement in the pound. If it falls, he makes a loss. So his total return is a combination of the **yield** he can get by investing in Britain and the profit or loss he makes on the currency.

Whatever the level of interest rates in Britain, overseas investors will not invest if they expect the currency itself will fall sharply for other reasons. But interest rates are still an important weapon the government can use in defending the currency by attracting investors to buy pounds to invest in Britain.

Effects of rising interest rates

Now look at some of the effects of a rise in interest rates across the financial system. In describing these effects different newspapers will highlight different aspects, according to where their readers' interests lie.

Higher interest rates probably mean:

- an increase in **borrowing** costs for industry, meaning that profits for many companies will be lower than they would otherwise have been and that companies may be less keen to borrow money to invest in new projects

- a rise in the **opportunity cost** of holding non-yielding assets such as gold or commodities (it becomes theoretically more expensive to own them because, at higher interest rates, you lose more by not taking the opportunity of earning interest on your money)

- higher monthly **mortgage payments** for homebuyers, soaking up more of their available income and leaving them less to spend

- more expensive **overdrafts** and **personal loans**, and higher **credit card** interest rates, possibly causing consumers to spend less

- a fall in the value of **gilt-edged securities** or other **fixed-interest bonds** on the stockmarket, unless investors think the rise in interest rates is very temporary or unless prices have already fallen in anticipation

- a possible fall in the value of **ordinary shares** on the stockmarket (though the mechanism here is more complicated than with the gilt-edged market – see below)

- an increase in the returns that **investors** and **savers** can expect to earn on their money

- a strengthening (all else being equal) in the **value of the pound sterling**, as overseas investors buy pounds to invest in Britain and get the advantage of the higher returns from depositing money in Britain or buying sterling bonds.

In the popular press it is the effects on the individual, and particularly the homebuyer, that are likely to make the headlines: 'Mortgage costs to rocket'. The quality press will probably mention the effect on mortgages, too. In a country where many people used to derive their main sense of economic security from selling their houses to each other at ever-rising prices, nobody is going to ignore the homebuyer. But the more serious papers will also be analysing the effects on sterling, industry, the stockmarket and on the outlook for economic growth. In the *Financial Times*, which regularly covers virtually every financial market, the ripple effects will spread to most corners of the paper.

Debt and equity

Much of the day-to-day comment in the financial press is concerned with the securities markets and the investments that are traded in them. And so far we have talked mainly of the bond market (the market in long-term debt: particularly the gilt-edged market in which the government's own debt is traded). But this leads to another fundamental concept: the difference between **debt** and **equity**.

Established companies usually generate part of the money they need from the profits they retain in the business. But, ignoring for the moment these **internally generated funds**, a company can raise money in a number of different ways. These are the main ones.

First, it can simply borrow money from a bank or elsewhere. Normally the money has to be paid back in due course, and meantime interest has to be paid to the original lender. The interest may be at a **variable** or **floating rate**: it rises or falls with changes in the general level of interest rates in the country. Or it may be at a **fixed rate**, in which case the interest rate remains the same for the life of the loan.

Second, the company can **issue a loan** in the form of a security. In other words, it creates an IOU and offers it to investors in return for cash, in the same way as the government does in the gilt-edged market. Normally the company agrees to repay – **redeem** – this loan at some future point. But the loan can usually be traded in the stockmarket in the same way as a gilt-edged security. The investor who originally put up the money does not have to hold on to his IOU until it is repaid. If he wants the money sooner, he sells the IOU to somebody else. He may get less for it than he paid, or he may sell it at a profit. The company simply pays interest to whomever owns the IOU when interest is due, and eventually repays the money it originally borrowed to the person who owns the IOU on the **redemption date**.

These loans may pay a fixed rate of interest or a floating rate. If they pay a fixed rate, they are very similar to a fixed-rate government bond. The rate of interest is known as the **coupon** and for convenience it is expressed as a percentage of the **nominal**, **par** or **face** value, which in Britain is taken to be a unit of £100, as with a government stock. The loans issued by companies go under various names such as **loan stock**, **industrial debenture** or **bond**. The value of fixed-interest loans is affected by movements in interest rates, but the health and standing of the company also plays a part. The company has to earn the profits to pay the interest and repay the capital, whereas with a gilt-edged security these payments are guaranteed by the government (see Chapter 13).

Third, a company may raise money by creating new **ordinary shares** and selling them for cash. This is quite different in principle from issuing a loan or borrowing from a bank, because ordinary shares – also known as **equity** – are not a debt of the company. They do not normally have to be repaid. The owner of a share becomes part-owner of the company. In return for putting up his money, he shares in the risks and rewards of the company's operations: hence the term **risk capital**. He is entitled to a share of everything the company owns, after allowing for its debts, and to a share of the profits it earns. If its profits increase he can normally expect higher **dividends** – income payments – on his shares.

A share is also a **security** of the company and can normally be bought and sold in the same way as a loan stock. In the same way, its price in the market depends on the interplay of buyers and sellers, not on the price at which it was originally issued or on its **nominal** or **par value** (see Chapter 6). An investor who wants his money back simply sells the share to somebody else; whether he gets more or less than he paid originally depends on what the market price has done in the interim. If profits of the company rise, it will probably pay higher dividends and – all else being equal – the value of the shares will normally rise. If the company gets into trouble, the owners of the shares or **shareholders** are the last people to get any money back. All of the loans and other debts have to be repaid first.

Interest rate effects on ordinary shares

Investors will generally accept a lower initial **yield** on shares than on fixed-interest securities because they expect their income and the capital value of the shares to rise. Take the earlier example of shares that could be bought at a price that offered a 3 per cent yield but which rose in value by 7 per cent over the year. The overall return to a buyer would have been 10 per cent. This is attractive relative to the 6.5 per cent return we assumed that he could get at the time on gilt-edged securities. The additional 3.5 **percentage points** allow for the risk element in the ordinary shares.

But investors do not know in advance what return they will get from ordinary shares. Even the 3 per cent dividend yield could fall if the company had to cut its dividend. And if it cut its dividend, the value of the shares in the stockmarket would almost certainly fall, too. Hence investing in shares involves a judgement about a company's prospects and its ability to earn the profits out of which the dividends will be paid.

However, share values may be affected by movements in **interest rates** as well. Let us take an extreme example and assume that prices of **gilt-edged stocks** fall so sharply that the yields on the stocks rise to 10 per cent. Investors would now almost certainly want a higher overall return than 10 per cent on ordinary shares to allow for the risk element. In the short run, the only way shares can offer a higher yield is if their prices fall in the market (you pay a lower price to receive the same dividend, so the yield to a buyer has risen), and this would probably happen. But the prices of shares in individual companies are also affected by the profits outlook for the company. In the very long run the return from shares will depend on the profits the company earns or is capable of earning, but in the shorter run, movements in interest rates can have an impact. A large proportion of the press's financial coverage concerns the profits companies earn and the profits they are likely to earn in the future.

Don't expect markets to be rational

One final word about **markets**. We can describe dispassionately how they operate and the main forces at work. This is not always how they present themselves in the short run to those who operate in them or those who comment on their day-to-day behaviour. Markets are moved by tips and rumours, by frenetic temporary enthusiasms and by devastating panics. They are creatures of mood and can sometimes be manipulated. Their enthusiasms and panics are frequently self-feeding, losing all contact with the underlying realities: the **fundamentals**.

Markets are a vital mechanism between investors with money and governments and companies that need money to put to work. But the average dealer in a City firm may rarely think about his function as a cog in this essential economic process. His business is dealing in shares and he has a gut feeling that share prices are due to rise, so he buys. He will usually find a reason afterwards for what he did. Do not take too seriously all of the reasons for market behaviour you find reported in the financial pages. Market professionals earn their bread from movements one way or another. If no logical reason for movement exists, they are quite capable of inventing one.

The financial institutions that make up the City of London provide the main mechanisms for distributing the flows of money. In the next chapter we look at the sources of money, the markets that distribute the money and the people you will meet in the financial pages who operate in these markets.

Internet pointers

There is a fair range of information on the investment basics available from different websites, though it tends to focus more on investment products than the principles themselves. Much of this is found on the personal finance sites, but try as well the share-ownership promotion organization ProShare at www.proshare.org.uk/ for some very basic fact sheets on stockmarket investment. More detail on sites with educational content is given in Chapter 23.

2 Money flows and the money men

When a financial journalist describes somebody as 'an eminent City figure', he probably means what he says. The man is perhaps a senior member of the banking establishment. If a journalist describes somebody as 'the controversial City financier', he's probably coming as close as he dares within the libel laws to calling him a financial spiv!

But what exactly is this 'City' which harbours these characters and many more? It is, of course, a geographical area on the east side of Central London, often described as the **Square Mile**. But 'The City' is more often used as a convenient blanket term for the commercial institutions at the heart of Britain's financial system. They do not necessarily operate within the square mile of the City of London, though a surprising number of them do. They provide the financial services that oil the wheels of industry and trade. They are not, however, concerned only with serving Britain's domestic economy. Much of the City's activity relates to international finance, trade and securities dealing, and many of the financial institutions that operate there are foreign owned. One of the more common criticisms of the City is that it is too remote from Britain's own productive industries. Whereas some parts of the City have always been international in outlook, the big change of the last 20 years is the internationalization of even the most traditional domestic institutions such as the London Stock Exchange. However, in looking at the City institutions we will be concentrating first and foremost on pinning down their importance to Britain's own economy.

The City is a major source of **invisible earnings** for Britain's **balance of payments**. Financial services generated net overseas earnings of almost £32 billion in 1998.

To put into context what we read about the City, we need some idea of the relative importance of different institutions and the sums of money involved. What follows in this chapter is an outline of the main domestic investment flows and the bodies that handle them. Some of these figures (together with other markets not covered here) are described in more detail in the chapters devoted to them.

The savings institutions

The City provides the mechanisms that channel money to where it can be put to work. The main external source of new long-term investment funds for business and government is the **savings** of private individuals, and in Britain these savings are channelled mainly through the large **financial institutions**: primarily the **pension funds** and **life assurance companies**. These two types of institution between them had almost £62 billion of new money to invest in 1999. They invest funds in companies by buying shares. By buying gilt-edged securities they supply much of the money the government borrows (in the years when it does need to borrow). The **London Stock Exchange** provides the main mechanism for these institutional funds to find their way into company securities and government and company bonds, and the financial institutions are the London Stock Exchange's largest clients (see Chapter 6).

The financial institutions also invest in **commercial property** and in **overseas securities and property**, and put money to work short term in the **money markets**.

A third type of investment institution is significant in the equity market: the **unit trust**. Unit trusts pool the money of individual investors to provide a spread of risk by investing in a range of shares, mainly via the stockmarket. **Investment trusts** perform a somewhat similar function, but there are important structural differences between the two types of trust (see Chapter 21).

The **building societies** also act as a funnel for the savings of individuals but the money they take goes primarily into providing **mortgages** for homebuyers. However, a proportion of their funds is invested in government securities via the stockmarket, where it can readily be turned into cash if needed. Building societies are less of a force nowadays, when many of the biggest have turned themselves into banks or been acquired by banks (see below).

Banking and money markets

The other major domestic source of external funds for business is the **banking system** and the **money markets** (see Chapter 15). The banks' main sources of funds are shorter term – the money of individuals and companies deposited with them (**retail deposits**) plus the **wholesale funds** they borrow in the money markets. The banks lend money in one form or another. The high-street banks in Britain do not, as in some other countries, invest in company shares to any significant extent. But they act as arrangers of finance as well as lenders by organizing and guaranteeing issues of various types of short-term IOU by companies. The banks also invest in government securities via the stock exchange. And they are the main participants in the **foreign exchange** or **forex** markets. Some of the banks are directly involved in the stock exchange through securities houses they own. The big banks are very active in buying and selling **derivative** financial products. Finally, they often deal quite actively in various financial markets on their own account in an attempt to boost their income.

Euromarkets

A third source of finance for business and governments is the **eurocurrency** market or **euromarket**, also known as the **international market**. Here the sources of funds were originally the deposits of currencies held outside their country of origin, in banks round the world. These days, however, this distinction has become a little unreal and the market is defined more in terms of its trading and issuing techniques, its structure and its international character. The users are borrowers round the world (in spite of the name, this market does not deal solely with deposits held in Europe). London is the main centre of this market, but Britain is neither the main supplier nor the main user of eurocurrency funds (see Chapter 17). The international market saw enormous growth in the late 1990s.

The market mechanisms

The London Stock Exchange, the banking and money markets and the euromarkets are the main markets for investment funds. But the City contains many other markets which provide services for business.

There is a range of markets concerned with the **management of risk**, in which investors or businesses can either **hedge** (protect themselves) against the risks inherent in their operations or opt for high risks and high rewards by betting on movements in prices and interest rates. These are increasingly referred to as the **derivatives** markets. They include the **traded options market** and the **financial**

futures market (which are now amalgamated) and a range of **commodities futures markets**. The **foreign exchange** market also comes within this category as a medium for hedging currency risks.

There is another aspect of risk management: a market in **insurance**. This divides into two parts: insurance provided by insurance companies (the **company market**) and the international insurance market operated under the aegis of **Lloyd's of London**, though the distinction between the two is less rigid than it once was.

Savings institutions and intermediaries

Occupational pension schemes – pension schemes provided by companies or industries for their employees – had (at end-1998) investments valued at some £699 billion and invested some £8 billion of new money in 1999. The contributions that companies and individuals pay into these schemes are invested in a fund to provide the pensions at the end of the day. Some pension funds manage their own investments – the biggest run into many billions of pounds. Others farm out the investment management, often to investment banks (see Chapter 6). Others are **insured** schemes where payments are made to an insurance company which contracts to provide the pensions.

Because **life assurance companies** provide pensions as well as life assurance, the distinction between the two types of investment is a little blurred and life assurance funds include a pensions element. The larger life assurance companies have also become more diversified investment management groups, offering unit trusts and other financial services. Life assurance is mainly a savings business as opposed to **general insurance** which provides cover against fire, theft and similar risks. The life assurance companies had (in 1998) existing investments of about £776 billion in their long-term funds and invested some £55 billion of new money in 1999.

Both the pension funds and life assurance companies are vehicles for **contractual savings**: money coming in under long-term savings schemes which can safely be invested for the long term because the savers have contracted to make regular payments.

Unit trusts cannot rely on the same regular inflow of funds, though part of the money they receive comes from regular savings plans. Investors tend to pile into unit trusts when the stockmarket is buoyant and may even withdraw funds when it takes a turn for the worse. But, overall, they have still shown strong growth in recent years, particular as investors could hold unit trust units in a **personal equity plan** – **PEP** – or **ISA** (see Chapter 21) and receive tax advantages. At end-1999 unit trusts held total funds of £254 billion, having invested a further £19 billion during the year. They are often operated by large **investment management groups** which market a range of savings products and services. **Investment trusts** were considerably smaller, with total funds of around £77 billion early in the year 2000.

The pension funds, life assurance companies and unit trusts between them own around half of all listed shares in British companies, and the first two have large holdings of gilt-edged securities.

Life assurance and unit trusts are sold direct by the organizations that provide them, but are also extensively marketed through **financial intermediaries** who operate on commission. These include **insurance brokers** and **independent financial advisers**. **Accountants**, **solicitors**, **bank managers**, **building societies** and **stockbrokers** may also sell these investment products.

The **building societies** at end-1999 had outstanding loans of some £129 billion, mainly mortgage loans to homebuyers. Their possible range of activities is now wider than in the past and the larger ones are allowed to offer a range of services including cheque accounts, personal loans, estate agency services and a variety of financial and savings products. But building societies are, regrettably, a declining force in the financial arena. Hitherto they have been **mutual** organizations – owned in theory by the people who deposit money with them and borrow from them – but the larger ones now have the option to become companies owned by shareholders or to acquire banking status. The Abbey National was the first to convert into a bank and launch on the stockmarket, and other major societies have either taken this course or allowed themselves to be taken over by banks. Since a building society's savers and borrowers normally receive a **windfall** payment in cash or shares when the society abandons its mutual status, short-term greed probably dictates that the mutual building society movement will contract still further.

The banks

At end-1999 **banks** in Britain had total deposits from UK residents of around £724 billion, of which £636 billion was in sterling. The bulk of this money is with the major **clearing banks** such as Barclays and Lloyds TSB, whose traditional deposit-taking and lending services are familiar enough. These are the banks whose branches you see in the high street and which are, indeed, also known as **high-street banks** or **retail banks**. Some of the clearing banks flirted in recent years with the world of the stock exchange via the acquisition of broking or, in some cases, marketmaking businesses, but with very mixed success and earlier grandiose plans were often watered down or abandoned.

Very different from the traditional clearing banks are the **investment banks** or **merchant banks**. Twenty years ago you would have used the term 'merchant bank', but many of Britain's traditional independent merchant banks with well-known names such as Kleinwort Benson and Warburgs have now been taken over by foreign banks and become part of much larger organizations. At the same time, foreign financial institutions have set up shop in London, with the American brokerage houses and investment banks particularly prominent.

Investment banks or merchant banks do not have a great deal of contact with the general public, except perhaps as fund managers and vendors of investment products. Nor do they necessarily have large-scale funds of their own even though they may nowadays have the backing of larger institutions. Their expertise lies in arranging finance, not necessarily in providing it. They are dealmakers whose **corporate finance** arms advise companies on stockmarket launches, capital raising, takeovers and on takeover defences. They may be active as marketmakers and dealers in the stockmarket and the eurobond market and many of them have a large **fund management** business – much pension fund investment is in practice managed by investment banks. The larger ones are global in their activities and outlook.

London is host to a wide range of **foreign banks** – around 550 at the last count – many of which were attracted by London's position as centre of the euromarkets though some of the larger ones also do significant domestic banking business in Britain and may be involved in stock exchange business.

The stock exchange

Britain's domestic **stock exchange** is one of the world's largest, ranking after those of the United States and Japan. At end-1999 the total market value of listed ordinary shares in UK companies was £1,820 billion, while UK government securities listed on the exchange had a value of £333 billion. In 1999 some £14 billion was raised by the first-time sale of shares in new and existing companies on the stockmarket. London Stock Exchange members may operate as **dealers** or **marketmakers**, acting as principals and putting their own money at risk, or they may confine themselves to the role of **agency broker.** Agency brokerage is the business of executing share trades for investors in return for a commission. Marketmaking in gilt-edged securities is undertaken by **primary dealers** known as **gilt-edged marketmakers.** There were 40 equity marketmakers in the main market of the domestic stock exchange at the end of 1999 and 16 gilt-edged marketmakers.

Most of the major London marketmakers and brokers are now owned by UK or foreign banks or other financial institutions and in some cases several firms have been brought together to form major **securities houses** which undertake all kinds of securities business. A number of major foreign banks and securities houses are now also active in the British market. Many of Britain's smaller brokers and **country brokers** remain independent, though some have got together into larger groupings. In recent years there has been growth in **execution-only brokers,** who provide a no-frills, relatively cheap share dealing service for the public and **Internet brokers** (who provide share-dealing facilities via the Internet) were becoming more established in Britain. They are already well established in the United States.

Most of the larger stock exchange businesses employ numbers of **investment analysts** who produce research into companies and other investment topics as a service to clients.

Venture capital businesses

By no means all investment in Britain passes through the stock exchange. An enormous growth area in recent years has been the provision of finance for businesses whose shares are not traded (or not yet traded) on the exchange. This can take the form of finance for **business start-ups**, **development finance** for growing private companies and finance for operations such as **management buy-outs.** **Venture capital groups** are the businesses that provide or arrange this kind of finance in return for a share stake. Some of these venture capital groups are stockmarket-listed companies in their own right. Others may be offshoots of other financial groupings such as banks, insurance companies or pension funds.

The professional back-up

The components of the other markets are described in the chapters devoted to them. But among the City figures encountered in the financial pages there is also a range of professional firms without which the City could not function: notably, accountants, actuaries, lawyers and chartered surveyors.

Accountants are a vital link in the financial chain, if only because they **audit** the accounts of companies (see Chapter 3). Their services are particularly vital in the preparation of a **prospectus** when shares are **marketed** (sold to a range of investors) for the first time. **Audit** and **tax** work is the traditional mainstay of the accountant, with **liquidation** work – **winding up** companies that have gone to the wall – as a specialist sideline for some of them. But the major international firms which number their employees in tens of thousands worldwide have pushed fast into areas which overlap with other established interests: **corporate finance** and all manner of **management advisory services**. Link-ups with firms of commercial lawyers are also being pursued.

Consulting actuaries are the firms that advise on the highly complex business of **pension funding** and **pension fund performance** and they crop up with some regularity when pension topics are discussed. This is in addition to the actuary's original function of assessing mortality risks, valuing life assurance assets and liabilities, and deciding on bonuses.

Commercial lawyers: few documents in the investment world can safely be prepared without the advice of a **commercial lawyer**, and the City boasts a dozen or so major firms specializing in commercial work.

Surveyors and **estate agents** act as intermediaries in the market in investment properties. But they do a great deal besides. **Valuations** of a company's properties may be needed in a new issue or takeover document. They will certainly be needed when finance is to be secured on properties. The chartered surveyor frequently helps to arrange finance for **development of properties**. He manages **property investment portfolios** for numerous institutions and is one of the main sources of information on conditions in both the **property investment market** and the **letting market** (see Chapter 20). But change is again in the air. Most of the largest firms have relatively recently surrendered their autonomy and are now part of larger international real estate and financial groupings.

Perhaps the **financial public relations** agencies should also rank as one of the City's back-up services. Many have a significant client list among stockmarket-listed companies. The reader of the financial press is not necessarily aware of their presence, but much of the routine information from companies – profit announcements and the like – reaches the journalist in the form of a press release on the paper of one of these agencies. They perform a more active role in publicizing the virtues of companies coming to the stockmarket, in helping to present the case for an aggressor or a defendant in a takeover bid, and generally in ensuring that information which could be good for the share price of a client company does not remain hidden under a bushel.

Finally, there are the **regulators** whose job is to supervise these diverse bodies and interests and ensure that they remain on the straight and narrow. The main regulator is now the **Financial Services Authority**. Since the regulatory system is complex, and currently undergoing significant change, we will deal with this topic where it crops up, and in a distinct chapter, towards the end of the book (Chapter 22).

Internet pointers

Most of the organizations mentioned in this chapter, or their professional bodies or trade associations, now have websites where further details and contact information are provided. These are listed in Chapter 23. For further information on the City and its components try first the Corporation of London-City of London website at www.cityoflondon.gov.uk/. This provides background and links to the main organizations operating in the City of London. Statistical and research material is available at the BI (British Invisibles) site at www.bi.org.uk/. At the Bank of England site at www.bankof england.co.uk/ you can find and download free *The City Handbook* of City organizations with their addresses and contact details (this is not available in printed form).

3 Companies and their accounts

Financial journalists write extensively about **companies**: companies that are growing, companies that are contracting, companies that are taking over other companies, companies that are going bust. They tend to approach company affairs from one of two angles (or, most usefully, from both). Take two examples:

'Mark Hustler, the thirty-year-old accountant who took charge at Interpersonal Video Systems earlier this year, has not let the grass grow under his feet. Following the purchase of Insight Compact Discs in June he plans a further important acquisition in the interpersonal systems field to consolidate the company's lead in this fast-growing business. The shares are acquiring a strong institutional following and at 180p – up from 60p earlier this year – look one of the best bets in the high-technology sector'

What do we deduce from this? First, that the writer thinks Interpersonal Video Systems is a good thing, because he is advising you to buy the shares. Second, that he is suggesting the investing institutions are buying the shares, which should help the price to rise. Third, that the shares have already risen strongly, presumably since Mark Hustler took charge. Fourth, that Mark Hustler is expanding his company by buying other companies. Fifth, that the company is a leader in interpersonal systems and that these are a high-technology area. Finally, we might suspect that the writer probably hasn't the faintest idea what an interpersonal video system is, whether it is a growth business, whether Mark Hustler is paying too much or too little for the companies he is acquiring or who the institutions are that are supposed to be following the company. In other words, the writer has clearly had a **tip**. It's not necessarily to be sneezed at. If enough people follow the tip and buy the shares because they think they are going up, they will go up. For a time at least.

Now take the following:

'Interpersonal Video Systems, the manufacturer of visual sales aids for the toothpaste industry, reports turnover up from £18m to £27m for the year to end-March. Pre-tax profits have risen from £2m to £4.3m, including a first-time contribution of £1.5m from Insight Compact Discs, acquired for shares last June, and earnings per share are up from 10p to 12.5p on the enlarged capital. If the company meets its target of 15 per cent a year internal growth, the 25p shares at 180p are on a prospective PE ratio of only 12.5, which is below the sector average. They look undervalued.'

In fact, the message from the second writer is essentially the same as that from the first: the shares should be bought. Not because Mark Hustler is a great guy, not because another important acquisition is planned, not because institutions are rushing to buy the shares. But because the conventional **investment arithmetic** says that they are cheap. We also learn roughly what Interpersonal Video Systems does and we have an indication – since earnings per share have risen – that it probably didn't pay too much for Insight Compact Discs.

Neither approach is totally satisfactory on its own. It is useful to know who runs a company. It helps us to get a feel for the operation if we know it plans expansion via takeover. It is useful to know (if, in fact, it is true) that institutions are investing in the company. But it is also useful to know what it does, how much it earns and how it is rated on accepted investment criteria.

Phrases like 'PE ratio' and 'earnings per share' are part of the currency of the investment business. But what do they mean? This requires a gentle incursion into company accounts.

Limited liability

First, what is a company? It is a trading entity that belongs to its shareholders and the **Ltd** or **plc** after the name indicates that it has **limited liability**. The plc also indicates that the company is a **Public Limited Company**: one whose shares or other securities may be held by the investing public and traded on a market. In either case the liability of the owners is limited to the amount of money they have put into the business. Unless they give **personal guarantees** for the debts of the business, the **owners** or **shareholders** (**members**, in the legal jargon) of a limited company cannot be called on to meet the company's debts where these exceed its assets. Only the money put into the company can be lost. Anybody who operates a business as a **sole trader** or as a partner in a **partnership**, on the other hand, is liable for all the debts of the business.

Voting and control

The owners of the **ordinary shares** in a company normally have the power to **control** the company if they act together, though the directors and managers – who may or may not be shareholders – run the company. Usually each ordinary share carries one **vote**. Owners of more than 50 per cent of the votes will thus – if they all vote the same way – control the company. In practice, shareholders can influence the way a company is run primarily by voting on the appointment or dismissal of directors and on certain other major policy matters that have to be presented to shareholders at a formal meeting of the company. Certain major resolutions – to change the aims and objectives of a company, say – will require that 75 per cent of the votes cast are in favour.

Most of the time shareholders vote the way the directors advise them to, especially at the **annual general meeting** or **AGM** of the company, which is normally a non-contentious event where the required resolutions are duly passed. The press will generally pick up the occasions when there is dissent between different groups of shareholders or between shareholders and directors. This is where the question of voting power becomes interesting.

Content of the accounts

Ordinary shareholders are entitled to receive **accounts**. As a rough rule (it's not technically quite correct) companies are required to produce a set of accounts each year. This is a legal requirement. The stock exchange further requires that listed companies produce figures showing profits at the **half-year** stage (in America they produce them each **quarter**).

The best way to look on accounts is as a sort of shorthand for what is really going on in a company. The bare figures don't conjure up the smoking chimneys or the salesmen out on the road. But once you are reasonably familiar with the basic figurework you can begin to look at what lies behind it.

The main items in the accounts are a **profit and loss account**,

a **cash flow statement** and a **balance sheet**. Under current accounting rules, the company should also include a **statement of total recognized gains and losses** and a **note of historical cost profits and
losses** – but we do not need to bother too much with these for the
moment. Various other bits of information required by law, by the
accounting standards of the day (or by the stock exchange in the case
of a listed company) are usually contained in the **directors' report**
or in the detailed **notes to the accounts**. In practice, the report and
accounts of stock exchange-traded companies normally contain a lot
more information in the form of a chairman's statement, a review of
the year's trading and statements of compliance with various codes
and practices that companies are meant to observe. Lavish colour
illustrations may also bulk out the document.

Role of the auditors

With the accounts will come an **auditors' report**. **Auditors** are firms
of accountants who hold a watching brief on behalf of the owners of
the company (the shareholders). The directors of the company prepare
and sign the accounts. It is the auditors' job to certify that these
accounts present a **true and fair view** of the company's profits and
financial position, or to point out any failings where they do not. The
auditors are meant to be independent of the company's management,
though obviously need to work quite closely with the managers in
agreeing the form of the accounts. The managers appoint them, though
the shareholders approve their fees. There is normally a certain amount
of give and take when opinions vary on the presentation of different
items. An auditors' report which says the accounts do not give a 'true
and fair view' or that they do so only with important **qualifications** will
normally be picked up by the press as a strong warning bell.

Company reporting

Companies that are quoted on the stock exchange need, we have
seen, to provide their shareholders with more frequent information
than that supplied by the legally required annual accounts. Some
weeks after the end of the first half of the company's year it will normally produce an **interim profit statement** (or **interim**) giving
unaudited first-half profit figures. The statement also normally gives
the size of the **interim dividend** (see below) and includes some comment on trading and prospects from the company.

Some time after the end of the full year a **preliminary**

announcement (prelim) will usually be published, giving the profits for the year and often a lot of background information. This appears some weeks before the full report and accounts are posted to shareholders. Most daily press comment on the company's figures is based on the interim and preliminary statements which have greater news value – though less depth of information – than the full accounts.

Profit and loss account

A **profit and loss account** shows the results of a company's trading over the past financial period. Usually this means a year, though the year can run to whatever date the company chooses. December 31 and March 31 year-ends are popular, though it could be April 1 or November 5. The profit and loss account thus shows the effect on the company's revenue account of all the transactions over the past year. If a company made profits of £20m in the first ten months of its year and losses of £22m in the last two months, the profit and loss account would show a loss of £2m: the final outcome. It would not by itself reveal that the company had been trading profitably for much of the period.

Cash flow statement

Profits are not necessarily the same as **cash flows,** and the differences can sometimes be revealing. Take just one example. A company lends £10m to another company for two years at 10 per cent a year interest but agrees that the interest will only be paid when the loan itself is repaid after two years. In its profit and loss account at the end of the first year the lending company will include in its profits the interest of £1m which has **accrued** (built up) by that point. It has earned this interest. On the other hand, it has not yet received any interest in cash, so the £1m will not feature in its **cash flow statement** for that year.

Companies go bust primarily because they run out of cash. The cash flow statements that they have been obliged to publish since the early 1990s make it far easier to see the early warning signs (see also Chapter 4).

Balance sheet

The **balance sheet** is a totally different animal from the profit and loss account and cash flow statement. It gives a snapshot of a company's financial position on one particular date: the last day of its financial year. Everything the company owned on this date and everything it owed on this date will be shown in the balance sheet, grouped under a number of different headings. The balance sheet is usually the best measure an investor has of a company's **financial health**. But it needs interpreting with caution. The position it shows on the last day of the company's year could be very different from what it would have shown if drawn up three months earlier or would show if prepared three months later. Where companies deliberately bring forward some items and delay others, so that the balance sheet gives a picture which is totally untypical of the company's position at any other time during the year, it amounts to excessive **window-dressing**. **Creative accounting** has a similar implication. It usually means that figures have been twisted beyond the bounds of decency to present the picture the company wants.

Note the difference between a balance sheet or **parent company balance sheet** and a **consolidated balance sheet** or **group balance sheet**. Most companies listed on the stock exchange are not, in fact, single companies. Bloggs Engineering plc may be a group of companies consisting of Bloggs Engineering plc, Scraggs Scrap Ltd and Muppet Metalbashers Ltd. Bloggs Engineering is the **parent company** or **head company** and controls the other two by owning all or a majority of their shares. They are therefore **subsidiary companies**. The head company of a group is also sometimes called the **holding company** because it holds the shares of the subsidiaries.

A parent company balance sheet shows the detail for Bloggs Engineering alone; its ownership of the other two companies is represented merely by the **book value** (value for accounting purposes) of its interest in these subsidiaries, which is generally pretty unhelpful. A consolidated balance sheet, on the other hand, treats the three companies as if they were a single entity. The assets and liabilities of all three are grouped together. Thus, if Bloggs owned buildings valued at £2m, Scraggs's buildings were worth £1m and Muppet's worth £1.5m, the figure for buildings (or 'properties') in the consolidated balance sheet of Bloggs Engineering plc would be £4.5m.

Companies are normally required to present both a balance sheet and a consolidated or group balance sheet, unless there are no subsidiaries, in which case only parent company figures are given. The consolidated balance sheet is the important one and virtually all press comment will be on the consolidated figures. Companies are not required to publish a parent company profit and loss account (unless the business consists of a single company), only a **consolidated** one which shows the aggregate of the profits and losses of all the different companies in the group.

Where the money comes from

In looking at a company's finances as shown by its balance sheet (and when talking of balance sheets from now on we'll be referring to consolidated balance sheets) it is vital to distinguish the different **sources of money** the company uses in its operations. There are three main sources. First, money put up as **permanent capital** by the owners (the shareholders) of the business. This is the company's own money, usually put up in the form of **ordinary share capital** when it is also known as **equity capital**. Then there is the part of the profit the company earns which it **ploughs back** into the business rather than paying out by way of dividend to shareholders. This also becomes part of the equity funds of the business, because it belongs to the shareholders and is shown as **reserves**. Third, there is the money the company borrows and which it will have to repay at some point. The general term for this is **debt** or **borrowings** but it can take a lot of different forms: **overdrafts**, **term loans** (both of these are bank borrowings, which are not securities) or **debentures**, **loan stocks**, and so on (which are securities of the company).

The main balance sheet items

The easiest way to understand the various accounting terms that crop up in press reports is to take a sample set of accounts. The accounts – for a mythical John Smith & Co Ltd – are slightly simplified to emphasize the main items: some of the complexities that will crop up are examined later in Chapter 5. In the interests of clarity the presentation may also differ slightly from what you will see in a real set of published accounts, though you will be able to make the transition easily. In particular, we have shown the detail of 'Current liabilities' or 'Creditors due within one year' on the face of the accounts – with a real set of accounts you probably need to turn to the notes to get this detail. First, the **balance sheet** (see Table 3.1). Assume that John Smith is a young company which makes, say, metal paperweights.

In fact, John Smith & Co was set up only a year ago by four friends who decided there was a future in paperweights. Each put £10,000 into the business by subscribing for 10,000 £1 ordinary shares and the company borrowed the rest of the money it required. Let us take the main balance sheet items in order.

Fixed and current assets

First come the **assets** of the business: what it owns. Assets are defined as **fixed assets** or **current assets**. Fixed assets are not necessarily fixed in a physical sense. A company operating oil tankers would show them as a fixed asset. They are 'fixed' because they are not something the company is buying and selling or processing in the course of its normal trade. They represent mainly the buildings and plant in which or with which the company produces its products and services. In this case John Smith's only fixed assets are £28,000 worth of paperweight-making machinery (we must assume that it rents rather than owns its premises). Originally John Smith paid £30,000 for this machinery, but out of its profits it has set aside £2,000 to allow for a year's **depreciation** or **amortization** of the equipment and written down the **book value** by this amount. This recognizes that machinery will eventually wear out and need to be replaced.

Fixed assets are divided between **tangible assets** (things you can touch like buildings and machines) and **intangible assets**. John Smith has only tangible assets. Intangible assets could be things like trade marks or patent rights which have a clear value but no physical presence other than the paper they are written on. But the most common form of intangible asset is general **goodwill**. We will come back to this later.

Current assets are the assets which are constantly on the move – stocks of raw materials that will be turned into products, stocks of products that will be sold to customers, money owing to the company by customers, money temporarily held in the bank that will be withdrawn as it is needed in the business. If there were a company whose business was buying and selling oil tankers, the tankers would be shown under current assets as 'stocks', and not under fixed assets.

John Smith has **stocks** of £50,000. These comprise mainly stocks of raw metal from which the paperweights will be made and stocks of finished paperweights that have not yet been sold.

The **debtors** item shows the money that is owing to John Smith, probably by customers who have bought paperweights they have not yet paid for. In effect, John Smith is making a temporary loan of £35,000 to its customers, on which it receives no interest. **Trade credit** of this kind is a fact of business life, but it poses problems, particularly for younger companies. John Smith has had to bear the costs of producing the paperweights, which soaks up its available cash, and does not get paid by customers till some time later.

John Smith & Co. Ltd.
Balance sheet as at 31 December

	£	£
FIXED ASSETS		
Tangible assets: plant and machinery		28,000
CURRENT ASSETS		
Stocks	50,000	
Debtors	35,000	
Cash at bank	5,000	
	90,000	
CURRENT LIABILITIES		
(Creditors: amounts due within one year)		
Trade creditors	20,000	
Tax payable	6,000	
Dividend proposed	4,000	
Bank overdrafts	8,000	
	38,000	
NET CURRENT ASSETS		52,000
TOTAL ASSETS LESS CURRENT LIABILITIES		80,000
CREDITORS (Amounts due in more than one year)		
Term loans		30,000
NET ASSETS		50,000
Represented by:		
SHARE CAPITAL		
(£1 ordinary shares)		40,000
RESERVES		
Profit & loss account		10,000
SHAREHOLDERS' FUNDS		50,000

Table 3.1 Balance Sheet

Finally, current assets include £5,000 of **cash** sitting in the bank until it has to be spent.

John Smith's total assets are therefore £118,000: the £28,000 of fixed assets and £90,000 of current assets. This figure is known as the **balance sheet total**. It represents everything John Smith & Co owns.

Current liabilities

Next we have to knock off everything the company owes. The short-term debts are shown as **current liabilities** or **creditors: amounts due within one year**. These are the counterpart of current assets and are therefore deducted from current assets in the balance sheet to give **net current assets** (or **net current liabilities** if current liabilities exceed current assets).

The first item under current liabilities is **trade creditors** of £20,000. This is the counterpart of debtors. It represents money the company owes for goods and services it has received but not yet paid for. In other words, it is much like an interest-free loan to the company: **trade credit** from which the company benefits.

Each year a company has to make provision from its profits for the **corporation tax** it must pay on these profits. But corporation tax is payable by instalments and at any time there is likely to be some tax which the company knows it will have to pay but which has not yet been handed over. This therefore appears as a liability of £6,000 under the heading **tax payable**.

Next comes the **dividend** the company plans to pay. A company usually seeks approval from its shareholders for the dividend it intends to pay, and until they have voted to approve the dividend at the **annual general meeting** (**AGM**) which takes place at least three weeks after they have received the accounts it remains a short-term liability: something that will need to be paid in the near future. A public company normally pays its dividend in two parts: an **interim dividend** in the course of the year and a **final dividend** (which is the payment on which shareholders normally vote) when the profits for the full year are known. It is therefore the cost of this final dividend that will appear as a liability.

Finally, the company owes £8,000 it has borrowed by way of **overdraft**. Since an overdraft is technically repayable on demand, it has to be shown as a current liability.

Deducting the current liabilities of £38,000 from the current assets of £90,000 gives a figure of £52,000 for net current assets.

Longer-term debt

Fixed assets plus net current assets give the figure described as **total assets less current liabilities**. From this figure of £80,000 we still have to knock off any **medium-** or **long-term debts**, which are shown under the heading of **creditors (amounts due in more than one year)** before arriving at a figure for net assets. In the event, John Smith has borrowed £30,000 in the form of a **term loan**. This is a bank loan, typically for a period of three to seven years, and normally repayable in instalments.

The net asset figure

After knocking off everything the company owes, we find John Smith is 'worth' £50,000: the **net asset** figure. This is the value for accounting purposes of the **shareholders' interest** in the company, though it probably does not tell us anything much about what the company might be worth in the stockmarket. It equates to the £40,000 the four founder-shareholders provided by subscribing for 40,000 £1 shares at par, plus the £10,000 of profits the company has earned and **retained** in the business rather than paying out as dividends. The two items together constitute the **shareholders' funds** of £50,000.

After looking at the individual items, translate them into a picture of the company's financial position. It has assets of £118,000 (fixed assets plus current assets). Where did the money come from to acquire these assets? It has effectively borrowed (partly as trade credit) the £38,000 shown as current liabilities. It has a longer-term borrowing of £30,000: the term loan. Knock these two items off the assets figure and you are left with £50,000. Where did the money come from for this remaining £50,000 of assets? The answer: £40,000 was put up as share capital by the original shareholders and £10,000 was 'saved' out of the profits of the year's operations.

Gearing

The relationship between **borrowed money (debt)** and **shareholders' money (equity)** in a business is important. Borrowed money has to be repaid at some point, though it might be a long way off. More important in the short run, interest has to be paid on borrowed money, and it has to be paid whether the company is earning good profits or not. A company that existed largely on borrowed money could be in bad trouble if it ran into losses for a year or so. If it was unable to pay the interest, the lenders could ask for their money back, which would usually result in the business folding up.

Equity finance does not carry this danger for the company. In the good times the shareholders reap the rewards of the company's success, usually in the form of rising dividends. But if the company should run into trouble and make losses, it does not have to pay any dividend at all on the ordinary shares. Equity capital is also called **risk capital** for this reason: the shareholder is at risk.

The relationship between borrowed money and equity money in a business is referred to as **gearing** (or **leverage** in the United States). It is a term that crops up in other contexts as well. A **high-geared company** is one which has a large amount of borrowed money in relation to its equity or its shareholders' funds. A **low-geared company** has a large equity and few borrowings. The appropriate mix of borrowings and equity depends on the type of business (see Chapter 4). If a journalist points out that a company is high-geared, he is probably suggesting that this is a good thing for shareholders if the company is doing well. If the company is doing badly, he is probably sounding a warning.

The main profit and loss account items

Next, look at the record of the company's profits for the past year, as shown in the profit and loss (P&L) account: see Table 3.2.

John Smith & Co Ltd
Profit and loss account for the year ended 31 December

	£
TURNOVER	200,000
OPERATING PROFIT	24,000
Less	
INTEREST PAYABLE	4,000
Leaving	
PROFIT ON ORDINARY ACTIVITIES BEFORE TAX	20,000
Less	
CORPORATION TAX	6,000
Leaving	
PROFIT AFTER TAX ATTRIBUTABLE TO SHAREHOLDERS	14,000
Less	
DIVIDENDS	4,000
Leaving	
RETAINED PROFIT	10,000
Earnings per ordinary share:	35p
Dividends per ordinary share	10p

Table 3.2 Profit and loss account

Turnover and profit

Most of these terms are pretty much self-explanatory. They don't all have a precise legal or accountancy significance and some can be used in slightly different ways. The **turnover** of £200,000 is the total value of all goods and services sold by the company to third parties in the normal course of trade – it is sometimes called **sales**, instead. It does not usually include any taxes (like VAT) charged on these goods or services.

The difference between turnover and the **operating profit** of £24,000 is the costs incurred by the company in its operations during the year: wages, rent, raw materials, distribution costs, and so on. These will be broken down to a greater or lesser extent in the **notes to the accounts** (which contain a lot of important information and are sometimes more revealing than the accounts themselves). The costs also in this case include the **directors' salaries**, the **auditors' fees** and the amount set aside to provide for **depreciation of plant and equipment** (these items will also be shown in detail in the notes to the accounts). The operating profit is what remains after these costs have been deducted.

The next deduction is the interest the company pays on its borrowings of all kinds (for convenience we've ignored the fact that it may also have received a little interest on its temporary bank balances). In the notes this interest should be broken down between interest on short-term borrowings and interest on long-term borrowings. An overdraft is technically a very short-term borrowing.

After deducting the interest paid we are left with a figure of £20,000 for **profit on ordinary activities before tax**. Mercifully this can be abbreviated to **pre-tax profit** and is the most frequently quoted measure of a company's profit, in the press and elsewhere.

The tax take

Next, the tax man has his cut. Companies pay **corporation tax** on their profits, after all other costs except dividends have been deducted. Tax rates change relatively frequently and examples can be soon outdated. For consistency we have taken a 30 per cent corporation tax rate throughout this book (except where specifically noted) because this is the rate applying from the 2000–01 financial year. But the exact rate that companies pay on their profits will depend on a number of factors, including the proportion of profits earned overseas and various allowances that may be available. We have also ignored the fact that there is a lower rate of corporation tax that applies in practice to small companies like John Smith.

The company tax system used to incorporate a complexity that was often puzzling to the layman. It concerned **Advance Corporation Tax** or **ACT**. Though this has been abolished from 1999 (at considerable cost, incidentally, to companies and their shareholders) you will still read references to the old **imputation tax system** that incorporated ACT and a brief explanation is therefore needed. Under this system, the corporation tax paid by the company covered the basic rate income-tax liability on the dividends that shareholders received. So a basic rate taxpayer did not have to pay additional tax on his dividends – the corporation tax paid by the company was deemed to cover it. Shareholders who were not liable for tax at all – in particular the **pension funds** – could use the **tax credit** voucher they received with their dividends to claim back the tax that was deemed to have been paid by the company on their behalf. When the tax credit was equivalent to 20 per cent of the gross dividend payment, this meant that an 80p dividend received by a pension fund was actually worth 100p once it had claimed the tax back.

Now that ACT has been abolished, non-taxpayers no longer have a tax credit they can reclaim. The value of an 80p dividend to a pension fund thus reduces from 100p to 80p – a severe cut in its income. But while nobody (except charities, for which there are temporary transitional arrangements) can now claim back tax on dividends, a residue of the old system remains. The rate of income tax on dividends for standard rate taxpayers is now 10 per cent and for higher rate taxpayers is 32.5 per cent. The corporation tax paid by the company is deemed to cover this standard rate 10 per cent liability. A standard-rate taxpayer therefore does not have to pay tax on the dividends he receives and a higher rate taxpayer can offset this 10 per cent against the total tax due on his dividends.

Equity earnings, dividends and retentions

The **profit after tax attributable to shareholders** or **net profit** is much what it says. Provided there are no further deductions, it belongs to the shareholders or owners of the company and may be referred to as **equity earnings**. But it is up to the company to decide, probably with the approval of its shareholders, how much of this profit is to be paid out as dividends and how much should be kept in the business to help finance its expansion. Most companies in their

early stages need all the money they can get and tend to keep most
of the profit in the business. In the case of John Smith & Co the company has decided to pay out under a third of its profits – £4,000 – as
dividends and to 'plough back' the remaining £10,000 which is
therefore described as **retained earnings** or **retentions**. The amount
of cash a company has available and the amount it needs to retain for
the business will affect the dividend decision, which does not depend
solely on the level of profits earned. Note that occasionally companies pay cash to shareholders in forms other than a dividend: this is
covered in Chapter 9. Sometimes, too, shareholders are given the
chance of taking their dividend in shares rather than cash (a **scrip
dividend** – see Chapter 9). See also **foreign income dividend** in the
glossary. But there are no such complexities with John Smith & Co.

Remember, the £10,000 of retained earnings belongs to the
shareholders just as much as the £4,000 they actually receive as dividends, which is why it was shown in the balance sheet as part of
shareholders' funds, under the heading of **revenue reserves** or **profit and loss account reserve**.

The £4,000 paid as dividends is divided equally among the
40,000 £1 shares in issue. Normally, the dividend is expressed as an
amount (in pence) per share. In this case the dividends are equal to
10p per ordinary share.

Minor complexities

The figures shown for John Smith & Co are obviously simplified. They
illustrate the main figures on which the investment ratios explained
later are based. But a few technicalities must be mentioned briefly.

If John Smith has **interests in associated companies** or **related companies** (companies which are not subsidiaries, but where it
has a significant shareholding – see Chapter 5) it will show as a separate item its proportionate share of the profits of these companies
and include them in the pre-tax profit figure.

The profit after tax will not always be the same thing as the
profit attributable to ordinary shareholders or **equity earnings**.
First, the company may have to make a deduction for **minority
interests** or **outside shareholders' interests**. These arise where a
parent company controls subsidiary companies but does not own all
the shares of all of them. Suppose John Smith had a subsidiary called
Super Stampings. Smith holds 70 per cent of the Stampings shares,

and the original founders of Stampings have held on to the other 30 per cent. So 30 per cent of the profits of Stampings belongs to these **minority shareholders**. Smith includes the whole of the Stampings profits in its own operating profit figure, but makes a deduction after tax for the amount of the net profit of Stampings belonging to the minority holders.

Second, the company may have **preference shares** in issue (see Chapter 5). In this case the dividends on the preference shares must be deducted from the net profits. Both minority interests and preference dividends must be allowed for before arriving at the net profits or earnings that belong to Smith's ordinary shareholders.

Third, the aim of any investment commentator is to assess a company's earning power, present and future. This means he may need to adjust the published profit figures to exclude 'one-off' items that distort the profits in a particular year. Again, a little history helps to explain the position. In the past, these items usually appeared under the heading either of **exceptional items** or of **extraordinary items**. They could include items such as costs incurred in closing down a subsidiary business or windfall profits on the sale of a surplus factory. Neither item would have been a normal feature of the company's trading.

Exceptional items were added or subtracted in the published accounts **above the line**: before reaching a pre-tax profit figure. Extraordinary items, however, did not affect the published pre-tax profits or published earnings but were deducted **below the line** after striking a **net profits after tax** figure. What was 'exceptional' and what was 'extraordinary' was a matter for some debate. What often happened in practice was that companies treated favourable items such as windfall profits as 'exceptional' and therefore included them in published pre-tax profits. Unpleasant one-off items such as factory closure costs were more likely to be treated as 'extraordinary' and deducted after tax where they would not be so easily spotted.

But this form of **window-dressing** did not escape the accounting authorities and a new accounting standard, **FRS 3**, came into force which obliged companies to treat virtually all one-off items as 'exceptional' and add or subtract them before arriving at pre-tax profits and earnings per share. While this remedied the earlier abuses, it also resulted in earnings that were sometimes a lot more volatile and did not necessarily reflect a company's on-going earnings power. So, alongside the volatile **FRS 3 earnings**, investment analysts normally calculate an earnings figure for the company's on-going operations, which excludes the one-off items. Many companies themselves publish an on-going earnings figure – sometimes referred to as **headline earnings** – as well as the obligatory FRS 3 earnings.

The FRS 3 accounting standard also obliged companies to show the division of their profits between continuing operations, profits from new businesses acquired during the year and profits from businesses that were subsequently closed or sold. But the new millennium is likely to see still further changes in the way companies are required to present their performance. Discussions are under way about a new form of performance statement which would show not only profit as defined in the current form of profit and loss account but also changes in the value of the business resulting from revaluation of assets and similar developments.

Accounting systems and inflation accounting

The accounts we have looked at are prepared according to the **historical cost convention**. This is the traditional way accounts are prepared and is the form required for most taxation and legal purposes. It means that most items – particularly fixed assets and stocks – are normally shown at what they originally cost, less provisions for depreciation or other necessary write-offs. The main exception is that properties are sometimes revalued, with the new values included in the balance sheet.

In a period of high inflation, historical cost accounting may be misleading. Plant and equipment will cost more to replace than was paid for it originally. Stocks of raw materials will cost more when they have to be replaced.

To overcome this problem, various forms of **inflation accounting**, including **replacement cost accounting**, have been developed to supplement or replace historical cost accounts. Before reaching a profit figure, deductions will be made for the higher costs of replacing fixed assets and stocks (there are other adjustments, but these are usually the most important). The result for most companies is that profits will be lower than those shown under the historical cost convention. You still occasionally see references in the press to inflation accounting. But with the lower rates of inflation that prevailed in the 1990s, some of the steam has gone out of the debate on the merits of different accounting systems. The accounting authorities have, however, been examining the possibility of requiring companies to show more items in their accounts at present values and fewer at historical cost.

Internet pointers

There are any number of websites that impinge on companies and their affairs. First, most major listed companies have their own websites which are often informative and provide the latest figures. You may access them easily via the Peter Temple linksite at www.cix.co.uk/~ptemple/. Details of listed companies from an investor's viewpoint are available at the Hemmington Scott website at www.hemscott.net/. The Companies Registry has a website at www.companieshouse.gov.uk/ where certain basic information on all limited companies is provided free and you can find out how to obtain the more detailed information. And information on the accounting standards to which companies must conform are on the Accounting Standards Board's website at www.asb.org.uk/. The ProShare organization at www.proshare.org.uk/ offers a very basic guide to published accounts.

4 The investment ratios

After a first look at the main accounting items, we can see how they translate into comment on a company's standing and prospects. The figures are used in two main ways to produce the ratios on which investment judgement is often based. Take an example:

> 'Following the rights issue in July last year, Super Silicon has £4m in cash or near-cash form to see it through the planned expansion programme, and borrowings as a percentage of shareholders' funds are down to 14 per cent.'

This makes it clear that Super Silicon is unlikely to run out of cash (which is a good thing) and that its gearing is low (which is probably also a good thing). What it does not do is to tell you whether the shares look cheap or expensive at their current level. Next take this:

> 'With the benefit of interest on the proceeds of last year's rights issue, Super Silicon should achieve earnings of 12p per share on the enlarged capital. With the shares at 180p this suggests a prospective price earnings ratio of 15, which is well below the sector average'.

The difference is that the second piece does not merely comment on Super Silicon's prospects. It relates these prospects to the market price of the shares so that readers can form a view on whether the shares are cheap or expensive.

Two types of financial ratio

An investment is only a good investment if you buy it at the right price. Super Silicon may be a superb company and may have proved it over many years. This does not mean, however, that its shares are always a good buy. As with anything else, there are times when you could pay too much even for the best – though it is obviously better to pay too much for something that is intrinsically good than for a load of rubbish.

So there are two layers of **financial ratios** applied to companies: the ones that tell us something about the operations and health of the company itself and the ones that relate the company's performance to the price you would have to pay for the shares.

Profit margins

First, let's look at the company itself. Look again at the profit and loss account for John Smith & Co (Table 3.2). It is making a profit, but how can that profit be quantified in such a way that it could be compared with the profit performances of other companies? One of the more common measures is the **profit margin**. If we take the pre-tax profits of £20,000 and the turnover of £200,000, it is clear that 10 per cent of what the company gets for its products after all costs and overheads have been paid is profit. So the **pre-tax profit margin** is 10 per cent. This figure does not mean a great deal by itself. But if we compared it with other companies in the same field, it could be informative.

Assuming there is another paperweight manufacturer, and that it earns a pre-tax margin of only 6 per cent, we might reckon that John Smith & Co is the more successful company. If the following year's accounts show that John Smith's profit margin has increased to 11.5 per cent, we might deduce that it is strengthening its competitive position still further. If, on the other hand, turnover has doubled to £400,000 but the profit margin is down to 9 per cent, it might seem that John Smith has decided to sacrifice a bit of profitability in order to increase its turnover – possibly by reducing prices or offering bigger bulk discounts. If turnover had dropped to £180,000 and profits were down to £9,000 (a pre-tax margin of only 5 per cent) it would be clear that something had gone wrong: possibly the competitors had hit back with lower prices themselves and made a big dent in John Smith's business.

No ratio on its own will give the full picture, and it can be dangerous to jump to conclusions. But taken together with other indicators from the accounts, and with whatever else we can learn about the company, they can provide valuable clues.

Income gearing

The next ratio to look at is the **gearing** or in this case **income gearing**. How much of the company's operating profit goes to pay interest charges? John Smith produces an operating profit of £24,000, and £4,000 of this goes in interest charges. This is important because the company has to pay the interest whatever profits it makes. Income gearing is normally calculated by expressing the interest charge as a proportion of the profit before interest is deducted: in this case, £4,000 as a proportion of £24,000 or 16.7 per cent. Another way of expressing the relationship is to say that **interest cover** is six times (24 divided by 4) – the company could cover its interest bill six times from its profits.

At all events, John Smith's income gearing is fairly low, and to see the full significance of gearing we need a more extreme example. Take a company whose profit and loss account looks as shown in Table 4.1.

	£
OPERATING PROFIT	100,000
less	
INTEREST PAID	50,000
leaving	
PRE-TAX PROFIT	50,000

Table 4.1

Then assume that the company does not increase or reduce its borrowings and that interest rates remain unchanged. Assume also that the company increases its operating profit by 50 per cent to £150,000. The profit and loss account then looks as shown in Table 4.2.

	£
OPERATING PROFIT	150,000
less	
INTEREST PAID	50,000
leaving	
PRE-TAX PROFIT	100,000

Table 4.2

So for an increase of only 50 per cent in operating profit, pre-tax profits have risen by 100 per cent. Since the profits, after tax has been deducted, will belong to the owners of the company, the gearing is working very much in favour of the shareholders. But do the same sum assuming a 50 per cent fall in operating profits (see Table 4.3).

	£
OPERATING PROFIT	50,000
less	
INTEREST PAID	50,000
leaving	
PRE-TAX PROFIT	NIL

Table 4.3

It has only taken a 50 per cent fall in operating profit to wipe out completely the profits that belong to the shareholders. If operating profits fell by more than 50 per cent, the company would be making losses.

The appropriate level of gearing will vary between companies in different fields. But as a general rule, high gearing might be appropriate for a company whose income is very stable and on a rising trend: a property company deriving its income from rents on good commercial buildings, for example. It would not be appropriate for a company whose profits are liable to shoot up one year and down the next.

Effect of changing interest rates

One final point about income gearing. It is not simply that a company's operating profits can shoot up or down. The interest charge could also vary up or down as the general level of **interest rates** changes. This is why you have to look more closely at a company's borrowings. Has it borrrowed its money long-term at a **fixed rate of interest** (in which case the interest charge will not be affected if interest rates rise or fall)? Or are its borrowings at **variable** or **floating** rates of interest, which will change with general movements in interest rates?

In the example we have taken, a doubling of the rate of interest the company has to pay would be just as serious as a halving of its operating profits. So **high income gearing** based on variable-rate loans can be dangerous in a period of sharply rising interest rates. When interest rates do change dramatically, investment analysts and the press tend to comb the gearing statistics for companies that will suffer badly from a rise in interest rates or benefit from a reduction. But nowadays they need to be a little careful. The company might have used various techniques to protect itself against a rise in interest rates – more of this later.

Earnings per share

The next calculation concerns the **profit after tax** or **net profit**. In the case of John Smith & Co, this is the same thing as **net profit after tax attributable to members** or **available for ordinary shareholders** or **equity earnings**. Again, it is not very useful in isolation, though in subsequent years we can chart its rise or fall. But the key information is the amount of profit the company is making for each share in issue. And to get at this we simply divide the net profit by the number of shares in issue; the result is normally

Figure 4.1 Dividend yields since 1965 How average dividend yields have varied with the state of the stockmarket – the line shows the average yield on shares in the FTSE All-Share Index. The spike in 1974 marks the collapse in share prices of that era and the smaller but faster jump in 1987 reflects the stockmarket crash in October of that year. By the millenium yields were looking very low indeed (i.e share prices were very high) on historical criteria. Source: *Datastream.*

expressed in pence. John Smith has 40,000 shares, for which it earns £14,000 or 1,400,000 pence. This works out at 35p for each share.

This 35p is the company's **earnings per share** or **eps** and its rise or fall over the years is an important measure (perhaps the most important measure) of how good a job the company is doing for its shareholders. Where a company has one-off profits or losses in its accounts, you would probably use the adjusted earnings per share (which eliminate these items) rather than the official FRS 3 earnings per share. Why is the earnings per share figure more important than the simple profits figure? Again, an example helps.

Suppose John Smith & Co decided to take over another company exactly similar to itself, in exchange for shares. It creates 40,000 new shares and swaps them for shares in the company it is taking over. The enlarged John Smith now has combined net profits of £28,000 (its own £14,000, plus £14,000 from its acquisition). Its net profits have therefore doubled, which looks impressive. But the number of John Smith shares in issue has also doubled to 80,000.

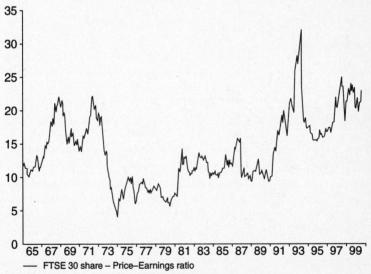

Figure 4.2   How price-earning ratios have varied over the years The average price-earnings (PE) ratio is quite a good guide to the mood of the equity market, though it needs interpreting with a little care. If the average PE ratio (in this case on the FT 30 Share Index) is rising, it means that share prices are rising faster than company earnings, which was the case in the 1990s. The drop to an average PE ratio of less than 5 in 1974 reflects the severity of the share price collapse of that period, while the peak in the early 1990s reflects a sharp fall in company earnings in the recession rather than a stockmarket share-price boom. Source: *Datastream.*

Divide the £28,000 net profits by the 80,000 shares and you get earnings per share of 35p. In the short run at least, a John Smith shareholder is no better off.

When looking back over a company's profit record it is easy to miss the fact that much of the growth might have come from **acquisitions** or issues of additional shares for cash. But look at the record of earnings per share and you have a far better picture of whether the company is really increasing the amount of profit it earns for shareholders.

Writers tend to talk of **internal growth** or **organic growth** for the profits growth the company generates from its existing activities, and **growth by acquisition** or **external growth** for increases in profit resulting from the purchase of other businesses.

Dividends per share

The figure for the cost of dividends – £4,000 in the case of John Smith – is also normally expressed as an amount per share. Divide it by the 40,000 shares in issue and you get a figure of 10p per share. Remember that the dividend no longer has a voucher allowing non-tax payers to reclaim tax paid by the company. But shareholders paying tax at the standard rate do not have to pay further tax on the 10p that they receive. For the implications of this, see the Glossary entry **grossing up**.

Dividend cover

Remember, too, that it is up to the directors to decide what proportion of profit is paid out as dividend, though shareholders generally have a chance to approve the decision. In this case £4,000 has been paid out of a net profit of £14,000 available for the ordinary shareholders. **Dividend cover** is thus 3.5 times – this is the result of dividing the £14,000 available profit by the £4,000 paid out. Dividend cover is an important measure of the safety of the dividend – the more strongly it is covered, the less chance that the company will have to reduce or **pass** (drop altogether) its payment if profits fall. In practice, companies do sometimes continue to pay a dividend even if they are temporarily making losses – it then comes out of **reserves** (see below). But they cannot do so indefinitely. The figure for dividend cover also gives an indication of the maximum dividend a company could have paid if it had distributed all of its profits.

Retained profit and cash flow

The final item in the profit and loss account in Table 3.2 is **retained profit** of £10,000. This is money **ploughed back** into the business. But the **depreciation** (£2,000 in the case of John Smith) is also money ploughed back into the business, though it is ploughed back to allow for the gradual wearing-out of plant and equipment. The term **cash flow** is frequently used for the combination of depreciation and retained profits, since both represent money that is retained in the company out of its profits and can be used for any of its various needs. If you know John Smith will need to spend £10,000 on new plant and equipment over the next year, you might look at its cash flow to see if the company can cover this **capital expenditure** from the money it is generating internally. With a cash flow of £12,000, it can (provided it maintains this level in the coming year), though it will probably need further money for additional **working capital** (to finance higher levels of stocks, and so on).

Cash flow statement

These sums are a little rough and ready. With the requirement for companies to publish a **cash flow statement** each year in addition to a profit and loss account, it is now possible to look in more detail at their cash-generating ability. A cash flow statement starts with the cash that a company generates from its operating activities – basically, its year's trading. Next comes a section headed 'returns on investments and servicing of finance' which deals with interest paid and received, dividends received from joint ventures, and so on. After that is a taxation section where corporation tax paid (not the tax due, note) at home and abroad is shown. We then move from 'revenue' items to 'capital' items with a section 'Capital expenditure and financial investment' which shows amounts spent on acquiring (or cash received from the sale of) fixed assets and similar items. If the company has bought or sold businesses for cash over the year, the relevant cash inflows and outflows will also be shown as a separate section. Then comes the amount paid out in cash dividends to shareholders over the year (which will probably be the previous year's final and the latest year's interim, as the latest year's final will not have been paid within the financial year). At this point a line is drawn and all the cash inflows and outflows are totted up to give a figure for the **net cash inflow** or **outflow** 'before use of liquid resources and financing'.

The final section shows how the company has managed its liquid resources over the year and also the effect of financing operations: cash raised from new loans or the sale of bonds or shares and cash laid out to repay existing debts.The effect of all items in the cash flow statement is aggregated in a final line showing the increase or decrease over the year in the amount of cash held by the company.

There is often a great deal of useful information for investors here. In particular, the cash flow statement highlights occasions where the cash generated is markedly different from the profits shown in the profit and loss account and allows the reasons to be deduced. A useful way to look at the statement is to start with the cash generated from operating activities and interest received, etc., then knock off the cash paid out in interest charges, tax and dividends. This shows whether the company is generating enough cash to cover its annual running costs, including the payment to shareholders. If it is not, you might want to probe a bit deeper. Then you can see if there is enough of a cash inflow left after allowing for these outflows to cover the cost of capital investment during the year as well. Do not necessarily worry if there is not – it may be perfectly reasonable for an expanding company to run down its cash resources or raise fresh cash from outside to finance investment in fixed assets. But if the company is going overboard in splurging out on new assets, the cash flow statement will help to highlight this and you might begin to question whether it is expanding too fast. The final sections of the statement will give you an idea of how soundly the company is financing whatever investment it is making, or whether its cash resources are coming under pressure.

Stockmarket ratings

The next stage is to take some of the figures we have worked out and relate them to the price of the company's shares in the stockmarket. Assume, for this purpose, that John Smith's shares are quoted on the stockmarket and that the current market price is around 500p. This market price is determined by the balance of buyers and sellers in the stockmarket and has nothing to do with the **nominal** or **par value** of the shares, nor with the amount of money subscribed for them originally by the founding shareholders – more of this later.

Yield

An investor who bought a share for 500p would stand to get a dividend of 10p, or an initial return of about 2 per cent on his outlay

(10 as a percentage of 500). This is the current **yield** on the shares and it will change slightly each time the share price changes on the stockmarket, which will be frequently. It will also change when the other component of the equation – the dividend – changes, though this will obviously not happen so often. The formula to calculate a dividend yield is simply:

$$\frac{\text{Dividend per share}}{\text{Share price}} \times 100$$

What is the significance of the yield? Clearly, it gives the investor an indication of the income return he might expect on his shares. An investor mainly concerned with income might select **high-yielding** shares. And it is one of the characteristics on which one company can be compared with another. But as such it is an imperfect instrument.

In theory, a **low yield** should suggest a fast-growing company and a **high yield** would indicate a company that is probably not going to increase its profits very fast or a company that carries an above-average risk. Investors are prepared to accept a low income today if they think the income will rise rapidly in the future as the company earns larger profits and pays higher dividends. If the dividends are not going to rise much, they will want a higher yield today.

The theory holds good up to a point. Unfortunately, it is completely arbitrary how much of its profit a company pays out as dividend. One cynical financial journalist habitually defines a dividend yield as 'five clowns sitting round a boardroom table'. And because the dividend is arbitrary, the dividend yield is an imperfect way of comparing two companies. Look at John Smith again. At 500p the shares yield 2 per cent on the 10p dividend. But out of its profits John Smith might quite easily decide to pay a dividend of twice as much: 20p. In this case the yield would be 4 per cent if the share price were still 500p. Yet it is the same company, earning the same profits.

Price-earnings ratio

To overcome this problem when comparing one company with another, there is another measure which is not affected by the dividend decision. It is the **price-earnings ratio** or **PE ratio**. Whereas a dividend yield is a fact, though an imperfect comparison tool, a PE ratio is a theoretical concept but much more useful for comparisons. In essence, it is a way of measuring how highly investors value the earnings a company produces. It is derived by dividing the **earnings per share** or **eps** figure into the market price of the shares. If John Smith has earnings per share of 35p and the market price is 500p, the shares are on a PE ratio of 14.3 (500 divided by 35). Other common ways of saying the same thing are: 'the shares sell at 14.3 **times earnings**' or 'the shares are on a **multiple of** 14.3'.

Why is this relevant? The thinking goes something like this. The amount a company earns determines ultimately the maximum dividend that it will be able to pay out of its earnings. If its earnings are growing, there is a good chance that dividends will rise in step. Earnings which are likely to grow fairly fast are therefore more valuable than static earnings, because they point to higher income in the future. Thus, in relation to what a company currently earns, investors will pay more for the shares if they think the earnings will rise rapidly. The investor is buying the right to a future flow of income and what he is prepared to pay today depends on what income he thinks he will get in the future. The way of quantifying this is by relating the earnings per share to the share price.

High and low PE ratios

All else being equal, a **high PE ratio** suggests a growth company and a **low PE ratio** suggests a company with a more static profits outlook or a company in a high risk area. It is not quite as simple as this, because a high PE ratio could indicate a company which had suffered a sharp temporary profits fall (reducing the 'E' element of the PE ratio) whereas the share price (the 'P' element) had not fallen in step because investors expected earnings to recover the following year. But the principle holds good.

Share price tables

Most 'serious' papers and magazines that quote share prices will show a yield and PE ratio as well (the *Financial Times* and some other papers give quite a lot of additional information which we will come to in a moment). These figures will not always be worked out in exactly the same way. For example, the dividend used could be the total dividend the company paid for its last financial year (the **historical dividend**). It could be the sum of the last two half-yearly

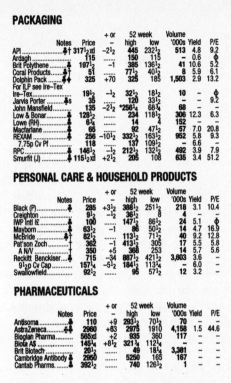

PACKAGING

	Notes	Price	+ or −	52 week high	low	Volume '000s	Yield	P/E
API	♣†	317½ xd	−2½	445	232½	513	4.8	9.2
Ardagh		115	......	150	115	−	0.6	φ
Brit Polythene	♣	197½	−1	385	136½	41	10.6	5.2
Coral Products	♣†	51	......	77½	40½	8	5.9	6.1
Dolphin Pack	♣♦	325	+70	325	185	1,503	2.9	13.2
For ILP see Ire−Tex								
Ire−Tex		19½	−½	32½	18½	10	−	φ
Jarvis Porter	♣s	35	......	120	33½	−	−	9.2
John Mansfield		135	−2½	*256¼	68¾	68	−	−
Low & Bonar	♣	128½		234	118½	306	12.3	6.3
Lowe (RH)		6¾	......	14	4	152	−	−
Macfarlane	♣	65	......	92	47½	57	7.0	20.8
REXAM	♣	256	−10½	332½	163½	952	5.8	9.3
7.75p Cv Pf	♣	118	......	137	109½	−	6.6	−
RPC	♣	146½	−½	212½	132½	492	3.9	7.9
Smurfit (J)	♣	115½ xd	+2½	205	108	635	3.4	51.2

PERSONAL CARE & HOUSEHOLD PRODUCTS

	Notes	Price	+ or −	52 week high	low	Volume '000s	Yield	P/E
Black (P)	♣	285	+3½	388½	251½	218	3.1	10.4
Creighton		9½	−½	36½	8	4	−	−
IWP Int'l IE		100	......	147½	86½	24	5.1	φ
Mayborn	♣	63½	−1	86	50½	14	4.7	16.9
McBride	♣†	82½	......	113½	71½	40	9.2	12.8
Pat'son Zoch	♣†	362	−1	413½	305	17	5.5	5.8
A N/V		350	+5	368	253	14	5.7	5.6
Reckitt Benckiser	♣	715	−34	887½	421½	3,603	3.6	−
9½p Cv Cap		157¼	−5½	184½	113¼	−	6.0	−
Swallowfield		92½	......	95	57½	12	3.2	−

PHARMACEUTICALS

	Notes	Price	+ or −	52 week high	low	Volume '000s	Yield	P/E
Antisoma	♣	110	+9	293½	70½	70	−	−
AstraZeneca	♣♣	2960	+63	2975	1910	4,158	1.5	44.6
Bioglan Pharma		565 xd	+2	935	360	117	−	−
Biota A$		145¼	+8½	321¾	112¼	−	−	−
Brit Biotech		20½	......	49	18¼	3,381	−	−
Cambridge Antibody	♣	2960		5250	165	167	−	−
Cantab Pharms	♣	392½	......	740	126½	1	−	−

Example 4.1 Share price information. Source: *Financial Times.*

payments (perhaps the past year's final and the current year's interim). Or it could be the dividend the company has forecast for its current year (the **forecast** or **prospective dividend**). Hence the terms **historical dividend yield** and **prospective dividend yield**. Be a bit wary of some prospective dividend yields, because they might also be based on the writer's own estimate of what the company is likely to pay, though possibly with a nod and a wink from the company itself; the context normally makes this clear.

You will also come across **historical PE ratios** and **prospective PE ratios**. The principle is the same. The first is based on actual earnings, the second on forecast or estimated earnings for a year for which the figures are not yet available.

Remember that yields and PE ratios move in opposite directions. A low yield and a high PE ratio probably indicate considerable expectations of growth. If the share price rises, the yield will fall further and the PE ratio will rise further. If the share price falls, the yield will rise and the PE ratio will fall. If a share price in a newspaper has **xd** after it, this stands for **ex-dividend**, and means that the buyer does not acquire the right to the recently announced dividend. **Cum dividend** means the buyer gets the dividend.

The way in which share price information is presented evolves constantly and anything we say on this point is likely to be fairly rapidly outdated. But a glance at the *Financial Times* late in 1999 gives an idea of the range of information available. The *FT*'s Monday coverage differs from its coverage during the rest of the week since there have been no previous day's dealings and the opportunity is taken to give more background information. On Tuesdays to Saturdays the *FT* lists against each share its price at the previous day's market close (this is a **middle price**, remember) and its movement (if any) the previous day. Next comes a historical record of the highest and lowest price reached over the past 52 weeks. This is followed by the **volume** of shares traded the previous day. After this come the basic investment yardsticks: **yield** and **price-earnings (PE) ratio**. Quite a bit of additional information is given via symbols and notes, including details of how you can get more information on some of the companies – it is worth noting the *FT*'s service for providing company reports.

On Monday the tables give the Friday closing price and the change over the week. This is followed by the amount of the annual dividend in pence, the dividend cover and the **market capitalization** of the company. This is the total value of all shares in the company, taken at the market price and is a useful guide to company size. You will see that it varies from less than £1m to many billions of pounds. The last date when the shares were declared **ex-dividend** is also provided. At the end of each entry there is an identification number you can use to get latest price information via a premium-charge telephone service.

Yield and PE ratio yardsticks

Not only are the yields and PE ratios of individual shares constantly changing. Average levels of PE ratio and yield change with the market cycle and investors' outlook. It is worth noting, incidentally, that where share prices in the past have risen to a level where the average PE ratio goes above 20 or so, a heavy fall in the market has often followed before too long. In the late 1990s this rule seemed to have been suspended – for a time at least. Thus, anything we say about PE ratios may be outdated even more rapidly than our comments on share price presentation, and it is the relative PE ratios rather than the absolute levels that we need to focus on.

For an idea of typical levels of yield and PE ratio, look at the table headed **FTSE Actuaries Share Indices** in the *Financial Times*. Like the share prices, it appears in the 'Companies & Markets' section of the paper. If you had been looking at this late in 1999 you would have seen that the average PE ratio on the privatized water companies was a low 7.95 and the average yield a fairly high 6.14 per cent. Water is a solid, safe earner, but unlikely in Britain to be one of the great growth industries of the future. Neither are investors looking for great growth from tobacco. The average yield on tobacco companies at this time was 4.92 per cent and the PE ratio 16.05. Compare this with the 44.10 average PE ratio and 1.6 per cent average yield on media companies at the same time. Investors were clearly looking for more growth here. Across the whole market the average PE ratio of industrial and commercial companies (excluding financial stocks) was 30.4 at this point and the average yield 2.16 per cent.

What we have looked at are only averages, and within each sector there will be a wide variation in the ratings of individual companies. Don't be thrown, incidentally, by an occasional rating that looks way outside the normal range. It could be, as we have seen, that profits have suffered a very temporary setback. It could also be that the market thinks the company might be taken over and has chased the share price up way beyond the levels it could sustain on the normal investment yardsticks.

Share price indices

We have mentioned the **FTSE Actuaries Indices**, but without explaining first what an index is. Take a very simple example. Suppose a stockmarket consists of just three companies whose names and share prices at the starting date for the index are as shown in Table 4.4. You could construct a very rudimentary index by simply adding the three share prices together to make 1,566p, then dividing by 1,566 and multiplying the result by 100. This would give you an index with a starting level of 100.

	Price	Index
	(p)	
Nuggins Nuts plc	450	
Ollie Oil plc	720	
Wilmington Widgets plc	396	
	1566	100.00

Table 4.4

The following day, say, the share prices of two of the companies rise
while one falls. Again, add up the three prices, divide by 1,566 and
multiply by 100 (see Table 4.5). This gives the new index figure of
102.3. You could therefore say that the market as a whole has risen
by 2.3 per cent, though Ollie Oil's price dropped against the trend.

	Price	Index
	(p)	
Nuggins Nuts plc	480	
Ollie Oil plc	700	
Wilmington Widgets plc	422	
	1602	102.30

Table 4.5

In practice, the construction of an index is vastly more complex than
this and the arithmetic is rather different. For a start, you probably
want to ensure that a movement in the share price of a large company has more effect on the index than share price movements of small
companies. But you only need to glance at the statistics pages of the
FT to realize that investors nowadays are index-mad. There is an
index for every conceivable purpose and for every possible category
of company. We cannot hope to cover them all here so we will simply mention some of the more significant.

The one you do not hear so much about nowadays is the old
FT 30-Share Index, also known as the **Financial Times Ordinary
Share Index**. The index, started in 1935 with a base of 100, is com-
piled from the share prices of 30 leading British companies and calculated as a geometric mean. It is biased towards major industrial
and retailing companies – the traditional **blue chips** of the stockmarket – though now includes financial stocks, oil, pharmaceuticals

FTSE Actuaries Share Indices										UK series
Produced in conjunction with the Faculty and Institute of Actuaries										

	£ Stlg Jun 26	Day's chge%	Euro Index	£ Stlg Jun 27	£ Stlg Jun 28	Year ago	Actual yield%	Cover	P/E ratio	Xd adj ytd	Total Return
FTSE 100	6313.5	-1.0	7868.8	6375.3	6405.2	6307.1	2.08	1.72	28.06	72.48	2893.84
FTSE 250	6578.4	+0.1	8198.9	6573.1	6566.9	5851.4	2.48	1.91	21.12	78.35	2976.11
FTSE 250 ex Inv Co	6602.7	+0.1	8229.2	6596.8	6589.6	5911.9	2.64	1.97	19.28	61.93	3005.06
FTSE 350	3084.1	-0.8	3843.8	3109.5	3121.5	3026.9	2.13	1.75	26.77	35.58	2891.37
FTSE 350 ex Inv Co	3073.9	-0.8	3831.2	3099.3	3111.2	3031.8	2.16	1.76	26.39	35.75	1478.56
FTSE 350 Higher Yield	2884.8	-0.5	3595.5	2900.8	2912.0	3016.1	3.22	1.73	18.00	49.63	2355.63
FTSE 350 Lower Yield	3302.4	-1.1	4115.9	3338.6	3351.5	3028.9	1.04	1.82	52.82	25.02	2477.84
FTSE SmallCap	3364.46	-0.1	4193.25	3367.97	3367.90	2651.18	2.72	1.86	19.73	46.05	3098.47
FTSE SmallCap ex Inv Co	3323.66	-0.2	4142.40	3328.99	3331.32	2621.82	2.89	2.00	17.32	48.54	3102.95
FTSE All-Share	3029.00	-0.8	3775.15	3052.98	3064.26	2941.39	2.16	1.76	26.36	35.20	2883.03
FTSE All-Share ex Inv Co	3017.73	-0.8	3761.11	3041.89	3053.20	2948.86	2.18	1.77	25.89	35.39	1478.28
FTSE All-Share ex Multinational	1042.19	-0.3	1076.57	1045.50	1050.76		2.50	1.74	22.99	12.61	1060.51
FTSE Fledgling	2189.50	+0.1	2728.86	2186.24	2184.77	1470.11	2.69	0.49	76.27	33.44	2570.44
FTSE Fledgling ex Inv Co	2230.99	+0.1	2780.56	2229.56	2232.36	1479.45	2.92	0.44	77.47	39.04	2839.14
FTSE All-Small	1992.09	-0.1	2482.81	1993.19	1992.89	1507.42	2.71	1.60	23.04	27.80	2341.80
FTSE All-Small ex Inv Co	2013.43	-0.1	2509.41	2015.89	2017.49	1517.75	2.90	1.73	19.95	30.29	2390.24
FTSE AIM	1722.6	+0.1	2146.9	1721.4	1723.2	1013.9	0.44	‡	‡	4.08	1595.84

FTSE Actuaries Industry Sectors										
RESOURCES(14)	5890.77	-1.8	7341.87	5996.67	6080.76	5286.01	2.26	2.00	22.14	77.15	2860.20
Mining(4)	4307.31	+0.2	5368.36	4298.48	4221.46	4039.77	3.04	2.09	15.75	84.80	1465.32
Oil & Gas(10)	6845.54	-2.1	8531.84	6989.79	7121.49	6094.41	2.14	1.98	23.62	81.80	3411.36
BASIC INDUSTRIES(66)	2102.88	-0.4	2620.89	2110.96	2104.86	2303.96	3.56	1.91	14.85	39.07	1330.00
Chemicals(16)	2318.94	-0.3	2890.18	2324.92	2325.48	2479.92	3.83	1.53	17.06	38.13	1283.83
Construction & Bld Matls(46)	1837.66	-0.4	2290.34	1845.08	1838.77	2027.29	3.76	2.56	10.37	39.90	1081.19
Forestry & Paper(2)	8393.52	-0.3	10461.15	8415.53	8388.74	7321.41	3.96	1.22	20.63	183.71	4140.16
Steel & Other Metals(1)	2347.04	-1.0	2925.20	2371.11	2335.00	3057.96	0.00	-	‡	0.00	1632.82
GENERAL INDUSTRIALS(83)	2540.86		3166.76	2541.84	2536.95	2166.88	2.90	1.96	17.57	33.30	1590.27
Aerospace & Defence(10)	2419.75	-0.5	3015.82	2431.25	2422.41	2429.80	2.28	2.04	21.53	32.38	1661.13
Diversified Industrials(0)									-	0.00	0.00
Electronic & Elect Equip(20)	7663.48	+0.8	9551.27	7604.60	7582.07	3403.12	2.04	2.00	24.50	29.46	4405.70
Engineering & Machinery(33)	2420.92	-0.4	3017.28	2429.58	2433.47	2702.20	4.74	1.89	11.16	47.49	1685.81
CYCLICAL CONSUMER GOODS(7)	5937.31	-1.8	7399.88	6045.43	6171.66	6942.80	1.66	3.21	18.73	42.03	2424.26
Automobiles(2)	4227.63	-1.9	5269.05	4311.12	4410.84	5081.53	1.28	4.90	15.96	18.63	2404.23
Household Goods & Textls(6)	2218.56	-0.1	2765.06	2221.09	2217.58	2062.25	5.94	‡	‡	71.51	1064.57
NON-CYCLICAL CONS GOODS(72)	5887.30	+0.9	7337.56	5832.78	5801.55	5615.07	2.22	1.54	29.27	71.59	2443.76
Beverages(8)	3380.38	-0.6	4213.09	3399.32	3426.32	3784.61	3.43	1.77	16.48	34.63	1410.71
Food Producers & Processors(19)	2793.97	-0.8	3482.23	2817.55	2830.27	3288.79	3.31	1.88	16.04	51.76	1434.23
Health(13)	2973.75	-0.5	3706.29	2989.01	2933.07	2496.46	1.67	1.94	30.85	31.32	1984.95
Packaging(6)	2081.55	-2.7	2594.31	2141.35	2135.35	2066.09	2056.98	6.40	1.80	8.71	80.23	1060.61
Personal Care & Hse Prods(4)	2080.93	-4.0	2593.54	2168.67	2182.01	2045.73	3.79	0.29	80.00†	38.49	949.20
Pharmaceuticals(19)	11369.60	+1.9	14170.35	11156.19	11062.21	9853.47	1.55	1.41	45.75	107.53	4220.64
Tobacco(3)	5750.12	-0.9	7166.58	5802.05	5752.89	7389.76	5.19	1.42	13.57	167.17	1810.62
CYCLICAL SERVICES(226)	4005.95	-0.3	4992.76	4016.71	4050.94	3813.17	2.05	1.77	27.60	45.87	2303.44
Distributors(17)	2768.15	+0.9	3450.04	2743.78	2783.57	2326.88	2.49	1.77	22.68	45.61	1169.53
General Retailers(43)	1676.00	-0.1	2088.86	1673.98	1678.78	2237.73	3.21	1.78	17.54	29.98	1086.26
Leisure Entertnt & Hotels(35)	3608.26	+1.3	4497.11	3561.48	3639.17	3707.82	2.19	1.96	23.30	60.24	2147.49
Media & Photography(45)	8173.56	-0.7	10187.01	8233.49	8326.22	5351.90	1.01	1.48	67.01	41.80	3193.26
Restaurants & Pubs(15)	3255.95	-0.3	4058.00	3265.58	3280.58	3791.74	3.08	2.04	15.89	46.68	1767.90
Support Services(45)	5185.76	-0.1	6463.20	5192.63	5213.72	4659.83	1.77	2.37	23.81	49.72	3526.49
Transport(27)	2761.02	-0.9	3441.22	2787.20	2788.35	3655.78	3.54	1.50	18.78	51.39	1306.79
NON-CYCLICAL SERVICES(23)	4527.09	-3.4	5642.28	4684.98	4709.98	4143.25	1.06	1.43	66.17	15.21	2565.69
Food & Drug Retailers(10)	2638.71	-1.1	3288.72	2667.43	2691.43	2666.25	2.98	1.93	17.42	52.71	1907.77
Telecommunication Services(13)	7281.95	-3.6	9075.76	7551.25	7589.18	6502.39	0.89	1.29	60.00†	14.05	3630.73
UTILITIES(10)	3681.18	-0.1	4587.99	3686.40	3701.45	3968.95	3.90	1.40	18.33	53.92	1894.90
Electricity(3)	3656.78	-0.5	4557.58	3675.85	3687.20	4258.45	4.18	0.80	30.09	64.29	2327.39
Gas Distribution(2)	4270.29	+0.6	5322.22	4246.54	4267.89	3537.73	1.61	2.53	21.84	40.48	4364.63
Water(5)	2417.27	-0.4	3013.35	2427.94	2439.67	3178.24	6.88	1.78	8.15	40.39	1647.93
INFORMATION TECHNOLOGY(67)	3445.84	-0.2	4294.67	3451.18	3483.48	1691.26	0.31	6.84	47.62	7.76	3487.95
Information Tech Hardware(9)	7653.38	+0.9	9538.68	7587.62	7737.22	1798.04	0.36	8.81	31.73	17.82	7735.78
Software & Computer Services(58)	2815.34	-1.1	3508.86	2845.93	2846.01	1678.66	0.26	4.36	90.00†	6.12	2847.61
NON FINANCIALS(583)	3168.73	-1.0	3949.30	3201.94	3218.05	2981.77	1.95	1.76	29.10	31.45	2702.62
FINANCIALS(233)	5432.70	+0.1	6770.97	5425.41	5418.97	5744.29	2.91	1.75	19.67	94.61	2662.70
Banks(11)	7626.11	+0.4	9504.69	7597.81	7565.87	8961.39	3.35	1.91	15.59	147.60	2837.56
Insurance(12)	2195.91	-1.4	2736.84	2226.66	2190.50	2255.18	3.32	0.47	63.83	53.74	1958.50
Life Assurance(8)	7226.04	+0.5	9006.07	7192.01	7263.50	6878.62	3.06	1.70	19.17	133.37	3408.46
Investment Companies(131)	5330.30	-0.5	6643.34	5356.53	5372.42	4150.85	1.41	1.08	65.82	43.02	2013.58
Real Estate(43)	1960.03	+0.3	2442.85	1954.00	1961.62	2033.28	2.59	1.83	21.15	28.17	1361.84
Speciality & Other Finance(28)	4903.64	-0.3	6111.58	4917.38	4885.11	4166.70	1.63	2.52	21.75	46.74	3128.18

Example 4.2 FTSE Actuaries UK share indices. Source: *Financial Times.*

and telecomms, which have assumed greater importance. Its ups and downs reflect the mood of the market, but it would not be a good index against which to measure the performance of a typical investment **portfolio** ('portfolio' is simply the collective term for the shares an investor or a fund owns). However, its venerable age makes it useful for historical tracking of share price trends.

As a yardstick against which to measure actual portfolios, the **FTSE Actuaries Indices** are a great deal better. First, they reflect the movements of almost 800 shares, representing more than 98 per cent by value of the London market. Second, each company in the index is weighted according to its market value. A movement in the share price of a large company has more effect on the index than movement in a small one.

The **FTSE Actuaries All-Share Index** (the **All-Share**) is the most representative of all, reflecting the full near-800 companies.

The **Non-financials Index** includes all except financial and property companies and investment trusts. The indices are in turn further broken down into a number of broad categories where you may see a distinction between cyclical and non-cyclical businesses. Thus you have utilities and you also have both cyclical consumer goods and non-cyclical consumer goods. Then the broad categories are broken down into individual business sectors so that, for example, you can find under non-cyclical consumer goods the sub-indices for beverages, food producers, health, packaging and several more. Thus there is an appropriate yardstick against which you can compare the rating and share price performance of an individual company in virtually any line of business. Not only do the indices give a measure of price movements but they also show average yields and PE ratios and a measure of the **total return** offered by the constituent companies (total return combines share price movement with income received as dividend). On Saturdays additional information is published on the **highs** and **lows** for each sector.

But the index most commonly used nowadays to measure and report on daily or hourly market movements, in the press and on the broadcast media, is the the **Financial Times Stock Exchange 100-Share Index** (**FTSE 100** or **Footsie** index). This started with a base of 1,000 at end-December 1983 and reflects price movements of the 100 most significant companies on the London market. Because of the smaller number of companies it can be calculated in real time – it changes constantly throughout the day. It was initially introduced mainly as a basis for dealing in equity index options and futures (see Chapter 18). Then there is the **FTSE 250 Index**, launched in 1992, which comprises the next range of companies, immediately below the size that would qualify for the FTSE 100. The **FTSE 350 Index** combines the companies of the FTSE 100 and the FTSE 250 and is a benchmark for companies in which the market is most liquid. The **FTSE SmallCap** measures the performance of smaller companies which are included in the All-Share but do not make it into the FTSE 350. And to reflect the performance of the very small concerns which do not even make it into the All-Share there is the **FTSE Fledgling Index**. To slice the cake yet another way, there is a **FTSE All-Small Index** which combines the companies in the FTSE SmallCap and the FTSE Fledgling. And late in 1999 **FTSE techMARK** indices emerged to track the progress of technology-related stocks.

But investment nowadays is international. The *Financial Times* also publishes **FT/S&P Actuaries World Indices** of all major (and some minor) stockmarkets, expressed in terms of the local currency, of US dollars, yen, euros and of sterling. There is also a whole range of indices of European shares under the general grouping of **FTSE Actuaries Share Indices – European Series**, some of which include British shares, some of which do not, some limited to the markets in euro-zone countries, and so on. Probably the most frequently quoted are the **Eurotop 300** and the **Eurotop 100**. Needless to say, most overseas stockmarkets have their own indices, the more important of which are tracked daily in the *FT*. Those referred to most commonly in the British media are the **Dow Jones Industrial Average** for the New York Stock Exchange and the **Nikkei 225 Average** for the Tokyo market (often abbreviated simply to the 'Dow' and the 'Nikkei').

Journalists often refer to shares as cheap or expensive relative to their sector of the FT-Actuaries Indices. Movements in an index are frequently referred to in terms of **points**. If the FT 30-share index falls from 2,400 to 2,380 it has dropped 20 points and a point is also sometimes used to mean a 1p price movement in an individual share or a £1 movement for a gilt-edged stock. Why movements are not generally expressed more meaningfully as percentage changes is obscure – at least the *FT* does express movements in its All-Share and World indices in terms of percentages.

Matching the index

Institutional investors attempt to **beat the index** most relevant to their portfolios of shares, but on balance have difficulty in doing so. They control such large volumes of money that they find it difficult to buy adequate numbers of shares in some of the smaller companies represented, which often outperform those of their larger counterparts in certain market conditions.

Some of them do run portfolios which seek merely to match a particular index by buying the stocks which constitute the index in the same proportions as they are represented in the index, or by otherwise trying to mimic the performance of the index. It is more difficult than it sounds. But these **indexed portfolios** or **index-linked portfolios** (they are also known as **tracker funds**) mean that when a large company such as British Telecom launches on the stockmarket, many institutions are bound to buy its shares in large quantities simply to maintain the balance of their portfolios.

Balance sheet ratios

The balance sheet can tell you a great deal about the financial health of a company, but it doesn't throw up convenient investment ratios in quite the same way as a profit and loss account. There's one possible exception – the net asset value – which we'll come to later. But there are a number of items an investment analyst or a financial journalist will check.

Borrowings and balance sheet gearing

Back to John Smith & Co. One of the first things to look at is the company's **gearing**: the relationship between the **borrowed money** and the **shareholders' money** in the business. We've already touched on it briefly but now it can be reduced to a convenient formula.

The borrowings, in the case of John Smith, are the £8,000 bank overdraft and the £30,000 term loan, totalling £38,000. Trade creditors do not count as borrowings in this context, since they are not clocking up interest charges. The shareholders' money in the business is the £50,000 of **shareholders' funds.** The most common way of relating the two is to calculate **borrowings as a percentage of shareholders' funds** – a definition that can be a little confusing because it could suggest that borrowings are a part of shareholders' funds, which of course they are not.

In this case the £38,000 **gross borrowings** are equivalent to 76 per cent of the £50,000 figure for the shareholders' interest. This would be fairly high for an established stockmarket-listed company but by no means out of the ordinary for a private company. Sometimes the gearing is worked out on the **net borrowings** (borrowings less cash) instead. In this case the net borrowings are £33,000 after the £5,000 of cash in the bank is deducted, and the ratio is 66 per cent.

The 'borrowings as a percentage of shareholders' funds' ratio, whether worked out on the gross borrowings or the net borrowings, is referred to as the **balance sheet gearing** to distinguish it from the **income gearing**: the relationship between profits and interest charges that was discussed in the context of the profit and loss account. Both can be useful in estimating whether a company is **over-geared** or **over-borrowed**. High balance-sheet gearing matters rather less if a company is exceptionally profitable or if the borrowings are at a very low fixed rate of interest. John Smith is, as it

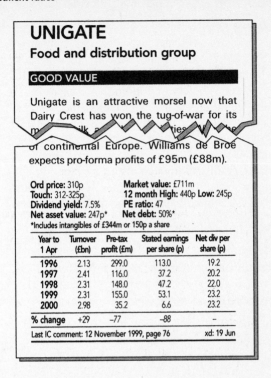

UNIGATE

Food and distribution group

GOOD VALUE

Unigate is an attractive morsel now that Dairy Crest has won the tug-of-war for its ~~milk~~ ~~ies~~ ~~e~~ of continental Europe. Williams de Broe expects pro-forma profits of £95m (£88m).

Ord price: 310p	**Market value:** £711m
Touch: 312-325p	**12 month High:** 440p **Low:** 245p
Dividend yield: 7.5%	**PE ratio:** 47
Net asset value: 247p*	**Net debt:** 50%*

*Includes intangibles of £344m or 150p a share

Year to 1 Apr	Turnover (£bn)	Pre-tax profit (£m)	Stated earnings per share (p)	Net div per share (p)
1996	2.13	299.0	113.0	19.2
1997	2.41	116.0	37.2	20.2
1998	2.31	148.0	47.2	22.0
1999	2.31	155.0	53.1	23.2
2000	2.98	35.2	6.6	23.2
% change	+29	–77	–88	–

Last IC comment: 12 November 1999, page 76   xd: 19 Jun

Example 4.3 Company performance and the main investment yardsticks.
Source: *Investors Chronicle.*

happens, quite highly profitable so interest charges only take a fairly small proportion of profits despite high balance-sheet gearing.

Bankers and other lenders always look for a **cushion** for the money they advance. In income terms the cushion is the level of profit out of which the company pays the interest charges. John Smith's profit would have to fall a long way before it was unable to pay its interest, so there is a comfortable cushion for the lender. In balance sheet terms, the cushion is the shareholders' funds. If the company starts losing money, it is the shareholders' funds that will be depleted first, so in John Smith's case there is (on paper, at least) a reasonable margin before the lender might be at risk of losing his money.

Security for borrowings

The other thing a lender normally requires is **security** for his loan in the form of a **charge** over some or all of the assets of the company.

The principle is similar to taking a mortgage on a home. If the borrower fails to keep up his interest and capital payments, the lender – the building society – can sell the house and recover its loan from the proceeds. With a company the charge may be a **fixed charge** on specific assets – its machinery or buildings, for example – or may be a **floating charge** on all the assets of the business including the current assets. The lender has priority for repayment out of the proceeds of selling the assets over which he has a charge. The importance of this in practical terms is that a company, particularly a smaller company, may find it difficult to borrow further money when it does not have enough reasonably saleable assets to provide adequate security for the loan. And since banks will usually take a floating charge when they lend money to a business, the **unsecured creditors** (who are probably mainly the suppliers who have not yet been paid) come at the bottom of the creditors' pile when a company goes bust. They do, of course, still rank ahead of the shareholders.

John Smith's financial position

From John Smith's gearing and from our knowledge of the business we might deduce the following. The company is likely to expand further in the current year, which means it will need yet more money to finance higher levels of stocks and debtors (see below), and it may need to install additional machinery to meet the demand for its paperweights. It generated a cash flow of £12,000 last year (on the crude measure of retained profits plus depreciation) and, assuming profits continue rising, the cash flow ought to be higher in the current year. But it is unlikely to be enough to provide all the money John Smith will need. It could probably increase its borrowings a little. But if it were a stockmarket-listed company, it would almost certainly be thinking of raising further equity capital by issuing additional shares for cash. This would reduce the gearing by increasing the proportion of shareholders' money in the business. And, quite apart from bringing in money for the immediate needs, by increasing the size of the equity 'cushion' it also prepares the way for bringing in additional borrowed money in the future.

Remember that fast-growing companies tend to use up cash faster than they can generate it from their profits. The expansion means that they are having to tie up more and more cash in higher and higher levels of stocks and debtors: their **working capital** need rises rapidly. A company that expands too fast may be described as **overtrading** (trading beyond its financial resources). It can go bust simply because it runs out of cash to pay its bills, even though it may have been operating at an 'accounting' profit.

Investment analysts therefore check the accounts to see if a company has adequate resources to finance its business and whether it would be able to raise any additional money needed. In the short run, a rights issue to raise further money from the sale of shares (see Chapter 9) often depresses the price of the shares because it increases the number in issue.

While looking at John Smith's borrowings, we would also check whether they are long term or short term and whether they are at fixed or variable rates of interest. The overdraft has to be counted as short term and the interest rate will be variable. The term loan, we might learn from the notes, has to be repaid over seven years, which would normally be classed as 'medium term'. The interest rate could be fixed or variable – the notes should say. But nowadays you need to be a little careful, because a large company may have borrowed floating-rate money and **swapped** it for fixed-rate, or *vice versa*. It could also have bought a **cap** or some other hedging instrument to limit its exposure to rising interest rates on floating-rate borrowings (see Chapters 15 and 17). Companies are getting rather better at giving detail of arrangements of these kinds in the notes to their accounts, but you cannot always rely on it.

Net assets per share

Next, look at the £50,000 figure for shareholders' funds: the book value of the shareholders' interest in the company. Divide the ordinary shareholders' funds by the number of ordinary shares in issue (£50,000 divided by 40,000 shares) and you get £1.25 (or 125p as it is usually expressed). It corresponds in this case, though not always, with the £1 the original investors subscribed for each share plus the 25p of retained profits attributable to each share.

It is very important to grasp what this **net asset value** or **NAV** figure means. The £50,000 of shareholders' funds on which it is based is very much an accounting figure and does not usually tell you anything much about the value investors are likely to put on the company in the stockmarket, which normally depends far more on the profits the company is capable of earning. First, John Smith & Co has no intention of closing down the business, selling the assets, paying the debts and returning what is left to shareholders. Even if it did, what was left would be very unlikely to amount exactly to £50,000. The paperweight-making machinery **stands in the books** at £28,000, but would a buyer necessarily pay exactly £28,000 for a used paperweight-making machine? It is highly unlikely. Would stocks of raw materials and half-finished or finished paperweights actually bring in £50,000? Again, unlikely.

When a long-term investor buys shares, what he is really buying is the right to a flow of income (by way of dividend) in the future, and generally he is buying shares in companies which he hopes will provide a rising income. If the income rises there is a good chance that the capital value – the market value – of the shares he holds will rise too.

Some companies are capable of providing an increasing flow of earnings without owning anything much in the way of assets. A successful advertising agency, say, might rent the offices it operates from and hire its photocopiers, typewriters and other equipment. Apart from a few sticks of office furniture and whatever cash it had accumulated from its profits, it might own virtually nothing. Its 'assets' are the people who work for it, its reputation in the business and its client connections – items which do not normally appear in a balance sheet. Yet the stockmarket might put a high value on the shares purely because of the profit-earning potential. This is why a yardstick that relates to earnings rather than assets – the price-earnings ratio – is the main one that investors use.

Asset-rich companies

But there are certain types of company where the assets, or a fair proportion of the assets, can be reasonably accurately priced and easily sold. Companies whose main business is owning property, owning shares in other companies (**investment trusts** – see Chapter 21), or which have a lot of cash or investments in the balance sheet are the main examples. Others in this category are companies carrying on a trade that involves owning large amounts of property: some stores groups, hotel companies and breweries which own large numbers of pubs.

In these cases the **net asset value** can and does affect the price investors will pay for the shares in the stockmarket. The shares are commonly described as standing **at a premium to** (above) the net asset value, or **at a discount to** (below) the net asset value. The size of the premium or discount is expressed as a percentage. If XYZ Holdings has net assets per share (or an NAV) of 100p and the shares stand at 90p in the market, the shares are at a discount to assets of 10 per cent. If the market price is 108p, the shares stand at a premium to assets of 8 per cent. For taxation and other reasons, the shares of **property investment companies** and single-tier investment trusts normally stand at a discount to assets except at times of market euphoria.

Readily saleable assets are most important when takeovers are in the air. A company with high earnings but few assets may try to acquire an **asset-rich company** to give it more substance. And the company at the receiving end of the bid will argue (not always successfully) that the takeover price should be at least as high as the value of its assets.

Return on assets

This brings us to another commonly used ratio: a company's **return on assets**. This is a measure of the profits the company earns relative to the capital employed in the business. As such, it can be used as a measure of the efficiency of one company against another, though it needs using with care. And it is not specifically a stockmarket measure: it does not reveal anything about the return the company earns on shareholders' money. It measures the return on all money used, whether derived from loans or from the shareholders. A company such as our successful advertising agency, with very few assets, will be earning a very high return on capital employed, simply because very little capital is employed. The return on assets is used mainly to compare one company with another in the same or a similar business.

To calculate the return on assets you take the profit before tax and before the interest on longer-term debt and express it as a percentage of shareholders' funds (less goodwill – see Chapter 5) plus long-term loans, deferred tax and minorities (again, see Chapter 5).

The return on assets figure can sometimes provide useful clues for a **stockmarket predator**: a company on the look-out for other companies it might take over. Suppose a retail stores group which owns most of its shops is showing a return on assets of only five per cent. Clearly, it is not a very efficient trader: it could make this level of return simply by renting its shops to other retailers. It is earning very little profit from the trading operation. A predator might reckon he could take over the retail stores group and vastly improve the return it earned by supplying more retailing flair. And it might be possible to recoup part of the costs of the takeover by selling some of the properties or selling them and leasing them back (a **sale and leaseback** transaction – see Chapter 20).

Internet pointers

Any number of sites provide recent share price and index information (see Chapter 23). For the basic facts and figures that you need for fundamental analysis, go to the Hemmington Scott website at www.hemscott.net/, the *Financial Times* site at www.ft.com/ (look in the 'company briefs' section) or to individual companies' websites. Detailed (and rather technical) information on the construction of the FTSE indices is available from FTSE International at www.ftse.com/. The London Stock Exchange site at www. londonstockexchange.com/ has statistical information on names and numbers of companies traded in its various markets.

5 Refining the figurework

There are a few more terms relating to company accounts that will crop up fairly frequently in the press commentary and the best way of illustrating what they mean is with another sample balance sheet (see Table 5.1).

This time we have taken a more mature company: call it Jones Manufacturing. Its assets are in the millions rather than the thousands. It owns the properties from which it operates: note the £3m item for land and buildings included under fixed assets. And, partly because it has been ploughing back a proportion of its profits over many years, its shareholders' funds are a substantial £11m.

Goodwill

We have already mentioned the topic of **goodwill** in a balance sheet, but without explaining what it is or how it is likely to have arisen, and it now features in the Jones Manufacturing accounts. Suppose Jones had recently taken over another business – call it Bonzo Beading – for a price of £3m. Bonzo Beading's net assets at the time of the takeover were only £2m. Thus, over and above the price it was paying for the Bonzo Beading assets, Jones Manufacturing paid £1m for the goodwill of the business it was acquiring – in other words, it was paying extra for the company's reputation, trading connections, profit-earning capability, and so on. After the takeover, Bonzo Beading's £2m of net assets were incorporated in the Jones Manufacturing group balance sheet. But the £1m of goodwill in the price also had to be accounted for, so it was shown as a separate item under the general heading of **fixed assets** and the subheading of **intangible assets**.

The accounting treatment of goodwill is complex and had, in the late 1990s, been changed by a new accounting standard. Previously, goodwill acquired in the course of a takeover had normally been written off against reserves and did not show on the balance sheet. After the change, acquired goodwill of this type appears in company accounts. But there is a further complication. Tangible fixed assets need to be **depreciated** each year to recognize the reduction in their value from wear and tear. What about intangible assets like goodwill? Do they lose in value and need to be depreciated?

The broad answer is 'yes', unless it can be demonstrated that the goodwill in the acquired businesses is holding or increasing its value. So you will find a range of treatments. Sometimes depreciation of goodwill is provided out of the year's profits, sometimes it is not.

Note that it is only 'acquired' goodwill that is shown in the balance sheet. Most successful businesses are actually worth a lot more than the mere value of their assets – in other words, their value (on the stock market or elsewhere) includes a large element of goodwill. But this goodwill that the business has generated internally does not normally appear in its accounts. It is up to the market to decide, in the value it puts on a company, what the goodwill of the business is worth. It is not for the company to try to estimate this in its accounts.

Note that goodwill is not the only type of intangible asset. Other items such as patents, trade marks and royalty agreements sometimes appear under 'intangible assets' in a company's accounts. Investment analysts will normally exclude goodwill when calculating a company's net asset value, which strictly ought to be expressed as **net tangible asset value**. They will not necessarily exclude items like patents which can have a definable market value.

Associated companies

The next item is **investments in associated companies** or **interests in associates**; sometimes associates are also called **related companies**. The definition of an **associated company** is open to interpretation. But in general it would be a company which was not a subsidiary, but in which Jones Manufacturing had an interest amounting to between 20 per cent and 50 per cent of the share capital and over whose affairs it exerted some management influence. In other words, Jones Manufacturing does not hold the shares in the associate simply as an unrelated investment, as it might own a holding of government stock.

There is probably some trading relationship between Jones Manufacturing and its **associate**. The associated company might, say, be an important supplier of components to Jones, or it might be an important customer for Jones's products – in either case it could be of benefit to Jones to be able to exert some influence over the associate's affairs. In accounting terms, the interest in the associated company will normally appear in the balance sheet at a figure representing Jones Manufacturing's share of the net assets of the associate. If the associated company or companies had net assets of £10m and Jones Manufacturing owned a 30 per cent stake, the figure in Jones's balance sheet would be 30 per cent of £10m, or £3m. An interest in an associate is different from a mere **trade investment**: a shareholding in a company with which there is probably no particular management involvement or influence.

Varieties of debt

Jones Manufacturing's **sources of finance** are also more varied and a little more complex than those of John Smith & Co. There is a bank overdraft, though small in relation to the company's size. But there are three types of medium-term or long-term debt under the heading of **creditors due in more than one year**. First comes the familiar term loan: again fairly small at £800,000.

The other two items – the **debenture stock** and the **convertible loan stock** – are in a different category of borrowings, because they are **securities** issued by the company rather than loans from a bank. Much as the government does when it borrows by issuing a gilt-edged stock, Jones Manufacturing has raised money by creating different forms of loan stock and selling them to investors: the familiar principle of issuing an 'IOU' note in return for cash (see Chapter 13). These stocks, once issued, will normally be traded in the stockmarket. Investors who paid cash to the company for them when first issued can either wait till the date they are due to be repaid by the company, or can sell them to other investors in the stockmarket. Both in this case pay a fixed rate of interest.

The **debenture stock** will probably be secured on specific assets of the company. Provided the assets are of good quality, it should thus be a safe form of investment for buyers. It is a form of long-term borrowing. It is not due for repayment until 2014, and when first issued it may have had a **life** of 25 or 30 years – possibly more.

The convertible loan stock is almost certainly an **unsecured loan stock**. It is not secured on the assets of the company, and to this extent it is a little less safe than the debenture. But its most important feature is that it is **convertible**. At some stage of its life, and probably right from the outset, it can be exchanged for ordinary shares according to a pre-arranged formula. This gives it some of the attributes of a loan and some of the attributes of an ordinary share, though in legal and accounting terms it is a loan. Until it is converted, it pays a fixed rate of interest like the debenture stock. Once it is converted into ordinary shares, the shares are identical to the other shares in issue and receive the same dividend.

Jones Manufacturing
Consolidated balance sheet as at 31 December

	£'000	£'000
FIXED ASSETS		
Tangible assets:		
Land and buildings	3,000	
Plant and machinery	5,600	
		8,600
Intangible assets:		
Goodwill		1,000
INVESTMENTS IN ASSOCIATED COMPANIES		3,000
CURRENT ASSETS		
Stocks	5,000	
Debtors	3,500	
Cash at bank	500	
	9,000	
CREDITORS – AMOUNTS DUE WITHIN ONE YEAR (Current Liabilities)		
Trade creditors	3,000	
Tax payable	600	
Dividend proposed	400	
Bank overdrafts	800	
	4,800	
NET CURRENT ASSETS		4,200
TOTAL ASSETS LESS CURRENT LIABILITIES		16,800
CREDITORS (AMOUNTS DUE IN MORE THAN ONE YEAR)		
Term loans	800	
9% Debenture stock 2014	2,800	
6% Convertible Loan Stock 2010	1,500	
		5,100
PROVISIONS FOR LIABILITIES AND CHARGES		500
MINORITY SHAREHOLDERS' INTEREST		200
NET ASSETS ATTRIBUTABLE TO JONES MANUFACTURING		11,000

SHARE CAPITAL

Equity share capital (20p ordinary shares)	1,500	
Non-equity share capital (£1 preference shares)	500	
		2,000
RESERVES		
Share premium account	1,650	
Revaluation reserves	1,950	
Profit and loss account (revenue reserves)	5,400	
		9,000
SHAREHOLDERS' FUNDS		11,000
Analysis of shareholders' funds		
Equity		10,500
Non-equity		500

Table 5.1 Consolidated balance sheet.

If the stock is not converted into shares during the **conversion period**, it may revert to being a simple unsecured loan stock, paying the fixed rate of interest until it is eventually repaid in 2010. Whether or not holders of the stock exercise the right to convert it will depend on how successful Jones Manufacturing is. The **conversion terms** were probably pitched originally at a level somewhat above Jones Manufacturing's share price at the time of issue (the **conversion premium**). If the share price at the time had been 80p, the terms of the loan might have stipulated that £1 nominal of the loan could be converted into one ordinary share, meaning that anyone who paid £100 for £100 nominal of the loan would be paying £1 for a share if he exercised his conversion rights – a conversion premium of 25 per cent at the time of issue. Five years later, if Jones had increased its profits and dividends at a good rate, the share price might have risen to, say, 180p. At this level there is clearly a value in the right to exchange £1 nominal of loan for a share worth 180p.

Because of this **conversion value**, the price of the convertible loan stock itself would have risen in the stockmarket. Investors would have been prepared to pay more than £100 for £100 nominal value of the loan, when they knew that each £1 nominal could be converted into a share worth 180p. The calculations that give the likely price of a convertible loan stock in the stockmarket, relative to the price of the ordinary shares, are quite complex. In general, a convertible loan rises in value to reflect the rise in value of the ordinary shares, but rises at a slower percentage rate than the ordinary shares. On the other hand, it normally provides a higher and more secure yield than the ordinary shares, at least in the early years until the dividend on the ordinary shares catches up.

For the company the main advantage of the convertible loan is that the interest rate it needs to pay will probably be lower than for an ordinary unsecured loan stock. Investors will accept the lower interest rate because of the possibility of capital gains if the share price rises and the market value of the convertible stock follows it. The convertible also represents a form of **deferred equity**. If the company had issued ordinary shares instead, its earnings and dividends would immediately be spread over a larger number of shares: the earnings would be **diluted** over the larger capital immediately.

Convertible stocks with considerably more complex features have also been commonplace in recent years, particularly in the case of issues made through euromarket mechanisms (see Chapter 17) and you find preference shares (see below) that are convertible into ordinary shares as well as loans that are convertible. One particular type of complex convertible needs mentioning here: the **premium put convertible** which also surfaced in an even more tortuous form as the **convertible capital bond**. The 'premium put' feature is an option for the investor that allows him to require the company to buy the stock back at a premium over its issue price after, typically, five years if the share price has not risen sufficiently to make conversion worth while. This feature appealed to euromarket investors who are generally bond-oriented rather than equity-oriented. The disadvantage for the issuer is that he is not sure when issuing the stock whether he is raising permanent capital or whether he will have to find the money to redeem the issue at a premium after a few years, possibly at a time when he is far from flush with cash.

Diluting earnings and assets

By issuing the convertible loan, Jones Manufacturing can offset the interest cost (the cost of **servicing** the loan) against tax, whereas dividends on ordinary shares or on convertible preference shares would have to be paid out of taxed income. By the time the loan can be converted, earnings should have risen significantly and the company's asset value should also have risen. Investment analysts, journalists and the companies themselves often refer to **fully diluted earnings per share** and **fully diluted assets per share**. This means they have calculated what the earnings per share would be on the assumption the stock was converted and current earnings (adjusted for the disappearance of the interest charge on the convertible) were spread over the larger number of shares. They have also done the same sums for the NAV (see below). As we have seen, companies may issue **convertible preference** shares (see above) instead of convertible loan stocks. They may convert into ordinary shares in much the same way, but the dividend on the convertible preference is not tax-deductible as the convertible loan stock interest is. On the other hand, convertible preference rank as share capital rather than debt.

Provisions

There are two other unfamiliar items. The **provisions for liabilities and charges** of £500,000 has to be knocked off the assets figure before arriving at a net asset value. It may consist mainly of **deferred tax**, which is tax that might become payable in the future but is not yet a sufficiently certain liability to be provided for under current liabilities. It would also include sums the company had earmarked to meet certain known future costs, such as the cost of closing down or reorganizing one part of the business.

Minority shareholders

The second item, **minority shareholders' interest** or **minority interest**, was mentioned in Chapter 4. Where Jones does not own all the shares of all of its subsidiaries, this figure represents the assets attributable to the shares in these subsidiaries that are held by other parties. Since this value does not belong to the shareholders in Jones it has to be deducted before reaching the figure for the net assets attributable to Jones Manufacturing's owners.

Capital commitments

Two further items that could affect the balance sheet in the future appear in the notes to the accounts but not in the accounts themselves. One item is **capital commitments**. This is expenditure on assets that the directors have authorized or contracted for but which has not yet taken place. It can be useful in giving an idea of the company's investment plans and whether these would be covered by the cash flow.

Contingent liabilities

The other item is **contingent liabilities**. Jones Manufacturing might provide a **guarantee** for the bank borrowings of one of its associated companies. Or there might be a legal case pending against Jones, in which the other side is claiming £500,000 of damages, though Jones denies liability. In both cases Jones does not expect any liability to arise, but it might. So the liabilities are not provided for in the accounts themselves but the company notes that they might arise in the future.

Preference shares

Back to the balance sheet itself. The make-up of shareholders' funds is also more complex than in the case of John Smith & Co. First, Jones Manufacturing has two classes of share capital: **preference shares** as well as **ordinary shares**.

Companies with **preference share capital** often have it for historical reasons, though issues of preference shares (particularly convertible preference) have regained popularity in recent years. Various mutations of preference capital may also crop up in the financing of young businesses which are not quoted on a stockmarket and in the financing of **management buy-outs** (see Chapter 11). Preference shares usually pay a fixed dividend and in this respect are more like a loan stock than an ordinary share. But the dividend has to be paid out of profits that have borne tax, whereas interest on a loan stock is allowable against tax. Against this disadvantage, preference shares will not normally be counted in the **gearing** of a company whereas loan stocks will. And they are safer in that the company risks being closed down if it cannot pay interest on its loans whereas it could miss dividends on the preference shares without the same risk.

Preference shares are part of **shareholders' funds** but not part of **ordinary shareholders' funds**. They are **share capital**, but they are not **equity share capital**. They do not share in the rising prosperity of a company, because their dividend is fixed and does not increase with rising profits. But they are entitled to their dividend before the ordinary shareholders get anything, so the dividend is safer than that of an ordinary share. And if the company should be **wound up** (closed down), preference shareholders are normally entitled to be repaid the par value of their shares (usually but not necessarily £1) before the ordinary shareholders get anything. This is assuming there is something left after loans and all the other debts of the company – which rank before preference shares – have been repaid. Preference shares do not normally carry votes unless the dividend is **in arrears** (the payments have not been kept up). Note that if an issue of preference shares has the word **cum.** in its title, this stands for **cumulative**. It means that, if the company is not able to pay a dividend on the preference shares in some years, these dividends still roll up and must be paid when the company is able to do so. If the word **red.** appears in the description, this means that the shares are **redeemable** – they will be repaid at some stated future date.

One technicality you may come across occasionally: certain types of preference share issued by subsidiary companies rather than by the parent company, but guaranteed by the parent, may have more of the characteristics of a loan than of share capital and may need to be treated as a liability rather than as capital in the consolidated accounts.

Less usual types of share

We have only shown preference shares and ordinary shares, but there are various other less common forms of share capital that companies may issue. These are variations on the theme of equity or preference. **Deferred ordinary shares** probably do not **rank for dividend** until converted into ordinary shares at some future date. **Preferred ordinary shares** will get a minimum dividend before the ordinary get anything, and probably share in ordinary dividends thereafter. **Participating preference shares** may be similar; they get a fixed dividend plus an extra dividend on top that depends on profits. **Convertible preference shares** may convert into ordinary shares, and so on.

Par values

Look next at the **equity share capital**. Note that Jones Manufacturing has **issued ordinary share capital** of £1.5m, but that this is divided into units of 20p each. In other words, each pound of nominal capital is divided into five shares, so there are 7.5m shares in issue, each with a **nominal**, **par** or **face** value of 20p. The meaning of the par value sometimes causes problems. It has nothing to do with the price at which the shares may be traded in the stockmarket and for most practical purposes you can forget it – American companies often have ordinary shares (known as **common stock**) with **no par value**.

Many British companies have shares of 25p par value and the other common denominations are 5p, 10p, 20p, 50p, and £1. But this is relevant mainly for certain accounting purposes and for a technical **Companies Act** requirement that companies may not issue shares at prices below their par value. What interests investors is the price at

which a share is quoted in the stockmarket, and it is perfectly possible
to have a 5p share quoted at 400p or a £1 share quoted below its par
value at 80p.

Authorized and issued capital

One other facet of a company's capital crops up in press reports, particularly of take-over offers. As well as the figure for **issued capital**
(the nominal value of the shares in issue) you will see references to
authorized capital. This is the maximum amount of capital that the
company has authorization from its shareholders to issue. Jones
Manufacturing might have an authorized capital of £3m, divided into
£500,000 of preference capital (all of which is issued) and £2.5m of
ordinary capital. Since only £1.5m of ordinary capital is so far issued,
there is £1m of **authorized but unissued capital** in existence, equivalent to 5m 20p shares. The directors could thus issue a further 5m
shares without needing to get shareholders to vote an increase in authorized capital first. In fact, 1.5m of these unissued shares are already earmarked for the eventual conversion of the convertible loan stock.

Institutional shareholders in companies are generally a bit
uncomfortable when the directors have the power to issue large numbers of new shares without consulting shareholders first. They could,
for example, go on a wild takeover spending spree using new shares as
currency, without needing to consult shareholders. So, quite apart from
the amount of authorized but unissued capital that a company has, the
institutions insist that the company regularly update its **authority to
issue new shares** under **Section 80 of the Companies Act** and they
impose a maximum limit on the number of new shares that might be
issued. These resolutions, seeking the authority to issue new shares
when required, are therefore a common feature of the agenda for company annual general meetings (AGMs). The usual rule is that the institutions will vote in favour of the authority to issue new shares provided the new shares would not add more than a third to the existing
issued share capital. This amount may represent the difference between
the company's authorized and issued capital anyway, or it may mean
that directors do not have permission to issue all of the authorized but
unissued shares without further consulting shareholders. If directors
subsequently want to go beyond the approved limit they will need to
call a meeting of shareholders to approve the move. This is one of a
number of ways shareholders may exercise control over the companies
they invest in.

Warrants

Apart from shares there is another type of quasi-security that a company may issue, which will be referred to in the notes to the accounts but which will not appear as share capital in the balance sheet. This is the **warrant**. A company may issue warrants which give the holder the right to **subscribe** at a fixed price for shares in the company at some future date. The **subscription price** will usually be fixed above the current price of the shares when the warrant is issued, so at this stage any value in the warrant is simply hope value.

Suppose a warrant is issued which gives the right to subscribe for one share at 180p at some point in the future. The current share price is 150p and there is no **intrinsic value** in the warrant. But if the share price should rise to 250p, there is a clear value in the right to subscribe at 180p for a share that could immediately be sold for 250p, and the price of the warrant itself will reflect this value. The principle is much the same as for a **traded option** (see Chapter 18 for a fuller explanation). But a warrant gives the right to subscribe cash for a new share the company issues. An option gives the right to buy an existing share from its present owner and does not affect the finances of the company itself. American terminology sometimes confuses this distinction, however. Warrants are traded in the stockmarket much like shares themselves.

Warrants are sometimes issued to improve the attractions of a loan stock and are often referred to as an **equity sweetener** or **equity kicker**. Fixed-interest loans are unpopular in periods of high inflation, but if subscribers to a loan are given, say, one warrant for every £3 of loan, they have an interest in the increasing prosperity of the company, as reflected in its share price. When warrants are issued in this way, they are afterwards normally traded separately from the loan. Arriving at the theoretical value of a warrant, relative to the price of the ordinary shares, is a pretty technical process and best left to the experts. The actual value at a given time is set by the balance of buyers and sellers in the market, as with a share. Note, by the way, that warrants issued by a company are a different animal from **covered warrants** (see glossary).

Profit and loss account reserves

Jones Manufacturing's **profit and loss account reserves** (they used more commonly to be called **revenue reserves**) at £5.4m are considerably larger than its issued capital. This points to some years' worth of

ploughed-back profits (retained earnings) which are added to the profit and loss account reserve in the balance sheet each year. If the company went through a temporary bad patch in which it did not earn any profits it could, if it chose, use part of these ploughed-back profits of previous years to pay a dividend (always assuming it also had enough cash as well). And in a loss-making year the revenue reserves will be depleted by the amount of the net losses plus the cost of any dividends paid.

Share premium account

The **share premium account** is part of shareholders' funds, but needs rather more explanation. It arises when the company issues new shares at a price above their par value (and in the case of an established company, the shares will almost always be worth more than their par value and new shares will be priced accordingly). Assume that in the past Jones had decided to raise money by offering new ordinary shares to its existing shareholders (a **rights issue** – see Chapter 9). Its share price at the time was 110p and it issued the new shares at 80p. Since the shares have a par value of 20p, each new share was being sold at a **premium** of 60p to its par value. So for each new share sold the company added 20p to its nominal capital and accounted for the additional 60p by adding it to the share premium account.

The share premium account has a special position in law in that it cannot be **written down** without the permission of the courts (it could not be used to cover **operating losses**, for example, without this permission). Since it arises from the issue of capital, it is treated rather as if it were part of the company's capital – part of the 'cushion' of equity that provides protection for creditors.

Revaluation reserves

Revaluation reserves are usually created or added to when the company revalues some of its assets upwards, probably the properties that it holds as fixed assets. Suppose Jones had commissioned a professional **revaluation** of its buildings ('Land and buildings') which showed them worth £1.95m more than their book value of £3m. It would have increased the value of properties in the accounts by £1.95m and added £1.95m to capital reserves to show that this extra value (the **surplus over book value**) belonged to the shareholders. Balance sheets must balance!

The revaluation of properties is often referred to in the context of takeover bids. If a company owns properties that were last revalued ten years ago (not Jones Manufacturing in this instance), a press report might say: 'the book net asset value [of the company being bid for] is 250p per share against the offer of 275p per share. But if properties are now worth £3m more than the book value, the net asset value would rise to 310p and the offer would look to be on the low side'. Thus the writer is mentally adding £3m to the value of properties, increasing revaluation reserves (and therefore shareholders' funds) by a like amount, and working out his net asset value figure on the result. He would apply the same arithmetic if the company owned investments that were worth more than the figures at which they were **stated in the books**.

Adjusting the net asset value

Finally, the **net asset value** for Jones Manufacturing. There are two complications. First, remember that goodwill is normally excluded to produce a figure for **net tangible asset value**. Second, the preference shares are not part of the ordinary shareholders' funds, and also have to be excluded from a calculation of assets attributable to the ordinary shares. So the sums go as shown in Table 5.2:

	£'000
SHAREHOLDERS' FUNDS AS STATED IN THE ACCOUNTS	11,000
less	
GOODWILL	1,000
less	
PREFERENCE CAPITAL	500
ORDINARY SHAREHOLDERS' FUNDS	9,500
Divide by the 7.5 million shares in issue	
NET TANGIBLE ASSET VALUE PER ORDINARY SHARE	126.7p

Table 5.2

The other complication is the existence of the convertible loan. As an added sophistication, we can work out the **fully diluted** net asset value per share for Jones – what the position would be if the loan were converted now. Take the £9.5m adjusted ordinary shareholders' funds (after excluding goodwill and preference capital). Add in the nominal value of the convertible loan stock – £1.5m – since this will cease to exist as a liability when converted, and therefore shareholders' funds will increase by £1.5m. Then divide the result by the enlarged number of ordinary shares: 7.5m plus the 1.5m arising on conversion. The result: £11m divided by 9m shares = £1.222 or 122.2p. So conversion of the loan stock will **dilute** assets per share from 126.7p to 122.2p. A fairly minor **dilution** as it happens, but worth bearing in mind.

Internet pointers

See end of Chapter 3 – the same pointers apply.

6 Equities and the stock exchange

Stock exchanges are not what they once were – and that may be no bad thing. Stock exchanges used to be clubby institutions, dealing mainly in the shares of domestic companies and largely protected from competition. That meant that the people who ran the club could dictate what clients paid for their services and the terms and conditions that they applied. No longer. Today's major exchanges are run more as businesses, increasingly competing with each other and increasingly responsive to the demands of their major clients. With the growth of international securities trading, no exchange can rest on its laurels and assume that it has permanent access to a captive clientele. If it does not give the clients what they want, the chances are that some other exchange will. There is no God-given rule that says that shares of British companies may be traded only in Britain or of French companies only in France.

But the change is not without its problems. The ideal market (and a stock exchange is only a market) brings together all prospective buyers and sellers of the product, allows the price of the product to be determined by the interplay of all these buyers and sellers, and ensures that this mechanism for establishing prices is transparent and visible to all. If you split the buyers and sellers between competing markets, you may find that the mechanism for establishing prices comes under threat.

This is less of a problem than it once was, however. The growth of electronic communications has revolutionized the picture. Stock exchanges used to be physical marketplaces where buyers and sellers (or their agents) came together on a **trading floor**. Today, computers have increasingly replaced the trading floor. A computer with electronic links to the market's clients can bring together the orders of all would-be buyers and sellers more efficiently than any physical marketplace. Moreover, it does not matter where these clients are physically located. Provided they can tap in to the market via computer and telephone line or satellite they can participate in the market as easily as an investor located on the market's doorstep.

The next question will be: do we even need formalized markets, operating their own proprietary computer systems? The Internet provides a resource available to anyone with a telephone and a computer that potentially can bring together buyers and sellers of anything from anywhere on the globe. What the Internet cannot provide, however – or not yet, anyway – are the rules, regulations and supervision that established markets operate for the protection of their users. So the initial impact of the Internet has been as a medium for disseminating information on the established stock exchanges and the stocks and shares that are traded on them. It also provides a channel of communication for would-be buyers and sellers of shares to place orders. But the orders, at least in the initial stages, are being executed on the established markets.

Where does the **London Stock Exchange** (**LSE**) fit into this evolving picture? At the end of the 1990s it was the only stock exchange in Britain with which the general public was likely to come into contact, though technically it was not the only stock exchange. And it had changed and evolved mightily over the previous 20 years. Gone was the old trading floor off Throgmorton Street in the City of London where dealers had once met face to face. It had long been replaced by a central computer linked by telephone and further computers to the dealing rooms of the individual brokers and securities houses. Share purchases and sales took place over these telephones and computer links between the individual dealers' offices. Visitors to London who ask to see the stock exchange are invariably disappointed. There is nothing much to see. The closest they can get is to arrange a visit to the screen-studded dealing room of one of the market's major players.

The LSE has evolved in its scope as well as its technology. In terms of size, London ranks after the **New York Stock Exchange** (**NYSE**), the American **Nasdaq** computerized exchange and the **Tokyo Stock Exchange**. But in addition to its business in domestic shares it has also become the largest market for trading in international equities.

But even these changes are dwarfed by the proposal that surfaced in the year 2000: a full merger between the LSE and the German stock exchange, **Deutsche Börse**. A new company would be formed, half owned by each party and called **iX** (for **International**

Exchanges). It would be based in London but with major operations in Frankfurt: notably the new market for high-growth technology stocks which was to be run as a joint venture with the American **Nasdaq**. A new electronic trading platform for all cash markets in the new grouping, known as Xetra, was also proposed. The new grouping would also include the Continental European **Eurex** derivatives market. In due course other European exchanges were expected to join iX in the push towards a true pan-European securities market. Initial reports that all trading might be in euros – even for the shares of British companies – caused some consternation in the UK. But it was later suggested that the trading currency would be the one which most suited the needs of investors and other market users and sterling prices would, in any event, continue to be available for private investors.

It will be some time before the full implications of the proposed merger – and the new trading platform – are apparent. In the meantime the London Stock Exchange has already evolved in terms of its trading methods. Twenty years back stock exchange members were divided between **jobbers** (**marketmakers** or **principals**) and **brokers** (**agents**) in what was known as a **single-capacity** system (we will explain what this meant in a moment). Both classes of stock exchange members had to be independent entities – they could not be owned by banks or other institutions.

In what came to be known as the **Big Bang** changes of the 1980s, this single capacity system was abandoned in favour of a system where firms could act both as marketmakers and as agents, and could also be owned by large financial institutions. It was at roughly the same time that trading moved from the physical marketplace of the stock exchange trading floor to a computer-and-telephone system.

Some eleven years further on, in 1997, yet another trading system was introduced for the shares of the largest companies. Buy and sell orders could be posted direct on a central computer, which would automatically execute matching trades.

Finally, the London Stock Exchange has changed greatly in terms of its membership. There are still independent brokers acting only as agents for investors. But most of the larger stock exchange member firms have been taken over by big financial institutions, mainly retail or investment banks from Britain or abroad. At the same time, established overseas financial institutions, particularly the

American investment banks, have become members of the LSE. The biggest of these groupings form major **securities houses** which offer the whole range of financial and investment services, including marketmaking, agency brokerage, organizing and underwriting of securities issues, eurobond dealing, money market and foreign exchange services, and so on. The **corporate finance** arms of the investment banks also orchestrate companies' takeover bids and bid defences and advise on anything concerning financial structuring. There may also be a large **fund management** operation, managing investments on behalf of clients (particularly the pension funds). Finally, the bigger brokers and securities houses employ large numbers of **investment analysts** who **research** the economy, the financial markets and the prospects for individual companies. The research is structured mainly as a service to the investing institutions whose stock exchange business the firm is anxious to secure. But investment analysts are also a prime source of information for financial journalists, and you will see their forecasts referred to frequently in the press.

The current structure of stock exchange member businesses poses some problems with terminology, particularly for financial journalists with memories of the pre-Big Bang days. Journalists often tend to talk of **brokers** and refer to them by their original names even when they are now part of a larger grouping. But the term **securities house** has gained ground when referring to the large concerns. **Marketmaker** is normally used when referring to the specific function of making a book in shares.

The London Stock Exchange used to be a mutual organization, owned by its members. But this, too, neeeded to change for ambitious plans such as the iX merger to be practicable. Hence the plan to allow its shares to be transferable, thus breaking the link between usage and ownership of the exchange.

Structure of the exchange

But before looking in more detail at recent developments we need to set the London Stock Exchange – as it exists today – in context with a few facts and figures. First, like most stock exchanges, it is both a **primary market** and a **secondary market**. It is a primary market in which securities may be sold for the first time to the investment community to raise cash for businesses. And it is a secondary market in which existing securities may be bought and sold between investors. The LSE's domestic market also breaks down into two main parts.

There is the market in company shares, known as the **equity market**. And there is the market in bonds which is known as the **fixed interest market** or the **gilt-edged market** (after the British government bonds or **gilts** which are its main constituent). But the range of securities that are dealt is wider than this. As well as ordinary shares in British companies there are shares in overseas companies listed in London, preference shares and more esoteric pieces of paper such as **warrants** and **covered warrants**. The market in **traded options** used to be part of the LSE but is now amalgamated with **Liffe** (the London International Financial Futures and Options Exchange – see Chapter 18). On the fixed interest side there are convertible loan stocks and straight fixed-interest bonds issued by companies (these may also be known as industrial debentures, industrial loans or corporate bonds). And as well as UK government bonds, loans issued by local authorities and certain bonds issued by overseas governments are also listed. Bonds issued in the **euromarket** may also be technically listed on the LSE.

The total value of shares listed in the market – £1,820 billion at end 1999 for domestic companies listed on the **main market** in London – is known as the equity **market capitalization**. The value of the annual **turnover** in shares was £1,385 billion for UK equities in 1999 and the number of bargains (a stock exchange transaction is called a 'bargain', whatever price you pay!) was 20.1m. Both figures included some trading that was purely between dealers, rather than with the public. In addition to its business in domestic shares, we have seen that the London Stock Exchange is the largest market for trading in international equities, using an electronic price quotation system called **SEAQ International**. Shares in any company listed on a stock exchange approved by the London Stock Exchange can be traded via this system. The total value of trades in 1999, at £2,420 billion, was considerably larger than that in domestic shares.

As a measure of the LSE's function as a primary (capital-raising) market, in 1999 some £14 billion was raised by the first-time sale of shares by new or existing UK companies and the figure rises slightly if domestic company bonds and other securities are included. But for bonds the domestic market is dwarfed by the **euromarket** or **international market**. In 1999 listed UK companies raised over £82 billion by the sale of eurobonds formally listed on the London market, though trading in these bonds is outside the domestic market (see Chapters 13 and 17).

As we noted earlier, the London Stock Exchange comprises more than one market. Companies that are **listed** on the stock exchange make up the **main market,** which is by far the most important component. The 'listing' refers to a **Listing Agreement** that companies have to sign, which governs aspects of their behaviour and their reporting to shareholders. Though the LSE has traditionally been the **Listing Authority** for UK companies wishing to market their shares, responsibility for this function is due to move to the **Financial Services Authority** (**FSA**). At the end of 1999 there were over 2,000 domestic listed companies. In addition, the shares of many overseas companies are listed on the London exchange as well as in their country of origin.

The **Alternative Investment Market** or **AIM**, which the stock exchange runs in addition to the main market, is designed for the shares of younger or smaller companies which might not qualify for a full listing. The idea, in catering for the funding needs of developing companies, is to keep the costs down and make the rules as simple as possible. As well as catering for complete market newcomers,

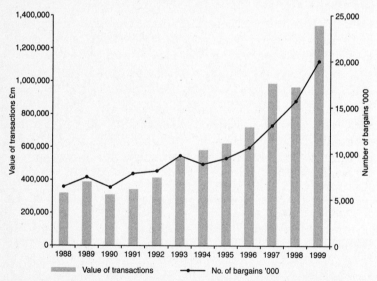

Figure 6.1 Stock exchange volumes in UK equities The second half of the 1990s proved a boom time for the London Stock Exchange, as well as for those who invested in the market. Strongly rising share prices were matched by rapidly increasing turnover on the market, both in value terms and in terms of the number of transactions ('bargains'). Our chart shows the volume for shares in UK companies listed on the main market and includes some trading between market members. Source: *Office for National Statistics: Financial Statistics.*

the AIM market was intended to provide a facility for companies whose shares were previously dealt under the stock exchange's Rule 4.2. This allowed dealing on a **matched bargain** basis (see glossary) in shares of companies that were neither listed nor quoted. The AIM companies, close to 350 of them at the end of 1999 and with the number rising sharply, do not fall within the definition of listed companies. Their shares may be described as being **quoted** or **traded** on the market.

This is not the stock exchange's first foray into the world of smaller companies. In 1980 it launched a second-tier market called the **Unlisted Securities Market** or **USM**, which has now been wound down. And for even more embryonic companies it had opened in 1987 an earlier version of a small-company market known as the **Third Market**. But this proved short-lived, closing after a few years.

While the LSE's AIM has filled a need, most 'junior' markets face a common problem. Cut back too far on the regulation and scandals erupt which damage the credibility of the market. Step up the regulation and the costs deter companies from joining. There is also a perennial problem in stimulating sufficient trade in the shares of small companies to ensure a reasonably liquid market.

There is one other market within the stock exchange that we should mention as you are likely to read a lot about it in the future. This is **techMARK**, announced towards the end of 1999. Technically, it is not a separate market but a grouping of technology companies within the main market, which will have rather different listing rules from those applying to the majority of companies (see Chapter 8). It also has its own indices.

The London Stock Exchange is not the only organization that has provided share trading facilities in Britain. There used to be a freewheeling and unofficial **Over-the-Counter** or **OTC** market, conducted over the telephone by **licenced dealers in securities**. Regulation was minimal, it was not part of the LSE and the LSE did not like it. It was pretty much killed off by the **Financial Services Act** of 1986 which made life very difficult for a marketmaker who was not part of a **Recognized Investment Exchange** or **RIE** – the London Stock Exchange is, of course, an RIE. Today there is an unregulated share trading facility outside the LSE called **OFEX** which facilitates dealing in small companies that are not listed or traded on the LSE, but that might previously have been dealt under

Rule 4.2. 'Indicative' prices for shares in these companies are listed in the *Financial Times*. OFEX is not a Recognized Investment Exchange and it is not technically even an exchange. But it does operate under the aegis of an LSE member company.

Who owns shares and who deals

Despite encouragement for the private investor from privatization issues and from the distribution of shares by former mutual building societies, today's stock exchange is dominated by the **financial institutions**. In the 1950s **private investors** owned more than 60 per cent of all shares directly. By 1997 their holdings represented less than 17 per cent of the total. Institutions (mainly the pension funds and insurance companies) owned around half of all shares in 1997, against some 30 per cent in the 1960s. But, reflecting the internationalization of securities ownership and trading, **foreign investors** have been the fastest-growing category in recent years, with 24 per cent of the London equity market in 1997 against only 7 per cent in 1963.

When it comes to **trading volumes**, private investors are still less significant than they are in terms of ownership. Though their deals account for a high proportion of all individual trades, this is misleading since their bargains tend to be small. Their deals accounted for under 7 per cent of the total in terms of value, according to a survey in 1999. Because their bargains are small, private individuals overall tend to pay average **commission rates** several times those paid by the institutions in percentage terms. But though percentage commission rates on big institutional deals are much lower, the actual commission earned may be much higher and it is not difficult to see where the market perceives its best interests. Large institutional deals are not necessarily more expensive to undertake and process than the small private-client deals and can therefore be vastly more profitable.

Figures for **share ownership** in Britain can therefore convey a very distorted picture of investment activity. Thanks largely to privatization issues and the arrival on the stockmarket of former building societies, the number of individuals owning shares directly rose from around 3 million in 1980 to a peak of over 14 million or so in 1997 and slipped back to around 12 million in 1998. But a majority of these shareholders own small amounts of shares in one or two privatization stocks or former building societies, rarely if ever use a stockbroker and are largely irrelevant to stockmarket activity. The organization

ProShare, which exists to promote share ownership, estimates that less than half of all shareholders own shares in two or more companies. The number of active or substantial private investors is probably numbered in the hundreds of thousands rather than the millions.

More on the trading systems

Twenty years ago, when a private investor – call him Joe Bloggs – wanted to buy 1,000 shares in ICI, he contacted his **stockbroker** with the order. The stockbroker or a member of his staff on the stock exchange floor went round the **pitches** (trading posts) of the various **jobbers** (**marketmakers**) who dealt in ICI shares till he found the one offering the best price. He bought the 1,000 ICI shares from the jobber and his firm's **back office** operations looked after the subsequent paperwork which was necessary to transfer the shares into Joe Bloggs's name. The jobbers acted as **principals**, buying and selling shares on their own account and hoping to make a profit in the process. They could deal only with brokers or with each other, not direct with the public. The broker, on the other hand, operated as an **agent** and could deal only with a jobber on behalf of his client, not direct with another broker. He was remunerated via a **commission** calculated as a percentage of the value of the transaction. **Minimum commission rates** were set by the London Stock Exchange and they operated on a sliding scale. The percentages were higher on small transactions, reducing on the large institutional trades.

This **single-capacity** system with two distinct classes of stock exchange member – jobbers acting only as principals and brokers only as agents – claimed a number of advantages for itself. Competition between the different jobbing firms would, in theory at least, ensure competitive pricing of shares. The presence of the jobber as marketmaker promoted a **liquid** market: one in which transactions could be undertaken easily without moving the share price too violently up or down. Since the jobber was always there to act as buyer or seller as required, a Joe Bloggs or his broker did not have to wait until a Bill Smith turned up wanting to sell 1,000 ICI shares before the transaction could go through. The jobbers would sell to Joe Bloggs and subsequently buy from Bill Smith when he emerged. But the system was also expensive. The jobber quoted two prices: a higher price (the **offered price**) at which he would sell and a lower price (the **bid price**) at which he would buy. The difference between the two was known as the **spread** or **turn**. Add the cost of the jobber's turn to the relatively high commission to the stockbroker and share dealing was not cheap. In the late 1970s there were signs that some institutional business was moving to the more liquid New York Stock Exchange, which had already abandoned fixed commission rates. This ultimately helped to spark changes in London.

As far as the private investor is concerned, however, the share dealing process – or the part of it that he can see – is not all that different today. He still approaches a broker to buy or sell on his behalf, though it could be a broker that he contacts via the Internet. But behind the scenes a great deal has changed. It happened like this.

Big Bang changes

In the first half of the 1980s the UK government threatened legal action against the London Stock Exchange unless it abandoned its restrictive practices, notably the fixed minimum commission structure. In the end the exchange bowed to the pressure and a deal was struck. It would abandon its fixed commissions in favour of **negotiated commissions**. But at the same time brokers, who foresaw a big drop in their income, insisted on the right to operate as marketmakers to try to recoup some of the shortfall. Thus the single-capacity system broke down. All stock exchange members would be able to elect to operate as **marketmakers**, with a duty to make a continuous market – be prepared to deal at all times during trading hours – in the shares in which they had opted to deal. Alternatively, they could operate as **broker dealers**, who could supply clients with shares that they held on their own books provided that the shares could not have been bought more cheaply from a marketmaker, but who had no obligation to make a continuous market. Both types could also act as **agency brokers** (like the old style stockbrokers), executing clients' buy and sell orders with the marketmakers and charging a commission (though in theory a negotiated commission) on the deal. Some brokers, particularly smaller ones, chose to confine themselves entirely to this agency role.

Accompanying these changes was another significant development: the abandonment of the rule against outside ownership of stock exchange firms. The partners of most of the big jobbing and broking firms were only too ready to sell out to the banks and other institutions that beat a path to their doorstep with pockets overflowing with cash, and many of them retired happy and rich. It was pretty clear at the time, and abundantly so with the benefit of hindsight, that most of the buyers overpaid vastly for what they were getting. But at least the presence of new owners with deep pockets added welcome liquidity to the market – it takes a great deal of cash for marketmakers to hold large stocks of shares on their books.

The most significant of these changes to the exchange's structure took place on 27 October 1986 on what was known as **Big Bang** day and the new players had roughly a year of buoyant share trading before Nemesis struck in the shape of the **stockmarket crash** of October 1987 (see Chapter 7b). Share-dealing volumes plummeted thereafter and took years to recover. Many of the new owners of stock exchange firms were forced to cut back their operations or abandoned the stock exchange altogether.

Computer systems

The post-Big Bang trading system relied heavily on computers once face-to-face dealing had been abandoned. At the heart of the new structure was a computerized system called **SEAQ (Stock Exchange Automated Quotation System)**, into which marketmakers fed the prices at which they were prepared to deal. This was planned initially as a **price information system** rather than an **automated dealing system**. The dealer used the SEAQ screen to see who was offering the best price in the stock that interested him. He then phoned the chosen marketmaker and arranged the deal. The rule was that the marketmaker must be prepared to deal up to a certain stated number of shares at the price he had quoted though he could, of course, adjust his quoted prices after he had done the deal. With larger deals above this stated number, the deal was subject to negotiation. In 1989, a fully automatic system for executing small transactions was introduced under the name of **SAEF (SEAQ Automatic Execution Facility)**.

While the principle of the London marketmaker system was competition between marketmakers in all shares, this proved unrealistic in the case of some very small or infrequently traded companies. For these there might be only one marketmaker or there might be no marketmakers quoting continuous prices. Here, a system called **SEATS (Stock Exchange Alternative Tracking Service)** displayed the marketmaker's quote (if any) and firm orders from member firms.

Marketmakers, brokers and some big institutional investors all had SEAQ screens in their offices. The screen showed them the marketmakers who were offering the most favourable prices in the share they were interested in at the given time. Big institutional investors with SEAQ screens in their offices had the option of dealing direct with the marketmakers at **net prices**, thus cutting out the agency broker and saving his commission. Small private investors needed, of course, to go via a broker.

Introduction of order book trading

Thus, following the Big Bang, the London Stock Exchange still had a **quote-driven** trading system (marketmakers quoted prices at which investors could choose whether or not to buy or sell). But the market players – or many of them – had changed and computers had replaced face-to-face trading. The next major move came in 1997 and involved the introduction of a totally different **order-driven** system (described as an **Order Book Trading** system), initially for the 100 most actively traded shares that constitute the FTSE 100 (Footsie) Index, plus a few others. The number of shares covered by the system was subsequently extended and is likely to increase further. But for the moment the new system runs alongside the marketmaker system for these actively traded shares while the less actively traded shares are dealt through the marketmaker system alone. The new system is called the **Stock Exchange Electronic Trading Service** or **SETS**. The big difference between SETS and the marketmaker system is that buyers and sellers are matched directly without the need for the trade to go through a middleman. They are also matched by a computer which can execute the trades rather than acting merely as a SEAQ-type, price-information system.

SETS works like this. An investor wants to sell, say, 100,000 shares in Payola Properties at a price of 200p or higher. His broker enters the sell order onto the SETS computer. If there happens to be an order already on the computer from an investor who wants to buy 100,000 Payola shares at 200p or less, then the computer can match the two trades immediately. The 100,000 shares are sold by one investor and bought by another and, since they have been satisfied in full, both orders can then be removed from the system.

In real life, things are rarely as neat as this. More likely is that one investor wants to sell 100,000 Payola shares at 200p or above and another investor wants to buy 60,000 Payola shares at a price not above 196p. The computer cannot match the orders and a trade cannot take place unless the seller decides to lower his asking price or the buyer raises the price he is prepared to pay (or other buy and sell orders at different prices are put on the system). Assuming seller or buyer (or both) adjust their prices to arrive at the same figure, the computer can then execute the trade, but not in its entirety. The seller wants to dispose of 100,000 shares, the buyer only requires 60,000 shares, so the buyer's order can be satisfied in full and will be removed from the system. The sell order will remain on the computer but be reduced in size from 100,000 to 40,000 shares.

We have taken the example of a single buyer and a single seller, but in practice numerous buy and sell orders in each of the shares traded through the SETS system may be entered throughout the day. An investor using the system (via his broker) has several options. He may:

- ask his broker to execute his order **at best**. This means that the order is to be executed immediately at the best price available on the order book computer at the time;

- give his broker an **execute & eliminate** order. This works rather like the 'at best' order, with the difference that the investor sets a price limit. The order will be executed wholly or in part only if this is possible at the specified price or better;

- give his broker a **limit order**. This means the buyer or seller specifies the price at which he is prepared to deal, how many shares he wants to deal in and a time and/or date when the order should expire. The order is put on the computer and executed immediately in full or in part if this is possible at the stipulated price. If not, the order remains on the order book until either it can be executed or it expires, at which point it is withdrawn;

- give a **fill or kill** order. In this case the order will be executed only if this proves possible immediately and in full. Otherwise, the order is removed from the order book.

The SETS system has not been completely problem-free in its early days. In particular, buyers and sellers may enter unrealistic prices, especially at the start of a day's trading when volume is thin. This may give a misleading impression of the true price level and persuade some investors to deal at unrepresentative prices. Steps were taken to mitigate this problem and soon virtually half by value of the trades in shares on SETS was being executed through this system with the remainder going through the older marketmaker system. Shares in companies not traded on SETS go through the marketmaker system as before. Marketmakers may, of course, themselves intervene to buy or sell shares via SETS when they see the opportunity of a profit.

Changes in settlement procedure

Private investors who always need to place their orders via brokers are somewhat removed from the mechanics of the dealing system and will not always have been aware of the introduction of SETS. For them, the two most noticeable changes of recent years are the abandonment of the old **stock exchange account** system and the introduction of a new **settlement** system.

In the past, the stock exchange's year used to be divided into two-week **accounts** (with the occasional three-week account at bank holiday periods). The usual account thus ran from the Monday of one week to the Friday of the following week. Anyone buying or selling shares during this period did not have to pay for the shares or deliver the shares he had sold until **settlement day** or **account day**, which was ten days after the end of the relevant account. A speculator could thus **deal for the account**. If he bought at the beginning of the account and sold before the end, he would never have to pay for the shares. He would simply receive or pay a cheque for his profits or losses. Trading in gilts, however, was and remains for **cash settlement** (in practice this means payment the day after you buy the stock). The old equity account system has now disappeared and been replaced by a system of **rolling settlement**. In 1999 the settlement period was down to five days, which meant that a buyer would normally have to pay for shares or a seller would have to deliver shares five days after the trade took place, and there were plans to reduce it further to three days.

The coming of CREST

After shares have been bought or sold, **settlement** must take place. This is the process of confirming the deal, collecting cash from the buyer, recording the change of ownership, and so on. It is part of the **back office function** in a broker's office. The big change in this area is the introduction of an electronic settlement system called **CREST**. To understand its impact we need to look at the old system first.

When an investor bought or sold a share, he was sent a **contract note** which gave details of the transaction and payment became due on settlement day. Once the contract note had been sent, the broker dealt with the subsequent paperwork – and the system used to be largely paper-based, even if computers were used to generate the paper. Purchases and sales had to be registered with the company whose shares were involved and the company eventually issued a **share certificate** to the new owner. British company shares are thus **registered** securities (though the identity of the real owner is sometimes cloaked in a **nominee name**). It is a Companies Act requirement that a company keep a **register of shareholders**, and the public has the right to inspect the register on payment of a fee. In some countries shares in **bearer** form are more common. The certificate alone is proof of ownership, which does not have to be registered with the company.

This system of share transfer, coordinated through a stock exchange computer system called **Talisman**, was lengthy and time consuming. Talisman has now been replaced by the more efficient **CREST** electronic system for most shares. Shares within CREST are held in electronic form and the beneficial ownership can be transferred from a seller to a buyer with a few clicks of the computer keyboard. The lengthy paper-based process is cut out.

The concept of an electronic share registry is difficult to grasp at first encounter, so let's start from the principles. As noted earlier, shares may be held in the name of a **nominee company** rather than in the name of the beneficial owner. This is a convenience often used by investment managers who hold shares for a number of different investors. The shares owned by these investors legally belong to a nominee company run by the investment manager: call it Whoopee Nominees Ltd. There might be, say, 100 different investors whose shares are held by Whoopee Nominees. In the registers of the companies whose shares are held by the nominee company, Whoopee Nominees will appear as the registered owner. However, the people who really benefit from the ownership of these shares are the investors on whose behalf Whoopee Nominees holds them. They are the **beneficial owners**, though not the registered owners, and have the right to receive dividends and proceeds from sale of the shares. The advantage for the investment manager is that shares may change hands between the investors within the nominee without each change of ownership needing to be registered in the shareholder list of the company concerned. If Mr Smith and Mr Jones are both clients of Whoopee Nominees and Smith sells 1,000 Payola Properties shares to Jones, Whoopee Nominees remains the owner of these shares as far as Payola is concerned. Only the beneficial ownership has changed.

This is the principle behind CREST. A large number of financial institutions and brokerages run **nominee accounts** in CREST in which the shares that are beneficially owned by their clients are held.

The nominee company is thus the legal owner. The shares are held as electronic records rather than as pieces of paper. If one investor sells a share and another buys it, only the electronic records need to be amended. It is rather like the electronic message that would be sent if you and I used the same bank and I transferred money from my bank account to yours. Of course, as in banking, a clearing system is needed when shares are transferred from one institution's nominee account to that of another, and CREST provides this; it ensures that the seller or buyer is never out of both stock and cash during settlement.

In practice the system is more complex than this and investors have a choice. The shares they own can be held in a nominee account run by, say, their stockbroker. The advantage here is that they do not need to bother with share certificates and when they buy or sell shares the transfers can be registered electronically, which reduces dealing costs. The disadvantage is that they will not automatically receive annual reports and other communications from the companies they invest in. These will go to the nominee company as the legal owner of the shares. And votes in company affairs will be exercised by the nominee company rather than by the individual investor. However, the **ProShare** organization set up to encourage share ownership does promote a system whereby investors may receive annual reports even when their shares are held in a CREST nominee account. Many stockbrokers pass on benefits and voting rights to their beneficial shareholders – you should talk to your stockbroker about the services he offers.

A second option for the investor is to become a **personal** (previously called **sponsored**) **member of CREST** in his own right. In this case the investor remains the legal owner as well as the beneficial owner of his shares, while still benefiting from electronic settlement through the CREST system. And he retains the right to receive company information and vote on company affairs. Settlement and transfer arrangements are looked after by the client's broker and, needless to say, there is a price to be paid for this service which may discourage many private investors from using it. However, at the end of January 2000 over 10,000 shareholders had taken up this option.

Finally, the investor may choose to stay outside the CREST system altogether, retain his share certificates and have his purchases or sales of shares registered each time with the company concerned, as in the past. Transactions will be more expensive and take longer than those going through the CREST system, but this may not be too much of a problem for existing private shareholders who deal only infrequently.

Conflicts of interest

The emergence of large securities houses spanning a whole range of financial and stockmarket activities has its advantages: most types of financial service can be provided by a single organization. But it is not without its problems. Paradoxically, several of these disciplines ought to be kept well clear of each other. The investment management arm must not know if the corporate advice arm is counselling ABC Industries on a planned takeover of XYZ Holdings. If it knew, it could make large profits by buying the shares of XYZ before the bid became public. The marketmaking arm must not know if Myopic Mutual Assurance has approached the agency brokerage arm to acquire a couple of million pounds' worth of shares in ABC, though the information would assist the marketmaker considerably in adjusting the price it quoted. The marketmaking arm must not learn of the intentions of the fund management arm, nor of ABC's plan to take over XYZ. And so on.

To deal with the possible **conflicts of interest** and to convince the outside world that no improper use is being made of information available in different parts of the organization, safeguards are required. Securities houses have **compliance departments** or **compliance officers** with a brief to ensure the confidentiality rules are observed. Within the organization there are **Chinese Walls**: barriers that are supposed to exist between different arms of a securities house to prevent information from passing between them. Sometimes they are invisible walls. Sometimes the different arms are physically separated. Cynics claim they've never met a Chinese Wall that did not have a grapevine growing over it. Or, more succinct if less politically correct, that there's no Chinese Wall without a chink.

Bullish and bearish

Much of the old stock exchange terminology survives the structural changes in the London market. Somebody who sells shares he does not own in the hope that the price will fall and he will be able to buy them more cheaply before he has to deliver has undertaken a **bear sale** or a **short sale**. The investor is **short** of the shares – he does not own them – at the time he sells them. Short selling can be a dangerous game. If the price rises instead of falling, there is theoretically no limit to the price that might have to be paid for the shares that are required for delivery. Marketmakers have to sell shares they do not own in the course of their daily trading. The disappearance of the account system makes it more difficult for private individuals, though there are now opportunities for betting on a price fall with traded options or even via stockmarket index betting systems run by traditional 'bookies'.

The term **bear** (see Chapter 7a) is used not only to cover a short seller but anyone who expects the market to go down. By extension, a **bear market** is a falling market and a **bearish** news item is one that might be expected to cause the market or an individual share to fall.

The opposite of a bear is a **bull**, who expects prices to rise. A **bull market** is a market on a long-term rising trend and **bullish** news is news that is likely to push prices up. **Long** is (self-evidently) the opposite of short. Somebody who is long of a particular share owns the share in question – possibly with the implication that he holds large quantities which he intends to sell rather than holding for the long term. A **stale bull** is somebody who bought shares in the hope of a price rise, has not seen the rise and is tired of holding on.

Bid and offered prices

Though the newspapers normally quote only a **middle price** for a share, we have seen that the marketmaker quotes a price at which he will sell and a price at which he will buy. The marketmaker's selling price is the **offered price** (the higher of the two, and the price at which the investor will buy). The marketmaker's buying price is the **bid price** (the price at which an investor can sell to him). The difference between the two is the **spread** or **turn**. Different marketmakers may quote a different range, depending on the state of their books and whether they want to encourage investors to buy from them or sell to them. Thus you might see:

	Marketmaker A	*Marketmaker B*
Offered	102p	103p
Bid	100p	101p

The spread is the same in both cases (though it need not be). The likelihood is that marketmaker A is long of the particular share. He wants to encourage investors to buy from him so that he can square his book, so he is prepared to sell to investors at 102p. Marketmaker B is probably short of the share, so he will only sell at the higher price of 103p to discourage still more investors from buying from him shares that he does not have. But he is prepared to offer investors

101p if they will sell to him, thus hoping he can pick up the shares he needs to square his book. An investor who wanted to buy would naturally get the best price from marketmaker A and one who wanted to sell from marketmaker B. The difference between the lowest offered price and the highest bid price (in this case 1p) is known as the **touch**.

The stock exchange publishes a **Daily Official List** of prices of all shares traded on the stock exchange or the Unlisted Securities Market. But since it gives the highest price and the lowest price at which dealings took place during the day, the spread is unrealistically wide. In an adjusted form, however, these official prices are relevant for some tax purposes, particularly probate. Of more interest is the information in the Official List on prices at which deals actually took place. Details of price, size and time of transactions allow the day's performance to be tracked.

Stockbroking for private investors

In the past many would-be small investors were deterred from direct buying and selling of shares by the 'clubby' nature of the stock exchange and the feeling that their business would not be welcomed. They may have been right, though the LSE has for a long time been prepared to provide a list of brokers who would accept **private client** business. Today the position is rather different. There are now a considerable number of brokers, including subsidiaries of major high-street banks, prepared to offer a 'no frills' share buying and selling service at relatively low cost. This is usually described as an **execution only** service, as it does not include the traditional investment advice and hand-holding. Some of these brokers use the Internet as a channel for orders, though a distinction needs to be made between those that simply accept instructions by, say, e-mail and those that allow investors to place buy and sell orders on-line: the true **Internet brokers**. Needless to say, any broker will want a certain amount of information from a potential client to enable him to establish the client's *bona fides* and ability to pay. In turn, the client needs to satisfy himself in advance as to the precise service he is getting and the amount of commission he will pay. Though commission is usually expressed as a percentage of the value of the trade, there will probably be a minimum commission per transaction which can make very small deals relatively expensive. However, with many brokers these minimum commission levels are considerably lower than in the past.

Internet pointers

Needless to say, the world's major stockmarkets have their web sites on the Internet and generally provide useful background and news of up-to-the-minute developments in the market structure. The London Stock Exchange is at www.londonstockexchange.com. In addition to the traditional fare, the site now provides a section on the new techMARK market in technology stocks. The New York Stock Exchange is, unsurprisingly, at www.nyse.com/ and the US Nasdaq market at www.nasdaq.com/. Links to the sites of these and other world stockmarkets can be found at the Peter Temple Associates Linksite at www.cix.co.uk/~ptemple/. ProShare, the organization promoting share ownership in the UK, provides quite a bit of very basic investment guidance at www.proshare.org.uk/. The Ofex quasi-market has a site at www.ofex.co.uk/. More information on the UK's CREST electronic settlement system can be found at www.crestco.co.uk/ and there is information on safeguards for stock-market investors at the Securities and Futures Authority site at www.sfa.org.uk/. For results of an annual survey ranking UK invest-ment analysts, go to www.primarkextelsurvey.com/results/.

Share prices both for UK and overseas companies are available at a wide range of sites. The usual position is that you have to pay for 'live' prices, but prices with a built-in delay of 15 or 20 minutes are available free (this should be quite adequate for most private investors). The Peter Temple Linksite provides pointers to a number of sources. It also provides a useful list of links to UK and US stock-brokers' websites, with an indication of whether they provide web-based dealing services. For comprehensive details of UK stockbro-kers and an indication of their services and charges, go to the *Investors Chronicle* site at www.investorschronicle.co.uk/ (be careful not to confuse this with an American newsletter site with a somewhat similar name!).

7 What moves share prices a: In 'normal' times

'Observers attributed the lacklustre tone to the absence of any market-affecting news'.

Share prices had been slipping slightly, activity was very low, and the reason – we are told – was that there was no reason on this particular day for things to be otherwise.

The quotation comes from a report on the French stockmarket, but might have been written about other markets, too. News – good or bad – is what brings out the buyers and sellers. Without the buyers and sellers, there is no activity. Markets thrive on activity and for the professionals, the brokers and marketmakers who derive their living from market activity, no news is very definitely bad news.

But in London, where shares of over 2,000 UK and many overseas companies are traded, there is no such thing as a day without news, and even if there is not much going on in London there will be plenty happening in other markets that affect London. The daily **stockmarket reports** that feature in the financial pages of the press and the Internet record both the ups and downs of the markets and the movements of individual shares. At their best, when they give background information on reasons for price movements, they are essential reading. At their most turgid, they are simply a list of price movements in narrative form, stretching the writer's imagination to find synonyms for 'rose' and 'fell'. Most of what they contain is self-explanatory, but a few technical terms crop up. More serious, the general tenor may be difficult to grasp without some knowledge of the influences that move share prices.

Looking at the stockmarket from a turn-of-millennium perspective, there has as yet been no movement in share prices to compare in terms of drama with the events of 19 and 20 October 1987. The later 1997 crisis in the Far-Eastern markets failed to spark a comparable panic in the West and Russia's problems in 1998, together with the near-collapse of a large American hedge fund, caused only a temporary blip. But on those two days back in 1987 the London equity market fell 20 per cent. Since stockmarket crashes contain useful lessons for the future, we will look in the second part of this chapter at the facts behind world stockmarkets' fastest ever bust. But the events of Autumn 1987 will be easier to understand if we look first at the influences that operate on share prices in more normal times.

Bull and bear markets

When the new millennium dawned, investors in Britain could look back on many years of sustained share-price growth. This was very different from much of the post-war period, when share prices had followed a regular cyclical pattern of **bull markets** (prices in a rising trend for a year or so) followed by **bear markets** (where prices were falling). The highs and lows of each cycle generally mirrored the **stop–go** pattern of the British economy itself. The stockmarket **peaks** and **troughs** normally preceded those in real economic activity, because stockmarket prices always look forward a step. In the depths of a recession, share prices begin to rise to reflect the coming upturn. At the height of a boom they tend to become weak in anticipation of the next downturn. But over the post-war period as a whole, the movement in prices was upwards until the 1973–75 financial crisis brought a horrendous stockmarket collapse, with prices falling to scarcely a quarter of their previous peak.

It took some time to recover fully from the events of 1973–75. But the 1980s, with the Thatcher Government in power, were to see a sustained boom in share prices that was broken only by the crash of 1987. Even this event, dramatic as it was at the time, in practice wiped less than a year's growth off share prices. It was remarkable more for the speed with which it happened than for the size of the fall. The recession of the early 1990s was the real price paid for the excesses of the 1980s, and its effects were felt far more widely across the economy. But the stockmarket suffered far less seriously than other areas such as the residential and commercial property markets. Though share prices underwent a couple of severe dips and several more minor ones, they were generally on an upward trend between 1988 and 1993, with the stockmarket looking forward to economic recovery long before it was discernible to the man in the street. And by 1995 shares were setting off on a five-year bull rampage which, with only the one serious blip in 1998, was to carry them up to the millennium. If you adjust for inflation, at the end of 1999 shares had been on a rising trend since 1982. If you take unadjusted prices they had been rising since 1975. It was tempting to believe that in the 1990s business cycles had become a thing of the past. Not everybody was quite so sure.

Whatever view you take on this point, it is clear even from this brief background that stockmarket movements need to be seen on at least three levels. First, there is the long-term trend of the equity market, second the short-term fluctuations up and down within this trend, and third, the movements of individual shares within the movement of the market as a whole.

Share prices reflect earnings growth

Investors buy **ordinary shares** mainly because they expect share values to increase. Over a long period, what causes share prices to increase is the increasing **earning power** of companies, and their ability to pay higher **dividends** out of these increased earnings. But in the short run a lot of other factors can distort the picture.

An example helps. Suppose that companies on average pay out half of their earnings as dividends and the average **yield** on ordinary shares is 3 per cent and the average **PE ratio** is around 17 (in practice the PE ratio was considerably higher at the turn of the millennium – this is just for illustration). Suppose also that, on average, companies are increasing their earnings and dividends by 7 per cent a year. Share prices might be expected to rise by 7 per cent a year to reflect the underlying growth in profits and dividends.

How shares are re-rated

Over a long period this may well happen. But the example assumes that investors always expect – again on average – that ordinary shares will yield 3 per cent and that investors will be prepared to buy shares at a price equal to 17 times current earnings. In practice there will be some times when investors expect higher yields and others when they will accept lower yields – times when a PE ratio of 17 looks too high and others when it may seem on the low side.

Why is this the case? It is easier if we now come down to a single company. Call it ABC Holdings and assume it is totally typical of the market averages: the ABC shares at 100p are backed by earnings of 6p per share, offer a yield of 3 per cent on the 3p dividend and stand on a PE ratio of 16.7. If ABC's earnings and dividends grow at 7 per cent a year, a buyer of the shares can expect a 10 per cent a year overall return: 3 per cent of income and 7 per cent of capital gain from the rise in the share price. But suppose something happens to alter the outlook for ABC's future profits: it comes up with a new product that should help raise the future growth rate from 7 to 9 per cent. Earnings will now rise faster in the future than had been expected. And, all else being equal, investors will be prepared to pay a higher price for the shares today because they are buying the right to share in a more rapidly rising flow of future earnings. The share price might rise from 100p to 120p, where the yield drops to 2.5 per cent and the PE ratio rises to 20.8. The share has been **re-rated**.

Remember, however, that share prices can be **re-rated downwards** as well as upwards. One of the quickest ways for investors to lose money is to buy a highly rated growth stock that suddenly goes 'ex-growth'. The late 1990s threw up several examples of this phenomenon, with once highly-rated household-name companies such as Sainsbury and Marks & Spencer seeming to lose their growth formula. But it is easier to demonstrate the process with our mythical ABC Holdings. Suppose its profits fall heavily and its earnings per share drop from 6p to 3p. At the same time, investors take the view that a rapid profits recovery is unlikely and future growth prospects are much worse than had earlier been thought. The share, they now decide, is not worth a PE ratio of 16.7 but something more like 10. To provide a PE ratio of 10 with earnings per share of only 3p, the shares would have to stand at 30p. Anyone who had bought at 100p would have lost more than two-thirds of his money as the shares were re-rated downwards.

Searching for value

The aim of investment analysts and managers, and of commentators in the financial press, is to find companies that are **undervalued** relative to their growth prospects. The writer who spots that a company is due for an **upward re-rating** before other people realize that its earnings prospects are better than expected is (if he is right) offering his reader the chance of a capital profit. And, as we have seen, it is equally important to spot companies whose growth prospects are diminishing and whose shares are likely to be **re-rated downwards** – astute investors will want to sell before the share price adjusts downwards. But warnings of this nature are a lot less common in print than the buy recommendations. And press commentators along with most other investment advisers are much less adept in forecasting major turning points in the market as a whole than they are at predicting price movements in individual shares. Don't necessarily expect a press warning ahead of a major fall in the stockmarket!

When interest rates change

Now take a totally different aspect, which we touched on in Chapter 1. ABC Holdings at 100p (we will assume it has not gone ex-growth!) yields 3 per cent and stands on a PE ratio of 16.7. With expectations of 7 per cent a year growth in earnings, the overall return is 10 per cent if the share price rises in line. An expected overall return of 10 per cent might look about right if, at this time, investors could get a redemption yield of 6.5 per cent on long-dated gilt-edged securities. It would not look nearly so good if interest rates rose so that gilt-edged stock prices fell till they offered a risk-free 10 per cent. Investors would want a higher return on the ordinary share, so its price would have to fall. Nothing has necessarily happened to alter the outlook for ABC's profits. But the price falls because the returns available on other forms of investment have increased. So the price of any individual company's shares – relative to others – will reflect the growth prospects of that company and therefore the **overall return** investors can expect. And the prices of ordinary shares as a whole will be affected by returns available on alternative forms of investment.

While these forces are always at work, they are not always so easy to spot in the reports of short-term price movements. Investors do not necessarily sit down and work out their assumptions on relative growth rates or returns available elsewhere before buying a share. But prices in the stockmarket reflect a balance of the (often instinctive) views of many thousands of investors. And it is noticeable that the ratings of individual companies do reflect their perceived growth prospects and that, over a long period, there is a remarkable correlation between movements in the yields on equities and those on fixed-interest investments (see Figure 7a.1).

Thus in a period of buoyant economic activity and rising company profits, the equity market as a whole might be expected to show a rising trend (though it will anticipate what is happening in the economy). And when we come down to the particular, any news about a company which adds to expectations of future growth will cause the share price to rise, and events which might depress earnings will cause it to fall, relative to the market as a whole.

If share prices in the long run depend on a combination of company profits and alternative investment returns, in the short term they can be moved by a variety of other factors. Many of these are purely technical. Investment comment draws a distinction between **fundamental** influences (those relating to company profits or assets) and **technical** influences (mainly those affecting the share price without reflecting on the trading position of the company itself). Here are some of the more important influences, mainly of a technical nature, that we have not yet covered.

Company profit announcements

Surprisingly, you will see from market reports that a share price often falls when a company reports good profits. A market report probably talks of **profit-taking**. The reason is as follows. In the weeks ahead of the profit announcement the share price rises as investors buy in expectation of the good figures. By the time these figures arrive, there is no reason for the speculators to hang on any longer, so they sell to take their profits. It is another example of the stockmarket **discounting** news well in advance.

Another type of announcement that very definitely affects the market price is the **profit warning**. If a company realizes that its profits for the year are going to be significantly lower than it had forecast or than the market was expecting, it will normally have to give advance warning to the stock exchange and therefore to investors. Sometimes investors already suspect that bad news is coming, but when these profit warnings emerge from the blue, the share price can fall very heavily.

Press recommendations

If the press or a firm of brokers **tips** (strongly recommends) a share, the price will usually rise. It will rise furthest if the shares are a **narrow market** – in other words, the recommendation relates to a company which does not have a great number of shares in issue or available on the market. In this case a small amount of buying would push the price up, whereas a recommendation for a large and widely traded company such as British Telecom might have relatively little impact on the price.

Don't assume, however, that all the price rise that follows a

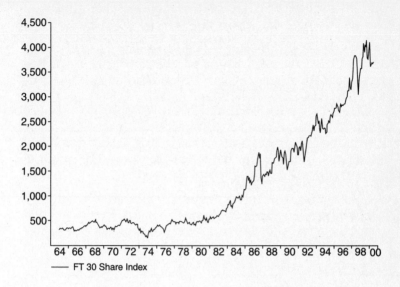

— FT 30 Share Index

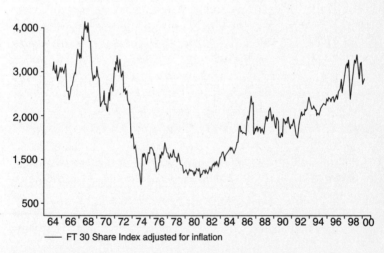

— FT 30 Share Index adjusted for inflation

Figure 7a.1 Share prices since 1964... and adjusted for inflation The top chart shows a long run of the FT 30 Share index, and pretty impressive it looks in recent years as a sustained bull market appears to have replaced the stop–go bull and bear markets of the 1960s and 1970s. The second chart, which shows the same thing adjusted for inflation, does not look quite so impressive, though it is still clear that anyone who bought shares in the early 1980s is likely to have done well. Source: *Datastream.*

press recommendation is the result of share buying. **Marketmakers** read the press too, and when they see a share recommended they will tend to move up the price they quote in anticipation of likely buying. Thus investors often find they can buy a share only at a price considerably above the one quoted when the recommendation was made.

Marketmakers' manoeuvres

You'll sometimes see reports such as 'marketmakers were short of stock, and prices rose as they balanced their books'. This simply means that marketmakers had sold shares they did not own – they went **short** – and later they had to buy the shares they needed to deliver to clients. This buying moved prices up.

Marketmakers and other dealers thrive on activity and when there is little activity they may attempt to stimulate it artificially. For example, at a time when there was little news to encourage investors either to buy or sell, they might move their quoted prices down to attract buyers and generate some action.

Bear operations

It is not only marketmakers that sell shares they do not own. Speculators in the market may also **go short** in expectation of a price fall. They sell shares in the hope they can buy them at a lower price before they have to deliver. The profit on a successful short sale is the difference between the two prices – though, as we saw, the manoeuvre is more difficult for private investors now that the fortnightly account system has gone and operations in the traded options market may be used instead.

Selling short is a dangerous manoeuvre. If the speculators get it wrong and the price rises rather than falling, there is no limit to their potential loss. They might sell shares at 100p in the expectation of a fall in the price to 80p. Suppose instead that there is a takeover bid for the company which forces its price up to 200p. They now have to buy shares at 200p to deliver the shares sold at 100p.

Short sellers have to buy to fulfill their contractual obligations to deliver the shares. If marketmakers sense there has been widescale short selling of a particular share they may deliberately move their quoted prices up, forcing the **bears** (those who had been trading on expectation of a price fall) to buy at an inflated price. This is known as a **bear squeeze**. Quite commonly you will see reports that prices rose on **bear covering**, even when the general trend of prices had been downwards. This simply reflects the forced buying by speculators who had earlier sold short and does not necessarily indicate a reversal of the market's downward trend.

A **bear raid** occurs when speculators descend on a company and deliberately try to force the price down, partly by short selling but possibly also by circulating unfavourable rumours about the company. They hope to buy the shares cheaply once the price has dropped. Bear raiders are, of course, vulnerable to being caught in a bear squeeze.

Technical corrections

Markets seldom continue up or down in an unbroken line. After a period of rising or falling prices you often see references to a **technical correction** or to the market **consolidating**. If prices have been rising for a long period, there will often be a break as some investors sell to take their profits and prices temporarily fall. They may well continue on up after the **shakeout** has taken place. A similar process takes place in reverse on the way down. The market tends to move in fits and starts, with investors pausing for breath at various points on the way up or down.

Chartist influences

There is a theory that you can predict from past price movements what a share price (or the market as a whole, as measured by one of the indices) is likely to do in the future. Whether you believe in this theory or not, you cannot ignore the fact that at times it has a strong impact on share prices. Commentators who base their forecasts on these theories are known as **technical analysts** or **chartists** (because they use charts to plot the price movements).

The theory is not as silly as it might sound. Suppose the share price of ABC Holdings had, over the past few months, fluctuated between 100p and 120p. This would suggest that each time the price dropped as low as 100p there were investors who considered it cheap at this price and were prepared to buy. Each time it rose as high as 120p a fair body of investors considered it was becoming expensive and therefore sold. So 100p and 120p became recognized as **resistance levels**.

If subsequently the price dropped significantly below 100p or rose significantly above 120p, this would suggest that something had happened to change investors' perception of the shares. The chartist would not need to know what had happened but simply that the price

– reflecting the balance of opinion among buyers and sellers in the market – had broken out from a resistance level and might be expected to continue in the direction it had taken until a new resistance level was reached.

This merely illustrates the principle – in practice, the chartist projections may be based on considerably more complex analysis. And nowadays share prices are probably plotted with the help of computers rather than on graph paper, and the computer can be programmed to give buy and sell prompts at appropriate points.

Since most **chartists** work on broadly similar theories, their predictions can be self-fulfilling. If all chartists reckoned the ABC Holdings share price had breached a significant resistance level when it rose through 120p to 125p, all who followed the theory would duly jump in and buy and the price might be carried up to, say, 140p. Chartist techniques are also widely used in other markets such as gold and foreign exchange.

Interest rate and currency movements

We have seen that a rise in interest rates will depress the price of gilt-edged stocks and may also depress equity prices by raising the returns available on other investments. But it will have different impact on different kinds of company. It might depress, say, housebuilders more than the average because higher interest rates mean higher mortgage costs and could deter housebuyers. It would depress highly-geared companies which use a lot of variable-rate borrowed money, because higher interest costs will depress their profits. It might actually help companies which are sitting on large amounts of cash and will therefore earn a higher interest income. But, all else being equal, higher interest rates raise the cost of borrowing for consumers and for industry and may be expected to damp down economic activity, which is bad for company profit prospects. This is quite separate from the purely technical factor that higher interest charges may depress share prices because of the higher returns available elsewhere.

The effect of **currency movements** is also complex. If sterling is strong (perhaps too strong, as it was in the later 1990s – see Chapter 16) the government will not necessarily try to counter any fall in the currency by raising interest rates. The fall might be welcome. But if sterling is weak and then falls further there will be the prospect of higher interest rates to defend the pound. This will usually hit gilt-edged prices and might be expected to have a knock-on effect on share values. On the other side of the coin, a lower level of sterling improves British industry's competitive position in home and export markets and thus improves profit prospects. So sometimes a weakening in sterling will depress bond prices but boost ordinary shares.

Weight of money argument

Share prices tend to rise when there are more buyers than sellers. If there is a lot of money available for investment in stockmarkets, prices would normally tend to rise – hence the **weight of money** factor. But, now that the British can invest freely abroad as well as at home (**foreign exchange controls** were suspended in 1979 and later abolished) and foreigners invest heavily in Britain, this factor is difficult to pin down. In the past you might have started with the amount of new money that the financial institutions would have available for investment. From this you would knock off the amounts that would be soaked up by new issues of government debt, by new share issues on the domestic stockmarket and likely sales by existing investors, by investment in property and overseas securities, and so on. What was left would be available for buying existing shares in the UK stockmarket, whose prices it would tend to push up.

If the sums are now more difficult to pin down, the weight of money factor should not be ignored. The Japanese stockmarket in the 1980s was carried up to unrealistic heights by the very high savings of Japanese families which were channelled into the market, leaving it very vulnerable when economic and financial problems erupted.

At a domestic level, the weight of money factor may be seen at work in some of the stockmarket's more excessive enthusiasms. Prices of Internet-related companies were roaring through the roof late in 1999, partly because private investors were prepared to pay virtually any price to get in on the latest hot stock. In other words, a vast weight of money was being thrown at the stockmarket's current fashion. In many cases the companies in question consisted largely of hope value and were impossible to value on normal investment criteria.

Too many shares

When a company raises capital by issuing new shares or issues shares in a takeover, the price will often fall. This is simply because initially there are not enough buyers around to absorb all the new shares. And if it is known that there are owners of large blocks of shares who want to dispose of them (possibly **underwriters** left with shares they do not want – see Chapter 8) the price may be weak until these have been disposed of. You will see references to large blocks of shares **overhanging the market**.

Politics

It used to be regarded as a general rule, particularly in the run-up to an election, that evidence that the Conservatives were doing well would boost gilt and equity prices and evidence to the contrary would depress them. This was never completely logical. Though, in the past, Labour governments might have been associated in the public mind with high inflation and high interest costs, shares had often performed well under a Labour regime. Sometimes share prices would rise in anticipation of a Conservative election win, but fall on heavy profit-taking when the expectation was fulfilled. Betting on elections was always dangerous. At millennium time, with a New Labour government in power but largely implementing Conservative economic policies, the odds looked more than usually difficult to call.

Sentiment

This is the indefinable factor. On some days investors feel cheerful and decide to buy. It may be good political or economic news, it may simply be that the day is sunny or England has won a game of cricket. But one strong and consistent influence on the London stockmarket is the performance of share prices in overseas markets. The behaviour of **Wall Street** has always influenced London. But with increasing globalization, the overseas influence today is often more than sentimental. The same world economic events may affect London as markets overseas. Shares that are quoted in New York or Tokyo may also be traded in London and a fall in the home market can trigger a fall in the UK. Though, for London, the Wall Street link is probably still the strongest, the crash of October 1987 (with its knock-on effect on all world markets) demonstrated how quickly market movements now travel across most frontiers.

Takeovers

We have left **takeovers** to last because at times they dominate stockmarket thinking. The assumption is that if Company A bids for Company B it will need to pay above the current market price of

Company B shares, though in practice the Company B share price often rises as a result of leaks or inspired guesses in the weeks before a bid is announced.

Actual takeovers, and rumours of takeovers, raise the prices of individual shares. Investors' thinking becomes obsessed with takeovers and they look for other possible bid candidates and force up the prices by buying the shares. The equity market as a whole is carried upwards by the takeover fever.

Price rises on takeover talk seem to fly in the face of the idea that a company's earnings prospects determine the value of its shares. This is not so. The bidder is simply paying a price that takes account of the expected earnings growth of the victim company over the next two or three years, the earnings he expects to be able to squeeze out of his victim (possibly with the help of creative accounting), or the possible cost savings from eliminating overlapping activities and jobs. Thus for any share there are at least two possible values. What it is worth in the market on its own earnings prospects – and the price a bidder might have to pay, which pre-empts a few years of earnings growth or which is based on the potential for **asset-stripping** (see glossary) or selling off the constituent businesses. Shareholders in the victim company get jam today rather than jam tomorrow.

Internet pointers

For an indication of what is moving share prices on any particular day, go to any of the sites that carry market reports and financial news. These include, of course, the *Financial Times* site at www.ft.com/ and the news agency sites (see Chapter 23). Many other sites include a feed of market reports and main financial news, including some of the personal finance sites and the portal sites such as Yahoo! on (for British readers) http://uk.finance.yahoo.com/.

7 What moves share prices
b: In the crash of '87

Investors have short memories. After every major crash in financial markets we read that lessons have been learned and taken to heart. The same mistakes could not be made in the future. Do not believe a word of it! Within ten years or so the crash is no more than a faint folk-memory. The same mistakes are resurfacing, perhaps in slightly different form. Once financial markets get a head of steam behind them, nobody wants to hear the words of caution. After the 1974–76 collapse in the commercial property market, for which the groundwork was laid by excessive bank lending, we were told that the same thing could never happen again. Between 1984 and 1990 the banks increased their property loans sevenfold. The early 1990s saw these same banks making provisions for their multi-billion pound property-loan losses as the bloated commercial property market once again collapsed.

Crashes in the stockmarket can be even more dramatic. For investors nurtured on the bull market of the 1980s the roof fell in on Monday 19 October 1987. And it was not only investors who suffered falling roofs. The Friday morning of the previous week (16 October), a once-in-a-century freak storm had devastated much of southern England, causing widescale property damage but also disrupting transport and all forms of communication. On that Friday the stock exchange in London had barely functioned. Many securities dealers had not arrived for work. The stock exchange's SEAQ price information system was out of commission much of the day and such dealing as took place reverted to old systems of direct contact. No stock exchange indices were calculated in London that Friday.

America was spared the storm, but nasty things had been happening on Wall Street. On Saturday 17 October the *Financial Times* had led with a story headed 'Wall Street ends two worst weeks with record daily fall'. The Dow Jones Industrial Average – the most commonly used index of the American market – had fallen over 17 per cent from its August peak. On Friday 16 October alone it had dropped almost 5 per cent. The *Financial Times*'s market report commented 'It

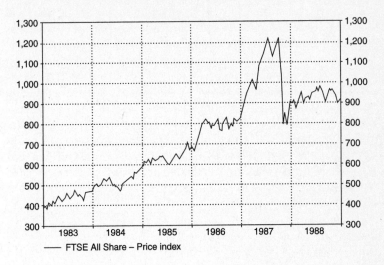

FTSE All Share – Price index

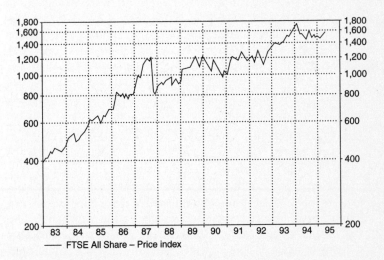

FTSE All Share – Price index

Figure 7b.1 How history lends perspective The top chart shows the boom in share prices in the 1980s which paved the way for the dramatic bust in October 1987. The bottom chart shows exactly the same thing, but has been updated to 1995 and uses a logarithmic scale. The '87 crash seems barely more than a blip. Be careful with charts: they can be designed to deceive. Source: *Datastream International.*

was not simply that the stockmarket fell ... It was more: last week the US stockmarket lost its optimism'.

Had London been fully functioning on Friday 16 October, and had share price indices been calculated, some indication of what was to come this side of the Atlantic might have filtered through. As it was, London was worried; but there was little sense of market cataclysm that weekend. Monday's *Financial Times* led with a story 'Bull yields to bear as Wall Street accepts the party's over'. But it was writing mainly of the United States. In Britain, the biggest-ever sale of government-owned shares was about to take place: the £7.2 billion offer of the government's stake in British Petroleum. Monday's paper contained a piece on the BP sale headed: 'A test for the bull market's resolve'. In Britain we were still talking of bull markets.

By Tuesday 20 October the worldwide bull market was history. At the close on Monday 19 October the London market was down almost 10 per cent from its close the previous Thursday, as measured by the FTA All-Share Index (as it then was).

But on that Monday the United States had again held centre stage. The Dow Jones Industrials crashed by over 500 points to 1738.42: a one-day fall of over 22 per cent, the worst of which happened after the London market had closed. By Tuesday's close London was a further 11.4 per cent down for a two-day fall of 20 per cent. And, with only modest occasional rallies, it continued down well into November. At its nadir the FTA All-Share Index was down 36.6 per cent from its July 1987 peak. Other markets worldwide had suffered a similar fate. On Monday 19 October and the following day the Tokyo stockmarket lost 17 per cent and the Australian market was down almost 28 per cent. Hong Kong could not be measured at this point. The market had closed.

Once the full extent of the market rout was apparent, the economic gurus were out in force to rationalize the week's events. The instability in the financial system as a result of world trade imbalances, and particularly the budget and trade deficits in the United States, was apparently to blame for the mayhem in the world's financial markets. The economists singularly failed to explain why, since these imbalances had been present for some considerable time, the crash had not happened before. There was in fact a far simpler and, at least with the benefit of hindsight, more accurate explanation of the week's events. Most speculative booms in stockmarkets end with a bust: what sparks the fall is almost irrelevant. Professor J K Galbraith summed up the

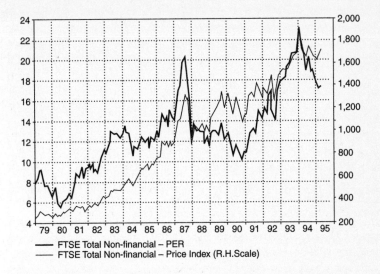

Figure 7b.2 The average PE ratio on shares of industrial and commercial companies (thick line and left-hand scale) rose to 20 in 1987 as share prices (thinner line and right-hand scale) boomed and lost contact with the fundamentals of company earnings. PE ratios returned to more normal levels and with subsequent crash in share prices. Source: *Datastream International.*

phenomenon in his book on an earlier and ultimately far more serious stockmarket crash in the United States, *The Great Crash 1929.* '... it was simply that a roaring boom was in progress in the stock market and, like all booms, it had to end. ...When prices stopped rising – when the supply of people who were buying for an increase was exhausted ... everyone would want to sell. The market wouldn't level out; it would fall precipitately'. On Monday 19 October 1987, this happened again on Wall Street – and in London and across the world.

The price falls in the 1987 crash were as nothing compared with the bear market of 1973–75, when share prices in the UK fell to around a quarter of their previous peak. It was the speed of the fall that created the drama. A decline in share prices that in previous decades might have taken place gradually, over a year or more, was telescoped into a day or a few days. Again, many explanations have been advanced for the suddenness of the fall, and computers (or the men and women who programme them) were singled out for a large share of the blame.

There was much talk of the perils of **programme trading**, though the phrase appeared to mean different things to different commentators. In the United States widescale **arbitrage** habitually took place between the cash market and the financial futures market, with computers signalling the minor discrepancies in pricing between the two that offered the chance of a profit (see Chapter 18). **Portfolio insurance** was also common in the States. This is a tactic by which major institutional investors may seek to lock into the profits on their portfolios. It can involve operations in the futures or options markets (the value of the futures or options positions rises if the value of shares in the portfolio falls). It can also involve a set programme for turning part of the share portfolio into cash if prices fall more than a certain amount. And on top we have the familiar **chartist** theories (see previous chapter) whereby a price fall can itself signal a larger price fall and stimulate selling which makes the prediction self-fulfilling.

All of these factors and more were probably at work on Wall Street during the crash. The interaction of the stockmarket and the futures market meant that a fall on one stimulated selling on the other, which in turn led to further selling on the first. And the use of semi-automatic programmes made the spiral twist even more rapidly down.

But perhaps this form of computerized trading (which in any case was not widespread in London at that time) was the least significant aspect of computers in the crash. More important was the instant dissemination of information across the world by electronic message and computer screen. The trader knew instantly what was happening in other financial centres and marked down share prices in his own in consequence. As panic spread through the world's financial centres it became clear that instant information had negative as well as positive features.

So much for the technicalities. Why had share prices been poised for a fall? If we take the London market in isolation (and many of its features were mirrored overseas) the charts tell much of the story. Look first at Figure 7b.1 on page 129, plotting the FTA All-Share Index since 1983. Share prices had been climbing steadily through to the end of 1986. In the first half of 1987 the rate of increase accelerated (a typical feature of the late days of a bull market) as more and more investors or speculators climbed on the bandwagon, attracted by the profits made from the market in recent years. By its peak in the middle of July, the index had climbed 48 per cent from its beginning of the year level. Then look at Figure 7b.2 on page 131, showing the average price earnings (PE) ratio on the FTA 500 Share Index.

The immediately striking point is that though on balance PE ratios were rising up to the end of 1986 – again, this tends to happen in a bull market – they were not rising anything like as fast as share prices. In other words, company profits and earnings were rising rapidly, providing part-justification for the increase in share prices. But the rise in share values in the first half of 1987 finally lost contact with the **fundamentals** – earnings, yield and alternative investment returns – which are the ultimate support for share values. Company profits did not rise 48 per cent in half a year, as shares did. Outright speculative fever had taken hold. If we look at Figure 7b.3 on page 134, showing average dividend yields against average redemption yields on gilt-edged stocks, we get another facet of the same picture. Up to the end of 1986, company dividends had been increasing fast enough to prevent a great drop in yields despite booming share prices. In 1987 share prices shot ahead of dividend growth and dividend yields fell sharply to below 3 per cent on average. In the process, as the chart shows clearly, the traditional relationship between gilt-edged returns and dividend yields was sharply distorted.

When prices began to fall, there was therefore nothing to stop the rout until a rational relationship with the fundamentals was re-established. In fact, for all the drama, the crash did no more than return share prices to their values of a year earlier, when the final speculative fever had taken hold. The crash was a vindication – not a negation – of the theory that company profits and dividends determine share values in the long run.

What of the aftermath? Company profits and dividends continued to grow after October 1987. The economic collapse, which many felt that the crash foretold or would cause, simply failed to happen over the following eighteen months. Shares again began to look quite attractive on the fundamental criteria. The crash was a pure stockmarket phenomenon: a bust following an excessive speculative boom. That is not to say that it did not have its economic effects. The authorities in Britain, it is argued, were terrified of any action that might provoke further mayhem on the markets. They therefore failed to act soon enough to damp down an over-heating economy, with the result that the 1980s boom ran totally out of control and the reaction – the recession of the early 1990s – was correspondingly more severe. But that is another story.

Even in the short term, however, the crash had left its scars. It largely destroyed the illusion, prevalent at the time of the Big Bang a year earlier, that the City could sustain its extravagant lifestyle with ever more frenetic dealing in shares. There was little more talk of expansion in the equity trading rooms; cutbacks became the norm. The

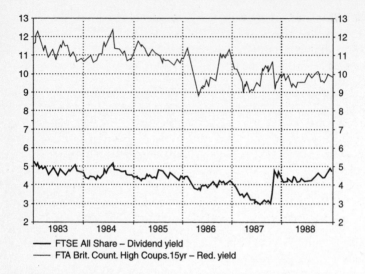

Figure 7b.3 The average dividend yield on shares (solid bottom line) normally maintains a relationship with the yield on gilt-edged stocks (light upper line). But in 1987 the final stages of the share price boom pushed dividend yields below 3 per cent and distorted the relationship. This relationship returned to a more normal pattern after share prices collapsed and dividend yields therefore rose again. Source: *Datastream International.*

liquidity of the market had been exposed as an illusion. The events of 1987 showed that shares were easy to buy and sell while prices were rising. But once the fall began, those who hoped to get out fast found they were lucky if they could get through to their broker or to the marketmakers. The trading system introduced in the Big Bang was already in need of revision.

Could a crash on a similar scale happen again? It will already be clear that our own answer is 'yes', though such a crash is most likely to come after a period of feverish speculative activity in the markets. Before the 1987 crash the British government had encouraged such speculative fever, by hyping privatization issues and by offering the taxpayer's assets to the public at below their worth. The illusion of the stockmarket as a source of instant profits had been created. It fuelled the boom that preceded the bust.

If such speculative fevers could be prevented in the future, perhaps crashes could be prevented as well. But once the stockmarket gets a head of steam behind it, nobody wants to miss the fun. Everybody holds on for the last five per cent of profit as the market approaches its peak, and everybody succumbs to the delusion that he or she will be able to spot the warning signs of the downturn ahead of the herd. The 1987 crash showed what happened when investors put this delusion to the test of reality and, in the event, all rushed to sell at the same time.

Ironically, when world stockmarkets were again put to the test almost exactly ten years later, the system managed to withstand pressures that had their root in real economic events. But the problem this time did not start on Wall Street or on the London Stock Exchange. Instead, it had its origins in the former **tiger economies** of Asia – notably Thailand and South Korea – whence it spread to the longer-established Far-Eastern financial centres of Malaysia, Singapore and Hong Kong. Japan itself – with enough problems in its own financial system – was further shaken, and in November 1997 witnessed the collapse of its oldest securities house, the once-proud Yamaichi Securities.

Initially, the storm did not spare the United States or Britain. In late October, Wall Street saw its biggest daily fall since the crash of 1987 – a decline of over 8 per cent in the Dow Jones index which triggered an automatic temporary closure of the market under the safeguards built in after the crash of ten years earlier. The fall was blamed on a further severe decline in the Hong Kong market. The London market responded with a fall of almost 10 per cent at one point the following day, but closed the day with a comparatively modest decline as Wall Street staged a sharp recovery. Europe's fledgling markets were hard hit, with Russian stocks falling almost 20 per cent in a day and further trouble to come.

The problems of the former tiger economies were ascribed largely to over-rapid expansion, financed extensively on borrowed money. They were exacerbated by some pretty ramshackle financial structures that had failed to develop to match the countries' very rapid industrial growth. Adding to the problems were corporate structures which lacked the accountability and transparency found among more mature Western corporations. The term **crony capitalism** (see glossary) was much to the fore.

Once growth slackened in the tiger economies, servicing the debt became difficult or impossible. The expansionary years had been accompanied by a boom in securities prices and real-estate values. With securities and real estate forming the security for much bank lending, financial institutions were in trouble when values turned down. Much of the security for the lending had disappeared.

Though considerably more robust than the younger tiger economies, Japan itself had a long-standing problem stemming from earlier excessive lending by its financial institutions against the security of inflated share and real-estate prices. A very high level of bad loans among its banks and other lending institutions was the inevitable result when share prices and real-estate prices fell after the 1980s boom, and the problem plagued the Japanese financial system for most of the 1990s. Bad loans in Japan were reckoned to be equivalent to about 10 per cent of gross domestic product, though the true figure could have been considerably higher. In common with the more youthful tiger economies, Japan had always lacked a financial system that matched the strength and sophistication of its industrial base. Share prices in Japan at the end of 1997 were less than half of their all-time high.

Share prices in the stockmarkets of the former tiger economies collapsed when the growth bubble burst. By December 1997, South Korean shares were lower than ten years earlier, thus wiping out the market gains from a decade of growth. But not only shares were under attack. Each country in turn saw its currency fall steeply in the foreign exchange markets as the speculators moved in. When Malaysia's currency came under attack, its prime minister accused the speculators of creating the crisis. His words found an echo amongst the population. Effigies of George Soros – king of the international currency speculators – were burned in Malaysia's capital, Kuala Lumpur.

After providing help for Thailand, the International Monetary Fund (IMF) was called in to South Korea to mount its biggest-ever rescue package at that date, a total of $US57 billion, to help the country to avoid defaulting on its short-term overseas loans. The package had a price: as a condition of the assistance, South Korea was required to implement far-reaching financial and economic reforms.

The big question in Western financial centres was whether the storms in Asia would inflict severe permanent damage on the more mature economies of North America and Europe. There was the fear that a default on its debt by any one country could have a knock-on effect on other economies, perhaps triggering further defaults. This could seriously destabilize the global financial system. It was clear, too, that the problems of Asia's former tiger economies would have a direct impact on Western companies that traded extensively with them. The problems would also restrict the Asian countries' ability to invest directly in manufacturing plant abroad, which was bad news for the West. Britain saw delays or cutbacks in planned investment by Asian groups such as the South Korean Hyundai. A general slow-down in world trade was feared.

In the event, once the initial shock had subsided, the stockmarket repercussions were largely confined to Asia and to emerging markets in Eastern Europe and South America. Rightly or wrongly, the London market showed considerable strength and was riding high as the millennium approached. Jobs in Britain had been lost from the investment cutbacks. But for much of the population the most visible effect of the turmoil was a flood of bargain-priced personal computers and similar products resulting from the very low level of many of the Asian currencies and from manufacturers' need to raise cash by offloading stocks.

8 Stockmarket launches

When the stockmarket is buoyant you can expect a spate of new companies **coming to the market** – achieving a **listing** or **quote** for their shares for the first time – encouraged by the high valuation that will be put on their shares and by investors' readiness to buy them. The term 'new companies' is perhaps misleading. They are not usually new businesses, but businesses which are new to the stockmarket. For the first time their shares can be bought and sold on the stockmarket. The larger ones may apply for a **listing** on the London Stock Exchange itself (the **main market**, which used to be known as the **official list**). Smaller or younger companies (or companies which wish to **float** only a small amount of their share capital) may apply for a quote on the **Alternative Investment Market** or **AIM**, which is also run by the LSE.

The rule used to be (and still generally is) that a company needs at least a three-year trading record before it can list on the main market. But times are changing. While it may take many years to build up a business in traditional manufacturing areas, Internet-based businesses can – and often do – have a much shorter gestation period. The **Freeserve** free Internet-access provider, established as a spin-off from the Dixons high street electrical and electronics retailing chain, was allowed to launch in its own right on the main market in 1999 when it had been operating for well under a year. It was valued at over £1.5 billion at the issue price, without at that time ever having made a profit. Freeserve may have been an exception at the time, but later in 1999 the London Stock Exchange announced the formation of a 'market within a market' called **techMARK**, to recognize the particular characteristics and needs of technology companies. Though techMARK is part of the main market, changes were proposed to the listing rules that would allow techMARK companies to join the market without the normal three-year trading record provided they satisfied certain other criteria. Some young companies in the technology area, which up to then had qualified only for an

AIM quotation, were expected to move up to the main market as a result.

For many individual investors, applying for shares in **new issues** was their first introduction to stock exchange affairs. They may have applied for shares with the intention of holding onto them as an investment. But they may also have **stagged** new issues by applying for shares in the hope that these could be sold at a profit as soon as **dealings began** (we will see later why this was often a good bet). But there have been changes here, too. The number of new issues which are thrown open for subscription by the public at large has declined drastically in recent years. With the major privatization issues now out of the way, the most likely route for many private investors to have acquired shares for the first time has been through the launch of former mutual building and insurance societies.

The Internet factor

The **Internet** is a natural medium for making information available to large numbers of people and the opportunities it offers for marketing shares have not been overlooked. But be a little careful. The international nature of the Internet also makes it an ideal medium for those attempting to promote shares in duff businesses that do not conform to the listing requirements of any reputable stock exchange.

However, if properly used the Internet could improve access to new share issues for the general public. Reputable on-line brokers and banks may have allocations of shares that are available for subscription by their clients.

The Internet has impinged on the new issue scene in another way, as the Freeserve example suggested. The run-up to the millennium saw a spate of new issues – mainly on the AIM market – of companies engaged in one type of Internet business or another. The inclusion of '.net' or '.com' in the company title seemed enough to secure a market capitalization of many millions of pounds for businesses which had never done anything as prosaic as earning a profit. Like most stockmarket fashions, the enthusiasm for the so-called **dotcom** companies showed every sign of running out of control. Investors tended to forget that the very nature of the Internet, which allows a novel idea to be exploited with startling rapidity, also allows competitors or imitators to join in and erode the position of the innovator equally fast. Trouble was widely predicted at the turn of the millennium, and seemed more than likely.

Type of launch

First, the mechanics of a new issue.

There are four main ways a company may float its shares on the market. (Flotations have traditionally attracted nautical metaphors just as takeovers attract marital ones, and a new issue may also be described as a **launch**. It is perhaps a pity that the more prosaic American term **Initial Public Offering** or **IPO** is now gaining ground). These launch methods are:

- The **offer for sale**. Shares are offered for sale to the public, partly via the medium of the newspapers which carry details of the issue. A full **prospectus** giving a great deal of information on the company, its financial position, its trading record and its directors and advisers is a legal requirement when shares are marketed, though it may be only an abbreviated **mini-prospectus** that appears in the press with details of where to get the full document. The offer for sale, though less common nowadays, is the method of most interest to the general public and we will look at it in detail later.

- The **placing**. In this case the company achieves an initial spread of shareholders by arranging privately to sell shares to a range of investors: usually several hundred of them. The placing is usually arranged by the company's broker and most of the shares will probably be placed with his clients. The general public who are not clients probably do not get a look-in at this stage. After the placing, permission is given for the shares to be traded on the stockmarket, and anybody can buy in the normal way, though the price has probably now risen above the placing price.

- The **intermediaries offer**. Shares are offered for sale to financial intermediaries for allocation to their clients. Again, investors who are not clients of the intermediaries in question cannot buy at this stage but have to wait until the shares are traded on the market.

- The **introduction**. An introduction is likely to be used when a company already has a large spread of shareholders and simply wants permission for the shares to be dealt in on the stockmarket. An introduction does not involve the raising of capital or the marketing of shares – though it could pave the way for raising additional capital in the future – and it is the cheapest way of coming to market. When a company moves up from the AIM market to the main market or when a former building society distributes shares to its members and seeks a listing, it will probably be by way of an introduction.

With the exception of introductions, combinations of these various issue methods may be possible.

Who is raising money?

In any report of an offer for sale, a placing or an intermediaries offer, one of the first points to focus on is: who gets the money from the sale of the shares? The shares may come from one of two sources:

- shares being sold by the existing shareholders – perhaps the founders of the company who built it up from its inception. In this case the cash raised goes to these original shareholders, not to the company;

- new shares created by the company. In this case the cash from the sale of the shares goes into the company's own coffers, not to its original owners.

In practice, the shares made available may be a mix. Some are existing shares sold by the owners and some are new shares sold to raise cash for the company. Be a little cautious if you see that all the shares are coming from existing shareholders and that they are disposing of a large part of their holdings. Why have they decided to cash in at this point? There may be a valid reason, but you would want to know.

Pricing an offer for sale

Offers for sale to the public are of two main types: **fixed-price offers** and **tender offers**. The fixed price offer is the more common. How is the price fixed?

Every issue requires **sponsors**. Traditionally, an issue would be sponsored by a broker or both an investment bank and broker might be involved. More recently, other types of institution – such as accountants – may apply for permission to act as sponsors. And on the AIM market the role of **nominated adviser** is substituted for that of sponsor. Normally – though not always – a company coming to market makes in its prospectus a **forecast of profits** and **dividend** for the current year, as well as giving details of its historical profits. Working with these figures, the sponsors will look for existing quoted companies in a similar line of business. By reference to the **ratings** (**PE ratio** and **yield**) that these companies enjoy – and adjusting for the superior or inferior **growth prospects** of the new-comer – it should be possible to fix the appropriate rating, and there-fore the price, for the shares of the newcomer. Much the same pricing process is at work whatever issue method is used. In the case of larger issues, the advisers to the company may also sound out major investors as to how many shares they would be prepared to take at what price – a process known as **bookbuilding** (see glossary).

Two points should be borne in mind. The sponsors want to make sure the new issue gets off to a good start: in other words, when trading begins in the shares the price in this **aftermarket** should not be below the offer for sale price and preferably should rise some way above it. So they will try to pitch the shares at a price a little below what they are likely to be worth. Too far below and they will be accused of failing to get a sufficiently good price for their client. The **dotcom** companies that were launching in profusion around the turn of the millennium were a bit of an exception. In many cases shares shot way above the issue price in first dealings – but there was no rational way of valuing them anyway.

Second, the company itself almost certainly errs on the side of caution in arriving at its profits forecast. There is nothing worse for a market newcomer than to fail to meet its **prospectus forecast**. So the forecast will be pitched some way below what the directors expect profits to be.

The first point means that – unless the sponsors have got their cal-culations badly wrong or the stockmarket drops sharply between the price being fixed and the start of dealings – the shares are being sold at less than their likely value and there is therefore a very good chance of a quick profit for **stags** who manage to secure an allocation of shares. The second means that you should not take too seriously the reports that appear later when the company publishes its first profit figures after going public. They are often headed something like 'XYZ Holdings exceeds forecast' as if this implied unexpectedly good performance. The truth in most cases is that investors should have been worried if the company did not exceeed its forecast. It had planned to do so.

The tender offer

Some companies are almost impossible to value – for example, there may be no comparable quoted company – and in these circumstances a **tender offer** can make sense. Investors are invited to apply for the number of shares they want and asked to state what price they are prepared to pay above a stipulated minimum. Assuming the issue is **fully subscribed** – applications are received for at least the total number of shares on offer – the sponsors will calculate at what price all the shares available can be sold. This becomes the **striking price** and anybody who applied for shares at this price or above has a chance of getting some. The shares are often allocated at the striking price, even to those who bid at a higher price, though sometimes applicants are required to pay the price that they bid instead. Those who bid below the striking price get no shares.

The striking price will not always be the highest possible price at which all the available shares can be sold. As this becomes a bit complicated, an example helps. Suppose XYZ Holdings offered 10 million shares to the public and invited tenders at a price of 120p or above. Applications were received as shown in Table 8.1:

No. of shares applied for at each price	Price	Cumulative total of shares that could be sold at each price
2,000,000	140p	2,000,000
3,000,000	135p	5,000,000
5,000,000	130p	10,000,000
2,000,000	125p	12,000,000
4,000,000	120p	16,000,000

Table 8.1

The right-hand column shows that, at a price of 130p, all of the 10 million shares available could be sold, since there were applications for 5 million at 130p, 3 million at 135p and 2 million at 140p. So 130p would be the highest possible striking price. But the sponsors may decide they would rather sell at a slightly lower price to ensure the shares get off to a good start when dealings begin. So they fix on 125p as the striking price. Since there were applications for 12 million shares at this price or above, not all the applicants will get all the shares they asked for.

Oversubscription and allotments

Sponsors pitch their price at a level that they expect will attract applications for more shares than are on offer. Or, with a tender offer, they may settle for a striking price below the highest possible. If they are right and there are applications for more shares than are on offer, the offer is **oversubscribed**. Press reports normally give the extent of the oversubscription.

Then comes the problem of deciding who gets shares, and how many: the **allocation** or **allotment**. This depends on policy and on the extent of oversubscription. It may be decided to hold a **ballot** of all applicants, with the successful ones receiving a standard allocation, whatever they applied for. Or those applying for large numbers (over 100,000, say) may have their applications **scaled down** to, perhaps, 10 per cent of what they asked for. Those applying for fewer than 100,000 might each get 100 shares, or might be put in a ballot with the successful ones getting 300 shares each and the remainder nothing. It depends on the spread of shareholding that the company and its sponsors want (the big initial privatization offers from the government for companies such as British Gas tended to be structured so as to favour small investors).

Underwriting an issue

Most offers for sale are **underwritten**. This means that big investors – particularly institutions – agree for a fee to buy any shares that are not bought by the public if the offer is **undersubscribed**. The vendors – the company or its original shareholders – are thus sure of getting their money. The investment bank sponsoring the issue takes a fee (a percentage of the value of the shares on offer) and pays part to **sub-underwriters** – investors who agree to take a certain maximum number of shares if required to do so. **Underwriting fees** are a useful source of income for investment banks and investing institutions and the City does not like tender offers (which are not invariably underwritten).

It is unusual for the underwriter or sub-underwriters to be called on to take up shares. But if an offer for sale is undersubscribed and **left with the underwriters** you may see references in the press to shares **overhanging the market**. This may mean that underwriters, who were forced to take up more shares than they wanted, will want to sell them (**lighten their holdings**). The share price is unlikely to rise far until these shares overhanging the market have been sold and end up in **firm hands**: with investors who want to keep them.

For the most dramatic case of an **issue flop** we need to go back to 1987 and the sale of the government's £7.2 billion stake in British

Petroleum in October that year. This was not technically a new issue, as BP's shares were already listed on the stock exchange. Rather, the government was disposing of its own large shareholding in the company via a **secondary issue**. But the issue coincided with – and probably helped to cause – the stockmarket crash of that month. As the share price in the stockmarket fell well below the offer price, most of the shares were left with the underwriters and sub-underwriters, who suffered massive losses. They would have suffered still worse losses if the Bank of England had not effectively re-underwritten the part-paid shares by offering to buy them at 70p – a startling case of government subsidy for the private-sector securities houses of Britain and North America. And, as a reflection on the financial sophistication (or lack thereof) of the British public, it is worth noting that over a quarter of a million people applied to buy the government's BP shares at the offer price, even when it was clear that BP shares could be bought at a much lower price in the stockmarket.

Sometimes, as in the BP case, underwriters earn every penny of their fees. But there has long been criticism of the City's underwriting system, though probably more in relation to underwriting rights issues (see Chapter 9) than new issues. Standard fees used to be 2 per cent of the issue proceeds and were, the critics argued, a form of cartel. The standard fee paid insufficient attention to the differing degrees of risk in different issues. Supporters of the system argued that the pricing of the issue should help to even out the risk factor, but they have been forced to give ground and accept more competition in setting the fees.

The offer for sale timetable

The sponsors of an offer for sale want as little time as possible to elapse between fixing the price of an issue and the receipt of applications. They are vulnerable if the market falls in the interim – as with the BP issue – and the shares on offer consequently look overpriced.

In the case of big issues a **pathfinder prospectus** is normally made available to major investors and the press some days ahead of the issue. This contains the details of the company and the offer, so that investors can assess them, but leaves blank the vital information on price and prospective yield and PE ratio. This information is then filled in just before the prospectus is officially published. Applications then have to be in, usually within a matter of days, and the basis of allocation is announced a few days later.

Allotment letters go out to successful applicants as soon as possible after the basis of allocation is decided, and unsuccessful applicants get their money back. The stock exchange fixes a date on which official dealings in the shares will start. In practice, shares may be traded in a **grey market** before shareholders get their allotment letters or even before the basis of allotment is known. In the *Financial Times* the prices of shares in newly floated companies are listed for a time in a special table in the 'Companies and Markets' section of the paper under the heading **Recent issues: equities**.

The major **denationalization** or **privatization issues** – British Telecom, British Gas and the like – worked to a longer timetable because of the size of the issues and the number of unsophisticated investors they were expected to attract. And when there are a lot of companies coming to market, the timetable may in any case vary a little.

Part-paid shares

Most shares are **fully paid**. In other words, suppose we are talking of shares of 20p par value being sold at 100p, the buyer or subscriber pays the whole 100p at one go. But sometimes – mainly with the privatization issues and in the case of some gilt-edged stocks (see Chapter 13) – the price is paid in two or more instalments. This means the vendor gets his money spread out over a period rather than in a single lump.

Thus when XYZ Holdings launches, it might decide to sell its shares at 100p but ask for 30p immediately, a further 30p in six months and the remaining 40p in a year. When only 30p has been paid, the shares will be **part paid**. The *Financial Times*'s **Recent issues: equities** table shows the amount paid for each share in a column headed **Amount paid up** (in pence). Usually the entry is 'FP' for fully paid, but not in every case.

Part-paid shares are speculative because they are **highly geared**. Suppose investors think the right price for XYZ shares is 130p: a 30p premium on the issue price of 100p. In their 30p-paid form, the shares might also be expected to stand at a premium of 30p, so the market price is 60p. This means that anyone who was allotted the part-paid shares at 30p has a 100 per cent profit on his outlay to date, though the shares are only thought to be worth 30 per cent more

RECENT ISSUES: EQUITIES

Issue price p	Amt paid up	Mkt. cap (£m.)	2000 High	Low	Stock	Close price p	+/-	Div	Div cov	Yld	P/E
123	F.P.	7.02	125½	107½	†Basepoint	107½	-	-	-	-	-
§	F.P.	23.8	14¾	12	†BrainDock.Com	14¾	-	-	-	-	-
§	F.P.	44.6	131½	110½	†BSoftB	122½	-	-	-	-	-
§70	F.P.	14.3	75½	52½	†Clipserver.com	59	+6½	-	-	-	-
160	F.P.	1,400	190	165½	‡EGG	171	-	-	-	-	-
2	F.P.	3.25	3½	3½	†Harrogate	3½	-	-	-	-	-
-	F.P.	8.85	38	28	†I Feel Good	28	-4	-	-	-	-
-	F.P.	501.2	358	205	Intec Telecom	337½	-1	-	-	-	-
95	F.P.	25.7	141	97½	†Inventive Leisure	126½	-	-	-	-	-
150	F.P.	36.5	178	175½	†Lok 'n Store	175½	-	-	-	-	-
100	F.P.	11.0	108½	106½	†Mettoni	106½	-1	-	-	-	-
§84	F.P.	67.4	102½	92½	†Newsplayer	102½	-	-	-	-	-
§24	F.P.	8.09	26½	17½	†Non-League Media	18	-	-	-	-	-
§25	F.P.	2.73	30½	28½	†Online Sports & Leis	30	-	-	-	-	-
§	F.P.	32.5	62½	47½	†Online Travel	47½	-	-	-	-	-
§185	F.P.	382.7	318½	200	Orchestream	313½	-	-	-	-	-
§100	F.P.	21.9	102½	99½	Quilter Gibl En Grd	100¼	-	-	-	-	-
§200	F.P.	-	199	195	Do Units	196	-	-	-	-	-
775	F.P.	704.5	1002½	800	TeleCity	995	+2½	-	-	-	-
25	F.P.	4.34	109	27½	†Tolmount	83½	-5½	-	-	-	-
§8	F.P.	13.6	10	7	†Weatherly Intl	7½	+¼	-	-	-	-
§	F.P.	0.73	2	¾	†Do Warrants	2	-	-	-	-	-

New issues within the last six weeks. † Alternative Investment Market. § Placing price. * Introduction. For a full explanation of all other symbols please refer to The London Share Service notes. ‡ When issued.

Example 8.1 Information on new issues. Source: *Financial Times*.

than their issue price. But it works the other way round, too. If the shares are thought to be worth only 90p against an issue price of 100p, in their 30p-paid form they might be expected to stand at 20p. At that point a subscriber has lost a third of his outlay to date. The problems of the BP issue in 1987 were exacerbated by the fact that only 120p of the 330p sale price was payable immediately, and the value of the part-paid shares roughly halved at one point.

New-issue fraud

Multiple applications for shares in an offer for sale are, at best, discouraged and in the case of the privatization issues those making multiple applications were threatened with prosecution. Some applicants, including a few moderately prominent figures, were actually prosecuted. A multiple application is when one person fills in a number of different application forms, perhaps with different names and addresses, hoping to get more shares or increase his chances of getting some shares. It is most likely to happen with a popular issue that is expected to be **heavily stagged** and where there is an almost certain profit when the shares begin trading.

The issuing bank's normal way of discouraging multiple applications in an offer for sale is to threaten that all cheques sent in will be cashed. If the multiple applicant has borrowed heavily to stag the issue, he is paying large interest charges until he gets the money back in respect of his unsuccessful applications. The Conservative government of the 1980s and earlier 1990s – perhaps because it was selling state assets at less than their true worth to attract the public into its version of popular capitalism – decided that one handout per person should be the limit. This is why it adopted the prosecution route for anyone who attempted to grab more.

Internet pointers

In the Internet world, new issues are frequently referred to as Initial Public Offerings or IPOs. So if you are looking for information on up-coming or recent issues, look for an 'IPO' button on your chosen website as well for 'new issues'. A lot of sites now incorporate some information under these headings, including personal finance sites, brokers' sites and the fundamental information site Hemmington Scott at www.hemscott.net/. A search of the whole web on 'IPO' will throw up quite a few leads, but much of the on-line information on new issues relates to the United States markets. The fact that you may see details of an issue does not, of course mean that you will necessarily be able to subscribe. However, Internet-based businesses that are planning to launch on the stockmarket often make use of their website to give information on the issue and arouse investor interest (there may even be preferential applications for their clients).

9 Issuing more shares – and buying shares back

There is an old principle, enshrined in British company law, that when a company issues new shares to raise cash, those shares should be offered first to the existing shareholders – the owners of the business – traditionally in the form of a **rights issue**. This is the principle of **pre-emption rights**.

The principle still holds to a certain extent, but in recent years it has been eroded at the edges. The rights issue process is lengthy and cumbersome, some companies and their banking advisers argue. Companies should be free to take advantage of temporary windows of opportunity in the financial markets by issuing shares as and where they see an opening. Companies in America have considerably more freedom in this respect and the principle of pre-emption rights counts for little. American companies may issue shares *en bloc* to a securities house, which subsequently sells them through its marketing network. This, it is claimed, is faster and cheaper for the company. And the people who make these claims are frequently the banks and securities houses that would earn most from this method of share distribution.

But there is a paradox here. How can a procedure be good for a company if it is not good for the existing shareholders who own the company? Echoes of this debate surface from time to time in the financial columns of the press. Generally the big investors – the insurance companies and pension funds – will argue strongly for a system which gives existing investors the first right to new shares. But they have compromised by allowing companies to make small issues of shares for cash without going through the pre-emption procedure. You will frequently see in companies' annual reports that they ask investors to vote them the powers to make limited share issues to buyers other than existing shareholders. It may be described as 'disapplication of the statutory pre-emption rights'.

Thus, anything we say about traditional methods of issuing new shares for cash must be read with a note of caution. Rights issues are no longer as common as they once were and **placings**, **open offers** and **vendor placings** are frequently encountered. It is the rights issue, however, that we need to look at first to grasp the principles.

Mechanics of the rights issue

The **rights issue** procedure – 'rights' because existing shareholders have the first right to put up the new money – goes like this. The company announces that it intends to raise a particular amount by creating and selling new shares. The new shares will be offered to the shareholders in proportion to their existing holdings. And they will virtually always be offered at a price below that of the existing shares in the market, to give shareholders an incentive to put up money for the new shares. If they are offered at a price way below the existing price – say, at half the market value – the issue would be described as a **deep discounted** rights issue or as having a very large **scrip** element (see below under 'The scrip issue'). But this is the exception rather than the rule. Discounts of 20 per cent or so are more common.

This is a point that often causes confusion. You will come across phrases in the press like: 'XYZ Holdings is offering shareholders one new share for every five held at the very favourable price of 200p against a market price of 400p' or 'XYZ Holdings is making a rights issue on very attractive terms to investors'.

This is usually sheer nonsense. The shareholders already own the company. The company cannot offer them anything that is not theirs already. The price at which the new shares are offered is a technicality, provided they are offered to existing holders. Investors are not getting anything on the cheap. An example illustrates the point.

Adjusting the price

Suppose XYZ Holdings, whose shares are quoted in the stockmarket at 260p, decides to raise £40m by creating and selling 20m new shares at 200p each. The shares are offered to shareholders in the ratio of two new shares for every five existing shares they hold (a 'two-for-five' rights issue). For an investor who decides to take up his rights, this is how the sums go. For every five shares worth 260p each that he holds, he buys two new shares at 200p each. The average value of his shares after the issue would be 242.9p:

		p
5 existing shares at a market price of 260p	=	1,300.0
2 new shares for cash at 200p	=	400.0
Total for 7 shares	=	1,700.0
Value of 1 share (1,700p / 7)	=	242.9

If all else were equal, 242.9p (call it 243p for simplicity) would be the price at which the XYZ shares would stand in the market after the rights issue. In other words, the market price would **adjust** down from 260p to 243p to reflect the fact that new shares had been offered below the previous market price. In practice, the general level of the stockmarket and the prices of individual companies are constantly moving up or down, so the sums may not be quite so clear cut. But the principle holds good.

It follows from this that the right to buy new shares at below market price has a value in itself, which is why it needs to be offered first to existing shareholders. A shareholder who simply ignored the rights issue would start with 5 shares at 260p worth 1,300p in total and end with 5 shares at 243p after the price adjustment, worth only 1,215p. In practice, when the shareholder does nothing the company will normally sell his entitlement to the new shares on his behalf and send the proceeds to him.

Cum-rights and ex-rights

When a company announces a rights issue, it says that the new shares will be offered to all shareholders on the company's **register of shareholders** at such-and-such a date. But since it can take time for purchases and sales to be reflected on the register, the stock exchange adopts its own different cut-off date. Anybody buying existing shares in the market before this date buys them with the right to subscribe for the new shares (**cum-rights**). Anyone buying on or after this date does not have the right to the new shares – this remains with the seller. The date is the day on which the shares go **ex-rights** for stock exchange dealing purposes, and it is therefore the day on which the market price will adjust downwards – from 260p to 243p in the example. After this date the share price in the Stock Exchange Official List and in newspapers will be marked for a time with an **xr** to tell buyers that they are not acquiring the right to subscribe for the new shares.

Dealing in rights

The rights to subscribe for new shares can be bought and sold in the
market in much the same way as shares, and the value of the rights
will be roughly equivalent to the **ex-rights price** (the price that has
been adjusted downwards to take account of the issue) less the subscription price for the new shares. In the example, the right to buy for
200p a new share which will be quoted in the market at 243p ex-
rights will be worth about 43p (243p minus 200p), though technical
considerations can affect this a little. Shareholders who do not want
to put up money for new shares will sell their rights and thus end up
with some cash plus a smaller proportionate stake in the company.

		p
Shareholder has 5 shares at 260p	=	1,300
Sells rights to 2 new shares at 43p	=	86
Retains 5 shares at adjusted price of 243p	=	1,215
Has shares and cash of	=	1,300
(adjusting for rounding-up errors)		

The rights themselves are a short-life high-geared investment rather
like an **option** or **warrant** (see Chapter 18), and often appeal to gam-
blers. Suppose XYZ's ex-rights share price rose 10p from 243p to
253p: an increase of 4 per cent. The value of the **nil paid** rights (the
subscription price for the shares has not been paid) might be expected to rise from around 43p to around 53p: an increase of 23 per cent.
Like all gearing, it works in reverse and the value of the rights can
disappear entirely if the XYZ share price suffers a sharp fall.

The *Financial Times* carries in its 'Companies and Markets' section a table of **rights offers** showing the prices (technically the **premiums**) quoted for rights to buy new shares. It also gives the price at
which the new shares are being issued (which would be 200p for
XYZ), the proportion of this price which has already been paid (if any
– see Chapter 8) and the highest and lowest price at which the rights
have traded. You can see that the percentage swings can be very large.
The **pm** after the price simply means that the price is actually a premium which the buyer pays for the right to subscribe to a new share.

The price for the new shares in a rights issue is normally
pitched sufficiently far below the market price to allow a bit of leeway in case the share price falls in the interim – investors will not put
up money for the new shares if they can buy existing shares more

RIGHTS OFFERS

Issue price p	Amount paid up	Latest Renun. date	2000 High	2000 Low	Stock	Closing price p	+or-
355	Nil	25/5	157½pm	41pm	Fairey Group	41pm	-5
127	Nil	22/5	13pm	1¼pm	JWE Telecom	2½pm	+½

pm premium.

Example 9.1 Stockmarket prices for 'rights'. Source: *Financial Times.*

cheaply in the market. Nevertheless, to make sure the company gets its money, the issue will normally be **underwritten** – institutions agree for a fee to put up the money for any shares the company cannot sell (see Chapter 8).

Deep-discounted issues

To XYZ Holdings it makes little difference if it issues 20m new shares at 200p each or 40m at 100p each. It still raises the £40m it needs. And if it pitches the **subscription price** at 100p against a market price of 260p for the existing shares, there is very little risk that the market price might fall below the subscription price and prevent the new shares from being taken up. A **deep-discounted rights issue** such as this would therefore not need to be underwritten – a considerable cost saving. In practice, very few companies follow the deep-discounted route. The reason usually given is that there is a slight tax disadvantage for some shareholders in the deep discount process. The City, for which **underwriting fees** are a useful and normally an easily-earned perk, does not encourage deep-discounters.

When XYZ's market price is 260p the company is being no more and no less 'generous' if it offers new shares at 100p than at 200p. Remember the principle. The company belongs to the shareholders and there is nothing they can be given that they do not already own. The only benefit they may derive is if the **dividend per share** is maintained on the increased capital, which has the same effect as a dividend increase. This is a totally different decision, but it is often confused with the rights issue itself. If XYZ was paying a 10p per share gross dividend before the issue, the yield on the shares at 260p would have been 3.8 per cent. If it paid the same dividend per share after a two-for-five rights issue at 200p, the yield at the **ex-rights price** of 243p would rise to 4.1 per cent.

Other share issue methods

As we have seen, the rights issue is not dead, but other methods of issuing new shares for cash have become increasingly common. The ones you are likely to read about include the following.

- The **placing**. This works in much the same way as a placing used as a method of bringing a new company to market (see Chapter 8). New shares are created and the company's financial adviser will sell them direct to a range of investors. The shares will probably be offered at a price a little below the market price, but not as far below as in a rights issue. Sometimes, all the new shares might be offered to investors on an overseas stockmarket. In the 1980s companies and their advisers frequently presented this as a way of gaining a wider geographical range of shareholders – useful to a company's international standing, they claimed. In practice, the overseas buyers who acquired shares below the market price frequently sold them to UK investors rapidly and at a profit (a process known as **flowback**). The guidelines imposed by institutional investors would normally allow a placing of only a small proportion of the company's capital unless there were **clawback** arrangements for existing shareholders (see below).

- **Placing and open offer**. This is a process which, up to a point, preserves the pre-emption principle and is increasingly commonly used instead of a rights issue. It can be described in slightly different ways. Essentially, new shares are created and sold conditionally (usually at a small discount) to large investors, mainly the institutions. But existing shareholders have the right to take up the new shares at the same price instead (this is the **clawback** feature). So the new shares will end up with the purchasing institutions only to the extent that existing shareholders decide not to take them up. Thus far, the result from the company's point of view is much the same as with an underwritten rights issue. The arrangement for the institutions to purchase the shares serves the same purpose as a conventional underwriting agreement: the company knows that it will get its money. But note that this does not produce the same result as a conventional rights issue for all shareholders. A holder who does not take up his entitlement under the clawback has no **rights** to sell for cash. The benefit of new shares at below market price goes to somebody else.

- The **vendor placing**. Suppose Company A wants to buy a division of Company B, and wants to use its own shares to pay. Company B, on the other hand, wants cash, not shares in Company A. Company A could, of course, make a conventional rights issue to raise the cash to pay Company B. But it might be quicker and simpler to issue new shares to the required value to Company B and at the same time make arrangements for all these new shares to be bought by institutional investors for cash. This would be a vendor placing (the shares are placed with institutions on behalf of the vendor). The purchaser thus pays in shares but the vendor receives cash. Again, the institutional shareholder rules place an upper limit on the size of transaction that can be undertaken in this way without the new shares being offered to existing shareholders by way of clawback.

- The **euroequity** issue. A company uses a securities house or a number of securities houses to market the new shares that it creates to investors in a range of overseas countries via the international market mechanisms (see Chapter 17). Such operations by UK companies will tend to be limited by the pre-emption rules.

- The **bought deal**. Instead of placing shares with a number of investors, a company can invite bids for all the shares from the **securities houses**. The securities house offering the highest price gets the business and pays cash for the shares, hoping to make a profit by selling them via its distribution network to a range of investors. This might be described as a 'primary' bought deal, and in Britain its application is limited by the pre-emption rules. But the principle of the bought deal is not limited to new shares a company creates. A company which held a large investment portfolio of other companies' shares that it wanted to dispose of could invite offers for the lot (a 'secondary' bought deal). Both types of business can be very profitable for the securities houses, though they are also very high risk – the buyer could lose heavily if the share price dropped between its buying the shares *en bloc* and selling them to the final purchasers. The operation requires large amounts of capital – one of the reasons why British securities houses need big financial backing to be able to compete with their American counterparts. Equally important, it demands a large efficient marketing department with a wide spread of investor contacts. The dangers of the bought deal procedure were underlined in

1990 when merchant bank Kleinwort Benson paid £138m (or 99p per share) to Burmah Castrol for its 29 per cent stake in Premier Consolidated Oilfields, hoping to distribute the shares quickly at a profit. Instead, the price fell heavily and Kleinwort eventually got out at 78p for a loss of £34m on the operation.

- **Euromarket convertible issues.** Companies may issue 'deferred equity' to international as well as domestic investors by issuing a convertible bond via the euromarket mechanisms (see Chapter 17). In the past, some companies used this route as a way of avoiding the institutional rules for new share issues. But the limits on the amount of new capital that could be offered to investors other than existing shareholders now apply to convertible issues as well as to direct issues of shares.

Pre-emption rights and the institutions' rules

In the case of a placing, a vendor placing or, particularly, a bought deal, the price for the new XYZ shares would probably be far closer to the market price than in the case of a conventional rights issue. But it will still normally be at some discount to the ruling market price. And this is where the controversy arises. It makes no odds, as we've seen, whether XYZ choses to offer its new shares at 200p or 100p as long as they are offered first to existing shareholders. But if they are offered below market price to investors who are not already shareholders in XYZ, there is a transfer of value from existing shareholders to the new buyers, which is a totally different matter.

The pension funds and insurance companies are the major existing shareholders in most larger companies, and they have not taken kindly to seeing their birthright eroded. They have therefore argued that most or all of the new shares sold via these techniques should be offered to existing shareholders as a **clawback** – the process we have already looked at.

In practice, as we have seen, they have had to compromise. Their rules – which are reinforced by the authority of the stock exchange – lay down that a company may not issue new shares for cash, without offering them first to existing shareholders, if the new shares represent more than a certain proportion of existing capital or are issued at a discount of more than a certain amount. In 2000 the rule was that new shares issued for cash, and bypassing existing shareholders, must not add more than 5 per cent to the company's capital in a single year or more than 7.5 per cent over a rolling three-year period, or be issued at a discount of more than 5 per cent to the market price. For vendor placings the institutions have their own slightly less restrictive guidelines. Here, in 1999 the limit on issues without clawback was 10 per cent in a year and at a discount of no more than 5 per cent. Even at these levels, issues over a period of years to non-shareholders can significantly dilute the existing shareholders' interest and the institutions are not entirely happy with the situation.

The scrip issue

From the new, back to the old. There is one further type of share issue that any reader of the financial press has to understand: the **scrip issue** or **capitalization issue**. It arises almost by historical accident, but poses a pitfall for the unwary. It is sometimes referred to in the press (and, even less excusably, by companies themselves) as a **free issue** or a **bonus issue** – again conjuring the vision of shareholders receiving something for nothing. In the case of the traditional scrip issue, this is misleading nonsense.

The historical accident is the fact that the nominal value of the share capital of British companies is distinguished from other funds belonging to shareholders and that the shares themselves therefore have a **par** value: 5p, 10p, 20p, 25p, 50p, £1 or whatever. The equivalent unit of **common stock** in American companies may not need to have a par value.

A scrip or capitalization issue in the UK is the process whereby a company turns part of its accumulated **reserves** into new shares. Suppose ABC Company's shares stand in the market at 800p and its **shareholders' funds** look like this:

	£m
ORDINARY SHARE CAPITAL (in 20p shares)	100
PROFIT AND LOSS ACCOUNT RESERVES	600
REVALUATION RESERVES	300
SHAREHOLDERS' FUNDS	1,000

Because the company has accumulated considerable **profit and loss account reserves** (also known as **revenue reserves**) by ploughing back profits over the years, the £100m of share capital gives little indication of the total size of the shareholders' interest in the company. Also, as profits have risen so the share price has risen, to the point where – at 800p – it is **heavy** by British standards. In many other countries, shares which each cost the equivalent of tens or hundreds of pounds are common. Britain has the tradition of units with a smaller value, and shares are considered to become less easily **marketable** (less easy to buy and sell in the stockmarket) when the price pushes up towards £10 or so.

So ABC might decide to convert part of its reserves into new shares. Suppose it decides to use £100m of its profit and loss account reserves for this purpose. It creates £100m nominal of new shares (500 million shares, since they are 20p units) and uses £100m of the profit and loss account reserves to make them **fully paid**. The new shares are distributed to existing shareholders (in this case in a one-for-one ratio) and the shareholders' funds after the operation look like this:

	£m
ORDINARY SHARE CAPITAL (in 20p shares)	200
PROFIT AND LOSS ACCOUNT RESERVES	500
REVALUATION RESERVES	300
SHAREHOLDERS' FUNDS	1,000

All that has happened is that £100m has been deducted from one heading (profit and loss account reserves) and added to another (ordinary share capital). It is a **book-keeping transaction**, pure and simple, and in no way affects the value of the shareholders' interest in the company nor does it raise money for the company. Shareholders' funds remain unchanged at £1,000m.

Adjusting the price for a scrip issue

In our example the shareholder now has two shares where he had one before. But since the value of the company has not changed, the market price will simply adjust to reflect the issue. Previously the shareholder had one share worth 800p. After the issue he has two shares worth 400p each. The greater number of shares in issue and the less heavy price may make them slightly more marketable.

A scrip issue need not be in the ratio of one-for-one (also referred to as a 100 per cent capitalization issue). It could be one-for-ten (a 10 per cent issue), two-for-five, two-for-one, and so on. The complication in each case is that the market price has to be adjusted for the issue. If the issue were one-for-ten, the market price would come back from 800p to 727.3p. The investor starts with 10 shares at 800p, worth 8,000p in total and he ends with 11 shares. Dividing the 8,000p by 11 shares gives a price of 727.3p.

As with a rights issue, the stock exchange sets a date after which a buyer of ABC's shares in the market will not acquire the entitlement to the new shares resulting from the scrip issue, and that is the day the price adjusts downwards. After the adjustment the letters **xc** will appear after the price, meaning **ex-capitalization**.

If a scrip issue by itself is significant only in a technical sense it can, like a rights issue, have implications for the shareholder's income. If ABC makes a one-for-one scrip issue and wants to pay out the same amount of money by way of dividend after the issue, it will have to halve the rate of dividend per share. The shareholder who received 10p on one share gets the same income from 5p on two shares after the issue. If ABC holds its dividend at 10p per share, it is effectively doubling the payment. Occasionally, companies increase their dividends by paying a constant amount per share, but making regular small scrip issues such as one-for-ten.

How scrip issues complicate comparisons

With a one-for-one scrip issue, when the market price halves, it is not easy to miss what is happening, though brokers still get calls from clients asking why their shares have performed so badly. A one-for-ten issue, with a comparatively minor downwards adjustment in the price, is far easier to miss. When tracking the performance of a share price over the years, the investment analyst or journalist has to **adjust** for every scrip issue. Not only must the price be adjusted. Previous years' earnings and dividends per share will also need adjustment. Suppose ABC earned 25p per share and paid a 10p dividend for the year before it made its one-for-one scrip issue, at which time the share price was 800p. In the year after the scrip issue the earnings per share were 15p, the dividend was 6p and the share price has touched 550p. What has really happened?

All of the earlier year's figures have to be adjusted for the issue:

One share at 800p	=	two shares at 400p
25p earnings on one share	=	12.5p per share on two shares
10p dividend on one share	=	5p dividend on two shares

Therefore, in comparing the previous year's performance with the latest one, we are comparing **effective** or **adjusted** earnings per share of 12.5p with the latest year's 15p, and an effective or adjusted previous year's dividend of 5p with a current one of 6p. The share price has risen from the **equivalent of** 400p to the current 550p. Net asset values must be adjusted in a similar way.

Discussions of company performance in the financial press are thus studded with words like 'effective', 'adjusted' and 'equivalent', and reflect this particularly irritating technicality of British company practice. In theory, all figures should also be adjusted for a rights issue at below market price, though practice varies. Certainly, a deep-discounted rights issue (which really contains strong elements of a scrip issue as well as a money-raising issue) requires adjustment.

Less common forms of scrip issue

Two other quirks of the scrip issue process crop up from time to time. Sometimes, companies give their shareholders the option of receiving their dividend in the form of a scrip issue of new shares in place of cash (a **scrip dividend**). Originally the new shares would have been issued only to the value of the net dividend (the dividend after basic rate tax has been deducted). But later we saw the **enhanced scrip dividend**, where the company offered a larger value in shares than in cash to persuade shareholders to opt for the former. But there are objections to scrip dividends. In effect, a company that pays most of its dividend in shares rather than cash is making a smallish disguised rights issue – boosting its cash resources by avoiding a cash outflow – often without adequately explaining the reasons. It was sometimes felt that this encouraged companies towards laxity in their cash management by removing the need to ensure that the cash was there for the annual dividend.

Second, in some of the government **privatization issues**, shareholders who retained their shares for a specified period were promised a **loyalty bonus** in the form of a scrip issue of additional shares. In this case the issue does have a value since it does not go to all shareholders alike. Those who receive the extra 'loyalty' shares are increasing their proportionate stake in the company at the expense of the other shareholders who do not qualify.

Getting money back to shareholders

As well as issuing new shares, companies sometimes buy back existing shares. And as well as raising money, they sometimes decide to return money to shareholders. The two operations are sometimes interconnected and have become a lot more common in recent years.

Take share **buy-backs** first. We said earlier that ordinary share capital – equity capital – is permanent capital. And so it usually is. Ordinary shares, unlike loans and some preference shares, do not have to be repaid. But a company may still decide that it is in its interests to reduce the number of shares in issue. And it can do this either by buying them in the market or by inviting shareholders to sell some of their holdings to the company. In Britain, the shares that are bought by the company will be cancelled, thus reducing the issued ordinary capital. In the United States, companies are allowed to buy their own shares and hold them as **treasury shares**, perhaps reissuing them again later. There has been talk of allowing British companies to do this, too, in the future.

Why would a company want to buy back its own shares? It may be simply that it thinks the shares are too cheap, and if it reduces the number of shares in issue the price will improve because investors will be chasing a smaller number of shares. It may be that the company has accumulated more cash than it needs and would like to return some of this to shareholders. This is often a good idea, because another way of getting rid of the excess cash would be to use it to make a takeover – and it is rarely sensible to make takeovers simply because you have cash burning a hole in your pocket. It may be that the company thinks its gearing ratios are wrong and it could operate more profitably with less equity and more debt. It may be that the company sees that it can improve its **assets per share** or **earnings per share** if it reduces the number of shares in issue.

Take an example of this last operation. A company has net assets of £13m and it has 10 million shares in issue. The net asset value per share is therefore 130p but the share price in the market is only 100p. So the company decides to use £1m of the cash it holds to buy back and cancel 1 million of its shares. The use of the cash reduces net assets to £12m, but the number of shares in issue reduces to 9 million. The £12m of net assets divided by the 9 million shares gives a new net asset value per share of 133.3p per share: a small but worthwhile improvement.

Because companies in Britain are not normally allowed to give financial assistance for the purchase of their own shares, they have to go through a fairly lengthy rigmarole to pave the way for a buy-back operation. You will notice in the annual reports of companies that a resolution is often proposed for the Annual General Meeting, asking shareholders to give the directors the authority to buy back the company's own shares, probably up to a maximum of 10 per cent of the issued capital.

The problem with returning cash to shareholders is that there may be severe tax obstacles. The cash is likely to be treated as a distribution – in other words it may receive the same tax treatment as a dividend. With the abolition of **Advance Corporation Tax** (**ACT**) in 1999, this may be less of a problem in the future, But it has generated some very complex transactions to return cash to shareholders in the most tax-efficient manner. One variant involved making a scrip issue to all shareholders of a new class of share that carried no rights to dividends or votes. These shares were then redeemed for cash by the company and cancelled, putting the cash in the hands of the shareholders.

Far simpler is for a company to return cash to shareholders simply by paying a **special dividend** in addition to the normal interim and final dividends. This special dividend is likely to be a lot larger than the normal annual dividend and, because it is a one-off, it will not of course be taken into account in calculating the yield on the shares.

Internet pointers

For statistical information on recent issues (both new companies that have come to the market and further issues by existing companies) you may download the monthly *Primary Market Fact Sheet* from the London Stock Exchange site at www.londonstockexchange.com. There is information on the institutions' guidelines on share issues at www.ivis.computasoft.com/.

10 Bidders, victims and lawmakers

Takeovers are the jam on the bread and butter of normal investment business. When Company A bids for Company B, it will almost always be at a price above that which Company B commands in the market on its own merits. Therefore there are instant profits for shareholders of Company B. Moreover, the **market professionals** have a strong vested interest in takeovers. They generate high share-dealing **volumes**, and activity is the lifeblood of brokers and marketmakers. They generate big fees for the **investment banks** who advise the companies involved in the takeover. And there are spin-off benefits for the accountants, solicitors and other professionals drawn into the affair. The City has a strong vested interest in a high level of takeover activity and there will be fierce resistance to efforts to curb it.

By and large the 'Anglo-Saxon' economies (which are deemed to include Britain, the United States, Canada and Australia) operate a stockmarket-based system for settling questions of industrial control. In other words, one company may attempt to gain control of another via the stockmarket, with or without the victim company's consent, by appealing direct to the victim's shareholders – anybody is entitled, on payment of a small charge, to access to a shareholder list. Weak or badly managed companies, so the theory goes, will thus be taken over by stronger and better managed concerns. Many other countries have traditionally operated rather different systems, where mergers were usually arranged between the companies themselves or by their dominant shareholders. In Japan and Germany, for example, **hostile takeover bids** were virtually unknown. But the end of the 1990s saw an explosion of takeover activity, much of it across national borders, as industries regrouped into larger and more international units. In the process the market-based system of deciding who should control companies was gaining ground.

The clash of cultures was seen very clearly in November 1999 in the world's biggest takeover bid up to that date: the £77 billion unsolicited offer from British mobile phone group Vodafone AirTouch for German group Mannesmann. Not only did Mannesmann cry 'foul' but the German chancellor himself weighed in, suggesting that hostile bids destroyed the culture of the target company which, in Germany, included worker representation on the board. It was entertaining to see one of the main proponents of the European single market rejecting so strongly the disciplines of the marketplace.

Not only did the end of the millennium see a very high level of takeover activity, there were also changes in the air on the policing of takeover activity: the European Union was imposing minimum standards of takeover practice in its member states. Britain, with long-established self-regulatory procedures in this area, hoped to avoid any weakening of its own codes (see below).

Who benefits from takeovers?

In the press, takeover activity is covered at several levels. There are the takeover tips: 'buy shares in XYZ Holdings; a predator is sniffing round'. There are the blow-by-blow accounts of disputed takeovers which can occupy many column-inches week after week. And there are the occasional more thoughtful pieces questioning whether frenetic takeover activity harms Britain's economy and dissecting some of the less desirable tactics employed. Much of this is self-explanatory, but a little background is needed.

Take the last point first. **Takeover activity** tends to go in waves and often reaches its peak when share prices are also close to their peak after a prolonged bull market, as was the case towards the end of the millennium. At these times takeover considerations can almost totally dominate stockmarket thinking as a form of collective fever takes hold. Everybody is looking for the next takeover victim, buying its shares and forcing prices up. The process becomes self-fuelling. Financial journalists catch the fever like everybody else. Remember this when reading the financial pages: some of the comment on share prices loses all contact with fundamental values that are based on dividends and earning capacity.

As we have seen, a common justification for takeovers is that they increase industrial efficiency. Sleepy companies are gobbled up by more actively managed **predators** which can get better returns from the victim company's assets. In some cases this may be true. But there is little if any consistent evidence that takeovers improve industrial and commercial performance in the long term. And in pure stockmarket terms, the shareholders in the company that is bid for are usually shown to have come better out of the affair than the shareholders of the bidder when subsequent performance is monitored. Takeovers may, however, suit the biggest owners of British companies: the **insurance companies** and **pension funds**. Finding it difficult to exert positive influence to improve management in the companies they invest in, they may welcome a takeover approach from an actively managed company that will do the job for them. The other side of this coin is that the management of major British businesses is often settled by nothing more than the relative levels of two different share prices in the market on a particular date.

Opposition to excessive takeover activity that sometimes finds its echo in the financial pages homes in on other arguments. The threat of takeover induces short-sighted attitudes in company managements. They will not undertake long-term investment if the cost threatens to depress profits before the benefits appear. Depressed profits depress the share price and make the company vulnerable to takeover. Institutional investment managers, too, are being forced to take a short-term view of their performance: **short-termism**. If they are judged over a three-month period on the performance of the investments they manage, they will be inclined to back a takeover which shows them short-term profits.

How accounting blurred the issues

Finally, there are criticisms of the way that the outcome of takeovers has been presented in accounting terms in the past. The profits of the combined group were often presented in an unduly rosy light after the takeover. This was frequently achieved under the system of **acquisition accounting** by making large **provisions** at the time of the takeover to cover reorganization costs and even future trading losses of the company acquired. Effectively, these provisions were treated as a deduction from the value of the assets acquired. Company A paid £50m for Company B, which had £30m of net assets. Company A then made provisions of £10m to cover reorganization costs and future trading losses, reducing the net value of the assets acquired to £20m. Since Company A had paid £50m for net assets of £20m, it had paid £30m for goodwill which it immediately wrote off against reserves under the accounting practice of the day. The £10m provisions never affected Company A's profit and loss account and, by using up the provisions, it could present Company B as making a contribution to profits from day one. The reality may have been that it was loss-making at this point.

Accounting's standard-setting body, the **Accounting Standards Board**, was concerned by these abuses and two recent accounting standards – **FRS 6** and **FRS 7** – have gone a fair way towards eliminating them. Now, if Company A wants to make provisions against reorganization costs in Company B, these provisions have to go through the profit and loss account of the combined group after the takeover. And provisions against future trading losses are now ruled out entirely. Thus, published profits of the combined group are reduced by the amount of the provisions and the outcome of the takeover is presented in a more realistic light. Moreover, the method of accounting for acquired **goodwill** has changed. Instead of being written off against reserves it is now taken onto the balance sheet of the combined group and may have to be depreciated each year in the same way as tangible assets (see Chapter 5). This change, too, may present the group's profits in the years after the takeover in a less flattering light and brings British accounting closer in line with practice in the United States.

The new standards also greatly restrict the use of another way of accounting for takeovers – **merger accounting** – which sometimes presented an unrealistic view, too. Note that except in this context the word **merger** does not normally have a precise technical meaning (see below).

Takeover mechanics

Takeovers in Britain are fought within the framework of formal rules, rather like the moves of medieval combat. As with most rules, frequent revisions of the detail are needed as new techniques emerge. We will come to the more important ones later, but the point to grasp at the outset when reading of any takeover is that a form of corporate democracy prevails. Company A gains **control** of Company B by persuading the holders of at least 50.01 per cent of the Company B **votes** to sell to it or accept its offer. If it already owns some shares in Company B it may require fewer votes to take it to the magic control point. Most companies have a one-vote-per-ordinary-share **capital structure**, so in practice Company A usually has to secure just over 50 per cent of the Company B shares.

Within this general rule there are numerous permutations. The first thing to look for in the press report is whether the bid is agreed, defended or contested.

- The directors of Companies A and B may have met and decided that a merger is in the interest of both parties. In this case the bid for Company B will be **agreed**, though this is not a guarantee that it will succeed. The shareholders, not the directors, have the ultimate word. An agreed bid between two companies is often referred to as a **merger**.

- Company A may announce that it is bidding for Company B and the Company B directors may decide to try to fight off the bid. In this case it is **defended** or **contested**. It is certainly **hostile**.

- Two or more companies may bid at about the same time for Company B, which perhaps does not want to be taken over by either of them, or might back the bid from Company C against that from Company A. This will be a **contested** bid. A company at the receiving end of an unwelcome bid often searches for a **white knight**: an alternative bidder that would be acceptable to it and might keep it out of Company A's clutches.

While the directors of a company that is bid for have a duty to act in the best interests of their shareholders, it would be unrealistic to suppose that they always entirely ignore their own interests. A bidder who would allow them to keep their jobs after the takeover might have greater appeal than one who would want to substitute its own management. On the other hand, directors who are ousted after a takeover frequently walk away with very large cash sums – **golden handshakes** – in compensation for early termination of their employment contracts (see Chapter 12).

Form of the offer

When Company A bids for Company B, it has several options. It can make a:

- **Cash offer**. In this case it simply offers a certain amount in cash for each Company B share. Shareholders in Company B who decide to accept have no further interest in the combined group. But acceptance counts in much the same way as if they had sold their shares for cash in the stockmarket, and they may be liable to **Capital Gains Tax** on profits.

- **Paper offer**. Company A offers to swap its own shares in a certain proportion for those of Company B. This will also be referred to as a **share exchange offer**. Company A might offer three of its own shares for every five of Company B. If the Company A shares stand at 360p in the stockmarket, this puts a value of 216p on each Company B share. Sometimes a bid will provide a mix of cash and paper.

In a paper offer, instead of offering its own shares Company A might offer to swap some other form of security for the Company B shares. It might offer 216p nominal of Company A 6 per cent convertible loan stock for each Company B share, again valuing them at 216p if the convertible is worth its nominal value (there can be heated arguments on this point). Or it might offer a mix of convertible and shares, or a choice between the two. When the bid terms become very complex, involving rare and wonderful forms of security, these securities are sometimes referred to as **funny money** (see glossary). When a company issues massive quantities of its shares in a succession of takeovers, the press sometimes talks in terms of a **paperchase** or makes references to **wallpaper**.

In the case of a paper offer from Company A for Company B, acceptance by Company B shareholders does not count as a disposal of their shares for tax purposes. But they may be liable for tax if they subsequently realize profits from the sale of the Company A securities they had received in exchange.

Note that with any share offer, the value of Company A's shares in the stockmarket determines the value of the offer for each share in Company B, and therefore the chances of the bid succeeding. Company A thus has every incentive to keep its own share price up, and its friends and associates may help its chances by buying its shares to **support** the price (see below).

In a paper offer, the bidder will often establish a floor value for its bid by arranging **underwriting** for the shares it offers. Take the share exchange offer we looked at earlier. Company A offers three of its own shares for every five in Company B. With Company A at 360p Company B shares are valued by the offer at 216p. But Company A arranges with institutions that they will agree to buy any new shares it offers at, say, 340p cash if the recipients want to sell or perhaps it offers a 340p cash alternative from its own resources. So a shareholder in Company B who accepts the Company A offer knows he can take 340p in cash per company A share, which gives an

underwritten cash value for the bid of 204p per Company B share (340p multiplied by three equals 1,020p for five Company B shares or 204p for one share). Of course, if the Company A share price stays high after the bid, he would do better if he wants cash by taking the new Company A shares and selling them in the stockmarket.

Market purchases

So far we have assumed that a takeover simply involves an approach by Company A to the shareholders of Company B outside the stock-market. But in many cases Company A will use the stockmarket as well. It will perhaps build up a stake in Company B by buying shares in the stockmarket before it makes a formal offer. Or, once an offer has been made, it will increase its chances of success by buying the shares of Company B in the market – the shares it acquires via **market purchases** can then be lumped together with acceptances by Company B shareholders to reach the magic control figure.

But there are rules governing market purchases in the course of a bid (see below), and Company A has to be careful. By buying in the market it may force up the Company B share price, which can make it more difficult or more expensive to gain control.

Rules of the game

Takeovers in Britain have been policed for more than three decades by the **Panel on Takeovers and Mergers** (the **Takeover Panel**) which applies the **City Code on Takeovers and Mergers** (the **Takeover Code**). The Takeover Panel has always been a non-statu-tory body with the main City institutions represented on its board, though it now has the backing of the Financial Services Authority and thus a new range of sanctions if it requires them. It has general-ly been one of the best examples of **self-regulation** at work. With a full-time executive, it can give quick judgements on contentious points arising in a takeover, and these are generally respected by the parties involved. In the more legalistic atmosphere which has evolved since the Big Bang there is perhaps a greater tendency for the contestants to bring their lawyers with them to discussions with the Panel, but there have been few legal challenges to Takeover Panel decisions. Certain aspects of takeovers are also governed directly or indirectly by the **Companies Acts**.

Most other European Union members have in the past had a far less developed system for policing takeovers and the EU's 13th Company Law Directive seeks to impose rules that would have to be implemented in all member states. Originally proposed as a detailed directive, it has evolved in the direction of a somewhat bland framework for regulating takeover behaviour and thus looks like imposing a low common denominator. This is partly because most EU members have put their own takeover legislation in place during the Directive's gestation period. Nonetheless, once the Directive passes into law Britain would have to put its own takeover policing arrangements onto a statutory basis. The hope is that this could be achieved by legislation that simply devolves the responsibility onto a non-governmental body – i.e. the Takeover Panel. This would allow the present flexibility to be maintained while continuing to impose tougher standards than the Directive demands. However, there were fears that if an ultimate right of appeal to the FSA was built into the arrangement, the present speed of decision-making might be impaired in some cases.

The Takeover Code has been expanded over the years to incorporate points raised by specific cases which have a general application. You do not have to understand all its ramifications to follow a press report of a takeover. But the rules can play an important part in some of the big contested bids and a general understanding of the principles, which are relatively simple, is useful.

Underlying the Takeover Panel's approach is the principle that all shareholders should be treated equally when one company tries to gain control of another. This is a counsel of perfection, but at least some of the worst abuses have been eliminated. In the bad old days of the jungle, before the Panel existed, one company might pay a high price for a controlling interest in another company, but make no offer to the remaining **minority shareholders**, who were left out in the cold. Those closest to the market would have the best chance of knowing what was going on and selling at the higher price. Therefore, much of the rulebook is concerned with preventing control from changing hands until all shareholders can see what is happening.

The trigger points

When a company acquires shares in another, it may come up against **trigger points** which affect its subsequent actions.

A company which builds up a stake of **30 per cent** in another is obliged to make a bid for all the shares in the target company unless specifically exempted by the Panel. This is because 30 per cent is pushing close to **effective control**: it is difficult for anyone else to bid successfully when one party has a stake of this size. So a **mandatory bid** normally follows acquisition of a 30 per cent stake. You will often see in the press that one company has built up a stake of 29.9 per cent in another: just below the level that triggers a bid.

When Company A builds up a stake of 30 per cent in Company B, the price it offers the remaining shareholders must usually be at least as high as the highest price it paid over the previous year. If, in the course of the bid, it buys Company B shares at a price above the bid value, it will have to increase the bid. In a voluntary bid, if the bidder acquires (or has acquired) 10 per cent or more of the voting rights during the previous 12 months, the offer will have to include a cash alternative at the highest price paid over the 12 months. In a voluntary bid where this 10 per cent has not been acquired, the bid must be on terms at least as favourable as the highest price paid over the previous three months.

There are also provisions designed to limit the speed with which Company A can acquire shares in the market before it has announced a firm intention to make an offer. With some exceptions, it is not allowed to buy more than 10 per cent of the voting rights of its victim in a seven-day period if this would result in its holding more than 15 per cent of the votes in total. When a company goes over a 15 per cent holding in another company, it must notify the stock exchange and the company concerned. These rules give the directors of Company B a breathing space in which to advise their shareholders on whether or not to sell (and if not, why not), and allow smaller shareholders as well as professional investors who are close to the market to decide whether to take advantage of the price the predator is paying. A **dawn raid** is when a company swoops on the stockmarket to buy a stake of up to 15 per cent in another company in double-quick time. Another means of acquiring a sizeable holding quickly, though it is less common, is to invite shareholders to tender shares for sale, up to the maximum required.

Conditions to be met

Takeover bids are **conditional** upon a number of factors. In other words, the bid may lapse unless the conditions are met. The most important conditions are those regarding **acceptances**. Normally the offer will lapse unless the bidder gets over 50 per cent of the victim. Between 50 and 90 per cent it has the option of letting the bid lapse or declaring it **unconditional** – except in a mandatory bid, where the offer must go unconditional at 50 per cent. Above **90 per cent** the bid has to become unconditional. The **Companies Acts** allow the bidder to acquire any remaining shares **compulsorily** when it already has over 90 per cent of the shares it bid for.

The other required condition built into a takeover is that the bidder must withdraw if the bid is referred to the **Competition Commission** (formerly the **Monopolies and Mergers Commission**) or the European Union competition authorities. If called on to do so, the Competition Commission will investigate a proposed takeover and may report against it, usually on the grounds that it would seriously diminish competition. Whatever its finding, its researches normally hold up a takeover for more than six months, and few potential predators are prepared to wait. The **Office of Fair Trading** recommends whether a particular bid should be referred to the Competition Commission, though the Industry Secretary has the last say. Policy in this area is not always wholly clear.

There are also important trigger points for **disclosure of shareholdings** in another company (most of these apply outside takeovers as well). Any person or company acquiring **3 per cent** or more of another company (this trigger point used to be **5 per cent**) must declare the holding to the company. You will often see references in the press to the fact that one company has acquired over 3 per cent of another, perhaps presented by the writer as a prelude to a possible bid. Following the Guinness affair (see below), the Takeover Panel tightened its rules to require disclosure of transactions which resulted in a stake as small as **one per cent** in the parties to a bid or which resulted in changes to stakes of over one per cent, once the bid had been announced.

Sometimes in the past, when Company A wanted to prepare the ground for a bid for Company B, it would persuade its friends, Companies C and D, to buy Company B shares, effectively **warehousing** them on its behalf. Nowadays, Companies A, C and D would be held to be **acting in concert** (or would constitute a **concert party**) and their shareholdings would be lumped together for the purposes of the various disclosure and trigger points. In practice it may be difficult to prove that parties are acting in concert, particularly when the beneficial owners of shareholdings are obscured behind overseas **nominee names**. Such activities might also be criminal **insider trading**.

Share price support

We have seen why it is vital for the bidder to maintain its own share price if it is offering shares. But there are limits – in theory at least – on what can be done by way of support.

First, all **associates** of the bidder must declare their dealings in the shares of either party. The most common forms of associate are the investment bank advisers and funds under their control.

Second, any buyer – even if he is not an associate – will have to declare his holdings if they pass one of the trigger points for disclosure.

Third, the company itself must not support its own share price with company money. This revolves on a **Companies Act** provision that companies may not, except with the permission of their shareholders and in very closely defined circumstances, give **financial assistance for the purchase of their own shares**. It was the main point at issue in the Guinness scandal (see below).

Again, the practice may diverge some way from the theory. In the course of a bid, **friends** of Company A may try to help by buying shares in Company A to boost its price and selling those in Company B to depress it. The friends could include friendly institutions and are often referred to as a **fan club**. Whether or not the help is given in the expectation of future favours (in which case the company might be deemed to be giving financial assistance for the purchase of its own shares) is often difficult to establish.

In the United States **arbitrageurs** or **arbs** made a business of acquiring large share stakes in takeover situations in the boom days of the 1980s. Sometimes they would simply gain by buying shares in the victim and selling at a profit. Less legitimately, it was suspected that some offered their services to support or depress a particular share price to aid or frustrate takeover ambitions. Though they have never been so active in Britain, they cropped up frequently in accounts of the Guinness affair (see below).

The bid timetable

To prevent bids from dragging on interminably, there is an established **bid timetable**. The Takeover Panel sets a time limit of 60 days for an offer or series of offers from the same party to remain on the table, starting from the day the **formal documents** go out. If the bidder cannot gain control within this time, he has to wait a year before making another attempt. However, if a second or subsequent competitive bidder emerges, it in turn has 60 days and its deadline also becomes the deadline for the first bidder.

A takeover often starts with a sustained rise in the price of the victim company's shares. Yet, for all the insider dealing penalties, it is by no means always the case that a bid remains unheralded until it is declared. However, legitimate buying by the prospective bidder could account for the movement, while some forthcoming bids are not too difficult for the market to spot in advance.

Then Company A announces to the stock exchange and to the press that it is bidding for Company B, usually giving the terms. Company B, if it resists, will usually rush out a statement describing the bid as inadequate and wholly unacceptable, and telling its shareholders to stay firm.

Some time later Company A posts its formal **offer document** to Company B shareholders, giving details of itself and of the offer and – with a paper offer – stressing its own management strengths, the (possibly dubious) **industrial logic** of the offer and the advantages of acceptance. Company B studies the offer and comes out with a formal **defence document**, knocking down the Company A arguments and extolling its own virtues, usually with the help of profit and dividend forecasts and, possibly, asset revaluations.

Salvoes of this kind may be fired by both parties several times during the course of the affair. The more important ones are reported in the press. By the **first closing date** of the offer, Company A must decide – if it does not already have control – whether simply to keep the offer open in the hope of further **acceptances**, raise the bid if it clearly needs to offer more or let it **lapse** if it does not fancy its chances of winning. If it lapses, any acceptances that have been received become void. Offers may be raised several times during the affair. Alternative bidders may appear at any point to complicate the decisions. Throughout, Company A and any competitive bidders may be buying Company B shares in the market and friends or associates of all the parties may be supporting the price of their respective protégés (such actions, as we have seen, are generally subject to public disclosure). But by the **final closing date** the bidder must announce that the offer is **unconditional** as to acceptances – the bid goes through if the other conditions are met – or allow it to lapse.

Throughout the **offer period** the price of Company B's shares in the stockmarket will give some indication of the expected outcome. If it lags just a little behind the value of the latest bid it can mean that the bid is expected to succeed. If it jumps ahead, the market is probably expecting a higher offer, though it could just possibly be that Company B has justified a higher price for its shares on their own merits.

The United States scene

The takeover scene is considerably rougher – as to the tactics permitted and employed – in the **United States** than in Britain. The Takeover Panel has been effective in preventing widespread use in the UK of some of the more questionable American techniques, of which **greenmail** – a form of corporate blackmail – is a prime example. A company builds up a large stake in a potential takeover candidate. It threatens to bid or sell the stake to another prospective bidder unless the target company buys the stake from it at an inflated price – possible, because of the greater freedom to buy their own shares enjoyed by American companies.

The **poison pill** bid defence is another American tactic which has also cropped up only in its milder forms in the UK. The target company builds in a tripwire to make itself less attractive to a bidder. It might, say, create a new class of stock which becomes automatically redeemable at a high price in the event of a successful takeover.

Geared or **leveraged** takeovers have also been less common in the UK where the bidder was a UK company, though the idea enjoyed some popularity in the late 1980s and leveraged bids to take public companies private (a **public-to-private deal**) have resurfaced in the later 1990s. In the typical leveraged takeover a bid is made using a high proportion of borrowed money. The resultant company is very highly geared and forced to concentrate on short-term profitability to meet the interest charges (see Chapter 11). Sometimes these bids involve borrowing money by the issue of **junk bonds** – bonds that offer a high rate of interest but that would not normally count as being of investment quality because they are issued in large quantity by relatively insubstantial companies.

We have already seen how the **arbs** took positions in takeover stocks in the late 1980s. But a series of high-profile arrests and court cases in the United States subsequently suggested that their success was based more on **insider dealing** – acting on confidential information, often unlawfully purchased – than on successful prediction, and their activities were consequently curbed.

Leverage and level playing fields

Cross-frontier takeovers are usually for cash; in the past, shares have rarely been a widely accepted currency outside their country of origin, though this might change with the global integration of financial markets. Thus, British companies have made major acquisitions for cash in the United States, and most large overseas bids for British companies are for cash. British companies at the receiving end of hostile takeovers from overseas have frequently complained about lack of **reciprocity** and the lack of a **level playing field**: the predator companies may be protected from hostile takeovers in their country of origin, though perhaps more by patterns of shareholdings and by local custom and practice than by specific legislation.

Overseas bids for British companies are frequently highly **leveraged** and a trend towards bids made with borrowed money was reinforced domestically by the growth in **management buy-outs** and **management buy-ins** (see Chapter 11), some of which were aimed at stockmarket-listed companies in the late 1980s and again in the later 1990s. There has often been no shortage of cash from the banks to back management teams dissatisfied with the share price performance of their company, or somebody else's company, who reckoned they could do better by buying it and taking it private (a **public-to-private** deal). If the company was listed, this involved making a takeover offer to its existing shareholders.

However, several high-profile leveraged acquisitions of this kind in the 1980s – including the takeover of the Magnet joinery and kitchens business and the Gateway supermarket group – went badly wrong and extensive capital reconstructions were required. The climate was therefore a lot less conducive to this kind of leveraged operation in the earlier 1990s – even had market conditions been right – though buyouts of private companies retained their popularity. By the late 1990s much of this caution had gone to the winds and the prices offered to buy listed companies and take them private were again often looking excessively high.

The Guinness affair

No review of takeovers is complete without a glance at the *cause célèbre* that filled so many column-inches of the financial press from late 1986 and is still frequently referred to today: the £2.6 billion **Guinness** bid for whisky giant Distillers in 1986.

Drinks group Guinness was competing with the Argyll supermarket business to take over Distillers, which backed the Guinness offer. The Guinness offer was mainly in shares and its value – and therefore Guinness's chances of beating Argyll – depended heavily on the Guinness share price. Having been below 300p in January 1986, the Guinness share price staged a remarkable rise to over 350p at one point. The value of the Guinness offer surpassed that of Argyll's offer and Guinness won the day.

The revelations which followed the appointment of **Department of Trade inspectors** to investigate Guinness's affairs at the beginning of December 1986 made it clear that there had been a massive support operation to boost the Guinness share price. More serious were the allegations that Guinness had used its own money in one way or another to recompense those who bought its shares on a large scale and boosted the price: by paying them fees, by making large cash deposits with them or by guaranteeing to cover any losses they might suffer on the shares. Resignations and sackings – at Guinness itself and at its then investment bank advisers, Morgan Grenfell – preceded the DoT inspectors' findings. Criminal charges against some of the main players followed later and three of them served sentences in Ford open prison.

The Guinness affair provided a field day for the financial press and – taken with allegations of insider trading elsewhere in the City – considerable embarrassment for a government which had been selling the benefits of stockmarket investment to the public. There have been fewer major dramas in the takeover field since, and public cynicism about City and business affairs has anyway found a new focus: the spiralling pay and perks in British boardrooms.

Internet pointers

News of current takeovers and mergers features strongly on all of the sites providing market reports and financial news (see Chapter 23), and the *Financial Times* site at www.ft.com/ is a good starting point. Analysis of recent mergers and acquisition activity (M&A) is available from a number of sources, including accountants KPMG at www.kpmg.co.uk/ (look for the 'Dealwatch' surveys).

11 Venture capital and leveraged buy-outs

The 'small is beautiful' cry has been heard frequently in British business over recent decades, and various initiatives have emerged to provide finance for smaller companies and start-up enterprises. Several of the more serious national daily papers regularly carry features on small businesses.

Bank loans and overdrafts traditionally provide the finance for businesses in their very early years and the stockmarket allows more mature companies to raise debt or equity capital. But between the two, it is argued, lies a **financing gap**. Businesses that are too large or too fast-growing to subsist on bank finance, yet too small to launch on the stockmarket, may be held back by lack of funds. In particular, smaller businesses find it very difficult to raise equity finance as opposed to loans.

Management buy-outs

We have seen, too, the phenomenon of the **management buy-out** or **MBO**. A group of managers within a large industrial company, say, decide that they would like to own the particular part of the business they run and to operate it as an independent entity. It may suit the large company to sell it to them if the division in question is peripheral to its main business. Alternatively, managers might put in a bid for parts of a business when the parent group has got into trouble and landed in the hands of the receiver.

Sometimes, too, an existing business is acquired with a view to putting in a new management team not previously associated with it who will have a stake in the operation (a **management buy-in**). A variation on this theme occurs when a new management team links with existing managers and employees to acquire the business. The name for this operation – **buy-in management buy-out** – may, we suspect, have been chosen mainly for its usual acronym of a **BIMBO**. Finally, in another variation, the managers of a listed company may decide they would like to run and part-own the whole of the enterprise they currently manage on behalf of the public shareholders by turning it back into an unlisted company in a **public-to-private** deal (see below).

But in all cases we have described, the managers themselves rarely have the money to acquire an established business and they require help in the form of outside equity and loan finance.

Venture capital and development capital funds

To satisfy these different financing needs, there has been rapid growth in **venture capital funds**: organizations that provide finance – sometimes a mixture of equity and loans, but often just one or the other – for unquoted companies. Because it is provided to finance unlisted companies, equity finance of this kind is often referred to as **private equity**. Many of the venture capital funds are offshoots of existing financial institutions: clearing or merchant banks, insurance companies or pension funds. Around the turn of the millennium there were over 120 full members and a roughly equal number of associate members (the latter including advisers and companies for which venture capital is not the principal business) of the **British Venture Capital Association (BVCA)**, the umbrella body for these funds in the UK.

According to BVCA figures, the British venture capital industry has invested over £35 billion (of which £29 billion was in the UK) in around 19,000 companies since 1983. In 1999 alone a record £7.8 billion was invested. Since these figures represent mainly the equity element of the investment, which will generally be geared up with bank loans, the scale of total investment is considerably higher and funds committed to private equity now bear comparison with money raised for listed companies on the stock exchange.

The biggest venture capital organization in the UK, however, has a longer history than the BVCA. It is the **3i** group (previously **Investors in Industry**), whose original venture capital arm was known as Industrial and Commercial Finance Corporation (ICFC) and was founded shortly after the last war. Originally wholly owned by the clearing banks and the Bank of England, but now with a stock exchange listing, it currently provides most forms of banking and finance service, other than overdrafts, and in 1999 had gross assets of around £5.25 billion. It has invested more than £10 billion in over 13,000 businesses during its life.

The funding process

The typical **venture capitalist** puts up money for a growing business or to finance a management buy-out in return for a proportion of the share capital. Individual funds rarely want control of the companies they back, and where the funds required are large the financing may be **syndicated** among a number of venture capitalists. Each puts up part of the money and collectively they may control the enterprise they finance.

The original entrepreneurs, or the managers in the case of a buy-out, thus concede a large part of their ownership of the business in return for the money that they needed to buy it in the first place or the additional finance they need if it is to grow. Often their eventual stake in the business is geared to how well it performs (a **ratchet** arrangement). The venture capitalists usually want to cash in on their stake in successful businesses after five years or so and at this point will want an opportunity of selling the shares – a **take-out** – possibly via a **stockmarket launch** of the company. Alternatively, the company may seek a **trade buyer**: another company that is prepared to offer a good price for the business.

In the most successful buy-outs the managers who backed the venture may emerge as multi-millionaires within a relatively short period as the revamped business is floated on the market or sold to a trade buyer within a few years. If some of these 'instant riches' stories seem incomprehensible, just think how the gearing works when all goes well. Suppose the buy-out of a £100m business is financed with £20m of equity funds and £80m of debt. After three or four years, say, the business has prospered and is now worth £160m and the debt remains unchanged. Thus that £20m of original equity is now worth £80m. The venture capital investors are delighted and the managers – who may have paid relatively little for their original share stake – can be very rich indeed.

However, there are failures as well as successes in the management buy-out business, and the returns that venture capital funds seek are quite high – perhaps in the region of 30 per cent – to compensate them for such failures. While the participating venture capital fund (or funds grouped under a lead fund where the finance is syndicated) may provide only the equity portion of the money required, they will probably also organize the bank loans that complete the package. You might read in a description of a £10m buy-out that £3m of the money required was provided as equity by a venture capital fund and that the remaining £7m came from a bank loan.

With a large buy-out the structure could be more complex with, say, 30 per cent of the money coming as equity from venture capital funds, 60 per cent coming as **senior debt** from a consortium of banks and 10 per cent provided as **mezzanine debt**. This mezzanine layer is a form of halfway house between debt and equity: debt offering a high return which may also include some rights to share in equity values. The ratio between debt and equity will vary with market conditions. In a recession where business confidence is low the proportion of equity may need to rise as the banks will be less willing to take risk. Be a little careful, too, when you read that 30 per cent of the money for a buy-out was provided as **equity**. The term is used in a somewhat loose sense in the buy-out world. It is unlikely in practice that all of this 30 per cent was subscribed as ordinary capital. For structural and taxation reasons it is more likely to have been provided by the venture capitalists as a mixture of ordinary share capital and preference capital or subordinated loans. It is, however, all risk money.

Most of the major venture capital funds do not consider it worth investigating a **financing proposal** unless the sums involved are quite large and they are generally wary of business **start-ups** (entirely new businesses) where the risk is highest. Occasionally, however, a venture capitalist might be prepared to provide some **seedcorn capital** to see a new project through its very early stages. In general, venture capitalists prefer to provide money to buy an existing business or **development finance** for companies that are already past the initial stage and need more equity if they are to advance to a bigger league. The same is generally true of another type of fund providing capital for unquoted companies – the **Enterprise Investment Scheme** fund – although these funds will sometimes provide finance in smaller quantities.

Leveraged buy-outs and takeovers

Leveraged buy-outs and **leveraged takeovers** were very popular in the United States in the late 1980s. Fortunately, perhaps, the principle spread rather late to Britain, just as America was beginning to worry about some of the consequences around the turn of that decade. 'Leveraged' simply means 'geared up' in British terminology.

As we have seen, most buy-outs and buy-ins are geared or leveraged to some extent in that bank loans are used as well as equity capital. But the term **leveraged buy-out** or **public-to-private** deal is used particularly to describe an operation where an investor group, using mainly borrowed money, makes a public takeover bid for a listed company with a view to taking it private. The amount of equity finance used may be very small. Typically, the debt portion will be in several layers: **senior debt** which is reasonably well secured, some intermediate layers and perhaps an issue of high-yielding high-risk **junk bonds** (see Chapter 10, and below).

A company acquired by way of a leveraged bid (80 per cent and sometimes a lot more of the finance may be in the form of debt) finds that interest charges absorb most of its profits and it is probably under pressure to dispose of parts of its business to raise cash to reduce its borrowings as rapidly as possible. Leveraged buy-outs are a very high-risk game whose dangers become more apparent when economic activity turns down, the cost of servicing bank debt rises and it becomes impossible to raise cash by selling parts of the business at acceptable prices. The biggest leveraged operation of the late 1980s was the $25 billion buy-out of food and tobacco group RJR Nabisco in the United States. It turned out to be less than an unqualified success.

The biggest attempted leveraged bid for a UK company – Sir James Goldsmith's 1989 attempt to acquire and break up the BATS tobacco-to-financial-services group – was eventually abandoned in the face of regulatory hurdles in the United States and lack of enthusiasm in the UK. Experience with leveraged bids for UK listed companies that did go through was far from reassuring, as we saw in the previous chapter. But there was, nonetheless, a resurgence of this type of activity in the UK in the late 1990s and high-yielding (not to say junk!) bonds sometimes played an important part in the financing. Industry watchers shook their heads at the high prices paid and the financing methods used, and predicted trouble if economic activity turned down.

Enterprise Investment Scheme

Of the tax-favoured schemes to encourage investment in growing businesses, the **Enterprise Investment Scheme** (or **EIS**) has the longest history. It is a replacement for the earlier **Business Expansion Scheme** (or **BES**), which itself first saw the light of day in 1981 as the **Business Start-up Scheme**.

The idea is to encourage higher-earning individuals to sub-scribe for new 'full risk' ordinary shares in private trading compa-nies. Anyone with a sufficiently high income can gain income tax relief on up to £150,000 a year invested in this way. But the income tax relief is not at the higher rate and the shares must normally be retained for at least five years to gain the full relief. If the investor holds the shares for the qualifying period he would not normally pay capital gains tax on any profit, while losses he makes (less the origi-nal tax relief) would be offsettable against taxable income or against gains elsewhere for capital gains tax purposes. The scheme also offers some rollover capital gains tax reliefs for investors who put the proceeds of another profitable investment into an EIS investment or who cash in on one EIS holding and reinvest in another.

Those who are already directors or employees of a company cannot qualify for tax relief under the EIS when they invest in that company – the idea is to bring in new money from outside rather than give tax relief to those who may already have an interest. But there are provisions to allow **business angels** to invest in a private compa-ny and benefit from the EIS, provided they were not already con-nected with it. These 'angels' are individuals who want to invest in a company and also have something to offer by way of business exper-tise. They may both invest and become paid directors.

As far as the company is concerned, to rank for the EIS it must carry out, normally for at least three years, a qualifying activity. This broadly rules out a number of financial and investment activities and dealing in securities or property, plus the investment in rented resi-dential property that had been allowed under the BES. The company must not be listed on the stock exchange though it may be traded on the AIM market. The new ordinary shares it issues to EIS investors must not have any preferential rights.

How does the prospective EIS investor locate a suitable com-pany? Ideally he would know of one from his personal experience. In practice, many investors will invest via the medium of an **EIS fund**: a fund set up to invest in a range of qualifying companies. The investor still receives his tax relief and has the advantage of a spread of risk and more or less professional management. Unfortunately, as with many tax-favoured investments, things are not always as rosy as they seem. Investment in unquoted companies, direct or through a fund, carries a fair degree of risk. And there is a danger, as with any form of subsidy, that the price charged for the product rises to take some account of the tax relief available to the buyer.

Venture capital trusts

Another tax-favoured investment vehicle designed to encourage risk investment in private businesses is the **venture capital trust**. A venture capital trust needs to hold at least 70 per cent of its investments in unquoted trading companies: broadly, the same sort of company as would qualify for EIS investment. Not more than 15 per cent may be in any one company. But the trust is not limited to investing in equity. Up to half of its investment in qualifying companies can be in the form of loans with at least five years to run. If the companies in which it invests subsequently float on the stock market, the trust can count them as unquoted for a further five years.

The venture capital trust itself is much like an ordinary investment trust and must be quoted on the stock exchange. Within prescribed limits – investment of £100,000 in a year – investors in the trust pay no tax on dividends received or on capital gains arising on disposals of investments. Probably more significant, if subscribing for new shares issued by a venture capital trust the investor receives tax incentives similar to those for the EIS.

Given the costs of researching investments in smaller, unquoted companies, venture capital trusts are generally set up under the auspices of existing venture capital organizations or fund management groups rather than as stand-alone operations. There were around 45 of them in the year 2000 and the British Venture Capital Association reckoned that they had raised funds of over £900m in total at that point.

Loan Guarantee Scheme

Another government initiative was aimed at helping small companies that had found it difficult to borrow money from normal banking sources, often because neither the company nor its founders could provide the **security** considered necessary for a loan. Most owners of small companies which want to borrow money are required to offer their houses and other assets as security for the debts of the business.

The scheme – the government small firms **Loan Guarantee Scheme** or **LGS** – does not itself provide money for businesses but it removes part of the risk for traditional lenders. A bank can advance a loan of up to £250,000 to an existing small business or £100,000 to a new business starting up, secured on the assets of the business but without personal guarantees from the owners. The bank charges its normal interest rate plus a premium of one-and-a-half percentage points on the loan (or half a percentage point if the rate of interest is fixed), which goes to the government to provide the guarantee element. In return, 70 per cent (or 85 per cent for loans to existing businesses) of the value of the loan is covered by the **government guarantee**. Businesses in qualifying inner-city renewal areas receive broadly the terms applying to established businesses, even if they are start-ups, and the interest rate is also lower. If the business goes to the wall and the whole of the loan is lost, the government reimburses the lending bank 70 per cent or 85 per cent of its advance.

The LGS has undoubtedly helped some businesses that would not otherwise have got off the ground. Its terms have been frequently amended since it was first established in 1981. The main disadvantage of the LGS is that it supplies loan finance in circumstances where equity is often what is needed, with the result that the business becomes excessively highly geared, which may hasten its demise. Failures among companies taking advantage of the scheme were high in the early years.

Internet pointers

The British Venture Capital Association is the representative body for UK providers of venture and development capital. Its website at www.bvca.co.uk/ provides some statistical background to the business and some information on the Enterprise Investment Scheme and on venture capital trusts. It also provides pointers for entrepreneurs towards venture capital sources of finance and business angels. For small and medium-sized businesses looking for sources of financial advice or help, the Department of Trade and Industry website at www.dti.gov.uk/ provides a fair bit of information and also links to other sources. Among related sites offering help or information in the same areas are those of Business Link at www.businesslink.co.uk/ and the Enterprise Zone at www.enterprisezone.org.uk/. Details of the Small Firms Loan Guarantee Scheme are available on the DTI site at the address www.dti.gov.uk/support/sflgs.htm. There are also a number of individual websites offering to put (mainly high-tech) entrepreneurs in touch with sources of finance.

12 Pay, perks and reverse capitalism

We have looked at companies, but what of the men and women – and at the new millennium it was still predominantly men – who run them? The escalating **pay and perks** of the directors of listed companies had been a major political issue for much of the decade. A little background helps in understanding the frequent press and television reports on the pay and perks of board members, particularly in the previously nationalized industries. It also provides the background for the inordinately lengthy **corporate governance** statements and **remuneration committee** reports that nowadays occupy many pages of a listed company's annual report and accounts.

The starting point is a paradox that explains some of the confusion on this issue shown first by the Conservative government and later by its New Labour successor. Capitalism, by and large, is about allowing the owners of capital to enjoy the fruits of their capital. Yet, by amending the tax laws to promote executive share option schemes and the like, the Conservative government of the 1980s had paved the way for extensive transfers of value from the owners of a business (the shareholders) to the directors and managers (the senior employees who run the business on the owners' behalf). This process of 'reverse capitalism' – taking money from the owners to give to the senior employees – was a curious interpretation of the capitalist ethic.

Press reports tend to focus on massive jumps in boardroom pay or multi-million-pound profits made from the exercise of executive share options or long-term incentive plans. But the full picture is often more complex (and sometimes even more startling) than these reports would suggest. In the late 1990s, the directors of many of Britain's larger listed companies were rewarding themselves in five or six different ways, sometimes more, including:

- a basic salary

- a short-term performance-related bonus on top of basic salary, probably up to a maximum of 50 per cent of salary

- executive share options, which deliver profits when the share price rises

- longer-term incentives geared to performance over a three- or four-year period. These might take the form of cash payments or an outright grant of free shares

- a variety of benefits in kind such as cars, life and medical insurance and, in some cases, company-owned accommodation

- a pension based on final salary (sometimes with a non-tax-approved top-up scheme where the tax rules limited the amount that could be paid out by the main scheme)

- various generally less publicized devices such as employee share ownership plans (ESOPs) or phantom options (see below)

- the prospect of a golden handshake if the director is ousted for one reason or another.

How the reverse capitalism package works

Short-term bonuses or **annual bonuses** tend to be linked to a measure of short-term performance: perhaps the growth in earnings per share over the year. They account for many of the wilder percentage jumps in a director's pay – when a good year succeeds a bad one – that the press picks up. Sometimes they are actually paid a year later, when company earnings may have turned down again, making it more difficult for shareholders to discern a link between pay and performance.

The 1984 Finance Act smoothed the way for **executive share option schemes**, and most companies have adopted them. For no payment, a director used to be granted options over, say, a million shares, usually exercisable (see Chapter 18) at the market price at the time of grant. Normally, he had to wait three years before the options could be exercised. Suppose the share price was 100p at the time of grant and five years later had risen to 250p. The director had the right to buy a million shares (normally, new shares that the company created) at 100p each, costing £1m. He immediately sold them at the market price of £2.5m, making a profit of £1.5m. The creation and sale of new shares at a price below that in the market represented a transfer of value from the shareholders of the company to the director concerned.

Longer-term incentive plans (LTIPs) were introduced in the 1990s to counter some of the criticisms of executive share options (see below). In a typical scheme, a director receives a conditional gift of free shares. He actually receives some or all of these shares later if his company beats some pre-ordained performance target over, say, a three-year period. A popular performance trigger is the **total shareholder return** (or **TSR**) provided by the company to its shareholders over the three years, compared with that achieved by other companies. Total shareholder return is the combination of share price movement with dividends paid. Thus, a large company might compare itself to the other 99 constituents of the Footsie index. If the company is in the bottom half of companies in terms of total shareholder return, the directors get none of the free shares. If it is in the top 25, they might get all of the conditionally gifted free shares. In between, the number would depend on their position in the league.

The **benefits in kind** that directors receive are taken for granted nowadays and they excite little comment, but **pensions** are worth a closer look. Most schemes will pay a pension geared to final salary and it is noticeable that directors frequently ensure that their salaries are bumped up substantially in the years leading to retirement. The effect is to give the director a pension considerably larger than the contributions made to the scheme on his behalf over the years would justify. The cost therefore falls indirectly on the other scheme members. Where the tax laws limit the pension a director can receive from a tax-approved scheme, the company frequently contributes on his behalf to a separate non-tax-approved scheme. For pension calculations based on salary, however, bonuses are normally disallowed.

Phantom options and employee share ownership plans (ESOPs) rarely receive the attention they deserve, particularly as it may have been difficult in the past for a shareholder to find out anything much about them. A phantom option is an option on non-existent shares – but if that sounds crazy, wait a minute. The company tells the director, say: 'The share price is now 100p. We will grant you phantom options over a million shares, which you can exercise at any time over the next ten years. If, some years later, the share price has risen to 250p and you decide to exercise, the company will pay you the difference between 100p and 250p on a million shares. In other words, we will pay you £1.5m.' The effect is much the same as with the example we quoted of a traditional executive share option, but the tax treatment of the profits may be different and no new shares are created. Phantom options are sometimes used legitimately to reward directors of overseas companies who cannot benefit fully from a UK executive share option scheme. They have in the past been used more questionably to generate rewards for directors that shareholders know nothing about in advance.

ESOPs really deserve a chapter to themselves. They are **employee share ownership plans** or **employee share ownership trusts**. The type run by large companies is generally the so-called 'non-statutory ESOP', which attracts no special tax benefits. It works like this. The ESOP buys shares in the sponsoring company, financing them with bank loans guaranteed by the company or with loans from the company direct (in effect, the company buys its own shares). The shares are bought in the market, so no new shares are created. These shares are then available for allocation to employees as part of a bonus scheme, profit-sharing scheme, option scheme, or whatever. The rules will usually say that all employees can benefit from the ESOP, but in practice they are used predominantly to provide further benefits for directors and senior executives. They are not without risk to the company and therefore to its owners. If the share price falls, the ESOP may end up with shares worth less than the loans it raised and the loss will generally fall on the company in one way or another. This happened with, among others, a container-leasing group then called Tiphook, which suffered a share price collapse and had to write off more than £20m on guarantees for loans to its ESOP. ESOPs are sometimes used to acquire shares which are then used to satisfy share option schemes or LTIPs.

Golden handshakes also hit the headlines. Directors often used to be employed under **rolling contracts** of three years (**evergreen contracts**). This means that there would always be three years of their contract outstanding. Under institutional pressure this has tended to reduce to two years or even one year nowadays. If a director is forced out, he will be able (virtually regardless of the reason) to claim for most of what would have been due to him had he completed his contract. Companies are usually anxious to avoid litigation and want to wind the affair up as quickly as possible. Thus, even directors who have run their companies into the ground frequently depart with a 'golden handshake' of several years' salary. Cynical observers have a rule of thumb: the bigger the cock-up, the bigger the payoff (mainly because the company wants to get rid of the director in question rapidly and with the minimum of fuss).

Objections to incentive schemes

The declared objective behind bonus schemes and the like is to 'incentivize' management so that it produces improved performance from which shareholders and the economy also benefit. This poses a second paradox. Why is it that the highest-paid people in a company need extra payments to persuade them to give of their best?

But there are more detailed objections to some of the **incentive schemes** in force today and these are raised sometimes in the press. Annual bonuses focus on short-term performance, may encourage short-term attitudes, and the basis on which they are granted may be far from clear. It is also fairly easy to manipulate earnings per share in the short term, and this is often the measure on which the bonus is based.

Executive share options are open to the objection that they may reward even poor management when the share price is carried up by a bull market – though the company itself has underperformed. They also dilute the interests of existing shareholders and provide little long-term incentive since the director almost always immediately sells the shares he receives from exercise of his options. Institutional shareholders have pressured managements to introduce a further **performance criterion** before options could be exercised, but these criteria are often undemanding. Options can only be exercised if the rise in company's earnings per share has outpaced the rise in retail prices by a given percentage over a three-year period, and the like.

The **longer-term share incentive plans** (**LTIPS**) were introduced to counter some of the objections to share options though many companies operate the two in tandem. They do encourage a slightly longer-term view on the part of company management and sometimes introduce a more realistic performance criterion than share option schemes. But the criteria are again often relatively undemanding. Whether directors usually demonstrate confidence in their company by holding on to the free shares that they are given is questionable.

ESOPs are open to the objection that the company is exposing itself to a risk in the movement of its own share price. A second objection in the past was that they were often remarkably opaque – shareholders knew little if anything about them (but see below).

But the overriding criticism voiced of virtually all incentive schemes is that they offer directors a carrot, but no stick. Directors collect extra loot if the company or the share price does well. They do not suffer – as shareholders in the company suffer – if the company does badly. The frequent statements from companies that their schemes equate the interests of management and shareholders should therefore be viewed with a little cynicism. Incentive schemes may, it is sometimes argued in the press and elsewhere, encourage directors to take excessive risks with the company. If it works, they benefit. If it does not, shareholders suffer. And there is always the golden handshake at the end of the day as the ultimate reward for failure.

Corporate governance and disclosure

While shareholders do not have a great deal of direct influence on the pay and perks of directors, they had – by the end of the 1990s – a great deal more information than in the past. The **Accounting Standards Board** (ASB) and the related **Urgent Issues Task Force** (UITF) had done sterling work in insisting on more information on share options and ESOPs in the accounts.

The other pressures had come through the **corporate governance** process. It happened like this. A committee of the financial community's great and good – the **Cadbury Committee** – produced a code of conduct on the financial governance of company affairs: the **Cadbury Code**. It recommended, *inter alia*, openness by companies on directors' remuneration, though in terms so general that their effect was weakened. A later committee, the **Greenbury Committee**, was set up specifically to examine boardroom pay and perks in response to the Conservative government's embarrassment on the issue. Greenbury strengthened Cadbury's recommendations on **remuneration committees**, which were committees consisting mainly of independent non-executive directors who were charged with setting the remuneration of the executive directors. Reporting in 1995, Greenbury made a number of other recommendations including the phasing of share option grants and expressed a preference for longer-term incentive plans (LTIPs) over share options in any case. It also, crucially, required companies to disclose additional pension benefits acquired by directors over the year rather than merely the payments made into the scheme on their behalf. As we saw earlier, the two may be very different. Subsequently corporate governance was reviewed by yet another committee, the **Hampel Committee**. The strings of all these different recommendations were finally pulled together in a new **combined code** which drew its strength from the fact that its recommendations were incorporated in the **listing requirements** for companies on the stock exchange.

The effect of all these initiatives is as follows. Company reports now contain a great deal of information on directors' pay and perks plus numerous statements of compliance with various corporate governance requirements. There is a lengthy statement by the remuneration committee which sets out the policy on executive pay and gives some detail on incentive schemes in force. Either here or in the notes to the accounts you will find the nitty-gritty. The total remuneration received by each director has to be itemized. This will give his basic salary, bonuses received, benefits in kind and so on. Here or elsewhere you will also find the value of additional pension benefits acquired during the year.

There will probably be a separate item giving details of each director's interest in share option schemes. This shows options held at the beginning of the year, exercise prices, new options granted and existing options exercised during the year. Yet another table will give comparable information on the LTIP (if there is one): number of conditionally granted shares held on behalf of each director, and so on.

Finally, shareholders or journalists interested in knowing a little more about the directors' terms of employment than is disclosed in the report and accounts can take advantage of a long-standing provision of company law. The employment contracts of individual directors of a company must be available for inspection at certain times, notably during the annual general meeting and for a few weeks beforehand. A little digging may produce interesting insights which occasionally surface in the press.

Thus, shareholders have moved from being deprived of information to being swamped with it, and it is not always easy to interpret. Are share options a benefit in the year in which they are granted or the year when they are exercised? Likewise with free shares conditionally granted under an LTIP, which the director may or may not receive at a future date.

Moreover, many of the incentive plans devised by remuneration consultants for companies are extremely complex – company directors will sometimes admit privately they do not understand exactly what they are entitled to or in what circumstances – and no two are exactly the same. Analysts trying to compare boardroom pay and perks at different companies hit a problem similar to shoppers who are offered their money back if they can find the product at a lower price in another store. They will find the product is marginally different in weight, constituents or packaging in each outlet. And there is still the problem that the big bonus may actually be delivered at a time that company performance has already turned down.

Who monitors the managers?

Shareholders do not – as of the end of the 1990s – have an opportunity to vote directly on directors' pay levels, and there would be practical difficulties in giving them the right to do so. They can, of course, vote to remove a director, but in practice any pressure to moderate pay is more likely to come from the investing institutions and to take place behind the scenes. Shareholders have, however, always been required to vote on the establishment of an executive share option scheme, largely because it will normally involve the creation of new shares. And nowadays they will also have the opportunity to vote on the establishment of a new longer-term incentive plan (LTIP).

Individual shareholders are generally all too ready to take their directors' advice on how they should vote on company affairs and are rarely in a position to exercise much influence on boardroom pay levels – though there have been attempts. With less than a fifth of listed shares they are, anyway, a minor force.

UK institutions, with around 50 per cent of listed shares, should be in a far stronger position. But they are frequently reluctant to use their muscle. There are several reasons for this. First, they have a genuine belief that incentives will produce performance from which all shareholders will benefit. Second, they need to work with the City establishment, which will not thank them for rocking the boat. Third, the insurance groups which are major institutional shareholders are mainly companies with boards of directors of their own. These boards have their own pay and perks to consider and might not welcome excessive intervention in the pay affairs of other companies.

It is also questionable whether the system of remuneration committees has worked in the way that was ostensibly intended and sometimes the results have been hilarious. Many of the non-executive directors who sit on these committees are executive directors of another company and have very little interest in restraining boardroom pay levels. In addition, they tend to rely heavily in their deliberations on surveys of boardroom pay and perks produced by numerous firms of **remuneration consultants**. It is an unusually brave non-executive director who will insult the executives by suggesting that they should be paid less than the average for companies of a similar type and size. But if every executive director's salary is raised at least to the average by the remuneration committee, then it is a mathematical inevitability that the average itself must rise each year by leaps and bounds. There are strong grounds for thinking that the remuneration committee system has accelerated rather than moderated the explosion in boardroom pay and perks.

Where the press homes in

It is the pay and perks of the directors of previously nationalized companies – British Gas, the water companies and the electricity companies, in particular – that have attracted most media attention, and the reasons for these specific attacks on the reverse capitalism process need explaining. First, these directors were generally very badly paid by private industry standards when they were running their businesses for the state. Indeed, the prospect of moving over to a private-sector salary scale was a prime inducement for them to co-operate in **privatization** plans. Given the low starting point, the percentage increases in their pay were thus very large and caught the press's eye.

Second, share options for the executives were also built in at the time of privatisation. These have delivered far bigger profits for the directors than were ever envisaged, mainly because the businesses have proved far more profitable than had been expected and share prices have thus risen very rapidly. In many cases the government had seriously underestimated the cost savings to be made in the previously state-run businesses – mainly through sacking employees – and had therefore sold them much too cheaply. Via their share options the directors have benefited, whereas the taxpayer has lost out.

The directors claim they are running major competitive businesses and should be remunerated accordingly. Critics maintain they are running monopoly utilities with assured revenues and that there is no valid comparison with directors running competitive businesses in the marketplace. The debate is likely to rumble on and to be reported in the media for years to come.

Getting down to figures

But what are the private-sector salaries and perks that the utility bosses seek to match? Remuneration consultants New Bridge Street Consultants conducted a survey of the annual reports of the FTSE 100 and the FTSE Mid 250 companies in 1999. For the FTSE 100 companies the median base salary of the chief executive was £435,000 and for the next tier of companies it was £275,000. Annual bonuses added over 35 per cent in the case of the largest companies and over 32 per cent in the Mid 250 companies. Together with benefits in kind, this brought the median total pay of chief executives up to £586,000 in the biggest companies and £386,500 in the next tier. These figures are, of course, before taking account of additional benefits in the form of share option profits or free shares from an LTIP.

Analysis of incentive plans by New Bridge Street showed that 84 per cent of the Footsie 100 companies operated executive share option schemes, against 90 per cent of the Mid 250 companies. Among the largest companies, 71 per cent of the boards qualified for long-term incentive plans (LTIPs) against 52 per cent in the next tier, where share options are more commonly used. Some companies may use an LTIP to reward their top management and use options for those further down the line.

Finally, a search through the **Datastream** database of market, company and economic information in 2000 showed that over 70 companies paid at least one director £1m a year or more, excluding share option profits or LTIP benefits, and a further 181 paid their top-earning director between £500,000 and £1m. Since more than one director in a company may be earning a salary above these levels, the total number of super-earners is certainly higher.

How far will the pay explosion go?

High boardroom pay is frequently defended as the reward for high company performance. In practice, surveys on this issue frequently have problems in establishing a correlation. It is also justified on the basis that 'directors in other countries get more, and we would lose our top entrepreneurial talent if we did not match overseas pay rates'. Again, in practice it is difficult to compare pay and perks across frontiers as there are too many variables. While some UK executives undoubtedly have a value in the international marketplace, very many probably do not. Finally, there is the argument that, if pop stars can earn millions, why not the boardroom stars whose efforts are generally more important to the UK economy? But it is not unrealistic to ask – as the press occasionally has the temerity to do – if the performance of British industry would be one jot better or worse if company directors were paid a decent basic salary and 'incentives' were scrapped across the board.

Where will the pay and perks explosion stop? The median base salary of a chief executive in a Footsie 100 company is now about 21 times average pay across the population as a whole, or 28 times if his bonuses are allowed for. It is difficult to see what will limit further escalation.

The pattern of share ownership and control in Britain means that the owners of companies who foot the bill cannot (or are unlikely to) exert restraint on the directors they elect to manage their businesses. Thus, company directors themselves control the marketplace for their services – and the rates of pay. It is an odd interpretation of the free market philosophy. But the whole phenomenon of reverse capitalism is more than a little odd.

Internet pointers

It will come as no surprise that regular information on the pay and perks of UK company directors is one of the few topics which it is very difficult to find on the Internet. In whose interest would it be to provide it? Two organizations that sometimes provide information or conduct surveys on managerial pay, and also maintain websites, are Incomes Data Services at www.incomesdata.co.uk/ and the Trades Union Congress at www.tuc.org.uk/. For information on the investing institutions' attitude to various aspects of corporate governance, try www.ivis.computasoft.com/. If any reader knows of a source on boardroom pay, other than the occasional newspaper article or those mentioned above, we would be glad to hear of it.

13 Government bonds and company bonds

The government needs an efficient market in its own longer-term debt: this is the part of the stockmarket known as the **gilt-edged market** which we touched on briefly in Chapter 1. 'Gilt-edged stocks' or 'gilts' is simply the term used for British **government bonds** or **government stocks,** which are so called because they represent the absolute peak of quality and security. The government's agent in this market used to be the **Bank of England** but responsibility has passed to the UK **Debt Management Office (DMO),** which is now an executive agency of the Treasury. The DMO advises on debt issues and organizes the auctions of gilts on behalf of HM Treasury. The registration, servicing and redemption of government stocks is still carried out by the Bank of England's Registrar's Department. Settlement of gilt-edged transactions is due to move in the course of the year 2000 to the **CREST** electronic system (see Chapter 6). In 1999 the total **turnover of gilt-edged stocks** was £1,692 billion (about 36 per cent representing trades between marketmakers rather than with customers) and the total value of all stocks listed was some £333 billion at the end of that year.

New issues during the year totalled some £14.6 billion at market values, as new stocks were created to replace those that **matured.** But in effect the government was in the happy position of being a net repayer of debt in 1999, as redemptions of existing stocks at £18.8 billion comfortably exceeeded new issues. This was in marked contrast with most periods in the past. In the recession of the early 1990s the government's income from taxes and other sources fell while its spending on unemployment benefits and other items rose sharply. In 1993 it borrowed some £51 billion net via the issue of gilt-edged securities.

The high turnover in the gilt-edged market relative to the value of the stocks listed partly reflects massive and frequent **switching**

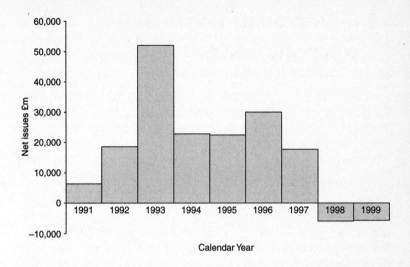

Figure 13.1 Net issues of government securities (£m) This chart reflects the big variations in the government's borrowing needs. In the early 1990s borrowing was rising sharply during the recession on account of flat tax revenues and high social security spending on unemployment benefits and the like. By the end of the decade the benefits of a healthier economy had fed through. The government was actually repaying more gilt-edged stocks than it was issuing and investors faced a shortage of stock to invest in. Source: *Office for National Statistics: Financial Statistics.*

from one stock to another, when a particular stock appears to offer a small interest rate or tax advantage to a particular class of holder. And recent changes to the structure of the market (see below) could make it still more liquid in the future.

Press coverage of the gilt-edged market is far more restricted than equity market comment. Except for comment of a highly technical nature, there is far less to say. There are no takeover battles. There are no profit announcements affecting individual stocks. The main news that moves the gilt-edged market is news of Britain's economic and financial outlook, boiled down to a view of likely movements in interest rates and inflation. Estimates of the government's borrowing needs, influencing the volume of gilts to be issued in future, and movements in government bond prices in overseas markets also play their part. Individual news items may affect one sector of the gilt-edged market more than another (see below) but comment on price movements in individual stocks is comparatively rare. This is also true of comment on the bonds issued by industrial and commercial companies, which operate in a similar way to government bonds and much of the explanation in this chapter applies to company bonds as well: certainly the basic price mechanism. But a few additional factors affect company bonds and these will be examined towards the end of the chapter.

Given the limited number of influences on the gilt-edged market, the press comment falls into three main categories. There are occasional pieces on the outlook for the fixed-interest market as a whole, usually sparked off by events that could mark a turning point. There are pieces on the DMO's intentions and techniques in its handling of the market. And there are the regular but brief reports of price movements of government stocks and fixed-interest bonds in general, plus the reasons for them, amplified where appropriate by news of new issues or changes in the DMO's issue techniques.

News that moves prices

If you remember the basic mechanism described in Chapter 1 – when interest rates go up, prices of fixed-interest stocks come down and when interest rates come down prices of fixed-interest stocks go up – much of this comment falls into place. Weakness in sterling generally rattles the gilt-edged market because it is feared that interest rates may have to rise or stay high to defend the pound. Domestically, fears of higher **inflation**, caused by overheating in the economy, or excessive earnings growth bring fears of higher interest rates. On the other hand, if sterling is strong and the inflation outlook is improving, lower interest rates might be expected and the prices of gilt-edged stocks could be expected to rise.

However, different factors affect different sectors of the gilt-edged market. Should the government need to defend the currency by raising short-term interest rates (which immediately affects the cost of borrowing money from the banks) the effect will probably be most marked on the yields expected from government bonds that have a short life to run (see below). This is because a bond with only, say, a year or two years of life before it is repaid has much in common with a bank deposit and the returns on the two different types of investment will influence each other strongly. On the other hand, when investors look at the returns on bonds with a longer life – say, ten years before they are repaid – they will probably pay more attention to evidence about inflationary trends in the coming years. This is because they are interested in the **real return** that the bonds offer over their life (the return after allowing for inflation). If evidence emerges to suggest that inflationary pressures will be higher than expected over the coming years, the markets expect that long-term returns will have to rise to compensate investors for the higher inflation, or alternatively that interest rates will need to be higher to restrain inflation. All else being equal, this means that the prices of existing longer-dated, fixed-interest bonds must drop until they provide the returns that investors now expect.

Remember that it is vital for investors to spot evidence of a change in expectations of inflation or interest rates. The **overall returns** can be very high for those who buy gilt-edged stocks just ahead of a major turning point when interest rates are about to move sharply down. This happened again in the recent past and a buyer of certain gilt-edged stocks in 1997 could have seen a return over more than 50 per cent in an 18-month period.

Technical influences on the market

The market is also affected by more **technical** factors. If a large amount of new stock is being brought to the market it may depress prices, because for a time the supply of stock will outpace investors' readiness to buy, though the DMO's methods of selling stock are intended to minimize the effect. A heavy flow of non-gilt sterling bond issues by companies and others may influence the market for government bonds. One other technical aspect of the market is now frequently remarked: investors have the opportunity to take a bet on movements in gilt-edged prices by buying or selling **financial futures contracts** in gilt-edged securities (see Chapter 18). Price movements in the very sensitive **financial futures market** can thus herald trends in the gilt-edged market itself, often referred to as the **cash market** when contrasted with the **futures market**.

Types of security

To understand the more detailed comment, we need to look a little closer at the structure of the market.

While the terms **gilt-edged market** and **fixed-interest market** are sometimes used almost interchangeably, they are not always quite the same thing. Not all government stocks carry a fixed rate of interest, though the vast majority of them do. And not all fixed interest stocks are government stocks. There are loans issued by industrial and financial companies (**corporate bonds, industrial loans, corporate loans** or **debentures**), loans issued by local government bodies (**corporation loans**) and loans issued in sterling by foreigners on the UK market (**bulldog bonds**). There are also the **convertible stocks** issued by companies, which were discussed in Chapter 5. Measured by the amount in issue, British government stocks predominate, but bonds issued by companies are also significant.

The life of a stock

Most gilt-edged securities are **redeemable**: the government will repay the stock at some point, but there are a few that have no fixed date for repayment. The notorious **War Loan** is probably the most familiar of these **undated** or **irredeemable** stocks. Irredeemable stocks have a value, because the right to receive interest each year has a value. But investors in these stocks who want their capital back can obtain it only by selling the stocks to other investors.

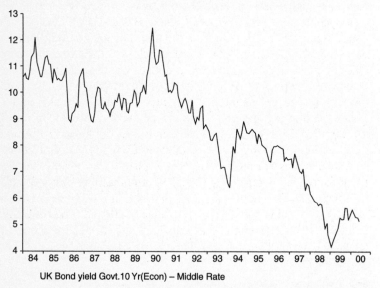

UK Bond yield Govt.10 Yr(Econ) – Middle Rate

Figure 13.2 The fall in bond yields as inflation came under control How longer-term yields have come down in Britain since the high-inflation days. The chart shows the yield on a 10-year government bond and reflects in part the declining influence of fears of inflation as the 1990s progressed. Companies pay a little more than the government when they borrow via bond issues, but it is clear that their long-term borrowing costs have come down dramatically. It is not all good news, however. Lower long-term bond yields mean that pensioners' savings buy a lower income in retirement. Source: *Datastream.*

The **dated** fixed-interest stocks are subdivided according to their **life** or **maturity**: how long they have to run until they are repaid. Those with a life of less than seven years (opinions vary – the *Financial Times* chooses five years) are classified as **shorts**, those with lives of seven to 15 years as **medium-dated** and stocks with more than 15 years to run as **longs**. These classifications reflect the current life of the stock, not its life when issued. A 25-year stock issued in 1987 – therefore repayable in the year 2012 – would initially have been in the 'long' category, but by 1999 it would have had a remaining life of under 15 years and would have been classified as a 'medium'. You will see how stocks are classified according to **redemption date** under the heading of 'UK Gilts Prices' in the 'Companies & Markets' section of the *Financial Times*.

How prices are quoted

If you had been looking at UK gilts prices in 1999 you would also have seen that prices quoted for conventional fixed-interest stocks were mainly in a range between about 100 and 140. Though the pound signs are omitted, these are the prices in pounds and decimals of pounds for a nominal £100 of the stock (the market traditionally used fractions such as 32nds of a pound, but decimals have now taken over). In practice the prices quoted are **middle prices**, between the buying and selling prices that marketmakers normally quote. Prices and interest rates are, as we saw earlier, expressed in terms of this nominal £100 unit of stock, though it does not mean that buyers or sellers have to deal in round amounts of £100 nominal. But a 6 per cent stock pays £6 of interest on every £100 of nominal value and the stock is normally repaid at this £100 **nominal** or **par value** at redemption. It was noticeable that, in 1999, almost all redeemable stocks were standing above their par value of 100 in the market. This is by no means always the case, but will happen when a period of lower long-term interest rates follows a period of high ones.

The range of coupons

The wide range of interest rates or **coupons** on the different stocks – ranging from under 3 per cent to over 13¾ per cent in 1999 – gives some indication of the interest rate the government had to pay when they were first issued and hence the very large movements in interest rates over the years. It is not a perfect guide, since stocks are often issued somewhat above or below their £100 **par value** (**at a premium** or **at a discount**) so that the yield to a buyer even at the outset is significantly different from the coupon rate.

The name is not important

You will also see from the *Financial Times* that stocks have somewhat curious names such as **Treasury**, **Exchequer** and **Funding**. Nowadays, 'Treasury' or 'Exchequer' is chosen as circumstances dictate to help identification if there are stocks of similar coupon maturing in the same year – 'Exchequer' is chosen if there is already a similar 'Treasury' stock. The word 'Loan' in the title indicates that the stock can be held in bearer form.

Regardless of the name, all the money raised goes into a central pool. What is important is the **interest rate** and the **redemption date**, which follow the name of the stock. Where two redemption dates are shown, the stock will not be redeemed before the first date and must be redeemed by the second. Thus, Treasury $5^1/_2$ per cent 2008–2012 pays £5.50 a year on every £100 nominal of stock (carries a $5^1/_2$ per cent coupon) and is due to be repaid (at the government's option) at the earliest in 2008 and the latest in 2012. Treasury 8 per cent 2013 carries an 8 per cent coupon and will be repaid in the year 2013.

Calculating the interest yield

But the interest rate or coupon is not the yield that a buyer of the stock receives, unless he happens to buy the stock at its par value of £100. The yield to the investor depends on the price of the stock in the market. And since it is easier to illustrate the principle with a stock that is standing below its par value, we will invent a convenient one. Let us call it Imaginary Treasury 3.5 per cent 2009 and assume that late in 1999 its price in the market was 90.

Thus, a buyer of the stock in 1999 would have been paying only about £90 to acquire stock with a nominal value of £100 and paying an income of £3.50 a year. A £3.50 income for an outlay of £90 represents a yield of 3.89 per cent on the outlay.

This is known as the **interest yield**, **income yield**, **flat yield** or the **running yield**. To calculate an income yield, you need to express the annual income as a percentage of the price the investor would have to pay. The sum to calculate an income yield is therefore simply:

$$\frac{\text{Interest (£3.50)}}{\text{Market price (£90)}} \times 100$$

giving the answer of 3.89 per cent.

What a redemption yield means

If Imaginary Treasury 3.5 per cent were an **undated** stock, this would be the end of the matter. But it is to be repaid at its nominal £100 value in 2009. Thus a buyer in 1999 could say to himself 'I'm paying about £90 for a stock that will be repaid to me at £100 if I hang on to it till 2009. In other words, I'll see a £10 capital profit in 2009, in addition to the income I've been getting. This £10 is really part of the total return I'll get on the stock if I hold on to it. If I apportion the £10 over the ten years that the stock has to run, it works out at £1 a year. So notionally I'm getting an extra £1 per year for my outlay of £90, which is about 1.11 per cent. This is my **gain to redemption**. If I add it to the 3.89 per cent yield I'm getting from the income, I have a notional combined yield of 5 per cent.'

In practice, an investor who did his sums this way would have grasped the general principle, but would be wrong on the detail. To calculate the total return requires a compound interest sum and is best done with a computer program or a sophisticated calculator. But he is right inasmuch as the *Financial Times* quotes two yields for each dated gilt-edged stock. First the **interest yield**, then the **redemption yield**, which combines the interest yield with the notional **gain to redemption** or **loss to redemption** (see below). When Imaginary Treasury 3.5 per cent 2009 at a price of 90 was showing an income yield of 3.89 per cent, in practice it would have given a redemption yield of about 4.78 per cent.

It is probably easiest to grasp the principles of fixed-interest stocks by taking – as we have done – a stock which stands in the market below its par value of £100 and where there is therefore a gain to redemption for the investor. What has happened here is that the stock was probably originally issued at a period of very low interest rates when investors would have expected a return of only 3.5 per cent. Even after some very sharp reductions from the considerably higher interest rates prevailing in the intervening years, by 1999 investors still expected a yield of more than 3.5 per cent on a ten-year bond. So they would not buy our Imaginary Treasury 3.5 per cent 2009 unless the price was down at a level that would show them a return

UK GILTS - cash market

	Notes	... Yield ... Int	Red	Price £	+ or –	... 52 week ... High	Low
Shorts" (Lives up to Five Years)							
Tr 13pc '00		12.96	5.92	100.28	–.02	108.02	100.28
Tr 8pc '00		7.93	6.00	100.85	–.01	104.15	100.85
Tr Fltg Rate '01		–	0.13	100.00	–.01	100.44	99.95
Tr 10pc '01		9.76	6.07	102.49	–.01	107.53	102.49
Cn 9½pc '01	✠	9.19	6.07	103.39	–.01	108.23	103.39
Cn 9¾pc '01	✠	9.38	6.07	103.90	–.01	109.02	103.90
Tr 7pc '01		6.92	6.10	101.14	....	103.84	100.05
Cn 10pc '02	✠	9.40	6.13	106.43	–.01	111.59	106.34
Tr 7pc '02		6.88	6.04	101.72	....	104.57	100.82
Cn 9½pc '02	✠	8.95	6.13	106.13	–.01	110.93	105.93
Tr 9¾pc '02		9.09	6.13	107.21	–.01	112.31	106.99
Ex 9pc '02	✠	8.47	6.13	106.28	....	110.83	105.74
Cn 9¾pc '03	✠	8.92	6.13	109.34	–.01	114.70	108.78
Tr 8pc '03		7.60	6.01	105.31	....	109.14	104.13
Tr 10pc '03		8.98	6.02	111.39	....	116.76	110.57
Tr 13¾pc '00–3	✠	13.68	5.89	100.54	–.02	109.02	100.54
Tr 6½pc '03		6.39	5.95	101.67	....	104.48	99.86
Tr 11½pc '01–4		11.08	6.06	103.77	–.01	110.11	103.77
Tr 10pc '04	✠	8.80	6.02	113.60	....	119.12	112.33
Tr 5pc '04		5.15	5.82	97.15	+.01	98.80	94.53
Fnd 3½pc '99–4		3.77	5.52	92.78	....	93.21	89.41
Cn 9½pc '04	✠	8.32	5.75	114.15	–.01	118.85	112.17
Tr 6¾pc '04		6.49	5.69	104.07	....	106.49	101.32
Five to Ten Years							
Cn 9½pc '05		8.23	5.76	115.49	+.01	119.94	113.23
Ex 10½pc '05	✠	8.67	5.76	121.12	+.01	126.32	118.78
Tr 12½pc '03–5	✠	10.45	6.02	119.61	–.01	127.01	119.29
Tr 8½pc '05		7.53	5.71	112.88	+.02	116.73	110.08
Cn 9¾pc '06	✠	7.99	5.59	122.04	+.05	126.07	118.84
Tr 7¾pc '06		7.00	5.66	110.77	+.03	113.66	107.25
Tr 8pc '02–6		7.72	6.26	103.61	–.02	107.43	102.84
Tr 7½pc '06		6.83	5.65	109.88	+.03	112.73	106.40
Tr 11¾pc '03–7	✠	10.39	6.13	113.14	–.01	120.04	112.97
Tr 8½pc '07		7.28	5.59	116.74	+.05	119.88	112.94
Tr 7¼pc '07		6.58	5.55	110.24	+.03	112.82	106.17
Tr 13½pc '04–8	✠	10.72	5.69	125.96	–.02	133.61	125.47
Tr 9pc '08		7.31	5.49	123.15	+.07	126.95	118.77
Tr 8pc '09	✠	6.74	5.39	118.75	+.13	122.22	114.68
Tr 5¾pc '09		5.53	5.22	103.91	+.10	106.08	99.10
Ten to Fifteen Years							
Tr 6¼pc '10		5.78	5.22	108.15	+.12	111.10	103.35
Cn 9pc Ln '11		6.86	5.25	131.16	+.16	135.49	126.26
Tr 9pc '12		6.73	5.20	133.77xd	+.18	138.51	128.45
Tr 5½pc '08–12		5.47	5.42	100.53	+.02	103.03	95.68
Tr 8pc '13		6.27	5.10	127.66	+.23	132.26	122.43
Tr 7¾pc '12–15		6.43	5.35	120.48	+.13	124.75	115.84
Over Fifteen Years							
Tr 8pc '15		6.02	4.93	132.94	+.28	138.53	127.70
Tr 8¾pc '17		6.03	4.85	145.09	+.30	152.40	139.82
Ex 12pc '13–17	✠	7.30	5.27	164.34	+.21	170.48	157.92
Tr 8pc '21		5.59	4.73	143.22	+.37	151.64	137.64
Tr 6pc '28		4.86	4.53	123.42	+.36	132.62	116.93
Tr 4¼pc '32		4.35	4.38	97.76	+.36	100.57	0.99
Undated							
Cons 4pc	✠	5.03	–	79.58	+.35	86.94	73.95
War Ln 3½pc		4.82	–	72.61	+.25	78.83	67.14
Cn 3½pc '61 Aft.	✠	4.14	–	84.61	+.25	90.83	79.14
Tr 3pc '66 Aft.	✠	5.38	–	55.79	+.21	60.59	51.78
Cons 2½pc	✠	4.93	–	50.75xd	+.22	55.55	46.78
Tr 2½pc		4.97	–	50.29	+.22	54.87	46.70

	Notes	... Yield ... (1)	(2)	Price £	+ or –	... 52 week ... High	Low
Index–Linked	(b)						
2½pc '01	(78.3)	3.19	4.11	210.26	+.08	210.26	201.90
2½pc '03	(78.8)	3.10	3.49	207.43	+.12	207.43	200.50
4⅜pc '04	(135.6)	2.73	3.01	130.56	+.10	133.51	127.26
2pc '06	(69.5)	2.30	2.49	235.08	+.27	237.89	229.47
2½pc '09	(78.8)	1.95	2.08	220.29	+.29	220.29	208.87
2½pc '11	(74.6)	2.00	2.11	233.80	+.34	233.80	219.11
2½pc '13	(89.2)	1.96	2.05	197.86	+.31	197.86	183.57
2½pc '16	(81.6)	1.92	2.00	219.51	+.33	220.12	203.03
2½pc '20	(83.0)	1.86	1.92	221.47	+.38	224.25	203.17
2½pc '24	(97.7)	1.72	1.77	196.20	+.38	199.43	176.32
4⅛pc '30	(135.1)	1.61	1.67	196.11	+.40	199.61	174.35

Prospective real redemption rate on projected inflation of (1) 5% and (2) 3%. (b) Figures in parentheses show RPI base for indexing (ie 8 months prior to issue) and have been adjusted to reflect rebasing of RPI to 100 in January 1987. Conversion factor 3.945. RPI for October 1999: 166.5 and for May 2000: 170.7.

Other Fixed Interest

	Notes	... Yield ... Int	Red	Price £	+ or –	... 52 week ... High	Low
Asian Dev 10¼pc 2009		8.09	6.20	126¾	....	130⅝	123
B'ham 11½pc 2012		7.88	6.10	146	....	153	140¾
Leeds 13½pc 2006		9.96	6.50	135½	....	142	132¾
Liverpool 3½pc Irred.		5.30	5.30	66xd	....	73	58
LCC 3pc '20 Aft.		5.26	5.20	57	....	64	50
Manchester 11½pc 2007		8.78	6.10	131	....	134½	127
Met. Wtr. 3pc 'B'		3.30	6.50	91	....	91½	85
N'wide Anglia 3⅞pc IL 2021		–	3.30	187½xd	....	200½	174 31/32
4¼pc IL 2024		–	3.20	183½	....	196¾	169

● Source: Debt Management Office (DMO). All UK Gilts are tax-free to non-residents on application. xd Ex dividend. Closing mid-prices are shown in pounds per £100 nominal of stock. Int yield: Interest yield. Red yield: Gross redemption yield. Prospective real Index-Linked redemption yields are calculated by HSBC Bank plc from GEMMA closing prices. ✠ Indicative price. Gilts "runners", the benchmarks and most liquid stocks, are shown in bold type.

Example 13.1 Price information on UK government bonds. Source: *Financial Times.*

on their outlay in line with what they could get on comparable stocks: we have taken about 4.8 per cent for purposes of illustration.

But, as we saw, in 1999 the majority of government stocks were standing above 100. The picture here is the reverse. The stocks were issued with high coupons at a time when interest rates were high. As the yields that investors can expect came down, they were prepared to pay more than the £100 nominal value for the stock. Where this is the case the buyer will, of course, register a capital loss rather than a gain when the stock is repaid at only £100 and in this case the redemption yield will be lower than the income yield. The income the investor receives over the years has to be high enough to compensate for this capital loss on redemption.

Take an example. Late in 1999, Treasury 9 per cent 2012 stood in the market at 134.22. It offered an interest yield as high as 6.57 per cent but a redemption yield of only 5.03 per cent when account was taken of the loss to the investor when it was redeemed at only 100 in the year 2012.

How tax affects the returns

Trading between one gilt-edged stock and another is often driven by considerations of tax. And the position is now a bit complex. Broadly, private investors pay tax on the income or notional income from a gilt-edged stock but pay no tax on capital gains (correspondingly, they cannot offset capital losses against gains elsewhere). Corporate investors, on the other hand, pay tax on the total return, regardless of whether it comes in the form of income or capital gain. Pension funds, of course, do not pay tax on income or capital gains, since they are tax-exempt.

This means that the difference between income yield and redemption yield is very important to investors (though slightly less so than when the highest income tax rates were well above 1999's 40 per cent). Let us look at it from the point of view of a private investor who pays top tax of 40 per cent and keeps only 60p of every £1 of income that he receives, but keeps £1 of every £1 of capital gain that he makes. Look again at Treasury 9 per cent 2012, quoted in the market at a price of 134.22. An investor is getting 6.57 per cent of income but suffering a notional 1.54 per cent loss to redemption to provide the combined 5.03 per cent redemption yield. To a private investor paying 40 per cent tax, the tax liability affects his return as shown in Table 13.1:

	Gross	Net of tax
	%	%
Income yield	6.57	3.94
Gain (loss) to redemption	(1.54)	(1.54) (no tax)
Total return	5.03	2.40

Table 13.1

So the **net return** is 2.40 per cent. Now look at another stock, Treasury 5¾ per cent 2009, which was standing in the market at 105.04 at the same time to give an interest yield of 5.47 per cent and a redemption yield of 5.10 per cent (see Table 13.2).

	Gross	Net of tax
	%	%
Income yield	5.47	3.28
Gain (loss) to redemption	(0.37)	(0.37) (no tax)
Total return	5.10	2.91

Table 13.2

The redemption yield on the 5¾ per cent stock is only marginally higher at 5.10 per cent than the 5.03 per cent obtainable on the 9 per cent stock. But the after-tax return to the private investor is significantly higher at 2.91 per cent than the 2.4 per cent he would get on the 9 per cent stock. This is because a smaller proportion of the return on the 5¾ per cent stock comes in the form of taxed income. The examples underline an important aspect of the gilt-edged market. No one government stock is quite like another. Different stocks are worth different amounts to different classes of investor.

Remember, however, that redemption yields of any kind are, to an extent, notional. The redemption yield is relevant to the investor if he **holds the stock to redemption**. In the interim its price will be determined by the interplay of buyers and sellers, though on balance it will obviously move closer to 100 as the redemption date approaches. This is known as the **pull to redemption**. But the redemption yield is the main yardstick for comparing one stock with another and for calculating the likely price a borrower would have to pay for raising money via a bond issue at a given time.

Interest rate effects

One more example will help to explain prices in the gilt-edged market (and other forms of bond market) and it will be easier again if we invent a theoretical case rather than taking actual stocks. Suppose that in 1999 the government had decided to issue three different stocks. One was short-dated with a life of only three years, one was medium-dated with a life of ten years and one was a 'long' with a life of 25 years. Suppose also that the government reckoned, given the structure of interest rates at the time, that it would have to offer investors a redemption yield of 4.5 per cent on each of the stocks to persuade investors to buy them (we have taken this figure for convenience, not as an indication of the precise interest rates at the time). Each stock was therefore issued at its par value of 100 with a 4.5 per cent coupon.

Now, these assumptions are, of course, a little unrealistic. It is very unlikely that the yields investors expected would have been exactly the same for a short-dated stock, a medium-dated one and a very long-dated stock. But they serve to illustrate our point. So we have our three stocks which we will give the names shown in Table 13.3:

	Price	Income Yield %	Redemption Yield %
Short-dated 4.5% 2002	100	4.5	4.5
Medium-dated 4.5% 2009	100	4.5	4.5
Long-dated 4.5% 2024	100	4.5	4.5

Table 13.3

With each of the stocks at a price of 100, income yields and redemption yields are exactly the same because there would at this point be no gain or loss to the investor on redemption.

Now suppose that a year later things have deteriorated in the UK economy. There is evidence of higher inflation in the pipeline and investors demand higher yields to compensate. If the government issued a new gilt-edged stock at this point it would have to offer a yield of, say, 6 per cent to persuade investors to buy. What happens to the market prices of our three stocks issued in 1999? The answer is clearly that no investor would buy them at a price of 100 where the redemption yield is only 4.5 per cent. The prices of the stocks will have to fall in the market until they reach a level where investors would buy them. What would this level be? It is the price at which they will offer the 6 per cent redemption yield that investors now expect. Again, we are being slightly unrealistic because it is doubtful if investors would expect exactly the same redemption yield from three stocks with different lives and different tax characteristics. But, to illustrate our point, the position would be as shown in Table 13.4 if each stock now had to offer a redemption yield of 6 per cent (remember that the remaining life of each stock is now a year shorter than when they were issued in 1999):

	Price	Income Yield %	Redemption Yield %
Short-dated 4.5% 2002	97.25	4.63	6.00
Medium-dated 4.5% 2009	89.80	5.01	6.00
Long-dated 4.5% 2024	81.20	5.54	6.00

Table 13.4

The example shows very clearly that long-dated stocks show much larger price movements for a given change in interest rates than short-dated ones. An investor in the short-dated stock who had bought at 100 originally and now needed to sell would have lost some money but not a massive amount. The investor in the medium-dated stock would have lost quite heavily and the investor in the long-dated stock would have fared worst of all. Investors in all three stocks would eventually be repaid at 100 if they hung on for redemption, but in the meantime the losses could be substantial. Thus, investors who are averse to risk and might want to get their money back in a hurry are more likely to buy the short-dated stocks. Those who want to tie their money up for a long time at a known return, together with the more adventurous or those who want to take a deliberate bet on favourable movements in interest rates are more likely to go for the long-dated stocks.

The **pull to redemption** is much greater with a short-dated stock than a long-dated one. When a stock is due to be repaid at £100 in the fairly near future, redemption is the dominant influence and its price will not fluctuate so widely in response to movements in interest rates. Nor, as the example shows, does it need to do so to accommodate investor's changed expectations of the return they should get. It is true that short-term interest rates can nowadays fluctuate very widely (perhaps by more than long yields), and will affect short-dated stocks more than the long-dated ones. Thus, as our example shows, price fluctuations can be quite marked even at the **short end** of the market. But the risk of capital loss is still a great deal lower than with long-dated stocks. Market reports will often highlight the different magnitude of price movements at the long and short end of the market. Investors switch between stocks of different maturities according to the way they expect long-term and short-term interest rates to move.

Cum-dividend and ex-dividend

Interest on most gilt-edged securities is paid twice a year. So between dividend payments it is **accruing** – building up – until the moment it is paid. Prices for gilts are now quoted **clean** (they exclude **accrued income**). But a buyer normally pays for (and receives the right to) any income that has accrued since the last dividend date, in addition to the price he pays for the stock itself. However, if he buys it once the stock has gone **ex-dividend** (see Chapter 4), the seller keeps the right to the forthcoming interest payment. Since the date that a stock goes ex-dividend does not correspond exactly with the end of an interest period, the seller pays the buyer rebate interest in respect of the period for which the buyer will hold a stock but the seller will receive the interest from the government. Yields on gilt-edged stocks are always calculated on **clean prices**. If the tax laws permitted (see below), it would benefit some higher-rate taxpayers to buy a stock just after it had gone ex-dividend and sell it shortly before the next dividend payment was due. In this way they receive no income, on which high rates of tax would be payable, but receive the benefit in the form of untaxed capital gain.

This practice, known as **dividend stripping**, has now been outlawed and the interest is normally taxed as income whether in fact it is received as interest or as capital gain. However, an exception is made for investors whose gilt-edged holdings total less than £5,000 at nominal values. These are taxed on an 'income received' basis.

The fact that interest on most UK government stocks is paid in two equal six-monthly instalments (paid **semi-annually**) introduces a slight complication when comparing gilts with bonds that pay interest as a single sum at the end of the year. The interest received after the first six months may itself be invested to earn interest for the second half of the year. Suppose an investor bought a gilt with a coupon of 5 per cent at its nominal value of 100. After six months he receives interest of £2.50 and may reinvest this at, say, the same 5 per cent rate to earn interest of 6.25p in the second six months. The total interest he receives over the year is therefore £5.0625, not £5, and the 5 per cent coupon on the bond is really worth 5.0625 per cent if compared with a bond paying interest as a single annual sum (see also Chapter 17).

Index-linked and other stocks

So far we've been talking of fixed-interest stocks. But there are, and have been, other types of government stock. For example, in 1996 a floating rate gilt was issued which was due to mature in 2001. The return to the investor varies with movements in interest rates in the economy.

There are also the **index-linked stocks**, which provide protection against inflation (act as an **inflation hedge**). They were initially introduced in 1981 for the pension funds, then made available to any type of investor – they now account for some 20 per cent of the gilt portfolio. With an index-linked stock, both the income and the price at which it will be redeemed are adjusted to take account of the movement in **retail prices**. In other words, both income and capital retain their **real value**. The price you pay for this protection is a much lower nominal coupon rate.

Say an index-linked stock is issued at its par value of 100, with a coupon of 2.5 per cent. Over the next five years, retail prices rise by 30 per cent in total, meaning that it would cost you £130 to buy goods and services you could have obtained for £100 five years earlier. So the price at which the stock will be redeemed rises to 130. The interest it pays must also rise by 30 per cent to maintain a real interest rate of 2.5 per cent. So the interest rate after five years will be 2.5 per cent on the new £130 redemption value (equivalent to 3.25 per cent on the original £100 nominal value).

Of course, if retail prices were to fall in year six, the redemption value could be adjusted down again from 130 and so could the interest. But in the more likely event that retail prices continue rising (though at different rates in different climates) the redemption value of the stock will continue to rise.

In practice, the redemption value of an index-linked stock does not match the movement in retail prices (as measured by the **retail prices index** or **RPI**) quite as closely as in the example because there is a time lag of eight months built in so that the size of the interest payment is known before the start of the interest period. This means that the return from the last eight months of the life of the gilt is not indexed and the real return will therefore vary depending on the future rate of inflation. In compensation, the investor is recompensed for inflation in the eight months before the stock was issued. The *Financial Times* quotes two possible real redemption yields, one on the assumption of 5 per cent inflation and the other on the assumption of 3 per cent (it is a measure of how much inflationary expectations have come down in recent years that these figures used to be 10 per cent and 5 per cent). The *Financial Times* also shows (in brackets after the name of each index-linked stock) the starting point for the indexation sum on the retail prices index or RPI.

The market price of the index-linked stock is, as with a fixed-interest stock, not directly determined by the redemption value, though this will begin to exert more influence as redemption comes close. Real redemption yields are very low (mostly in the region of 2 per cent late in 1999), partially reflecting the fact that most of the return comes in the form of untaxed capital appreciation. Index-linked stocks are not at their most attractive when **real rates of return** on conventional gilt-edged are high: in other words, when the nominal yields are well above the inflation rate. Index-linked stocks are more popular when inflation-fears rise.

Indices for government stocks

Price movements in the fixed interest market are measured on a number of indices. Separate **FTSE Actuaries indices** are published for a number of different maturity ranges of gilt-edged stocks, as well as for the **irredeemables**. There is also an **All Stocks Index** for gilt-edged as a whole. There are separate indices for index-linked stocks, again covering a range of different maturities, and there is a further index for index-linked stocks as a whole. The *Financial Times* also publishes its own longer-established **Government Securities Index** with a base of 100 in 1926. Market reports talk of price movements of a **point** or fraction of a point in individual stocks: a point in this context is one pound per £100 nominal.

New issues and dealing mechanisms

The mechanics of issue and subsequent dealing for gilt-edged stocks, as with equities, underwent some changes with the Big Bang. And in the second half of the 1990s further changes were made in the interests of a more efficient market and greater competitiveness with government bond markets overseas (see below).

In the past, when a **public offering of stock** was made, a minimum price was usually set and **tenders** were invited at or above that figure. All accepted bidders at tender paid a common price. The price might be due as a single payment, or payment might be made in instalments (see Chapter 8 for a description of **partly paid stocks** in the equity market, where the procedure is similar).

Stock that did not find buyers at a tender remained in the hands of the government and was subsequently made available to the market as and when there was a demand for it and when it suited the authorities to make further sales. Stock available for issue in this way is described as a **tap stock** because the supply can be turned on and off as required. A second source of stock that can be used as a **tap** is issues of small **tranchettes** of stock – possibly of a range of different stocks – which are available for sale to the market in the same way. Sales of tap stocks to the market are made via the DMO's dealing room, but they have become rarer since auctions for index-linked stocks were introduced (see below).

No issues of stock via the tender method have been made since 1991 and the more recent auction method is now the norm. This was first introduced in 1987 when the Bank undertook an experimental series of **auctions** for selling large amounts of stock, initially as a supplement to the tender method. The main difference between the auction and the tender is the implication, in the auction method, that there is the intention to sell all the stock on offer. Also, competitive bidders for conventional stocks are allocated stock at the price at which they bid, rather than at a common **striking price** as in a tender (see Chapter 8 for a description of the tender mechanism). But for small bids the facility exists for stock to be allocated non-competitively at the average of the accepted competitive bids. In the case of index-linked gilts, stock is allocated at the average price offered by successful bidders.

New gilt-edged stocks are created to satisfy the government's financing needs and the market's need for a balance of short, medium and long dates and index-linked stocks. The gilt auction operations by the DMO now take place according to a calendar determined a year in advance, with an indication of the identity of the stocks to be auctioned being given in advance of each quarter. The nominal size is announced in the week before an auction.

At times when the government is a net repurchaser of stock, one option open to the authorities would be to hold **reverse auctions** under which holders can offer to sell stock back to the authorities, who accept the stock offered at the most favourable price. As with the ordinary auction, there would also be facilities for small offers of stock.

Before Big Bang, gilt-edged stocks – once issued – were traded on the stockmarket via the **jobber/broker mechanism** as with equities. Nowadays the **marketmaking function** is undertaken by **primary dealers** known as **gilt-edged marketmakers** or **GEMMs**, of which there were 16 operating in 1999. They include former gilt jobbing and broking firms but also offshoots of banks and other financial institutions including a number of American, Japanese and continental European firms. These primary dealers have an obligation to maintain a market in all government stocks and have the right to deal direct with the Bank of England. They can bid for available tap stocks when they wish.

The market mechanism is eased by **inter-dealer brokers**, via whom the gilt-edged marketmakers can effectively deal with each other without disclosing their positions to their competitors. The primary dealers have access to a **price information system** via the **SEAQ** screens, but this is more rudimentary than the SEAQ equity service and they rely more heavily on screen-based price information supplied by the inter-dealer brokers. In order to cover their short positions, market-makers can also borrow (rather than buy) stock from **stock exchange money brokers**, who have increased in number since Big Bang.

Dealing in gilt-edged stock is for **cash settlement** (payment the next day), and major institutional investors are likely to deal direct at **net prices** with a primary dealer rather than going through an **agency broker**. Small private investors will go through a broker as before (though **commissions** are lower than on equities) or can buy through the **Bank of England Brokerage Service** (see below).

The winds of change

By the mid 1990s there were fears that Britain's gilt-edged market might be losing out in terms of competitiveness with some overseas government bond markets and change was once again in the air. One of the first steps to remedy this situation was the introduction of an open system of **repurchase agreements** (or **repos**) in the gilt market – they already existed in some of the more liquid overseas markets.

In a repo arrangement, the gilt-edged stock is sold with an agreement to buy it back later at a known price. Thus the seller is really arranging a short-term secured loan, with the gilts as security.

In effect, repos allow much easier lending of gilt-edged stocks and borrowing against gilt-edged stocks. Somebody with a bearish view of the market, for example, is able to sell stock that he does not own and temporarily borrow the stock that he needs to deliver. Alternatively, investors wishing to buy gilts may be able to borrow sterling more cheaply by using the gilts as security. Repos should thus add to the liquidity of the market.

The authorities also decided to reduce the number of individual gilts in issue and concentrate on a smaller number of larger (and therefore more liquid) issues. And settlement via the CREST system should also contribute to liquidity. Greater transparency and pre-dictability in gilt issuance has been achieved by advance publication of the issue schedule.

Introduction of strips

The other major change was the introduction in 1997 of a market in **financially engineered** government bonds known as **strips**. To grasp the principle, take a hypothetical example.

We will invent another government bond: call it Imaginary Treasury 6 per cent 2004. It pays interest twice yearly on 7 June and 7 December and is due to be repaid at its par value of 100 on 7 June 2004. Now suppose an investor bought this bond on 8 June 1999. The cash flows he can expect over the life of the bond are as shown in Table 13.5:

Income and capital payments on £1m face value of Imaginary Treasury 6% 2004

		Interest payment received £	Capital repayment received £
1999	Dec-07	30,000	
2000	Jun-07	30,000	
2000	Dec-07	30,000	
2001	Jun-07	30,000	
2001	Dec-07	30,000	
2002	Jun-07	30,000	
2002	Dec-07	30,000	
2003	Jun-07	30,000	
2003	Dec-07	30,000	
2004	Jun-07	30,000	1,000,000

Table 13.5

If our investor intends to hold the stock to redemption, it is clear that he can expect ten half-yearly interest payments of £30,000 and in June 2004 he can expect to receive £1,000,000 when the stock is redeemed. If the bond is 'stripped', what happens is that each of these receipts is treated as an investment in its own right. In other words, the right to receive a £30,000 interest payment in, say, June 2003 becomes a marketable investment. So do the rights to all the other interest payments. So does the right to receive the £1,000,000 capital repayment at the end of the day. So our bond with five years of life to run can be broken down into 11 different investments or **strips**.

But what are these rights or **strips** worth? They do not, after all, pay any income. They simply give the right to receive a certain sum at a certain date in the future. What this right is worth depends on the return you expect from your investment.

Remember the principle set out in Chapter 1. A sum of money that you will receive in the future is worth less than the same sum of money if you had it today. This is because, if you had it today, you could set it to work earning interest for you and it would therefore become worth more in the future. So we will assume that, in the market conditions of the time, you would expect a return of 4.8 per cent on your investment.

What, therefore, is £30,000 receivable in June 2003 – in four years' time if we are starting from June 1999 – worth in June 1999? It is worth whatever sum will grow to £30,000 in four years' time at a 4.8 per cent semi-annual interest rate (i.e. assuming interest paid in two equal annual instalments). The answer, as it happens, is £24,815. Another way of saying this is that £24,815 is the **present value** of £30,000 receivable in four years' time at a 4.8 per cent semi-annual discount rate. Work it out. At 4.8 per cent semi-annual compound interest, £24,815 grows to £30,000 in four years. The table below shows the present value of all 11 components into which our £1,000,000 of gilt-edged stock can be stripped, on the assumption of a June 1999 starting date and a semi-annual discount rate of 4.8 per cent. In practice, the market prices of strips are expressed in relation to a redemption value of 100. So if £30,000 receivable in four years has a current value of £24,815, the price of this strip would be expressed as 82.72, since £24,815 is 82.72 per cent of £30,000.

Discounted value of payments on £1m face value of Imaginary Treasury 6% 2004

		Number of years before payment received	Interest payment received	Present value of interest payment at 4.80% interest rate	Capital repayment received	Present value of capital repayment at 4.80% interest rate
			£	£	£	£
1999	Dec-07	0.5	30,000	29,297		
2000	Jun-07	1.0	30,000	28,610		
2000	Dec-07	1.5	30,000	27,940		
2001	Jun-07	2.0	30,000	27,285		
2001	Dec-07	2.5	30,000	26,645		
2002	Jun-07	3.0	30,000	26,021		
2002	Dec-07	3.5	30,000	25,411		
2003	Jun-07	4.0	30,000	24,815		
2003	Dec-07	4.5	30,000	24,234		
2004	Jun-07	5.0	30,000	23,666	1,000,000	788,861

TOTAL PRESENT VALUE:	263,924	788,861
Income and capital:		
TOTAL PRESENT VALUE:		1,052,785

Table 13.6

The calculations are inevitably a little technical, but they are necessary in order to explain the principle. If you want to do them yourself, incidentally (which you easily can do with a sophisticated calculator or a computer spreadsheet) look at the following formulae – skip the next few paragraphs if arithmetic turns you off, and continue at 'Attractions of strips'.

To calculate what sum £1 today will grow to in the future at an annual rate of interest, the formula would be:

£1 * (1 + interest rate) ^ number of years

We are using the computer symbols where an asterisk is a multiply sign, a slash is a divide sign and the pointed hat symbol means 'raised to the power of'. And the interest rate is expressed as a decimal: thus 4.8 per cent would be 0.048.

Since interest on gilts is normally paid semi-annually, we have to adjust the formula to allow for this. The formula used in the table is therefore:

£1 * (1 + (interest rate / 2)) ^ (number of years * 2)

So, if we want to know the value of £1 in four years time at 4.8 per cent compound semi-annual interest, the sum is:

£1* (1 + (.048 / 2)) ^ (4 * 2) or:

£1* 1.024 ^ 8 = £1.2089

If £1 will grow to £1.2089 in four years, then £24,815 will grow to £24,815 multiplied by 1.2089, which is £30,000 as near as dammit. If you want to do the sum in reverse and find the present value of £1 receivable at a future date at a given annual interest rate, the calculation is:

£1 * 1 / (1 + interest rate) ^ number of years

However, again we have to allow for the fact that interest on gilts is normally paid semi-annually, so the formula used in Table 13.6 is:

£1 * 1 / (1 + (interest rate / 2)) ^ (number of years * 2)

If we want the present value of £1 receivable in four years at a 4.8% semi-annual interest rate, the sum is therefore:

£1 * 1 / (1 + (0.048 / 2)) ^ (4 * 2) or

£1 * 1 / 1.024 ^ 8 = 0.82718

If £1 receivable in four years is worth only 0.82718 today at a 4.8 per cent semi-annual discount rate, then £30,000 receivable in four years is worth £30,000 multiplied by 0.82718, which works out at £24,815.

Attractions of strips

So nowadays larger investors have a choice. They can buy government bonds which pay them interest twice a year. Or they can buy strips which pay no interest but provide a return all the same because the sum you get at the end of the day is above the price you paid initially and this difference can be expressed as the equivalent of an annual rate of compound interest. Strips are therefore much the same as **zero coupon bonds**: bonds that were never intended to pay interest but provide their return from the difference between the issue price and the higher price at which they will be redeemed.

What is the attraction of strips as an investment? They enable you to tailor an investment to your own exact requirements and they give you absolute certainty as to the sum you will receive on a particular date. An insurance company knows, say, that it will have to pay out precisely £30,000 in four years' time under a savings plan it has sold. By buying the four-year interest payment strip, it knows it will receive exactly £30,000 at the relevant time so it will have the money to meet its commitment.

What is the difference between this and buying an interest-paying investment today (like a conventional unstripped gilt-edged stock) that will build up to £30,000 in four years? The problem is that you are never quite sure what return you will get on your money with an interest-paying bond. You may assume that, if you buy an interest-paying bond at a price that shows you a redemption yield of 4.8 per cent, then the return on your money will be exactly 4.8 per cent if you hold it until it is redeemed.

Unfortunately, this is not necessarily the case. The calculation of the redemption yield or **internal rate of return (IRR)** on a fixed-interest bond has to assume that the periodic interest payments that you receive can be reinvested at the same rate of interest as the redemption yield that you started with. In practice, this probably won't happen. Buying strips instead of interest-bearing bonds eliminates this uncertainty.

Since the return on strips comes entirely in the form of capital gain, is it tax-free to a private investor? Unfortunately no. Tax has to be paid annually on the notional return, as if the strips were sold at the end of each tax year.

Bank of England Brokerage Service

In Britain, the public has an opportunity to buy or sell the more liquid gilt-edged stocks without going through a broker at all, by using the **Bank of England Brokerage Service**. Commission charges on smaller transactions may be lower than a broker would charge. You may obtain a purchase form and a list of stocks available from a Post Office, by writing to the Bank of England's Registrar's Department or from the Bank's website at www.bankofengland.co.uk/. You send your order by post with a cheque and the Bank tries to carry out on the same day all orders that it receives by first post. However, it cannot undertake to buy or sell stock at a particular price or a particular time.

Corporate bond market

Companies as well as governments often want to borrow money for long periods at fixed rates of interest. And, just like governments, they can do so by issuing fixed-interest bonds which become **securities** of the company.

When a company issues a bond, a few additional considerations apply that do not crop up with government bonds. First, a company (even the best company) is not as secure as the government. Investors assume that the government will always be able to pay the interest on its debt and repay the debt at the end of the day. The government can ultimately tap taxpayers for the money it needs. A company, on the other hand, has to be able to earn the profit from which it will pay the interest and must find the cash to repay the debt eventually. Companies, even large and reputable companies, do sometimes get into trouble and even go bust. A bond issued by a company will therefore need to offer a higher return than one issued by the government to compensate investors for the higher risk. A very large and safe company may not need to pay a great deal more than the government would. A smaller and less secure company might have to pay considerably more.

Second, investors are prepared to lend to the government for 25 years or so, because they assume that one government or another will still be around in 25 years. They may be more reluctant to lend to companies for such a long period. Very well-established companies or those with assets such as property which investors expect to increase in value may be able to borrow for very long periods. Others may have to settle for somewhat shorter terms.

Third, when the government issues a bond it might issue several billion pounds' worth. Since there will be many thousands of investors in any single government bond, the bond will be easy to buy and sell in the **secondary market** without moving the price too much. In other words, it will be very **liquid**. Companies will normally issue bonds for rather smaller amounts and the bonds will not be quite so liquid. Again, investors expect some compensation for this factor in the form of additional return.

Deciding the coupon rate

But the rates of return on company bonds will take the returns on 'risk-free' government bonds as their starting point. If, at a particular

WORLD BOND PRICES

BENCHMARK GOVERNMENT BONDS

Jun 28	Red Date	Coupon	Bid Price	Bid Yield	Day chg yield	Wk chg yield	Month chg yld	Year chg yld
Australia	03/02	9.750	106.0287	5.95	+0.03	-0.03	-0.11	+0.85
	09/09	7.500	108.5604	6.26	+0.01	-	+0.02	-0.03
Austria	02/02	4.375	98.6800	5.21	+0.01	+0.08	+0.14	+1.99
	01/10	5.500	99.1500	5.61	+0.01	+0.05	+0.03	+0.85
Belgium	06/02	8.750	106.6500	5.12	+0.04	+0.06	+0.11	+1.95
	09/10	5.750	100.9300	5.62	+0.01	+0.07	+0.04	+0.78
Canada	12/01	5.250	98.9200	6.06	-0.03	-0.05	-0.21	+0.78
	06/09	5.500	96.8500	5.96	+0.02	-0.01	-0.14	+0.36
Denmark	11/01	8.000	102.6500	5.88	+0.02	+0.05	+0.27	+2.43
	11/09	6.000	101.9200	5.72	-0.02	+0.03	+0.01	+0.73
Finland	09/01	10.000	105.5970	5.03	+0.06	+0.05	+0.15	+2.27
	02/11	5.750	102.2120	5.47	+0.01	+0.05	+0.01	+0.70
France	01/02	4.000	98.4800	5.05	+0.04	+0.05	+0.16	+1.80
	04/07	5.500	100.9600	5.32	+0.02	+0.07	+0.06	+1.16
	04/10	5.500	100.5400	5.42	+0.01	+0.04	+0.03	+0.78
	04/29	5.500	98.3600	5.61	-	+0.05	-0.01	+0.14
Germany	12/01	4.000	98.5900	5.02	+0.01	+0.05	+0.14	+1.87
	01/07	6.000	103.7500	5.30	+0.02	+0.07	+0.04	+1.00
	01/10	5.375	100.6600	5.28	+0.02	+0.06	+0.02	+0.74
	01/30	6.250	111.5000	5.45	-	+0.05	-0.02	+0.02
Greece	01/02	7.600	101.7000	6.37	-0.04	-	-0.11	-0.94
	01/09	6.300	101.1500	6.12	-0.02	-	-0.09	-0.12
Ireland	10/01	6.500	101.6800	5.11	+0.03	+0.17	+0.18	+1.70
	04/10	4.000	88.6500	5.53	+0.01	+0.05	+0.04	+0.73
Italy	02/02	3.000	96.7000	5.16	+0.06	+0.09	+0.16	+1.80
	07/05	4.750	97.1800	5.40	+0.01	+0.07	+0.07	+1.41
	11/09	4.250	90.3900	5.59	+0.02	+0.07	+0.05	+0.80
	11/29	5.250	91.5100	5.86	+0.01	+0.02	-	+0.18
Japan	12/01	6.000	108.2580	0.32	-0.01	+0.01	+0.09	+0.02
	06/05	3.400	111.0480	1.10	-	+0.05	+0.09	+0.12
	12/09	1.900	102.1800	1.65	+0.02	+0.04	+0.03	-0.08
	03/20	2.500	106.2150	2.11	+0.01	-	+0.02	-0.57
Netherlands	02/02	3.000	96.8400	5.08	+0.05	+0.09	+0.13	+1.93
	04/10	7.500	115.4700	5.42	-	+0.03	+0.02	+0.57
New Zealand	03/02	10.000	104.8487	6.91	-0.12	-0.10	-0.24	+1.67
	07/09	7.000	100.9942	6.85	-0.08	+0.01	-0.14	+0.18
Norway	05/01	7.000	99.8200	7.16	+0.02	+0.22	+0.45	+1.74
	05/09	5.500	95.1500	6.23	-	+0.09	+0.09	+0.50
Portugal	03/02	5.750	100.8200	5.22	+0.03	+0.04	+0.14	+2.15
	05/10	5.850	101.3700	5.66	+0.02	+0.08	+0.04	+0.77
Spain	07/02	4.250	98.2600	5.15	+0.02	+0.07	+0.11	+2.03
	01/10	4.000	88.6200	5.56	+0.01	+0.07	+0.04	+0.73
Sweden	04/02	5.500	100.7560	5.03	+0.04	+0.05	+0.05	+1.16
	04/09	9.000	125.7330	5.26	+0.04	+0.06	+0.02	+0.17
Switzerland	07/02	4.500	101.2500	3.84	+0.01	-0.05	-0.03	+1.95
	08/10	3.500	95.6500	4.03	-	-0.01	-0.12	+1.16
UK	11/01	7.000	101.1000	6.13	-	-	-0.12	+0.68
	11/04	6.750	104.0000	5.71	+0.01	+0.04	-0.09	+0.17
	12/09	5.750	103.7800	5.24	+0.01	+0.01	+0.01	+0.11
	12/28	6.000	123.4200	4.53	-0.01	-0.05	+0.05	-0.21
US	02/02	6.500	99.9063	6.55	-	-	-0.19	+0.91
	11/04	5.875	98.0938	6.38	+0.01	-0.01	-0.25	+0.54
	02/10	6.500	102.7813	6.11	+0.02	+0.01	-0.22	+0.15
	05/30	6.250	103.9063	5.97	+0.03	+0.01	-0.09	-0.13

London closing * New York closing.   Source: Interactive Data/FT Information
Yields: Local market standard/Annualised yield basis. Yields shown for Italy exclude withholding tax at 12.5 per
cent payable by non residents.

Example 13.2 Yields on 'yardstick' government bonds. Source: *Financial* time, investors expect a redemption yield of, say, 4.8 per cent on a government bond repayable in ten years' time, what rate of return would the company have to offer? The company's financial advisers, who know the market well, might decide that the company would need to offer 100 **basis points** (one percentage point) more than the government to attract investors. If the government **benchmark gilt** – the one selected as a yardstick for medium-dated bonds – offers a redemption yield of 4.8 per cent, the company bond would therefore need to offer 5.8 per cent.

But bond prices can move up and down quite rapidly and it may still be a few days before the company bond is ready for issue. So the company or its advisers might say that the redemption yield on the new bond will be set at 100 basis points over the redemption yield on the benchmark gilt at 3 pm next Wednesday, the day of issue. If on that day the benchmark gilt is yielding 4.85 per cent to redemption, the new company bond will need to offer a redemption yield of 5.85 per cent.

This does not mean that the coupon will necessarily need to be 5.85 per cent. Instead, the company could issue the bond with a coupon of 5.8 per cent but issue it below its nominal value at a price (roughly 99.60 in this instance) which would provide investors with a redemption yield of 5.85 per cent over ten years. If the company making the bond issue were a smaller or lesser-known concern it would have to offer a higher yield – a greater **spread** over the benchmark gilt: say, 180 basis points. Its cost would thus be 7.65 per cent. The *Financial Times* publishes a table of yields on benchmark government bonds in different countries.

The credit risk

Once issued, company bonds respond to changes in interest rate expectations in much the same way as government bonds. But there is another factor that can affect their market price. Suppose something happens subsequently to affect investors' confidence in the company that issued the bond. A year after the bond issue the company begins making losses and investors start to question whether it will be able to pay the interest. The general level of yields in the market has not changed, let us suppose, and the benchmark gilt is still yielding 4.85 per cent. But buyers of the company bond in the market, which carries a 5.8 per cent coupon, would now demand a considerably higher return than 5.85 per cent to compensate them for the higher risk that they now perceive.

This means that the price of the bond must fall. Suppose it falls to a price of 70 before investors are prepared to buy it. At this level, with 9 years of life still to run, it offers a redemption yield of 11.28 per cent (provided it does, in the event, pay the interest): no longer 100 basis points over the benchmark gilt yield but 643 basis points above it. If the company returns to profit, buyers of the bond will see a handsome profit themselves. If the company goes bust they might lose the whole of their investment. Buyers of company bonds are not just at the mercy of changes in interest rates. They can be affected by changes in the **credit status** of the company and changes considerably less dramatic than that in our example are taking place much of the time.

For this reason, company bonds may carry a **credit rating** issued by one of the independent **rating agencies** (see Chapter 17). This rating aims to reflect the degree of risk and will be amended if the company's fortunes change.

Fixed-interest bonds issued by companies fall into two main categories: those that are **secured** and those that are **unsecured**. With a secured bond, the loan is normally secured on a specific asset or specific assets owned by the issuing company. If the company defaults on the terms of the bond, the asset or assets can be sold to provide the money to repay investors (though the position is slightly complicated by the 1986 Insolvency Act). This gives greater security than if the investors in the bond have to compete with other creditors for repayment if the company should get into trouble. It is similar to the system applying in the residential property market, where a lender to the homebuyer takes a **mortgage** on the property, which allows the home to be sold to repay the loan if necessary.

With an unsecured bond, the investor is relying mainly on the standing of the issuing company and its ability to earn the profits and generate the cash to pay the interest on the bond and repay it at the end of the day. Investors may insist on certain conditions or **restrictive covenants** to strengthen their hand. There might be upper limits on the amount of money the company could borrow and the company might have to stay within certain ratios between profits and interest charges.

All else being equal, a secured bond will normally be slightly cheaper for the issuing company than an unsecured one. In other words, the yield it has to offer to attract investors will be slightly lower. Traditionally, bonds issued in the domestic stockmarket were frequently secured whereas those issued in the **euromarket** or

international market (see below) tend to follow American practice and are usually unsecured. But the division is not rigid.

Bonds with a difference

There is another type of 'fixed interest' bond that you will come across sometimes, and that is the **zero coupon bond** which we mentioned briefly earlier. Its distinction is that it pays no interest at all during its life. The investor's return comes entirely in the form of a **gain to redemption**. A company issues a bond at, say, a price of 55 and agrees to repay it at 100 in ten years' time. In practice, this is much the same thing as a compound annual rate of interest of 6.2 per cent, but the investor has to wait for ten years to get this 'interest' as a lump sum.

Not all bonds offer a fixed return at all. Companies, like the government, have the option of issuing **floating rate** bonds instead and some types of company – particularly banks and other financial groups – use them a great deal more. The bonds, which are usually known as **floating rate notes** or **FRNs** pay a rate of interest that is geared to a widely accepted yardstick for interest rates such as LIBOR (see Chapter 15). The issuer agrees that the FRN will pay, say, 50 basis points (half of one percentage point) above the rate of LIBOR. In practice this means that the average rate of LIBOR will be taken over, perhaps, a six-month period. If average LIBOR was 6 per cent the FRN would pay 6 per cent plus the 50 basis points **spread** or 6.5 per cent in total in respect of that six months' period.

We saw that with a bond that has a fixed coupon, the price in the market has to change to accommodate changes in interest rates in the economy. With an FRN the interest rate itself can change so that the market price does not need to adjust in the same way. The price is likely to stay far closer to its nominal value of 100 and in this sense the risk for the investor is considerably less, as are the possible gains. But if something happened to damage the **credit standing** of the issuing company, the price in the market could, of course, drop for this reason.

New types of bond and FRN are constantly being developed and tailored to investors' requirements at a given time (see Chapter 17). And **convertible bonds** – bonds that may convert into shares – are a long-established part of the financing armoury (see Chapter 5). Nor do bonds necessarily need to be traded on a stockmarket at all.

Companies may make **private placements** of bonds that are **placed** with (sold direct to) big investing institutions who will often hold them until they are redeemed.

Tapping the bond markets

At times of high inflation when long-term interest rates are high, UK companies have generally been reluctant to raise capital by issuing long-term fixed-interest bonds. They do not want to commit themselves to paying very high interest rates for 20 years or so when there is a chance that capital might become considerably cheaper at a later date. And many investors are very reluctant to buy fixed-interest bonds when they think that inflation will seriously erode the real value of their capital.

Issues of fixed-interest bonds by companies virtually dried up in the high-inflation era of the 1970s and they have been unpopular at times of high interest rates subsequently. But the lower rates of inflation of the recent past have seen a resurgence of interest in the corporate bond market. For investors, **industrial debentures** or **corporate bonds** have the advantage of offering rather higher returns than the government's own bonds, still with quite a high level of safety.

UK companies are not limited to the domestic stockmarket when they wish to issue bonds. In the **euromarket** or **international market** the larger companies can issue bonds in sterling or in a range of other currencies. And they can also issue foreign-currency bonds in the domestic stockmarkets of a number of other countries, particularly the United States. The euromarkets need a chapter of their own (see Chapter 17). But it is important to note that many of the differences in issue and trading techniques for sterling bonds between Britain's domestic stockmarket and the euromarket have now broken down. Dealers tend to talk of the two markets almost interchangeably.

Internet pointers

The government's Debt Management Office at www.dmo.gov.uk/ is now the main official source for information on the gilt-edged market and the stocks in issue. Included in the publications listed on the site is a useful guide for private investors called *Gilts: An Investors Guide*, which may be downloaded free. Information on gilt-edged market turnover is available on the London Stock exchange site at www.londonstockexchange.com/. However, the Bank of England site at www.bankofengland.co.uk/ still carries a certain amount of historical information on gilts, including the introduction of gilt strips, and provides forms for those wishing to buy or sell gilts via the Bank's brokerage service. Investment websites in the UK are generally equity-oriented and information on gilts or bonds in general is more limited. But the *Financial Times* site at www.ft.com/ includes a 'capital markets' section that covers representative bond prices and yields. Information on the changes to the gilt settlement system may be found at the CREST site at www.crestco.co.uk/. Some background information on investment in gilts is available at the site of Kauders Portfolio Management at www.gilt.co.uk/. You may look at the bond yield curve for different countries in the 'international bonds' section of the international Bloomberg site at www.bloomberg.com/markets/. The Peter Temple Linksite at www.cix.co.uk/~ptemple/ also provides a link to a number of information sources on bonds.

14 Banks, borrowers and bad debts

Banks occupy a special place in the economic and financial system. Industrial companies may be allowed to go to the wall. Banks are normally viewed with a more protective eye by the authorities, although there is no such thing as a blanket guarantee of support for a bank in trouble.

Why the special treatment? First, there are not many aspects of economic life that can function without a stable banking system. Second, banking is a business that depends on confidence – allow the confidence to be destroyed and you are a fair way to destroying the banks. Third, banks play a vital role in the creation of money: something that governments like to keep within their control. Fourth, they play a central role in the operation of payment systems around the world.

To see two of these considerations at work, look back to the events surrounding the collapse of Barings, one of the City's oldest merchant banks, early in 1995. Barings had lost over £800m – considerably more than the total shareholders' money in the business – through wild and probably unauthorized gambles by a trader in the derivatives markets of the Far East (see also Chapter 18). The bank was bust. Should the Bank of England step in to save it with tax-payers' money?

After a week-end of intensive discussions with the London banking community (which was not on its own prepared to undertake a rescue while the size of the bill was still unknown) the Bank of England decided against bailing out Barings. On the one side was the desire to sustain the reputation of the City and confidence in its banking system. On the other, Barings was judged to be a fairly small player and it was not thought that there was great **systemic risk** in allowing it to fail. In other words, the knock-on effect on the banking system as a whole was judged to be fairly small. Later, the main operations of Barings were taken over by Dutch banking group

ING which was prepared to pump in cash to replace the missing millions. Consequently, while holders of the bank's shares and other securities lost out, there was no loss to Barings' depositors.

Deposits, advances and liquid funds

The best way to understand what is written about banking is to start by looking at what a bank is. This is particularly important now that the growth of telephone banking and Internet banking have concentrated attention on the techniques for delivering banking services, perhaps at the expense of focusing on the services themselves. At its simplest, a bank takes **retail deposits** from private individuals and others, and lends money (makes **advances**) to borrowers. A certain proportion of the money it takes in as deposits is held in **liquid** or **near-liquid** form: as cash or in a form in which it can readily be turned into cash. This is a safeguard in case some **depositors** want their money back. Another proportion will normally be held in the form of investments which are a little less liquid but can still be cashed in if necessary. The remainder can be lent to customers.

Borrowed money and shareholders' money

The detail may vary, but the principle is much the same for most **deposit-taking institutions**, including **building societies** which are really just a specialist form of bank whose business in the past has been to lend mainly to homebuyers. In practice, banks are not completely dependent on retail deposits because they also borrow **wholesale funds** in the money markets, which add to the money they have available to lend.

Like any company, a bank needs some money of its own – shareholders' funds – as well as the borrowed money it obtains from depositors or in the money markets. But banks are very much more **highly geared** than most industrial and commercial companies. They use a lot of borrowed money and relatively little of their own. How this structure translates into a simlified bank balance sheet is shown in Table 14.1:

The bank in the example in Table 14.1 has only £100 of its own money against £1,000 of borrowed money from depositors. Its total resources are thus £1,100. It holds £100 (equivalent to 10 per cent of its deposits) in liquid form, a further £250 as investments and lends the remaining £750.

ASSETS:

	£	
Liquid assets	100	
Investments	250	
Loans to customers (Advances)	750	
		1,100

FINANCED BY:

Current and deposit accounts	1,000	
Share capital and reserves	100	
(shareholders' funds)		
	1,100	

Table 14.1

The money creation process

How do banks create money? Assume that the bank in our example in Table 14.1 attracts a further £100 of deposits. It will hold £10 of this as cash and lend the remaining £90. The customer who borrows the £90 spends it on, say, a piece of office equipment. He pays the £90 to the office equipment supplier, who deposits it in his own bank. This increases the deposits of the supplier's bank by £90 of which the supplier's bank will lend £81, holding back £9 in cash form for safety. And so on. Since the money finds its way back into the banking system at each stage, that original £100 of extra deposits in the first bank actually generates – in this case – a further £1,000 of spending power in the economy.

If the proportion of their deposits that banks held in liquid form were lower (8 per cent, say) each additional £100 of deposits would create proportionately more spending power. One of the ways central banks sometimes try to control expansion of the **money supply** (see below) is by varying the permissible ratio between deposits and the amount held as **reserve assets**, which covers cash and certain other near-cash items (**reserve assets ratio**), though this system is no longer used by the British regulator.

The most commonly quoted measures of money supply in the press in Britain are M_0 ('M nought') and M_4 ('M four'). The M_0 measure comprises notes and coins in circulation plus banks' balances at the Bank of England. The broader M_4 measure covers notes and coins plus private-sector current and deposit accounts with banks and building societies and private-sector wholesale deposits.

A bank works on the principle that no more than a small proportion of depositors will want their money back at any one time and this calculation affects the proportion of deposits held in liquid form (the **liquidity ratio**). And a glance back at the simplified bank balance sheet in Table 14.1 shows the main ways a bank can get into trouble. If depositors suddenly lose confidence in a particular bank, they may all try to get their money back at the same time and a **run on the bank** develops. This does not mean that the bank is necessarily unsound, but may cause it to collapse all the same. The bank will not be able to get back rapidly the money it has advanced to customers and if it runs out of cash it may be forced to close its doors.

Whatever his problems, a banker is virtually obliged to maintain that his bank is totally sound until he has to close the doors. Any admission of difficulties will worry depositors and make them more likely to withdraw their money. So statements from bankers that everything in the garden is rosy must be treated with a large dose of salt. It may be true, but the banker would be equally obliged to say this if it wasn't.

This illustrates one of the paradoxes on which a banking system rests. Even the soundest of banks is sound only as long as its depositors think that it is sound. It explains why central banks play a vital role.

Rescues, recycling and lifeboats

To prevent a run if the bank is basically sound, the central bank will often organize a **recycling** operation. Banks which are not under any pressure from depositors will be persuaded to make deposits with the troubled bank to replace its vanishing deposits from the public. Such a rescue for third-tier money-lending institutions – euphemistically referred to as **secondary banks** – was organized in the 1973–75 period of **financial crisis** or **secondary bank collapse** in Britain. The clearing banks were dragooned into forming a **lifeboat** via which they made money available to secondary banks which had seen their normal deposits melt away.

Capital adequacy requirements

In reality, most of the secondary banks were not sound – their liabilities (what they owed) exceeded the real value of their assets (the money they had lent, much of which they lost). And this brings us to the second way a bank gets into trouble. The bank in our sample balance sheet in Table 14.1 could not lose more than £100 of the money it has lent without becoming insolvent. If it loses £100 of its £750 of advances, this completely wipes out the £100 of shareholders' money in the business. Any further losses and it will not be able to cover what it owes to depositors. The problems of the Barings bank in 1995 illustrated this process at work.

Again, a banker has to judge what 'cushion' of shareholders' money he needs to allow for any likely losses on his business activities. And the central bank normally makes doubly sure by imposing certain **capital adequacy ratios** which stipulate the amount of its own money a bank needs relative to its total assets. Since a bank that operated with less of its own money and more borrowed money could have an advantage over its competitors (though at greater risk), there have been moves in recent years to impose international standards for capital adequacy (see below).

This **capital ratio** or **solvency ratio** is not a simple calculation: the regulator will look at the make-up of a bank's business and decide that the risks that need to be covered are higher for some types of business than others. Mortgage loans on residential property, for example, are judged safer than lending to small businesses. And it will take into account some **off balance sheet risks** that do not appear in the accounts: forms of **guarantee** and **underwriting commitment** the bank may have undertaken or risks involved in **derivatives**. Nor are shareholders' funds the exact measure of the bank's own money that the authorities adopt. In calculating its **capital base** to arrive at a figure for primary capital a bank may be able to include certain **subordinated loans** (see glossary) but will have to make deductions for other items. A **risk asset ratio** shows **primary capital** as a proportion of risk-weighted assets. Capital ratios are part of what are normally described as **prudential ratios**: ratios dictated by banking prudence rather than by the central bank's need to control the money supply via the banking system.

Under the international agreement known as the **Basle Accord**, all banks are required to maintain primary capital equal to at least 8 per cent of their risk-weighted assets (mainly, the loans they make). Above this minimum, central banks may impose whatever ratios they consider appropriate to individual banks within their jurisdiction, to reflect differing degrees of perceived risk.

Banking in the new millennium

While the relatively simple business of taking deposits and making loans remains at the core of banking activities, banks are considerably more complex operations nowadays. There are six changes in particular to note.

- The dependence on retail deposits from the public has been reduced. Today's banks raise large amounts of the money that they need in the form of **wholesale funds** in the money markets (see Chapter 15).

- The process of **disintermediation** that we touched on earlier has brought big changes to the ways that banks operate. No longer do they simply borrow and lend. This is because many of their larger customers, instead of simply borrowing from a bank, raise money by selling **debt securities** in a market instead. To replace interest income that they have lost, banks need to be active in the markets in which securities are issued: underwriting the issue of securities, arranging their sale and distribution, etc. In this way they can earn fee income to replace some of the interest income. In practice, many have also tried to boost their income by more active dealing in securities markets (**own account trading**).

- The scale of loan required by major companies is often too large for a single bank to take on board. So **syndicated loans** have become more common. Suppose a company wants to raise £200m. An individual bank might be reluctant to take the risk of lending this amount to a single customer. Instead, a syndicate of, say, ten banks is put together, each of which contributes £20m of the loan, which is organized by one bank as **lead manager**.

- As we saw earlier, the changes brought about by the Big Bang in Britain allowed banks to own **stockbroking** and **marketmaking** businesses, thus introducing them to aspects of securities trading that had been closed to them before. Some plunged more enthusiastically into the new areas than others.

- Traditional banks with high-street branches have had to adapt to the information technology revolution and learn new ways of interacting with their customers. The first step was **telephone banking**, allowing customers to carry out transactions without going near a bank branch. This was followed by **Internet banking**, allowing customers to manage their accounts from a home computer. While traditional banks offered Internet services, the way was also paved for true **Internet banks**, operating only over the Internet and perhaps with no physical presence in the UK. And, at the same time, traditional banks faced competition from unusual sources as supermarkets offered savings and money-transmission services.

• Banks have had a central part to play in the development of the mushrooming markets in **derivatives** (see Chapter 18). Derivative products such as futures and options evolved as a way of hedging or reducing risk. Such contracts allow risks to be transferred to those best able to manage them. But the derivatives markets rapidly acquired a momentum as gambling markets where large amounts of money could be made or lost on small movements in the prices of commodities, currencies, bonds, equities and many other financial products. It was gambles in the financial futures markets that brought down the merchant bank Barings in 1995.

Off balance sheet risks

By no means all derivatives business takes place in the public markets. The big commercial banks are major vendors of **over-the-counter** or **OTC** derivatives products. These are products that can be tailored for (and sold to) individual clients. A company wants to arrange an inter-est-rate **swap** (see Chapter 17) or a **cap** on its borrowing costs (see Chapter 15). It goes to its bank. For a fee, the bank sells it the desired product. The bank might agree that it will accept the obligation to pay the interest on a £100m floating-rate loan the company has raised and charge the company a fixed rate of interest instead (a swap). Or it might agree to compensate the company for any rise above, say, 9 per cent in the interest rate on a £100m floating-rate loan (a cap). And vast-ly more complex hedging products than these can be devised.

Selling OTC derivatives products of these kinds had become very big business for the banks by the 1990s and there has been con-siderable comment in the press and elsewhere about the risks involved. What, for example, if interest rates rose sharply and the banks had to pay out under the arrangements whereby they had contracted to insure against increases in interest rates on floating-rate loans?

In practice, the banks lay off their risks. A bank may agree to pay the floating-rate interest on a loan and charge a fixed rate in a swap arrangement. But it will match this commitment by charging a floating rate of interest and accepting responsibility for a fixed rate of interest on a loan for another client. Provided neither client defaults (the **counterparty risk**) the two transactions simply cancel each other out, with the bank taking a small cut in the middle.

But as derivatives became more and more weird and wonderful, observers began to question whether the banks' arrangements for hedging their risks were likely to be proof against all eventualities. So complex were some of the derivative products dreamed up by the **rocket scientists** (mathematical geniuses) whom the banks increasingly employed that few if any in the upper echelons of banking could understand them or the risks they implied. The directors thus became increasingly dependent on the judgement of those rocket scientists and the computerized risk-matching systems that they devised.

The risks inherent in these derivative products are mainly **off balance sheet** for the banks: they do not appear in the main financial statements. For example, if you look at the accounts of Barclays Bank for 1998 you will see that loans made by the bank to customers were shown at about £96 billion in its group balance sheet. Excluded here was a further £1,600 billion of off-balance-sheet financial instruments entered into by the bank. This figure was, of course, the 'principal amount' of the contracts (the amount subject to interest rate or exchange rate undertakings) and not the amount at risk. And since many of the risks cancelled each other out, the 'fair values' of the bank's derivative positions were only around £14 billion on the positive side and £16 billion on the negative side.

Such figures are pretty typical of the major commercial banks. But, reflecting international evaluation of derivatives risk, press comment is increasingly homing in on the adequacy of risk-evaluation methods and control systems in the derivatives markets. Predictions of derivative-induced crises in the financial system are not uncommon.

Banking crises and banking cycles

A visitor from Mars who surveyed recent banking history could be forgiven for concluding that it consisted of periodic crises interspersed with relatively short periods of calm. In Britain we have had three major upsets in the past 30 years: the property and secondary bank crisis of the mid-1970s; the Latin-American debt crisis of the 1980s (very much an international problem); and the property and small business loan crisis of the early 1990s.

The secondary banking crisis we have already touched on. The **Latin-American debt crisis** or, in wider terms, the **Third World debt**

crisis had its roots in the 1970s when the major commercial banks, particularly in the United States, drew in deposits from oil-producing countries that had generated massive revenue surpluses from the oil price increases of that decade. Much of the money was lent to Third World countries – **less developed countries** or **LDCs** in the common banking euphemism – which seemed good business at the time. The total debt of the Third World was put in the mid-1980s at over $1,000 billion. For a variety of reasons – including high interest rates and low prices for basic commodities – many of these borrowers found themselves unable to **service** their loans (meet interest charges and capital repayments).

The outcome was an excellent illustration of the old banking adage that you are at your banker's mercy if you owe him £5 and he is at your mercy if you owe him £5m. A game of poker – for somewhat larger sums – ensued. If the banks admitted they would not get their money back and wrote off their loans, they would be shown to be insolvent or at least they would fail the capital adequacy tests. So they attempted to maintain the fiction that the loans were sound. To do so they frequently arranged a **rescheduling** of the original loans. At best this meant extending the terms of the loan to give the debtor countries more time to pay. At worst it meant lending them more money (which they were unlikely to be able to repay) to meet the instalments of capital and interest (which they could not otherwise pay) on the original loans. Without rescheduling, the debtor countries would be forced to **default** on the loans (fail to keep to the terms) and the lending banks would then be forced to classify the loans as **non-performing**.

The debtor countries in their turn had a difficult choice. If they simply defaulted, they would find it difficult to borrow again in the international capital markets. But the threat of default was a powerful weapon in bargaining with the lending banks.

The game of make-believe that rescheduling made possible was somewhat disrupted in May 1987 when Citicorp, one of the major American lenders, announced a $3 billion **provision** or **reserve** against its Third World loans. This meant it was not writing down the value of specific loans but was accepting that it stood to lose at least $3 billion of its Third World lending. Citicorp could afford to make the provision but it posed problems for some other lenders with less capital who were forced by Citicorp's action to acknowledge realities. The major British banks made similar provisions in due course. The banking emperors were not seen entirely without clothes, but were left looking distinctly chilly in their underpants.

The saga provided several insights into the nature of banking. First, banks do not always write off loans as soon as they suspect that the money is lost. While the banking authorities require banks to provide against losses on a prudent and timely basis, an observer might conclude that they sometimes fudge the realities until they have accumulated enough reserves to be able to afford the write-offs. Banking is not only a matter of confidence. The make-believe element is often important.

Second, 'profit' in banking is a more than usually nebulous concept. A bank declares good profits in the years that it makes the loans that will ultimately bring it severe losses. Third, dud loans can sometimes be sold – at a price. In the later years of the Latin-American debt crisis a **secondary market in bank debt** emerged. It worked like this: a bank with non-performing loans to the Republic of Erewhon might decide it would rather take its losses and get shot of the whole business. So it would sell the loans at, say, 50p in the pound to some other financial institution that was prepared to take a gamble on the amount it could recover. The prices at which the debt of different countries traded in this secondary market gave a pretty fair view of bankers' estimates of the likelihood of recovery.

No sooner was the worst of the Latin-American debt crisis out of the way than banks internationally were again lending very heavily for property development and purchase in the late 1980s (see Chapter 20). In Britain, very substantial lending on commercial property was exacerbated by a great expansion of lending to small businesses. In the severe recession of the early 1990s in Britain, property values fell like a stone and numerous small businesses went bust. Many billion pounds worth of lending had to be written off by the British clearing banks alone.

Rescues and reconstructions

There is nothing like a period of high interest rates accompanied by economic recession to expose the financing follies of the previous era. In the early 1990s companies that had expanded over-fast by takeover in the 1980s, and financed on borrowed money, were going to the wall like flies. In some cases there was no choice but to let the companies be wound up. In others, the lending banks decided that they would lose less in the long run by trying to keep the company going, probably with the help of a **capital reconstruction** or **capital reorganization**.

No two cases were quite alike, so we will take a hypothetical example to illustrate the main principles. Suppose Splurgeandspend Holdings had gone on a takeover spree in the great Thatcherite days of the 1980s and borrowed most of the money to do it. By 1991 the interest rate on its loans had more than doubled and, with the recession, its profits had halved. It faced an interest bill of £150m a year and had profits of only £70m before interest. Result: a pre-tax loss of £80m.

Splurgeandspend's total borrowings at this point were about £1 billion. The value of the businesses it had bought in the 1980s had slumped heavily and many of the assets required writing down to realistic values. Once these write-downs had been made, the value of the group's assets would have been £200m less than the money it owed to the banks. It had a **deficiency on shareholders' funds** of £200m. Add to this the fact that Splurgeandspend was running out of cash and had no way to raise more.

The lending banks knew that, if they closed the business down on the spot, they would get very little for the assets and would lose a large part of their loans. Since some of Splurgeandspend's businesses would have been quite promising in more normal economic conditions, they decided to try to keep the company going. First, they agreed to convert £300m of their loans into shares in the company at a price of 4p per share (the shares had, of course, slumped to virtually nothing in the market). This **equity-for-debt swap** would eliminate £300m of Splurgeandspend's borrowings and therefore also eliminate the interest charge on this amount.

Second, they converted a further £200m of their existing loans into a new kind of subordinated loan on which no interest would be payable for five years. Third, they agreed to waive the interest due on the remaining £500m of loans for one year to give the company a breathing space to sort itself out and sell some of its businesses (if it could) to raise cash. Finally, they agreed to make available a new overdraft facility of £30m to provide the company with a little cash to tide itself over.

Splurgeandspend thus has no interest bill to worry about for a year. For the following four years it will pay interest on only £500m of borrowings and thereafter on £700m. It has a chance of survival. But there is a price – banks are not charities. The company's share capital is massively expanded by the conversion of £300m of loans into shares. The original shareholders are left with only 5 per cent of the enlarged capital and are thus virtually wiped out. The rest belongs to the banks. If the company recovers, they will reap the rewards. The major British banks do not usually own shares in companies. But the early-1990s recession left them temporarily with quite significant shareholdings in troubled companies that arose through this kind of reconstruction.

The major problem in organizing a reconstruction of this kind, if the company has loans from many different banks, lies in getting all the banks to agree. Where the company has a syndicated loan from, say, 20 different banks there will often be some banks that want to close the company down immediately and recover what they can. Recognizing this problem, the Bank of England developed guidelines known as the **London Rules**, designed to persuade banks to give troubled companies a chance of surviving where possible. Some overseas banks with a different lending culture were not always easy to convince.

Banking supervision in Britain

In the past, banking institutions were regulated by the Bank of England and building societies had their own regulatory structure. The 1987 **Banking Act** had abolished an earlier distinction between banks and **licensed deposit takers** or **LDTs**, which had comprised mainly the less established or second-tier concerns. Under this Act, all but the smallest deposit-taking institutions were allowed to call themselves banks provided they satisfied prudential requirements as to the way the business was run (and provided the people running it were judged fit and proper).

But critics had long suggested that the Bank of England had a conflict of interest in that it was supervisor of the banks as well as being the body which advised on (and implemented) monetary policy. Cynics asked whether the Bank would really be prepared to advise the government to, say, raise interest rates at a time when this might damage the banks for which it had supervisory responsibility.

The position has now been resolved with the Bank of England acquiring greater responsibility for monetary policy but ceding its regulatory powers over the banks to the new 'super-regulator', the **Financial Services Authority** (see Chapter 22). The Bank still, however, has responsibility for the stability of the banking system as a whole. The **FSA** has also taken over responsibility for building societies.

Internet pointers

The major UK banks have their own corporate websites which are used both to promote their services to customers and to provide information to shareholders. Background information on banking in the UK is available at the British Bankers' Association site at www. bankfacts.org.uk/. The Chartered Institute of Bankers site at www.cib.org.uk/ is aimed more at those who work in banking. Needless to say, the Bank of England website at www. bankofengland.co.uk/ also contains information of relevance to the banking business. The European Central Bank site is at www.ecb.int/ and the European Bank for Reconstruction and Development at www.ebrd.com/. International banking and related organizations include the World Bank at www.worldbank.org/, the International Monetary Fund at www.imf.org/ and the Bank for International Settlements at www.bis.org/.

15 The money markets

Money market reports are an acquired taste. Few readers who are not in the money business will get completely to grips with their technicalities. But when the **money markets** are giving an important signal about likely trends in **interest rates**, a less technical interpretation of what is going on will probably appear elsewhere in the financial pages. Money markets are the markets in which money is borrowed and lent in large quantities for relatively short periods (often very short). Effectively they are a market in deposits and advances. But they are also a market in various forms of short-term security that are almost the equivalent of money.

Responsibility for the money markets is now divided (they used to be virtually the sole responsibility of the Bank of England). Supervision comes courtesy of the **Financial Services Authority**. The **Debt Management Office** (an executive agency of the Treasury) is responsible for managing the government's own cash flows and for issue of Treasury bills (see below). And the **Bank of England**, as before, operates in the money markets to implement monetary policy and smooth out cash imbalances between the Bank and the private sector. But it also does considerably more than this nowadays.

Very shortly after the New Labour government came to power in 1997, it handed over operational responsibility for monetary policy to the Bank of England. Interest rate decisions had previously been made by the government and simply implemented by the Bank. As from 1997, the government retained the right to intervene only in exceptional circumstances and for a limited period. The Bank's remit was to aim to hold the level of inflation, on a measure that excluded mortgage interest, at around 2.5 per cent. Since interest rates are the main instrument now used in the control of inflation, this means that the Bank's decisions on lending rates are crucial.

The extent to which interest rates are determined by the market or dictated by the authorities (in this case the Bank) often gives rise to

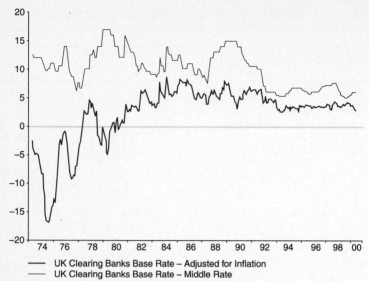

Figure 15.1 *Short-term interest rates: nominal and real* Short-term interest rates in Britain, as represented by the UK clearing banks' base rate, reflect the country's chequered economic history. The peak in 1975 reflects the runaway inflation of that period. The peaks in the earlier 1980s reflect the incoming Conservative government's attempts to squeeze inflation out of the system (which resulted in a greatly over-valued exchange rate for sterling), while the peak at the end of the 1980s is witness to the medicine applied to compensate for the runaway Lawson (or Thatcher?) boom. The heavier line shows the level of real interest rates, when inflation is deducted. Note that, even with high nominal rates, real interest rates were often negative in the 1970s because of the very high inflation of that era. Source: *Datastream*.

confusion. Basically, the position is as follows. Interest rates day to day are determined by supply and demand for money and by normal competitive pressures. The Bank of England does not directly dictate the rate that your bank charges on an overdraft! But private-sector commercial banks do, on occasion, need to borrow from the government via the Bank or may be put in a position where they need to do so (we will come to the mechanisms later). In other words, the Bank of England, as the country's central bank, is **lender of last resort** to the banking system. The level at which it is prepared to lend, and the terms, can be used to influence the level of interest rates across the economy.

Commercial banks are not willingly going to lend at a rate of interest below what they have to pay for money themselves. Thus, if the Bank of England raises the rate of interest at which it is prepared to lend money to the commercial banks, they in turn will normally need to push up the rates that they charge to customers. So a rise in the Bank of England's lending rate will work its way right through the banking system and will, in practice, probably mean that the rate you pay on your overdraft goes up too. Commentators on the broadcast media in particular are often less than precise when they talk about 'interest rates' going up or down, without making it clear what interest rates they are talking about.

The body that makes decisions on interest rates at the Bank is the **Monetary Policy Committee**. It comprises four Bank members and four outside experts, plus the Governor of the Bank. Decisions are made on a majority vote, with the governor having a casting vote in case of deadlock. It meets once a month and its decisions are published immediately. About 13 days afterwards, minutes of the meeting are published. The press comments extensively on the likelihood of a movement in official interest rates ahead of each meeting. Later, the minutes also come in for close scrutiny because they show how much agreement or dissent there was among the members and may therefore give a hint as to the most likely outcome at the next meeting. As we have seen, market rates of interest will reflect demand and supply in the market for short-term funds, but will also, of course, reflect expectations about future official rate moves. The publication of the Committee's minutes does help to lessen the uncertainties by providing an insight into its thinking.

Functions of the money markets

One function of the money markets is to transmit official interest-rate decisions. Why else are money markets needed? They are a form of short-term counterpart to the long-term investment markets of the stock exchange. The stock exchange funnels long-term savings into long-term investment. The money markets allow money which is available for shorter periods to be directed to those who can use it, and also have the virtue of transmuting very short-term deposits into money which can be lent for longer periods. As we saw, they are not just a market in deposits but also in a variety of forms of short-term IOU or **financial instrument** which are close to money because they are **marketable**. In other words, they can be turned quickly into money by a sale in the market. We will look at these later.

So the money markets fulfil several functions. First, at any one time there will be some banks which have a very temporary shortage of money and others which have a surplus: money has been withdrawn from one bank and deposited with another. A mechanism is needed so that banks which are temporarily short can borrow the funds they need, and those with a temporary surplus can put it to work.

Second, banks will in any case want to hold a proportion of their funds in a form which allows them to get at it quickly if needed. This means putting it on deposit with other institutions or buying short-term financial instruments.

Third, while banks derive a large proportion of their sterling funds from the accounts of individual depositors (**retail deposits**), they also borrow in very large amounts from companies, financial institutions and local government bodies that have short-term surpluses of cash to put to work (**wholesale funds**). Likewise, these bodies borrow in the money markets when short of cash.

Finally, we come back to the money markets as a bridge between the government and the private sector. A mechanism is needed to iron out imbalances in the supply of money between the **banking system** as a whole and the government. There will be times when the commercial banking system is short of money because, for example, individuals or companies are withdrawing funds from their bank accounts to pay their tax bills to the government. But the authorities can also influence the amount of money available to the commercial banking system *vis-a-vis* the government by selling gilt-edged stocks or Treasury bills to the private sector, which has to transfer money to the government to pay for them. However, if these are sold directly to the banks rather than to the **non-bank private sector** (to individuals and organizations other than banking institutions or government bodies) they will not directly affect broad money supply since they do not act on the liabilities of the banking system.

Operations such as these can create a shortage of money in the banking system. For example, suppose the government issues gilt-edged stock for sale to the public (see Chapter 13 for the mechanisms). To pay for, say, £500m of stock the public would have to withdraw £500m from its deposits with the banking system. Therefore this money would leave the commercial banks and be paid to the government. All else being equal, a shortage of cash would be created in the banking system which the Bank could use to increase its influence on the commercial banks.

The money markets provide mechanisms to cope with all these differing requirements. They fall into two main parts (we are talking now of the sterling money markets – a market in foreign currency deposits exists alongside them). There is the market that provides the interface between the government and the private sector, which used to be known as the **discount market** when it operated rather differently in the past. And there is the market in money between private-sector institutions, sometimes referred to as the **inter-bank market**, though its clientele is not limited to banks.

How the Bank influences interest rates

In the past, a specialist kind of bank called a **discount house** used to act as a buffer between the commercial banks and the Bank of England in its money-market operations. The discount houses made a living by borrowing surplus short-term money from the commercial banks and using it to buy **financial instruments** such as **Treasury bills**, commercial **bills of exchange** and **sterling certificates of deposit** (these are all forms of short-term IOU which we look at later). The money the commercial banks lent to the discount houses was **at call**. In other words, the banks could ask to have it back when they needed it. This could pose a problem for the discount houses if they had already used the money to invest in bills of exchange. So the Bank of England stepped in. When the discount houses were short of cash they had the right to sell bills of exchange, Treasury bills and local authority bills to the Bank (**rediscount** them with – sell them at a discount to – the Bank). This amounted to lending by the Bank to the discount houses and provided them with the cash they needed. And this cash found its way in turn into the banking system as it was used to repay what the discount houses had borrowed from the commercial banks.

The mechanism is rather different today because a far wider range of banks and financial institutions now have a trading relationship with the Bank of England and the discount-house monopoly has gone. But the principles remain much the same. These approved institutions have the right, in effect, to take a loan from the Bank of England when they find themselves short of cash. They take the loan by selling **financial instruments** to the Bank, as before. But the range of financial instruments that the Bank will accept has been widened, notably by the inclusion of **gilt repos** (see Chapter 13) and Bank of England **Euro Bills**.

The crucial point in all of this is the rate of interest at which the Bank is prepared to lend to the commercial banks – its **Official**

Dealing Rate – because this is what influences interest rates throughout the banking system. Nowadays, this rate is called the **repo rate** (we will come to the reason in a minute). So it is the repo rate that the **Monetary Policy Committee** announces after its deliberations each month and the repo rate is thus the measure of official interest rates in the UK. The Bank of England's lending rate had different names in the past, including **Minimum Lending Rate (MLR)** and, further back, **Bank Rate** and you will still see these terms referred to occasionally. Do not, incidentally, confuse Bank Rate with **Bank Base Rates**, which are covered later in this chapter.

Because of the constant flow of funds from private-sector institutions to the government and vice versa, the two will rarely be in balance and this creates the need for the Bank's **open market operations**. Early each working day the Bank of England estimates the likely size of the shortage or surplus in the money market on that day (a **shortage** is the amount by which the commercial banking system is likely to be short of money and will therefore have to borrow from the government) and may revise this estimate at later points in the day if necessary. Its estimates go out on the Reuters and Telerate screen information systems. It also publishes during the day the details of how it dealt with the shortage. It may have bought **bills of exchange**. It may have entered into arrangements to buy securities and sell them back later (**repurchase agreements** or **repos**) which act as a short-term loan. This is where we get the term **repo rate**, as it is effectively the rate of interest charged for this type of loan. These details will sometimes appear in the press's technical money-market reports, which often make rather dry reading.

The market participants therefore know the rates at which the Bank will be prepared to deal in the market. And the Bank posts the rates at which it has conducted its open market operations immediately after the completion of each round of operations.

Bills of exchange

The discount houses got their name because they **discounted** bills of exchange: they bought them at a discount to their face value. To see how the bill market works we need to examine the mechanism more closely.

Bills of exchange are a form of short-term IOU widely used to finance trade and provide credit. They work like this. Company A sells £1m worth of goods to Company B. It 'draws' (writes out) a bill of exchange for £1m which it sends to Company B. This bill is an acknowledgement by Company B that it owes the £1m, and Company B signs it to show that it accepts the debt. The bill may state that the money is not payable until some date in the future: perhaps in three months. The bill returns to Company A.

Company A then has a choice. It can hold on to the bill, in which case Company B will pay it the £1m in three months. Or, if it needs the cash sooner, it can sell the bill to somebody else. Whoever holds the bill when the three months are up gets the £1m from Company B.

Bills of exchange do not pay interest. But if Company A sells the bill before it is due for payment, it will receive less than face value. In other words, it **sells at a discount**. Remember the basic principle once again: money receivable in the future is worth less than money you have today. So if the bill is due for payment in, say, three months, the buyer might pay only £98.50 for every £100 of face value. The buyer is thus getting a profit of £1.50 per £100 when the bill is repaid at face value, which is equivalent to receiving interest: the discount is usually expressed as an annual rate of interest. When the Bank of England is said to have bought bills at 5.5 per cent, it means that the Bank bought them at a discount to their face value which equated to an annual interest rate of 5.5 per cent. Thus if interest rates generally come down, the prices of bills will rise (the discount will be smaller).

The bill described above is a **trade bill**, issued by one company to another. But a bill may be **accepted** by a bank, in which case it becomes a **bank bill**. By putting its name on the bill, the bank agrees it will pay the amount of the bill on maturity, even if the company which acknowledged the debt should default: it is therefore a form of guarantee. Accepting bills in this way was an important part of the business of the UK merchant banks in the past, hence the term **accepting houses** which used to be used for the top-tier merchant banks. A bill accepted by a bank, because of the security it offers, sells at the very lowest interest rates (i.e. the highest price). Any monetary sector institution may accept bills, but the Bank of England only buys or lends against bills accepted by **eligible banks**, hence the term **eligible bills**. The Bank maintains a published list of eligible banks; in general these are banks which have a substantial and broadly based sterling acceptance business.

Bank bills also provide a substitute for overdrafts in big company financing. A company arranges an **acceptance credit** with a bank, which allows the company to issue bills up to an agreed limit. Each bill is accepted by the bank in return for a fee and can be sold at a discount to raise cash for the company. The effective rate of interest may be lower than on other forms of borrowing.

Treasury bills

Treasury bills work in much the same way as commercial bills of exchange, but are issued by the government. They are sold at a discount, with an implicit rate of interest, via a weekly tender process, now managed by the Debt Management Office (it used to be the Bank of England). The amount supplied at the weekly tender varies to reflect government cash flows and to ensure a minimum stock of bills in issue. The *Financial Times* carries on a Monday a table with the result of the Treasury bill tender. As well as sterling bills issued by the DMO, bills denominated in euros are now in use. These **euro bills** are issued by the Bank of England.

Certificates of deposit

Certificates of deposit (**CDs**) are a method of **securitizing** bank deposits. A company with spare cash deposits £500,000 with a bank. It agrees to lock the money away for a year, thus getting the best interest rate. The bank issues the company with a certificate of deposit for the £500,000, stating the rate of interest payable and the date when the deposit will be repaid. If the company needs its cash before the year is up, it can sell the certificate of deposit in the money market. The buyer acquires the right to receive repayment of the £500,000 bank deposit (plus interest) when the year is up. Certificates of deposit may, like Treasury bills and eligible bills, be bought and sold by banks and other money market participants. But unlike Treasury and eligible bills, CDs cannot be used in operations with the Bank of England, whereby the market obtains funds through the Bank's open market operations.

The virtue of the certificate of deposit is that the bank (in our example) has acquired a deposit for a year and knows it will have a year's use of the money. But the company which lent for a year and received the CD can in practice have its money back at any time by selling the CD.

The inter-bank market

We started with the market in which the Bank of England deals with commercial banks (the former discount market) because it illustrates how the Bank can influence interest rates. But banks wanting to borrow and lend money in the wholesale markets are not confined to dealing with the authorities. They also operate in the other sectors of the money market, in which banks, local authorities, institutions and companies can borrow from or lend to each other rather than dealing with the government. The largest and most important of these markets is the **inter-bank market**, where banks and others deal with each other, often through a **money broker** who puts the parties together in return for a commission. The market divides further into the sterling inter-bank market and the inter-bank market in foreign currencies, particularly the dollar.

There has been enormous expansion in the use made of the money markets by large companies in recent years. And the 1989 Budget introduced changes that helped to break down the distinction between money markets and the established debt securities markets (stock exchange and euromarket) by allowing the issue of financial instruments with a life of up to five years. Thus a company wishing to borrow for five years should have the choice of following the securities market route or the money market route. Whereas the securities markets are open to private investors, the wholesale money markets are very definitely a 'professionals only' area.

Commercial paper and MTNs

Commercial paper is another feature of the money markets and an example of the **securitization** process. For companies it offers an alternative to bank borrowing or to an existing form of short-term security: the bill of exchange.

In essence, commercial paper is just another form of unsecured short-term IOU, issued in bearer form. It is normally issued at a discount rather than paying interest, with an initial life of up to a year, though three months would be more common.

The sterling commercial paper market got under way in London in May 1986 and initially was open only to very large established companies. These conditions have subsequently been relaxed, opening the way for medium-sized companies to tap the market.

The issue process goes as follows. A company wanting to tap the market gets a bank to set up a programme for it: say, £200m. This defines the maximum amount that the company may have outstanding at any one time. At the same time dealers are appointed. When the company wants to raise cash it alerts the dealers, or the dealers may take the initiative by telling the company that there is demand among investors for paper of a particular maturity. The dealers, who are constantly in touch with potential investors, find buyers for the paper. The paper is sold at a discount to its face value which provides the equivalent of a rate of interest. The buyers may be institutions or companies looking for a short-term investment.

When the original issue falls due for repayment, further issues can be made to replace it. Thus, though it is a very short-term market, by **rolling over** issues in this way companies may use it as a medium-term source of finance. In addition to the sterling commercial paper market there is an active international equivalent – the **eurocommercial paper market** – where companies can similarly set up programmes, perhaps allowing them to issue in a number of different currencies.

There is also now a longer-term form of money market borrowing in the **medium term note** or **MTN**, which has a life of one to five years. Like commercial paper, it has its euromarket equivalent in the **euro medium term note** or **EMTN**.

Multiple option facility

The **multiple option facility** or **MOF** is another form of arrangement for tapping the money markets which was popular in the late 1980s and might possibly see a resurgence. It emerged in various shapes but a typical arrangement might have been as follows.

A company got one particular bank to put together a panel of banks who agreed to make available a certain amount of loans – say £150m – for a period of five years. The rate of interest, which would be variable, was set at such-and-such an amount above the benchmark rate of interest when the loans were taken up (say, 20 basis points over the **London Inter-Bank Offered Rate** or **LIBOR** – see below). This £150m was what was known as the **committed facility** or **standby facility**.

Another group of banks was put together, comprising the original banks plus others which were recruited. They formed a **tender panel**. When the company decided it needed cash, the tender panel banks were invited to bid to provide the funds. Those that were flush with cash at the time would have responded, and the bank or banks bidding the lowest rate of interest would have made the loans to the company. If none of the tender panel banks bid at a rate below that on the standby facility, the company would have resorted to raising the money via this standby. Thus it was sure of getting its cash when needed.

The loans made under this arrangement would probably have been short-term: say, for three months. But as one loan fell due for repayment new loans could have been arranged, so for the company it provided the equivalent of medium-term borrowing at a competitive rate of interest. The 'multi-option' refers to the fact that the arrangement allowed for the money to be raised in a number of different forms, which might have included straight loans, acceptances (bills of exchange), foreign currency loans and so on.

Risk hedging

The money markets are also the home of many different types of instrument for limiting exposure to interest rate movements (**hedging** the interest rate risk). A **cap** is really an interest rate option. Say the benchmark interest rate is currently 6 per cent and you reckon a rise to over 8 per cent would seriously damage your business. You can buy a cap from a bank, under which you will be reimbursed for the effects of any increase in the benchmark interest rate above 8 per cent.

A **floor** is an option that works the other way. Suppose you agree with your bank that you will pay a minimum interest rate of 5 per cent, even if market rates drop below this level. The bank will pay you for agreeing this floor, in the same way as you pay the bank for providing a cap. So the proceeds from selling a floor can be used to offset at least part of the cost of a cap. An arrangement that includes both a cap and a floor is known as a **collar** or **cylinder** – it can be used to limit the interest you might have to pay within fairly narrow bands. Companies use these and similar instruments quite extensively to limit their interest rate exposure.

Perhaps **swaps** or **interest rate swaps** should be included in the same category of hedging instruments. For a description of how they work, see Chapter 17.

Interest rate indicators

You will find in the *Financial Times* a list of the interest rates for deposits and different types of short-term financial instruments under the heading of **London money rates**. For each, a range of maturities is covered. Thus, in the case of inter-bank deposits there is a rate for overnight money, for money deposited at seven days' notice, for a

UK INTEREST RATES

LONDON MONEY RATES

Jun 28	Over-night	7 days notice	One month	Three months	Six months	One year
Interbank Sterling	7⅜ - 5¾	6⅛ - 5⅞	6 1/16 - 5 15/16	6 3/16 - 6 1/16	6 5/16 - 6 3/16	6 17/32 - 6 13/32
BBA Sterling LIBOR	-	6 1/16 -	6⅛ -	6 7/32 -	6 11/32 -	6 9/16 -
Sterling CDs	-	-	6 - 5 15/16	6⅛ - 6 3/32	6 5/16 - 6¼	6 17/32 - 6 15/32
Treasury Bills	-	-	5 29/32 - 5 27/32	6 - 5 15/16	-	-
Bank Bills	-	-	5 15/16 - 5⅞	6 3/32 - 6 1/32	-	-
Local authority deps.	6½ - 6⅜	6 3/16 - 5 13/16	6⅛ - 6	6¼ - 6⅛	6 11/32 - 6 7/32	6 9/16 - 6 7/16
Discount Market deps	5 13/16 - 5¾	5⅞ - 5⅝	-	-	-	-

UK clearing bank base lending rate 6 per cent from Feb 10, 2000

	Up to 1 month	1-3 month	3-6 months	6-9 months	9-12 months
Certs of Tax dep. (£100,000)	2¼	5	5	5	5¼

Certs of Tax dep. under £100,000 is 2¼pc. Deposits withdrawn for cash 1¼pc.
Av. tndr rate of discount Jun 23. 5.8630pc. ECGD fixed rate Stlg. Export Finance. make up day May 31, 2000. Agreed rate for period Jun 26, 2000 to Jul 25, 2000, Scheme III 7.56pc. Reference rate for period Apr 29, 2000 to May 31, 2000, Scheme IV & V 6.307pc. Finance House Base Rate 6½pc for June 2000. SONIA Jun 28: 6.3515

Example 15.1 Rates of interest on deposits and money-market instruments in London. Source: *Financial Times.*

month, three months, six months and a year. You can plot the rates quoted for different maturities to produce a **yield curve**. Typically, this is a rising curve, showing that money deposited for short periods earns lower interest than money deposited for six months or a year. But when interest rates are expected to drop, there may be a **negative yield curve** with a lower rate of interest on money deposited for a year than money deposited for a month.

The London money rates table shows the rates of interest on **inter-bank deposits**, **sterling certificates of deposit**, **local authority deposits**, **discount market deposits**, **Treasury bills** and **bank bills**.

Note that the **inter-bank rate** (**sterling LIBOR**) is a far better measure of short-term swings in interest rates than the **bank base rates**. The latter are the yardstick rates of interest quoted by the commercial banks, to which deposit rates and borrowing rates for private individuals are normally geared (see glossary for more detail). Base rates are changed relatively infrequently, and normally to reflect changes in official interest rates by the authorities. The inter-bank rate, on the other hand, is the constantly changing measure of the cost of money in large amounts for the banks themselves.

In addition to sterling interest rates, the *Financial Times* provides a table of short-term money rates in the other major economies together with the rate of US dollar LIBOR. Interest rates for

WORLD INTEREST RATES

DOMESTIC MONEY RATES

Jun 28	Over night	One month	Three mths	Six mths	One year	Lomb. inter.	Dis. rate	Repo rate
Euro-zone	4⅜	4$\frac{7}{16}$	4$\frac{9}{16}$	4$\frac{23}{32}$	5	-	-	4.25
Switzerland	3$\frac{1}{32}$	3$\frac{1}{2}$	3$\frac{11}{32}$	3$\frac{17}{32}$	3¾	-	0.50	-
US	6$\frac{23}{32}$	6⅝	6¾	6$\frac{29}{32}$	7$\frac{5}{32}$	-	6.00	-
Japan	$\frac{1}{16}$	⅛	$\frac{3}{16}$	$\frac{9}{32}$	$\frac{13}{32}$	-	0.50	-
$ Libor BBA fixing*								
Interbank Fixing	-	6$\frac{11}{16}$	6$\frac{25}{32}$	6$\frac{15}{16}$	7$\frac{7}{32}$	-	-	-
US Dollar CDs	-	6.60	6.70	6.85	7.12	-	-	-
Euro Linked Ds	-	4$\frac{7}{16}$	4$\frac{17}{32}$	4$\frac{11}{16}$	4$\frac{31}{32}$	-	-	-
SDR Linked Ds	-	3⅜	3$\frac{17}{32}$	3$\frac{11}{16}$	4$\frac{1}{2}$	-	-	-
BBA Euro Libor	-	4$\frac{7}{16}$	4$\frac{17}{32}$	4$\frac{23}{32}$	5$\frac{1}{32}$	-	-	-
Euro Euribor	-	4.425	4.547	4.716	5.025	-	-	-
EONIA	4.38	-	-	-	-	-	-	-
EURONIA	4.3694	-	-	-	-	-	-	-

* London interbank fixing rate (LIBOR) is the BBA London rate, fixed at 11am (London time).
Mid rates are shown for the domestic Money Rates, US$ CDs, Euro & SDR Linked Deposits (Ds).

Example 15.2 Rates of interest in the domestic money markets of overseas countries. Source: *Financial Times.*

currencies traded in the international market (including eurocurrencies – see Chapter 17) are also provided.

The rates of interest on **floating rate bonds** are usually geared to the inter-bank **offered** rate: the rate at which banks will lend wholesale to each other. A bond might carry a rate of interest of, say, 50 **basis points** above the inter-bank offered rate. A hundred basis points is equivalent to one percentage point, so 50 basis points is 0.5 per cent. But the rate on an overdraft to a private individual will be related to the lending bank's base rate and expressed as so many **points** above base rate. A point in this case is a full **percentage point** so five points over base means 11 per cent when base rates are 6 per cent.

Thus the **London Inter-Bank Offered Rate** or **LIBOR** (see Chapter 17) is the usual benchmark rate of interest for wholesale funds, and is the rate in relation to which other floating rates of interest are set. **LIBID** is the equivalent **bid** rate or rate at which banks will offer to borrow. **LIMEAN** (pronounced 'lie-mean') is the rate mid-way between the bid and offered rates.

Internet pointers

The personal finance sites listed in Chapter 23 have details of the borrowing and lending rates that are of most interest to private individuals. The Bank of England site at www.bankofengland.co.uk/ has a lot of information on the Bank's operations in the money markets as well as the minutes of the meetings of the Monetary Policy Committee. The Debt Management Office at www.dmo.gov.uk/ is now the source for information on the Treasury Bill tender. The economic background which forms the framework for monetary policy may be found at the Treasury site at www.hm-treasury.gov.uk/.

16 Foreign exchange and the euro

If stockmarkets sometimes behave irrationally, they are a model of sanity compared with the **foreign exchange** or **forex** markets in which currencies are bought and sold. Not only are the swings in the value of one currency against another both frequent and dramatic; they also have vital implications for the economic prospects of the countries concerned and often for the prosperity of the whole free-world economy – remember the currency collapses among the one-time 'tiger economies' of Asia in 1997? It is no surprise that currency stories migrate so frequently from the detailed and technical **foreign exchange reports** to become lead items in the financial pages.

Where weighty issues of politics or nationalism are involved, currency stories will even make it to the general news headlines rather than confining themselves to the financial pages. The debate over Britain's joining – or not joining – the new European euro currency is a case in point. This has generated more heat (and, incidentally, more nonsense) than any other economic story in recent years. But before venturing into this territory later in the chapter, there are a few basic principles to examine.

It is precisely because the influences that move currency values are often so irrational that currency stories can be difficult to understand. Perhaps the easiest approach is to look on the major trading countries as if they were companies quoted on the stockmarket and on their currencies as if they were company shares.

Official intervention

As with shares, the value of each currency is determined by the balance of buyers and sellers in the market, at least since **floating exchange rates** were adopted in the early 1970s. But just as share prices may be **supported** by friends of the company, the value of currencies can be affected by **official intervention**: buying and selling by **central banks** to try to strengthen or weaken a currency.

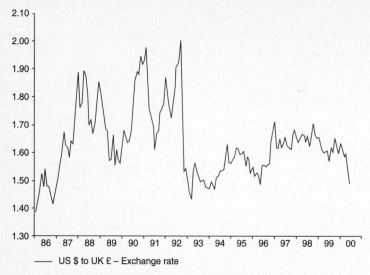

Figure 16.1 Dollars to the pound sterling Britain has seen some pretty wild swings in the value of its currency against the US dollar, though things have been calmer in recent years. Source: *Datastream.*

Where a currency is ostensibly **floating** (allowed to find its own level) but in practice being kept close to a particular value or **parity** in relation to other currencies by central bank intervention, commentators talk of a **dirty** or **managed float**.

But there is a limit to how far a currency value can be manipulated against the trend of market forces. If the central bank is using its **foreign exchange reserves** to support its country's currency when most other participants in the market are selling because they conclude from economic fundamentals that its value should fall in relation to other currencies, the central bank will in due course exhaust its available reserves, be forced to abandon the support operation and the value will then drop in any case. The market forces predominate. Successful intervention often requires concerted action by the central banks of a number of countries (see below). But even this will ultimately fail if the economic fundamentals are out of line.

The market forces

What are these market forces? Again, there is a parallel between a company and a country. If a company is trading successfully and increasing its earnings, all else being equal its share price will rise.

Successful countries which run a **current account balance of payments surplus** (sell more goods and services to other countries than they buy from abroad) and which keep inflation at a low level will also usually see their own currency strong or rising in value over time.

The effect of interest rates

Even if it is not trading spectacularly well, a company can try to make its shares more attractive to investors by increasing the dividends it pays. A country can also try to increase the attraction of its currency to international investors by increasing its **domestic interest rates**. This increases the returns investors can earn by depositing money in the country concerned or by buying bonds in that country. Suppose Britain is increasing its interest rates to attract overseas investors. To invest in Britain they will need to convert whatever currency they hold into pounds to deposit in Britain or buy British bonds. So they will be buying pounds, and when there are more buyers than sellers the currency should rise.

So far so good. But investors in the stockmarket will not buy a share if they are certain its value is going to drop, almost regardless of the income it offers. The income is of little use if the benefit is going to be wiped out by capital losses on the shares. The same applies to a currency. If international investors think the pound is going to fall heavily in value, they will be more inclined to sell it than buy it and the interest rates Britain is offering will only have limited effect. This process was very clearly demonstrated in September 1992 when successive rises in interest rates could not maintain the value of the pound sufficiently for it to remain within the **Exchange Rate Mechanism** of the **European Monetary System** (see below). Interest rate changes can and do influence the value of a currency and much of what the press writes about currencies is concerned with the way countries are adjusting – or being pressured to adjust – domestic interest rates to adjust the value of their currency. But interest rates are only one factor.

Swings in market sentiment

Increasingly, the vital factor is that indefinable element: **market sentiment**. If investors become enthusiastic about a share, they will buy it. Its price will rise and those who bought will show profits. This in turn may attract other investors to buy, the price rises still further and the process becomes self-fuelling. The same thing happens with currencies. Either longer-term investors or short-term speculators (or probably both) become enthusiastic about the dollar and buy it. Its value rises, which encourages still more investors to put their money in the dollar, so it rises still further. And the process can be self-perpetuating – until something happens to change sentiment or encourage investors to take their profit. When this happens, international investors can sell just as frantically as they previously bought, and the value of the currency can fall as fast as it had earlier risen.

The result is that currency swings can **overshoot**. That is, they can go much too far in one direction or another, creating havoc for businesses which trade internationally: they can never be certain what price they will receive for their goods when translated into their own currency. Here the analogy between stockmarkets and currency markets breaks down. In the stockmarket individual share prices can be carried ridiculously high or ridiculously low by swings in market sentiment. But at the end of the day there are some reasonably objective yardsticks: what the company earns and is capable of earning; the dividends it pays and therefore the yield it offers. Ultimately these **fundamentals** tend to reassert themselves and bring investors back to earth.

In the currency markets the fundamentals frequently exert less influence in the short term, so that the currency moves much further than is needed merely to adjust to trading realities. In the very long run the fundamentals will reassert themselves, but before this happens such overshooting may cause serious damage to a country's trading prospects.

How do we measure currencies?

There is another important difference to allow for before we can look more closely at the way currency questions are covered. In the British stockmarkets we measure securities prices in standard units: pounds and pence (though there's been talk of moving to euros!). But a currency is measured in terms of other currencies and all are moving relative to each other. The pound may be strengthening against the dollar but weakening against the euro. These **exchange cross rates** – values of each of the major currencies in terms of each of the others – are listed daily in the **currencies, money and capital markets** pages of the *Financial Times*, as are the values of major currencies in terms of the pound and of the US dollar, in somewhat more

POUND SPOT FORWARD AGAINST THE POUND

Jun 28		Closing mid-point	Change on day	Bid/offer spread	Day's high	Mid low	One month Rate	%PA	Three months Rate	%PA	One year Rate	%PA	Bank of Eng. Index
Europe													
Austria*	(Sch)	21.9795	+0.1086	699 – 891	22.0202	21.8824	21.9497	1.6	21.894	1.6	21.6938	1.3	100.0
Belgium*	(BFr)	64.4356	+0.3185	074 – 637	64.5550	64.1510	64.0321	1.6	63.8703	1.5	63.2745	1.3	99.0
Denmark	(DKr)	11.9170	+0.0665	115 – 224	11.9350	11.8578	11.8381	1.3	11.8237	0.9	11.7965	0.5	100.8
Finland*	(FM)	9.4972	+0.0469	931 – 013	9.5150	9.4550	9.4378	1.6	9.4139	1.5	9.3262	1.3	77.1
France*	(FFr)	10.4777	+0.0518	731 – 823	10.4971	10.4313	10.4121	1.6	10.3857	1.5	10.2889	1.3	101.7
Germany*	(DM)	3.1241	+0.0154	227 – 254	3.1308	3.1098	3.1045	1.6	3.0967	1.5	3.0678	1.3	98.4
Greece	(Dr)	537.624	+2.6360	219 – 028	538.527	535.521	536.047	-2.4	537.486	-1.9	535.21	0.0	58.0
Ireland*	(I£)	1.2580	+0.0062	574 – 585	1.2604	1.2524	1.2502	1.6	1.247	1.5	1.2353	1.3	87.6
Italy*	(L)	3092.83	+15.2800	148 – 418	3098.57	3079.16	3073.47	1.6	3065.71	1.5	3037.11	1.3	72.6
Luxembourg*	(LFr)	64.4356	+0.3185	074 – 637	64.5550	64.1510	64.0321	1.6	63.8703	1.5	63.2745	1.3	99.0
Netherlands*	(Fl)	3.5201	+0.0174	185 – 216	3.5266	3.5044	3.4981	1.6	3.4892	1.5	3.4566	1.3	97.8
Norway	(NKr)	13.0565	-0.0012	499 – 630	13.1314	13.0248	13.0645	-0.6	13.0822	-0.8	13.1856	-1.0	92.4
Portugal*	(Es)	320.233	+1.5830	093 – 373	320.824	318.816	318.228	1.6	317.424	1.5	314.462	1.3	89.2
Spain*	(Pta)	265.771	+1.3140	655 – 887	266.260	264.590	264.107	1.6	263.439	1.5	260.982	1.3	74.2
Sweden	(SKr)	13.3750	+0.0696	640 – 860	13.4276	13.2974	13.2811	2.2	13.2381	2.0	13.1111	1.5	83.8
Switzerland	(SFr)	2.4767	+0.0195	755 – 779	2.4829	2.4602	2.4512	2.9	2.4404	2.7	2.3971	2.4	106.1
UK	(£)	-	-	-	-	-	-	-	-	-	-	-	105.1
Euro	(€)	1.5973	+0.0079	966 – 980	1.6008	1.5895	1.5873	1.6	1.5832	1.5	1.5685	1.3	79.65
SDR	-	1.134800											
Americas													
Argentina	(Peso)	1.5106	+0.0116	101 – 111	1.5115	1.5027	-	-	-	-	-	-	-
Brazil	(R$)	2.7483	+0.0135	459 – 507	2.7507	2.7400	-	-	-	-	-	-	-
Canada	(C$)	2.2426	+0.0221	411 – 441	2.2441	2.2232	2.2203	0.1	2.2195	0.2	2.2173	0.1	79.7
Mexico	(New Peso)	15.0456	-0.0719	345 – 566	15.1403	14.9880	15.2396	-14.0	15.6282	-13.5	16.9835	-12.3	-
USA	($)	1.5109	+0.0116	104 – 114	1.5118	1.5030	1.5003	-0.8	1.502	-0.7	1.5112	-0.8	109.4
Pacific/Middle East/Africa													
Australia	(A$)	2.5132	+0.0139	102 – 161	2.5161	2.4949	2.4996	-0.1	2.4997	-0.1	2.5011	-0.1	77.9
Hong Kong	(HK$)	11.7778	+0.0921	731 – 824	11.7840	11.7160	11.6872	-0.1	11.6986	-0.4	11.7718	-0.7	-
India	(Rs)	67.4881	+0.5518	620 – 142	67.5142	67.1390	67.2638	-5.9	67.7321	-4.8	69.7707	-4.2	-
Indonesia	(Rupiah)	13114.62	+93.20	762 – 162	13141.62	13013.10	13089.68	-6.3	13251.26	-7.1	13956.4	-7.2	-
Israel	(Shk)	6.1834	+0.0643	738 – 930	6.1930	6.1738	-	-	-	-	-	-	-
Japan	(Y)	159.408	+1.2090	317 – 498	159.496	158.470	157.374	6.3	155.844	6.0	149.084	5.8	155.4
Malaysia‡‡	(M$)	5.7414	+0.0440	395 – 433	5.7447	5.7122	-	-	-	-	-	-	-
New Zealand	(NZ$)	3.2458	+0.0642	426 – 489	3.2489	3.1906	3.1833	-0.6	3.1869	-0.7	3.2079	-0.8	81.1
Philippines	(Peso)	65.1652	+0.6952	680 – 623	65.2623	65.0680	64.6474	-3.3	65.0181	-3.4	67.1827	-4.2	-
Saudi Arabia	(SR)	5.8667	+0.0435	646 – 688	5.6697	5.6373	5.6282	-1.1	5.6371	-1.0	5.6721	-0.9	-
Singapore	(S$)	2.6191	+0.0235	202 – 230	2.6230	2.6076	2.5906	3.5	2.5768	3.3	2.5191	3.0	-
South Africa	(R)	10.2923	+0.0858	813 – 032	10.3032	10.2067	10.2431	-4.3	10.3157	-4.3	10.7053	-4.9	-
South Korea	(Won)	1686.54	+10.0200	561 – 748	1687.48	1677.65	-	-	-	-	-	-	-
Taiwan	(T$)	46.5508	+0.3851	203 – 813	46.5813	46.3104	46.15	0.4	46.0907	0.7	45.846	0.7	-
Thailand	(Bt)	59.1291	+0.4390	717 – 864	59.1864	58.7220	58.6298	1.2	58.5737	0.8	58.5232	0.3	-

Bid/offer spreads in the Pound Spot table show only the last three decimal places. Sterling index calculated by the Bank of England. Base average 1990 = 100. Index rebased 1/2/95. * EMU member. The exchange rates printed in this table are also available on the Internet at http://www.FT.com.

Example 16.1 Exchange rates for different currencies against the pound, for immediate and for future delivery. Source: *Financial Times*.

detailed form. Note one complication: by convention the markets always talk of 'so many dollars to the pound' rather than 'so much of a pound to the dollar', even when talking of the value of the dollar rather than the pound. So the dollar's value in sterling terms is expressed as, say, $1.6235 to £1 rather than £0.6160 to $1.

In reports of currency movements there are two main ways currency values are expressed: in terms of another specific currency or in terms of a **trade-weighted index** where they are measured against a **basket of currencies**. In the second case, taking the value of the pound as an example, an index is constructed of the currencies of the main countries with which Britain trades, each weighted according to its importance in trade with Britain. This is expressed not as a monetary value but as an index with a base of 100 in 1990. Thus, on a particular day the pound might rise against the dollar from $1.6200 to $1.6300 (you get more dollars for a pound, so the pound has strengthened) but fall from 103.3 to 102.9 on the trade-weighted index. Overall, the pound was a little weaker against all currencies, but the dollar was weaker still so sterling improved against the dollar.

This is often rather badly reported in the media. You may read or hear that sterling rose one cent against the dollar whereas the reality was simply that the dollar was falling against most currencies and fell one cent against the pound. Again, the *Financial Times* shows sterling's value on the trade-weighted index (also known as the **sterling index** or the **Bank of England effective exchange rate index**) and similar indices for other major currencies. Dollar, yen, euro and Swiss franc values are frequently quoted.

The fundamentals

We have seen that the value of a currency might be expected – all else being equal – to rise if the country concerned is earning more from abroad than it is spending abroad. Other countries are having to buy its currency to buy its goods and it is adding to its **foreign exchange reserves**, which are roughly equivalent to a country's bank balance. A country may hold its reserves in the form of other currencies, **special drawing rights** (see glossary) or gold.

In theory, as the value of a country's currency rises in relation to other currencies, its goods become more expensive for foreigners to buy. So gradually it sells less abroad, earns less foreign exchange, and – all other things being equal – the currency begins to weaken until its goods become cheaper again and the cycle recommences. A country earning a surplus may also take deliberate steps to prevent its currency from rising too high: reducing interest rates to make the currency less attractive to foreign investors and to stimulate domestic demand so that more goods are consumed at home, more are imported and fewer exported.

In practice the phenomenon of **overshoot** means that self-correcting mechanisms may be rendered ineffective or only work with considerable delay. The problem is that there is no such thing as the 'right' value for a currency against any other currency. It can be argued that if the exchange rate is $1.60 to £1, an item which costs £1 in London should cost $1.60 in New York: the **purchasing power parity** argument. But such considerations clearly did not apply in the 1980s when the value of £1 fluctuated between more than $2.40 and little more than $1.00, which obviously did not reflect movements in the relative prices of goods in New York and London. Instead, when the dollar stood at $2.40 to £1 American goods were very cheap for the British and at just over $1.00 to £1 they were exceedingly expensive. Currency volatility exaggerates trade imbalances which in turn increase volatility.

Cross-border investment flows

We have talked so far mainly about the flows of money between countries that result from their trading performance. These are the **current account** flows which reflect what a country earns from selling goods and services overseas and what it spends in buying goods and services from overseas.

But there are also **capital account** flows, which we have encountered briefly in the form of speculative funds moving in and out of a country as a bet on a rise or fall in the value of its currency. Not all capital flows are purely speculative, however: they can also represent long-term investment in a country from abroad. And they can have a long-term effect on the values of currencies. Take an example. In the first half of the 1980s, the US dollar was rising for much of the time despite an escalating balance of trade deficit which passed $100 billion in 1985. This was mainly because of large inflows of investment funds from abroad, particularly from Japan, attracted by relatively high US interest rates. But in 1985, balance of payments worries plus concerted efforts among central banks to curb the dollar's strength proved all too effective and the currency began to fall even more rapidly than it had risen.

Why should countries worry if their currency becomes too strong? A strong currency can have beneficial effects such as reducing the cost of imported goods. Particularly in the case of a country like Britain, which imports much of the raw materials that it needs, the lower cost of imports helps to keep domestic inflation down. On the other side of the coin, a weak pound means higher import costs and, all else being equal, faster rising prices in Britain.

But if a currency becomes too strong, it can wreak havoc with the domestic economy. Manufacturers find that their products become too expensive to compete with those of other countries in export or home markets, so domestic manufacturers suffer severely. This happened in Britain in the early 1980s and UK manufacturers were again hitting problems as a result of the strong pound in the late 1990s.

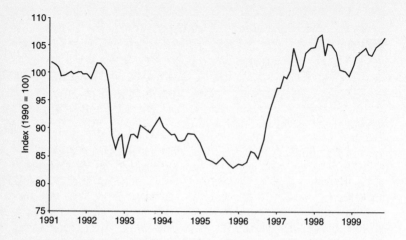

Figure 16.2 Sterling effective exhange rate The value of the pound sterling, as measured against a 'basket' of currencies by the Bank of England Index. The sharp drop in 1992 shows what happened when sterling failed to hold its place in the European Exchange Rate Mechanism. But the problem in recent years has been one of strength rather than weakness. The very high level of sterling in the late 1990s posed severe problems for British exporters and manufacturers. Source: *Office for National Statistics: Financial Statistics.*

Where trade imbalances and currency excesses require concerted action, they may be addressed by a meeting of the finance ministers of the major trading nations. These countries – the United States, Japan, Germany, France and Great Britain – are referred to as the **Group of Five** or **G5** and become the **Group of Seven** or **G7** with the addition of Canada and Italy and G8 with Russia.

European money

The start of 1999 saw the decisive step which locked 11 Continental European countries (but not Britain at that point) into a new single currency: the **euro**. But this was neither the first nor the last step in a process know as **Economic and Monetary Union** (or **EMU**) in Europe.

The precursor of full monetary union was a system called the **Exchange Rate Mechanism** (**ERM**) of the **European Monetary System** (**EMS**). The idea was to stabilize currencies between the European Union countries by limiting the extent to which each currency could fluctuate against the others.

Central to the system was the **ECU**, a notional European currency constructed from an amalgam of the currencies of all European Union members. Each country's currency was represented in the ECU with a weighting that roughly reflected the country's economic size. Thus, the German mark had the heaviest weighting within the ECU because the German economy was the largest, and movements in the value of the German mark would therefore be the greatest single influence on the value of the ECU.

Each currency started with an exchange rate against the ECU: its central rate. And the member countries were meant to manage their interest rates and economies in such a way that their currency diverged by no more than a small margin up or down from this central rate or the central rates of other currencies. A slightly larger margin of divergence was allowed for some more volatile currencies (such as the pound sterling when Britain joined the system in 1990 – see below).

Thus, if at any time the strongest currency in the system and the weakest one threatened to diverge more than was permitted against each other, the central banks of the two countries would need to take remedial action to bring them back into line.

If this happened, the central banks of the two countries would sell the strong currency and buy the weak one. In practice, a country whose currency was moving out of line might take action before this by buying or selling its own currency or raising or lowering short-term interest rates.

In other words, if speculators mounted an attack on a particular currency in an attempt to drive its value down, a concerted defence could be mounted. While this could help in the short run, it was not, however, a substitute for changes in economic or interest rate policy to correct the factors which had made the currency vulnerable in the first place.

As a last resort, if all the available measures failed to keep a currency within bounds, the EMS members might be forced to agree a formal **revaluation** which re-set the particular currency's central rate within the ERM.

The coming of the euro

There is a big difference between the Exchange Rate Mechanism and the move to full **monetary union** in most of Europe which followed it at the beginning of 1999. Under **EMU** the different participating currencies are locked together at a fixed exchange rate for all time (or that is the intention). The notional ECU is replaced by a real new currency: the **euro**. After a transition period of just over three years, the euro will replace the existing currencies for all purposes, and these traditional currencies will therefore disappear.

One currency for all brings with it one short-term interest rate for all. The newly constituted and independent **European Central Bank (ECB)** has taken over responsibility from the individual central banks, and sets a single short-term interest rate for all EMU participants.

We will look at the strengths and weaknesses of the new system in a moment. But first, a few of the practical details.

To qualify for participation in the euro, the individual European Union countries had to be able to demonstrate that they were moving roughly in step with each other. This involved meeting certain **convergence** criteria on matters such as inflation, interest rates, exchange rates and government borrowing. The assessment was undertaken in the spring of 1998 and (after a certain amount of fudging of the figures) only Greece failed to qualify.

Not all countries had wanted to join at that point, however. Initially, 11 countries both qualified and chose to join what came to be known as the **euro zone** or (more colloquially) **euroland**. They were:

Austria
Belgium
Finland
France
Germany
Ireland
Italy
Luxembourg
Netherlands
Portugal
Spain

Of the remainder, Denmark, Sweden and the United Kingdom chose not to join in this first wave, and thus deferred their decision, while Greece was not yet eligible.

The next important step took place at the end of 1998 when the exchange rate of each of the 11 currencies was permanently fixed in terms of the euro and of each other participating currency. A euro was (and is) worth, for example, 1.95583 German marks and 6.55957 French francs. When the financial markets reopened after the Christmas and New Year break on 4 January 1999, the new currency was a fact of life and trading in the euro could begin.

It might have been a fact of life, but there were as yet no **euro notes** or **coins**. These were not due to be issued until the start of the year 2002. Then, in the first six months of 2002, the old notes and coins would be phased out and replaced by euro notes and coins (during this six months, either old or new currency could be used). The notes would be issued in denominations of 5, 10, 20, 50, 100, 200 and 500 euros. The coins would come in denominations of 1 euro and 2 euros, plus 1, 2, 5, 10, 20 and 50 euro cents (there are, needless to say, 100 **euro cents** to a euro).

What about the three-year interim period between the creation of the euro at the start of 1999 and the issue of notes and coins at the start of 2002? During these three years, transactions could take place either in the old currencies or in the euro. Many government functions switched over to the euro (new issues of government bonds were to be denominated in euros) and other investments could substitute a face value in euros for the old national currencies. Euro-zone companies could chose whether to invoice in euros or the old currencies. As far as private individuals were concerned, if they had euro bank accounts they were at liberty to write cheques or undertake payment-card transactions in euros, though the absence of notes and coins ruled out euro transactions in cash until the start of 2002. Shops in the euro zone were encouraged to show prices in both old and new currencies to familiarize customers with the euro by the time the notes and coins arrived. During these three years, bank account holders could choose to convert their existing accounts into euros or they could stick with the old currencies. But at the start of 2002, any accounts not already converted would automatically be redesignated in euros. Likewise, many other forms of contract (savings and insurance contracts, for example) would automatically convert into the equivalent euro values.

For countries outside the euro zone, whether members of the European Union or not, the euro is just another foreign currency. British residents may open euro bank accounts if they choose, just as they may hold dollar accounts. But for a Briton a euro account will be a foreign currency account as long as Britain remains outside the

EURO SPOT FORWARD AGAINST THE EURO

Jun 28		Closing mid-point	Change on day	Bid/offer spread	Day's mid high	low	One month Rate	%PA	Three months Rate	%PA	One year Rate	%PA
Europe												
Czech Rep.	(Koruna)	35.7683	+0.0266	503 - 862	35.8410	35.6610	35.7974	-1.0	35.8396	-0.8	36.0321	-0.7
Denmark	(DKr)	7.4606	+0.0047	589 - 623	7.5033	7.4489	7.4629	-0.4	7.4724	-0.6	7.5247	-0.9
Greece	(Dr)	336.580	-0.0130	402 - 757	336.861	336.309	337.6398	-3.8	339.4042	-3.4	341.2833	-1.4
Hungary	(Forint)	260.075	+0.3470	953 - 197	260.320	259.650	261.4438	-6.3	264.0989	-6.2	273.7714	-5.3
Norway	(NKr)	8.1740	-0.0414	717 - 763	8.2201	8.1573	8.1882	-2.1	8.2212	-2.3	8.3599	-2.3
Poland	(Zloty)	4.1584	+0.0029	544 - 624	4.1635	4.1378	-	-	-	-	-	-
Romania	(Leu)	20121.66	+76.5300	717 - 615	20126.15	20117.17	-	-	-	-	-	-
Russia	(Rouble)	26.5373	+0.0164	297 - 448	26.6023	26.3830	-	-	-	-	-	-
Slovakia	(Koruna)	43.0465	+0.1055	866 - 064	43.2933	41.4487	-	-	-	-	-	-
Sweden	(SKr)	8.3734	+0.0021	684 - 784	8.4025	8.3520	8.3694	0.6	8.3630	0.5	8.3605	0.2
Switzerland	(SFr)	1.5506	+0.0046	502 - 510	1.5516	1.5435	1.5490	1.2	1.5460	1.2	1.5327	1.2
UK	(£)	0.6261	-0.0031	258 - 263	0.6291	0.6247	0.6269	-1.5	0.6285	-1.5	0.6343	-1.3
Americas												
Argentina	(Peso)	0.9457	+0.0026	456 - 458	0.9465	0.9397	-	-	-	-	-	-
Brazil	(R$)	1.7206	-	195 - 217	1.7249	1.7097	-	-	-	-	-	-
Canada	(C$)	1.4040	+0.0070	034 - 046	1.4046	1.3932	1.4056	-1.4	1.4087	-1.3	1.4203	-1.2
Mexico	(New Peso)	9.4193	-0.0920	145 - 241	9.4329	9.3595	9.5396	-15.3	9.7674	-14.8	10.7003	-13.6
USA	($)	0.9459	+0.0026	458 - 460	0.9467	0.9399	0.9477	-2.3	0.9512	-2.2	0.9659	-2.1
Pacific/Middle East/Africa												
Australia	(A$)	1.5734	+0.0009	719 - 748	1.5758	1.5628	1.5756	-1.7	1.5797	-1.6	1.5952	-1.4
Hong Kong	(HK$)	7.3735	+0.0213	722 - 747	7.3788	7.3268	7.3836	-1.6	7.4095	-2.0	7.5251	-2.1
India	(Rs)	42.2510	+0.1374	442 - 578	42.2891	41.9759	42.4780	-6.4	42.8655	-5.8	44.5669	-5.5
Indonesia	(Rupiah)	8210.41	+17.8500	536 - 547	8225.47	8162.10	8264.83	-8.0	8385.23	-8.5	8917.73	-8.6
Israel	(Shk)	3.8711	+0.0212	660 - 762	3.8762	3.8423	-	-	-	-	-	-
Japan	(Y)	99.7972	+0.2649	630 - 314	99.9000	99.2000	99.4239	4.5	98.7064	4.4	95.2817	4.5
Malaysia	(M$)	3.5944	+0.0098	940 - 948	3.5970	3.5717	-	-	-	-	-	-
New Zealand	(NZ$)	2.0320	+0.0303	305 - 335	2.0335	2.0038	2.0357	-2.2	2.0432	-2.2	2.0752	-2.1
Philippines	(Peso)	40.7967	+0.2348	451 - 483	40.8785	40.4909	40.9607	-4.8	41.2565	-4.5	42.9755	-5.3
Saudi Arabia	(SR)	3.5477	+0.0098	471 - 482	3.5507	3.5252	3.5558	-2.7	3.5705	-2.6	3.6254	-2.2
Singapore	(S$)	1.6413	-0.0067	408 - 418	1.6418	1.6304	1.6389	1.8	1.6341	1.8	1.6125	1.8
South Africa	(R)	6.4435	+0.0220	381 - 489	6.4489	6.3881	6.4754	-5.9	6.5380	-5.9	6.8434	-6.2
South Korea	(Won)	1055.86	+1.0600	551 - 621	1058.41	1055.51	-	-	-	-	-	-
Taiwan	(T$)	29.1432	+0.0975	306 - 557	29.1620	28.9600	29.1622	-0.8	29.1866	-0.6	29.3297	-0.6
Thailand	(Bt)	37.0178	+0.0923	902 - 454	37.0454	36.7971	37.0474	-1.0	37.1128	-1.0	37.4626	-1.2
UAE	(Dirham)	3.4742	+0.0096	736 - 748	3.9985	3.2713	3.4814	-2.5	3.4947	-2.4	3.5495	-2.2

Euro Locking Rates: Austrian Schilling 13.7603, Belgium/Luxembourg Franc 40.3399, Finnish Markka 5.94573, French Franc 6.55957, German Mark 1.95583, Irish Punt 0.787564, Italian Lira 1936.27, Netherlands Guilder 2.20371, Portuguese Escudo 200.482, Spanish Peseta 166.386. Bid/offer spreads in the Euro Spot table show only the last three decimal places. Bid, offer, mid spot rates and forward rates are derived from THE WM/REUTERS CLOSING SPOT and FORWARD RATE services. Some values are rounded by the F.T.

Example 16.2 Exchange rates against the euro, spot and forward. Source: *Financial Times.*

euro mechanism. What the money in it is worth in terms of sterling will fluctuate with changes in the sterling/euro exchange rate.

The coming of the euro has consequences for countries outside the euro zone, and particularly for businesses. Any company trading with a euro zone member must be ready to make and receive payment in euros. And the investment world in particular has had to adapt to the new currencies. Financial information and news agency group **Reuters**, for example, has had to translate all of its historical records of the 11 euro-zone currencies (and investment price information denominated in these currencies) into terms of the euro in order to provide meaningful price and exchange rate histories.

Will the euro work?

In Britain the public debate on Britain's joining or staying outside the euro has been conducted at a number of levels, not all of them very useful. The main strands – including the more fatuous ones often played up by the popular press – might be summarized as follows:

- Are we prepared to wave goodbye to our historic pound?

- Will we allow the Queen's head to be removed from our currency?

- Do we want our interest rates set by some faceless European bankers?

- Can we retain control over our own economic affairs if short-term interest rates are set elsewhere?

- Is the euro just a first step to full economic and political integration in Europe, removing individual countries' rights to set their own tax rates and manage many other aspects of national life?

- Would Britain lose in competitiveness (and, in particular, would the City of London lose its financial pre-eminence) if Britain stayed outside the euro?

- Will the euro system work?

Arguably, the last of these questions is by far the most important – there is not much point in debating the rest until you have formed a view of the likely success of the euro experiment. Yet it has probably been the least discussed aspect of the whole affair, certainly in the popular media.

By linking their currencies, the euro-zone members look for a number of advantages. The cost of financial transactions between member states will be reduced. While the euro will fluctuate against the world's other currencies, euro-zone members are spared disruptive fluctuations between member's currencies. A new Europe-wide financial and investment market is being created which should assist in attracting funds. Europe and its industries will form a powerful economic bloc, on a par with, say, the United States. And monetary integration is a necessary step towards the full economic and political integration that parts of Europe undoubtedly want.

The corresponding dangers have received less coverage. The 'one-interest-rate-for-all' strategy has its problems. What happens if one euro-zone member – Italy, say – finds itself moving into recession at a time when most of the other members are booming? The European Central Bank may see a need to raise interest rates to damp down activity and prevent overheating and possible inflation in the European economies as a whole. But Italy would be pleading for a reduction in interest rates to get its own economy moving, and a rise could push it deeper into recession. Could an Italian government survive the resultant rise in unemployment and the popular unrest that would probably accompany it?

The theoretical argument is that the unemployed Italians could seek work in the booming euro-zone member countries. But unless and until labour mobility in Europe improves greatly, this may be pie in the sky. It is possible to envisage euro-zone members being forced to drop out of the euro system if faced with insurmountable economic and political pressures at home.

And there are risks in the other direction. Ireland, which was enjoying a heady boom at the end of 1998, had to reduce its short-term interest rates in brief stages from over 6 per cent to 3 per cent – the starting rate for the euro zone – by the time that the new currency was launched. Thus it was obliged to reduce rates at a time when domestic considerations might have argued for a rise to prevent the economy from overheating. Early evidence suggested that the rate reduction had indeed fuelled the boom – particularly in the property market – in 1999 and that trouble might follow.

So there is no guarantee of success for the euro experiment. However, not too much attention should be paid to the comparative weakness of the euro against the dollar and sterling in the first year of its existence: one euro was worth around 71p at its launch and had fallen to about 62p by the end of 1999. While Britain's anti-euro brigade made much of this decline, it was probably what the euro-zone countries needed. A relatively weak currency increased their competitiveness and helped the climb out of recession. The real tests of the euro were yet to come.

Britain's currency turmoils

Britain has had severe currency and inflation problems since the Second World War. Usually these have been the problems of sterling weakness and an inflation rate well above that of our main competitors. But, as we have seen, there were also periods in the early 1980s and late 1990s where sterling's excessive strength was the problem.

In the early 1980s a combination of North Sea oil revenues, a high oil price and high domestic interest rates in Britain saw sterling

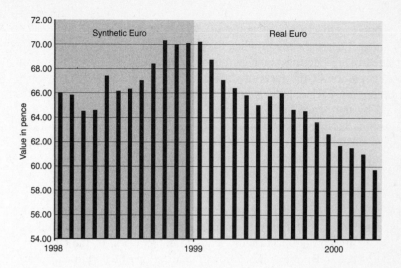

Figure 16.3 Value of one euro in UK pence This chart traces the steady decline of the euro from its launch at the beginning of 1999 (the 1998 values are for a 'synthetic' euro – what it would have been worth had it already existed). Here the euro is shown in terms of sterling, but its fall against the dollar was quite as dramatic. In other words, the problem was the euro's weakness rather than the strength of other currencies. But the euro weakness may have helped the main euro-zone countries in their climb out of recession. Source: *Office for National Statistics: Financial Statistics.*

climbing strongly and not only against a then-weak dollar. At one point the dollar exchange rate went above $2.40 to £1. The strong currency helped to curb Britain's domestic inflation. But it proved a severe blow for the country's manufacturers who found themselves unable to compete on price in home or export markets. Much manufacturing capacity was destroyed in consequence: some of it inefficient and deserving to go, some of it probably not.

But the strength was relatively short-lived and by the middle of the decade a strong dollar and weak sterling saw a pound buying little more than a single dollar. An improvement in government finances resulted in some strengthening of the pound again in 1987 and 1988, but then rising inflation and mounting balance of payments problems intervened.

Because Britain had such problems in controlling its inflation rate and maintaining its currency at a sensible level, there were obvious attractions in looking for help from outside. If the value of sterling could be linked into a strong currency system, this would both impose a discipline on domestic economic policy and provide for some concerted support when the pound came under attack. It would mean surrendering some autonomy. But up to a point this was a recognition of the facts of economic life. In an increasingly global economy, each country's interest rates and currency value are affected by the actions of others, and the scope for totally independent action is increasingly limited. Unfortunately, when Britain first looked for help from outside by joining the **European Exchange Rate Mechanism (ERM)** on 8 October 1990 with the wider 6 per cent fluctuation limit, it probably joined at the wrong exchange rate and at the wrong point in its own economic cycle.

To hold its position within the ERM, Britain would have needed to get its inflation rate in line with that of other EC members, since high inflation normally leads to depreciation of the currency. The hope in Britain had been that membership of a system dominated by the stability of the German mark would ultimately bring the benefits of low inflation that Germany had enjoyed. It was also hoped that the protection afforded by the ERM mechanism would allow Britain gradually to reduce its domestic interest rates and emerge from recession without sparking a run on sterling. In the event, the UK succeeded in cutting both its inflation rate and interest rates to a level consistent with other members of the ERM.

Unfortunately, this was not enough to allow sterling's continued membership. Germany's own position was affected by the way it chose to integrate the former East Germany. One consequence was that Germany felt obliged to impose considerably higher interest rates than normal to control domestic inflation. Because of Germany's dominant influence, this in turn imposed high interest rates on the whole ERM structure. The consequences were serious for Britain whose inflation rate had been brought under control but which then badly needed to pull itself out of the severe recession that the earlier government medicine of high interest rates had caused. The domestic situation in Britain therefore seemed to demand a further reduction in interest rates to stimulate economic activity but a cut in rates relative to the other European countries would cause sterling to weaken and might make it impossible for the pound to maintain its position in the ERM.

The events of September 1992 when sterling was obliged to drop out of the ERM have passed into financial folklore. Whatever the British government maintained, the speculators thought that the pound must fall: either through a formal devaluation within the ERM or by dropping out of the mechanism and finding its own level. And, as so often happens, government intervention to support the pound offered them a one-way bet. The authorities were there as buyer when the speculators wanted to sell. On 16 September the pound was at its lower limit within the ERM and at mid-morning the government announced that **Minimum Lending Rate** had been raised from 10 per cent to 12 per cent. But with everybody except the authorities betting on sterling's fall, this failed to lift it from the floor. As a final throw it was announced in the afternoon that MLR would rise again to 15 per cent the following day. Again, it failed to work. Sterling's suspension from the ERM was announced that evening and the MLR rise to 15 per cent was never implemented.

No longer supported, sterling fell 10 per cent more against the German mark from the level at which it had dropped out of the ERM, and the speculators collected their winnings – able to buy back more cheaply the pounds they had earlier sold short at the higher level. One so-called **hedge fund** (see glossary) had supposedly made $1billion on the operation. The Bank of England, according to the newspaper speculation of the time, had spent some £15 billion in its (ultimately unsuccessful) support of the currency, though only a fraction of this would have been money actually lost. Once attempts to maintain the pound's ERM parity were abandoned, interest rates in Britain were rapidly reduced in a series of steps.

Sterling was not the only currency to suffer from ERM turmoil at the time, though the mechanism ultimately survived to be replaced by full monetary union at the start of 1999.

Ironically, Britain enjoyed considerably more success in controlling its inflation rate in the 1990s than it had done previously. After sterling had dropped out of the ERM and short-term interest rates had been reduced, Britain eventually began to pull out of recession. When New Labour won the election of May 1997, it inherited a healthy economy and relatively low interest rates. As seen, one of its first actions was to surrender the government's responsibility for setting short-term interest rates to the Bank of England.

At the end of 1999 the British **repo rate** at 5.5 per cent was still well above the 3 per cent applied by the **European Central Bank** to all the euro-zone countries. The disparity illustrated one of the problems if Britain were to join the euro. Its economic cycle had been out of step with the economic cycles of the main euro-zone members. It had pulled out of recession and moved into a modest boom in the 1990s when the continental European countries, which moved later into recession, were still trying to climb out of it. The politicians, as usual, were not slow to interpret this to suit their own ends. The strength of Britain's economy was proved by the fact that it had the lowest unemployment rate in Europe, and so on. The reality was a little more complex. It would have been surprising if Britain's employment situation had not looked relatively rosy when it was near the peak of its own economic cycle and its European competitors were close to the low point of their own cycles.

Britain would clearly have problems if it were to seek to join the euro at a point when it reckoned it needed short-term interest rates of 5.5 per cent or more to keep its own economy in balance, but membership would imply rates of only 3 per cent. But there are structural problems as well as problems of timing. For example, Britain has an unusually high level of home ownership. Most homebuyers buy with the help of a mortgage loan, whose cost is linked to interest rates. A change in short-term interest rates can thus have a direct impact on a much larger proportion of the population than in many continental European countries.

Forward markets and hedging

Now that governments have only limited control over the value of currencies, it is up to businesses to protect themselves against the effect of wild swings as best they can. There are various ways they can **hedge** the **currency risk**.

There is a **forward market** in currencies as well as a **spot market**. In the spot market currencies are bought and sold for immediate delivery – in practice, delivery in two days' time – whereas in the forward market they are bought and sold for delivery in the future. You will see that the *Financial Times* table of the value of the pound against major currencies lists a spot price and prices for delivery in one month and three months and one year.

The forward price relative to the spot price reflects the **interest rate differential** between the countries concerned. Suppose, say, you hold sterling and are due to pay for goods in Swiss francs in three months' time. You are worried the value of the Swiss franc will rise, in which case you will have to pay more in sterling terms. So you might buy Swiss francs today for delivery in three months' time, which means you are **locking in** to a known exchange rate.

Suppose also that you can deposit money in Britain to earn 6 per cent and in Switzerland to earn only 2 per cent. For three months you have the benefit of the higher sterling interest rate, whereas if you had bought the Swiss francs immediately you would have been depositing the money at the lower Swiss interest rate until it was needed. So the price you pay for the Swiss francs for delivery in three months will be higher than the spot price by an amount that reflects this interest rate advantage – in other words, at the three months' price you will get fewer Swiss francs for your pounds than at the spot price. But if the currency you want to buy forward offers higher interest rates than in Britain, the forward price will be lower than the spot price (at a **discount** rather than a **premium**). Forward exchange rates are shown in the *Financial Times*, together with the annual interest rate differential they reflect.

In practice, hedging strategies in the foreign exchange markets may be a great deal more complex than simply buying or selling a currency forward, though this illustrates the principle. Currencies may be **swapped**, too (see Chapter 17) and banks offer a range of **OTC** currency hedging products. **Currency futures** may also be bought on certain financial futures exchanges and OTC currency options are traded in London (see below).

Who deals in the forex markets?

Foreign exchange is dealt in by the major banks and by specialist **foreign exchange brokers**, with the dealers operating from the screen-cluttered trading floors familiar from many film and television reports. Dealing is via these screens and telephones: there is no central marketplace.

London, conveniently placed to provide continuity between Tokyo and New York in the time zones, is the largest foreign exchange market. A Bank of England survey of 253 banks and securities houses and 10 brokers in 1998 estimated the average volume of the London market at $637 billion per day, with US dollar/sterling and dollar/deutschmark business accounting for 49 per cent of the total. As much as 65 per cent of that $637 billion represents **forward** business, mainly swaps, the remainder being **spot** (immediate delivery) transactions.

Was there really $637 billion of cross-border trade per day that required currency transactions in London? Of course not. More than four-fifths represented dealing between banks. Dealing with non-financial institutions was only 7 per cent of the total. Business with other financial institutions accounted for 9 per cent. Direct business with customers is thus a relatively small proportion of the total and the volume of speculative activity is high. However, each trade-backed transaction may in practice require a number of separate transactions on the exchanges as banks deal to 'lay off' the risk they have taken from the customer. **Arbitrage** (see glossary) evens out temporary disparities between rates for different currencies and ensures that interest rate differentials are reflected in forward rates. Currency dealers justify the vast speculative activity with the argument that it results in a highly liquid market in which necessary trade-backed transactions can be carried out with ease. In addition to foreign exchange itself, there is massive $171 billion daily trading in **over-the-counter** (OTC) derivative products. The market for interest-rate derivative products is about 2.5 times the size of that for currency products, though the latter were growing faster.

While the economists at the banks may seek to make rational forecasts of likely trends in a particular currency, the dealers have a much shorter-term view, taking advantage of temporary swings and anomalies. In the absence of rational reasons for currency swings, they may enlist the help of **chartist** techniques (see Chapter 7a) which indicate likely trends or turning points purely on the basis of chart patterns and profiles. It may add to the volatility of the market if large numbers of participants react to the same chart signals simultaneously.

Internet pointers

Exchange rates are obtainable at most of the investment or personal finance websites. The main source for more general information on foreign exchange is the Bank of England website at www. bankofengland.co.uk/, which also has a special section on the euro, and there is a UK government site on preparations for the euro at www.euro.gov.uk/. Most countries in the euro zone have their own euro sites, but the official European Commission site is at europa.eu.int/euro/. The value of the euro relative to other currencies is, of course, the concern of the European Central Bank at www.ecb.int/. Incidentally, the Internet is littered with organizations trying to persuade you to have a punt in currencies or their derivatives. Be a little wary.

17 International money: the euromarkets

By far the biggest **capital market** centred on London is the **euro-market** or the **international market**. The two terms do not mean exactly the same thing, but we will come to the differences later. You do not read a great deal about these markets day-to-day – except in the *Financial Times* and a few specialist publications – because they are markets for professionals, they have no central marketplace and they have not in the past directly impinged on many private investors in Britain. Yet, in terms of money raised, they completely dwarf Britain's domestic markets.

Moreover, now that inflation is under better control than in recent decades, both companies and investors are far more alive to the attractions of bonds, which are the mainstay of the international market. Add to this the explosion in takeover activity among very large companies, much of which is being financed by debt issues, and it should come as no surprise that activity in the euromarket has soared in recent years. The only fly in the ointment as far as Britain is concerned is the European Union's attempt to impose a withholding tax on savings, which could seriously damage the country's position as the centre of euromarket activity. This ongoing row surfaces frequently in the press: more of this later.

To understand the euromarket, start by thinking how markets evolve. A group of people have a need to come together to barter or sell goods. The market grows initially out of this need. It is probably informal, and some markets remain that way. But after a time – and particularly in financial markets – the participants may decide to introduce a more formal structure and a set of rules. It could help the market to function more effectively. It could reduce sharp practice and increase public confidence in the market. It could also, of course, allow the original participants to frame the rules so as to keep others out and to ensure that the market provides them with a good living.

At a later stage, governments may take a hand. Activity in financial markets can have far-reaching economic implications. The government may feel it needs to exert a measure of control. It may decide the market needs supervising by a governmental body. And so on.

Thus, most countries have domestic financial markets that are more or less closely regulated – directly or indirectly – by their respective governments. As we have noted, the trend in recent years has been to dismantle a great deal of this regulation – the **deregulation** process – and to throw domestic markets more open to competition. But this has not always been the case. And, when financiers have perceived a need or an opportunity that could not be exploited in the existing regulated markets, they have often tried to find a way round the problem, perhaps by operating in a new 'black' market of their own. The euromarkets have their origin in this sort of process.

The conventional explanation of the euromarkets used to be that they were an informal market in money held outside its country of origin. Thus, deposits of dollars in a European bank would be **eurodollars**, deposits of German marks in a British bank would be **euromarks**, and so on. This money could be borrowed and lent without going through the domestic financial markets of the country concerned and this is what, in fact, happened. Initially, much of the business was in dollars, hence the term **eurodollar market** in the early days.

Nowadays, when people talk about the euromarket they are referring not so much to the origin of the money that is borrowed and lent but more to the structure and techniques of the market in which it is traded. And the 'euro' part of the title is also misleading: the market is a market between banks worldwide. It is by no means confined to currencies held in European banks, or to European currencies. Nor does its origin have anything to do with the new European currency: the euro. There are **euroyen** and a 'euro' version of the Canadian dollar, and have been since long before such a currency as the euro existed. The market did, however, have its origins in Europe and more specifically in London, which remains the main centre – a factor that explains the presence of so many foreign banks. If we are drawing a distinction between the euromarket and the international market, we would probably say that the former covers transactions in the currencies of which there is a recognized 'euro' version and the latter term would also embrace dealing outside domestic markets in money or securities denominated in any currency. In practice, the two terms are often used virtually interchangeably.

INTERNATIONAL MONEY RATES

Jun 28	Short term	7 days notice	One month	Three months	Six months	One year
Euro	4⅜ - 4⅜	4⅝ - 4¹³₃₂	4¹⁵₃₂ - 4⅜	4¹⁹₃₂ - 4½	4²⁵₃₂ - 4²¹₃₂	5¹₁₆ - 4¹⁵₁₆
Danish Krone	4⅝ - 4⅜	4¾ - 4¹³₃₂	4²⁷₃₂ - 4²³₃₂	5¼ - 5⅛	5²³₃₂ - 5⁹₃₂	5³¹₃₂ - 5²⁷₃₂
Sterling	6⅜ - 6¼	6⅛ - 6	6³₃₂ - 5³¹₃₂	6⅛ - 6⅛	6⅝ - 6⅜	6¹⁷₃₂ - 6¹³₃₂
Swiss Franc	3⅜ - 2⅞	3¹³₁₆ - 3³₁₆	3³₃₂ - 3³₁₆	3⅜ - 3⁹₃₂	3¹⁹₃₂ - 3¹⁵₃₂	3¹³₁₆ - 3²¹₃₂
Canadian Dollar	5¼ - 5⅝	5²⁷₃₂ - 5¹¹₁₆	5¹⁵₃₂ - 5¹¹₁₆	5⁹₃₂ - 5¹³₃₂	6¹₃₂ - 5⅝	6¼ - 6⅛
US Dollar	6³¹₃₂ - 6⅞	6³¹₃₂ - 6⅞	6¹₁₆ - 6¹⁹₃₂	6¹³₁₆ - 6¹¹₁₆	6⅝ - 6¹⁷₃₂	7⁷₃₂ - 7³₃₂
Japanese Yen	⅛ - 1₃₂	⅛ - 1₃₂	⅜ - ¹⁵₁₆	7₃₂ - ⅛	¹¹₃₂ - ¼	7₁₆ - ¹¹₃₂
Asian $Sing	1¼ - 1	2⅞ - 2⅝	2¾ - 2½	2¹⁵₁₆ - 2¹¹₁₆	3 - 2¾	3¼ - 3

Short term rates are call for the US Dollar and Yen, others: two days' notice.

Example 17.1 Rates for borrowing and lending in different currencies in the international market. Source: *Financial Times*.

　　　The important point is that the international market does not belong to any one country, nor is the market as such regulated by any country's domestic supervisors (though London dealers in the market would come within the UK's regulatory structure). Dealing in this international market is not circumscribed by the local rules and regulations of a particular financial centre. To this extent it remains 'informal' or 'unofficial', though market organizations have agreed some rules of their own. If London is the centre of the international market, the market is by no means run mainly by British institutions, nor are British companies among the most important users of the market. American banks and their offshoots are dominant, and to a lesser extent the Japanese.

　　　Restrictions on capital-raising by foreigners in the United States domestic markets in the 1960s help to explain the establishment and growth of the international market in London, conveniently situated in the time zones. America imposed limits on the rates of interest that could be paid in its domestic markets and had levied a tax on foreign borrowers which made raising capital in New York uneconomic for them. London, on the other hand, offered a relaxed taxation and regulatory regime as far as the operations of the international market were concerned.

　　　Nowadays, the international market mirrors most of the facilities and forms of security available in domestic markets. Eurocurrencies can be deposited and borrowed for very short periods or for many years. Borrowers can take out the equivalent of a term loan in a eurocurrency. They can issue various forms of bond or 'IOU note' to raise money in a eurocurrency. And because the eurocurrency market is largely unfettered by national restrictions, many of the more innovative forms of financing are first devised in the eurocurrency market and often copied subsequently in domestic financial markets. It is a case of giving the market what it wants or selling the market what you think it will take. Recent years have also seen considerable growth in **euro-equity** issues – issues of company shares via the international market rather than in the domestic stockmarket of the company concerned.

It is important to note the difference between borrowing a eurocurrency and simply borrowing in an overseas financial market. A euroyen loan is a borrowing denominated in yen through the international market structure whereas a **samurai** bond is a yen bond issued by a foreigner in the Japanese domestic market. A **yankee** bond is a dollar bond issued by a foreigner in the United States domestic market and a **bulldog** bond is a sterling bond issued in Britain by a foreigner. The samurai, yankee and bulldog are not eurobonds.

Syndicated loans

Out of the original short-term market in eurocurrency deposits – the **inter-bank market** – grew the **syndicated loan** market. **Syndicates** of banks would get together under a **lead bank** or lead banks to provide medium-term or long-term loans running into hundreds of millions or billions of dollars – though the currency in which the money was borrowed would not necessarily be dollars. It could equally well have been Japanese yen. By each contributing part of the loan, the individual banks avoided too large a commitment to any one customer.

Eurobonds

Securitization of eurocurrency lending was the next step and the **eurobond** emerged. It is much like the bonds that governments and companies issue in their domestic markets (see Chapter 13), but the documentation and the issue techniques are somewhat different. It is also denominated in one of the eurocurrencies.

There are other differences, too. In Europe most domestic bonds suffer **withholding tax**. In other words, some income tax is deducted before the investor gets his interest. Eurobond interest is normally paid gross, without any withholding tax. The bonds are also issued in **bearer** form, rather than the **registered** form applying to UK domestic bonds, which gives them attractions for investors who do not intend being over-frank with the tax man (the tax advantages of eurobonds were probably a significant factor in the growth of the market). This is why Britain has been fighting to prevent the proposed EU **withholding tax** on savings and investments from applying to eurobonds. There is a very real risk that a significant part of the market's activity might transfer to a more tax-favourable climate.

Another difference between the euromarket and the UK domestic market: the interest is normally paid once a year rather than in two half-yearly instalments, as is normal for UK domestic bonds. This means that a coupon of 10 per cent on a eurobond is not generally the same thing as a coupon of 10 per cent on a UK domestic bond. With the UK bond the investor can reinvest the interest he receives after six months and earn interest on it for the second half of the year. It means that 10 per cent paid in two instalments is worth the same as 10.25 per cent paid only once a year. Coupons and yields on eurobonds therefore have to be adjusted to express them in the same terms as returns in the domestic market. So you may read of a yield 'equivalent to such-and-such an amount on a semi-annual basis'.

Issue techniques in the eurobond market are complex, and the way they work in practice is often somewhat different from the theory. At the two ends of the transaction you have the company or organization that wants to raise money via a eurobond issue (and needs to be sure of getting its money) and the end-investor in the bond (perhaps the proverbial Belgian dentist usually portrayed as the typical eurobond investor). Between is an array of banks. A lead bank (or group of banks) puts the issue together and agrees with the company the terms on which it will get its money. These banks need a good distribution network to be able to place a significant proportion of the bonds with investors. Other banks are brought in to take part of the risk of underwriting the issue (in theory, at least). Then there are other banks (the **selling group**) which are not part of the syndicate but which also use their extensive retail contacts to sell the bonds to the end-investors.

Once the eurobond has been issued in the **primary market** it can be traded in the **secondary market**, an **over-the-counter** or **OTC** market conducted by dealers over the telephone and television screen. In the early days the lead bank is allowed to **stabilize** (i.e. manipulate) the market in the issue by dealing itself. Whether or not it makes a profit on the issue depends on whether it can sell the bonds at a price that does not wipe out the fees it received. The secondary market can at times be a volatile market, partly because dealers (unlike market-makers on the London Stock Exchange) have not had an obligation to make a market. If times got tough in a particular sector they might

INTERNATIONAL BONDS

Jun 28	Red date	Coupon	S&P* Rating	Moody's Rating	Bid price	Bid yield	Day's chge yield	Mth's chge yield	Spread vs Govts
$									
EIB	01/09	5.250	AAA	Aaa	87.0046	7.35	+0.03	-0.26	+1.21
ABN Amro	06/07	7.125	AA-	Aa3	96.5229	7.79	+0.02	-0.31	+1.58
Quebec	02/09	5.750	A+	A2	89.6188	7.40	+0.03	-0.31	+1.26
Citicorp FRN	02/04	6.890	AA-	Aa3	99.6369	6.60	+0.02	-0.23	+0.22
C$									
Bayer L-Bk	08/04	9.500	AAA	Aaa	109.9308	6.65	+0.01	-0.18	+0.32
Toronto (M of)	05/04	8.500	AA+	Aa2	106.2180	6.63	-	-0.05	+0.30
Bell Canada	10/04	10.875	A+	A2	114.6514	6.79	+0.01	-0.06	+0.46
Deutsche B FRN	09/02	5.875	AA	Aa3	99.1229	6.70	+0.01	-0.13	+0.39
£									
EIB	12/09	5.500	AAA	Aaa	94.2000	6.33	-0.12	+0.07	+0.98
Boots	05/09	5.500	A+	A1	90.5000	6.97	-0.03	+0.08	+1.62
British Gas	07/08	8.875	A	A2	110.6500	7.09	-0.01	+0.10	+1.55
Halifax	04/08	6.375	AA	Aa1	97.6400	6.77	-0.04	+0.17	+1.23
SFR									
EIB	01/08	3.750	AAA	Aaa	96.7062	4.27	+0.01	-0.11	+0.31
Brit Columbia	02/02	3.250	AA-	Aa2	98.4751	4.23	+0.02	+0.02	+0.39
Hydro-Quebec	05/01	6.750	A+	A2	101.6148	4.81	+0.03	+0.11	+1.11
Gen Elect.	09/01	3.162	AAA	Aaa	99.7534	3.87	+0.03	+0.09	+0.17
YEN									
IBRD (World Bk)	03/02	5.250	AAA	Aaa	108.6200	0.21	-0.02	-0.03	-0.22
Spain (Kingdom)	03/02	5.750	AA+	Aa2	109.4028	0.27	-0.04	-	-0.16
KFW Int	12/04	1.000	AAA	Aaa	100.5812	0.87	-0.02	-0.09	-0.02
Eurofima	06/05	0.292	AAA	Aaa	100.0000	0.00	-	-0.99	-1.11
A$									
IBRD (World Bk)	02/08	6.000	AAA	Aaa	96.0693	6.67	-0.04	-	+0.41
Nw Sth Wales Tr	05/06	6.500	AAA	Aaa	99.4923	6.60	-0.02	-0.04	+0.42
S. Aus Gov Fin	06/03	7.750	AA+	Aa2	102.6308	6.75	-0.03	-0.08	+0.69
GMAC Aust	05/01	9.000	A	A2	101.7594	6.82	+0.01	-0.05	+0.86

Example 17.2 A sample of bonds denominated in different currencies that are traded in the international market. Source: *Financial Times.*

temporarily pull in their horns and the market would lose its liquidity.

Two organizations have provided clearance and settlement systems for international bonds and money-market instruments. These used to be **Cedel** in Luxembourg and **Euroclear** in Brussels though Cedel has recently merged with a German clearing house to form **Clearstream** and Euroclear has joined up with a French concern. The market's self-regulatory organization – the **International Securities Market Association** or **ISMA** – is based in Switzerland but has an office in London.

Variations on the bond theme

The original **straight** eurobond carries a fixed rate of interest. But forms of bond were developed which pay floating-rate interest, known as **floating rate notes** (**FRNs**). Some banks have issued **perpetual floating rate notes** or **perpetuals** which are never required to be repaid, though the value of these suffered a dramatic market collapse in the 1980s.

The complexities arise in the many variations of these basic themes, introduced to make eurobonds more attractive to issuers or investors (or both). First the borrower must choose what currency he will borrow in; the interest rate would be usually lower in a tradition-ally strong currency (as the Swiss franc usually is) than it would be in sterling, but if the Swiss franc rises, the debt could be a lot more expen-sive to repay. Some bonds (**dual currency bonds**) reduce the curren-cy exposure from the point of view of the investor: he puts up the money in one currency but is repaid in another at a rate of exchange fixed in advance.

Some eurobonds issued by companies incorporate an **equity sweetener**. Either the bond can be **converted** (wholly or in part) into the shares of the issuing company or it comes with **warrants** to sub-scribe for the company's shares. The principles are the same as those outlined in Chapter 5 in the context of convertibles and warrants issued by domestic British companies. And, as in the domestic bond market, eurobonds may be issued at a **deep discount** instead of paying a rate of interest (**zero-coupon bonds**).

The real complexities, however, concern the interest rate and the compromises evolved to obtain some of the advantages of both fixed-rate and floating-rate bonds. Hybrid bonds are issued which pay a fixed coupon initially, followed by a floating rate after a certain date. Or there may be an upper limit (a **cap**) to the interest rate payable on a floating rate note (a **capped floating rate note**) and sometimes a lower limit or **floor** as well. There are even bonds which pay higher interest as interest rates generally go down. And the investor might have a **put option** or the issuer a **call option**, allowing one or the other to force early redemption in certain circumstances.

Eurocommercial paper

Even in the field of very short-term securities, there are counterparts in the international market to the instruments found in domestic financial markets. You used to read about the **euronote**: an IOU with a life of under a year. Borrowers would arrange with a bank or dealer to sell or take up the notes they issued under arrangements such as the **revolving**

underwriting facility (RUF) or **note issuance facility (NIF)**. The borrower could thus issue further notes as he needed the money or as the earlier ones fell due. Nowadays the emphasis is on **euro-commercial paper (ECP)** which works in much the same way as commercial paper in the domestic market (see Chapter 15). A somewhat longer-term version is the **euro medium-term note** or **EMTN**. An ECP programme may give the borrower the option of raising money in a range of currencies, and a number of British companies have used it.

Euro and domestic markets in Britain

Of late the distinctions between the domestic market and the euromarket in sterling-denominated bonds have been greatly eroded. Much the same firms deal in securities in both markets, and the rules for the issue of domestic sterling bonds on the London Stock Exchange have been relaxed to bring them closer in line with those applying in the euromarket. There have been sterling issues for UK companies divided between a 'euro' and a 'domestic' component, with the domestic part in the form of registered bonds. Many major British companies have issued **convertible loan stocks** and **convertible preference shares** in the euromarket, and for larger companies the choice between the two markets often depends mainly on questions of tax, issue costs and the type of investor they are trying to attract.

While the UK domestic market is the main one for the issue of **secured loans** (eurobonds are usually unsecured) the 1980s saw rapid expansion of euromarket issues of **mortgage-backed securities** by British-based **specialist mortgage lenders** who competed strongly with the building societies and banks to provide housing finance. Large numbers of individual residential mortgages – typically a thousand or so – would be 'pooled' in a special-purpose company which then issued floating rate notes or bonds to investors at large, thus recouping the money originally lent to homebuyers. The payments of interest and capital by these homebuyers provide for the interest on the notes and for their eventual repayment. The process is a prime example of **securitization**: mortgage loans are transmuted into tradable securities. However, mortgage-backed securities lost a fair bit of their appeal after the early 1990s collapse of house prices in Britain, though they are gaining in popularity again now.

Setting the interest rate

The *Financial Times* carries a table of **international money rates**.

These follow but do not necessarily exactly match domestic interest rates within the countries concerned. Rates are given for a range of eurocurrencies for deposits ranging from very short term to periods of up to a year. Needless to say, rates are lowest for the strongest currencies.

The key rate is three-month or six-month **LIBOR**, which stands for **London inter-bank offered rate** (see Chapter 15). This is the rate at which banks will lend in the inter-bank market, and is adopted as the benchmark rate of interest. The interest on floating rate notes is usually set by reference to the average rate of LIBOR and expressed as 'so many **basis points**' (hundredths of one percentage point) above LIBOR.

Euroequities

The distribution networks used by major eurobond dealers to market loan and bond issues to investors are used on a smaller (but growing) scale to market ordinary shares in major internationally known companies. It may suit a company to raise cash by selling shares outside its domestic capital market when this is too small for its needs. Other companies may wish to attract shareholders in overseas countries where they trade. Such operations are known as **euroequity** issues. British companies that are already listed are generally prevented by the **pre-emption** rules from using this route to raise further cash – new shares have to be offered first to existing holders.

Size of the international market

For an idea of the size and make-up of the international market in 1999, look at Tables 17.1 and 17.2, based on figures supplied by Capital DATA Bondware and Loanware. Our figures were drawn up a week or so before the end of 1999, and up to that point bond issues in the International market had raised the equivalent of some $1,386 billion in 1999 against some $929 billion for the whole of 1998, thus comfortably exceeding the $1 trillion mark for the first time. Apart from the rate of growth, the notable feature of 1999 was the emergence of the **euro**, in its first year of existence and despite its weakness in the forex markets, as the most popular currency overall in which eurobonds were denominated. The euro narrowly pushed the US dollar into second place. Loan facilities were arranged for some $468 billion. In addition, European equity issues (both primary and secondary) in the international market totalled $179 billion in 1999, again using the Capital DATA figures.

International market: money raised from bonds and loans

	International bonds (US$ million)	Euromarket loans (US$ million)
1990	214,785	208,773
1991	285,835	149,395
1992	313,307	126,054
1993	441,238	148,703
1994	430,548	178,340
1995	464,284	323,650
1996	681,787	318,995
1997	749,032	364,462
1998	928,721	320,537
1999*	1,380,865	467,821

* To 16/12/99

Source: *Capital DATA Bondware and Capital DATA Loanware*

Table 17.1

International bond issues in 1999 (to 22/12/99)

Currency	Fixed rate bonds US$ million	Convertible bonds US$ million	Floating-rate notes US$ million	TOTAL US$ million	%
euro	398,155.88	26,892.72	202,724.80	627,773.40	45.30
US dollar	437,047.63	6,678.56	134,813.69	578,539.88	41.75
Sterling	69,649.11	2,237.28	25,112.39	96,998.77	7.00
Japanese yen	24,932.83	2,972.57	3,145.42	31,050.83	2.24
Swiss franc	20,461.76	615.08	2,494.18	23,571.02	1.70
Canadian dollar	5,800.03	0	0	5,800.03	0.42
Australian dollar	4,326.83	0	19.01	4,345.84	0.31
Hong Kong dollar	2,691.01	0	1,569.76	4,260.77	0.31
Greek drachma	2,347.31	0	199.43	2,546.74	0.18
New Zealand dollar	1,819.90	0	0	1,819.90	0.13
South African rand	1,492.71	0	115.69	1,608.41	0.12
Swedish krona	1,373.56	0	0	1,373.56	0.10
Norwegian krone	1,282.84	0	0	1,282.84	0.09
Polish zloty	1,121.84	0	0	1,121.84	0.08
Other	3,575.87	0	55.87	3,643.59	0.26
TOTAL	976,079.11	39,408.07	370,250.25	1,385,737.44	100.00

Source: *Capital DATA Bondware and Capital DATA Loanware*

Table 17.2

Interest rate and currency swaps

The form in which borrowers can most easily raise money is not always the form best suited to their purposes. Company A, say, finds it can easily raise fixed-interest money when it really needs floating-rate funds. Company B, on the other hand, has no problem in raising a floating-rate loan but its real need is for fixed-interest money which would be expensive for it.

The solution may be a **swap** – in this case an **interest rate swap**. Company A issues its fixed-interest bond and Company B issues a floating-rate loan. They then agree to swap their interest payment liabilities. Company A pays the floating-rate interest due on Company B's loan and Company B pays the fixed rate of interest on the Company A borrowing, with some adjustment to reflect the relative strength of the two concerns. By this mechanism, each ends up with money in the form in which it needs it, at a cheaper rate than if it had borrowed what it needed direct.

This is the principle: each company borrows the money in the form in which it has the greatest relative advantage. The mechanisms are in reality more complex. Companies will not normally seek the **counterparty** for the swap direct, but will arrange a swap with a bank, which can either find a counter-party for the deal (taking a small cut in the middle) or may act as counter-party itself. And swaps, once set up, may subsequently be traded or adapted as conditions change in the market.

The second type of swap is the **currency swap**. Company A may be able to borrow on the most advantageous terms in German marks, because its credit rating is high in Germany where it is known. But it needs US dollars. Company B can most easily raise money in US dollars, but it needs German marks. So Company A issues a German mark loan and Company B borrows dollars. They then swap so that each ends up with what it needs, paying the interest on the currency it swaps into. Since each is borrowing where its credit is best, both end up with cheaper funds than if they had borrowed direct in the currency they needed. Again, a bank probably acts as intermediary. With many swaps both interest payments and currencies are exchanged.

It has been estimated that at times as much as 80 per cent of the funds raised in the euromarket are immediately swapped.

Ranking of borrowers

The interest rate paid by a borrower in the euromarket depends partly on the borrower's standing. The main borrowers are governments, public bodies and internationally known companies, and companies known only in their domestic markets may be less well received.

Several organizations, including **Standard & Poor's**, **Moody's** and **Fitch IBCA** provide **rating services** which attempt to quantify the credit-worthiness of a borrower. The highest rating is AAA, hence the term **triple-A-rated** for the very safest borrowers. The same organizations provide ratings for short-term debt such as commercial paper.

Tombstones

Banks that are active in the euromarkets like to advertise their success in raising funds for clients. They do so partly by taking **tombstone** advertisements in the financial pages, particularly (in Britain) in the *Financial Times* and the magazine *Euromoney*. These advertisements announce that they appear 'as a matter of record only' (in other words they are not a solicitation to buy securities) and give the name of the borrower and brief details of the loan facility or bond issue arranged plus the names of the participating banks. The lead bank or banks which put the deal together appear at the head of the list and the remainder are normally listed in alphabetical order. The distinctive layout of these advertisements makes it clear why the term 'tombstone' is appropriate.

Press coverage

Domestic stockmarkets are usually hot on information and the press automatically receives details of most issues. The international market is rather different. The deals are between issuers and banks, rather than direct with the public, even though the public may end up owning the securities that are offered. There is no central stock exchange to impose disclosure rules. Details of a deal are frequently only publicized outside the market (see **tombstones**, above) well after it has taken place. Therefore, much of the information on what is happening in this mammoth market has to be picked up by specialist journalists with close contacts among the participating banks, who sniff out the rumours of a forthcoming deal.

The *Financial Times* publishes on a Monday a table of New international bond issues. On other working days its International capital markets page carries a smallish sample of international bonds denominated in different currencies, while its Euro markets page gives details of some major euro-zone bonds.

The monthly magazine *Euromoney* was set up specifically to cover the international capital market. Weekly news of new offerings, syndicated loan facilities and the rest appears in *International Financing Review*, aimed strictly at the financial community. And a variety of euromarket newsletters and news services such as the *Syndicated Lending Review* are also aimed principally at market professionals.

Internet pointers

The clearing houses for international bonds are Clearstream (formerly Cedel) at www.clearstream.net/ and Euroclear at www.euroclear.com/. The trade and self-regulatory organization for dealers in international bonds is the International Securities Market Association (ISMA) whose London operation has a website at www.isma.co.uk/. The magazine *Euromoney* is at www.euromoney.com and Euromoney Publications' associated company Capital DATA, which supplied the statistics for this chapter, is at www.capitaldata.com/. The three main rating agencies are Standard & Poor's at www.standardandpoors.com/, Moody's at www.moodys.com/ and Fitch IBCA at www.fitchibca.com/.

18 Financial derivatives and commodities

Every financial market involves risk for the market user, but there are some markets whose main function is the **redistribution of risk**. On the one hand, they are the riskiest markets of all. On the other, they are markets in which risks can be reduced or eliminated. These are the **options** and **futures** markets, which come under the general heading of markets in **derivative products** or **derivatives**. These markets are not the only places where derivative products are bought and sold. We saw earlier that the banks undertake large volumes of 'over-the-counter' derivatives business direct with their customers in products such as swaps and interest rate caps (see Chapters 14, 15 and 17). But it is the public derivatives markets that are most frequently reported in the press.

The customers who use these markets fall into two main categories: those who want to **hedge** (guard against) a risk to which they are exposed in the normal course of their business. And those who are prepared to accept a high risk in return for the possibility of large rewards: the **traders** or **speculators**.

Following the collapse in February 1995 of the City of London's oldest merchant bank, **Barings**, as a result of losses in the derivatives markets, awareness of derivatives has spread far beyond the readers of the financial pages. But judging from much of the press and television reporting at the time, there is considerable confusion as to what derivatives are. Yet the principle behind derivative products is a very old one. All that is new is the recent explosive growth in the derivative markets and in the range of products that are dealt in them. So let us start from basic principles.

First, why the term 'derivatives'? Answer: because they are financial products derived from some other existing product. Shares, bonds, currencies and commodities such as cocoa or zinc are all existing products. There are markets in which they can be bought and sold. It is not too difficult to understand what they are.

And today there are derivatives based on these existing products. The derivatives give the right (and perhaps the obligation) to buy or sell a quantity of one of these existing products at some point in the future. Or to benefit in some other way from a rise or fall in the price of one of these existing products.

The betting side of derivatives

Perhaps the best approach is to look at derivatives in terms of a bet (and there are, in fact, bookmakers who will offer you a bet on the movement in a market index). Suppose you think that share prices are going to rise. You could, of course, buy shares to make a profit from the rise that you think is coming. But you would need quite a lot of cash for a worthwhile investment. Alternatively, you could find somebody who is prepared to bet against your view of the market: somebody who does not think that the market will rise as fast as you do or who thinks it is going to fall. So you agree with this person that he will pay you £1 for every percentage point by which the generally accepted stockmarket index rises above an agreed starting point within, say, three months. The other side of the coin is that you agree to pay him £1 for every percentage point by which the stockmarket index might fall below an agreed starting point. In practice of course, you would probably be betting much larger amounts: perhaps £10,000 for every percentage point by which the index rises or falls. But the attraction of the system is that you do not have to put up much cash at the outset when you make your bet. You will be required to pay a small deposit or **margin** for safety. However, if the bet goes against you and the market starts moving in the opposite way to that you had expected, you might be required to provide considerably more cash or else cancel your bet and accept your losses to date. Equally, if the bet is going your way you could decide to take your profits at any time within the three months by cancelling it.

What we have described here is not the way the **futures markets** work in practice. The mechanics are rather different. But the principle and the effect are much as described in our example. There is an opportunity to make or lose very large sums of money very quickly for a relatively modest initial cash outlay. The same principle underlies many of the **over-the-counter** or **OTC** derivative products that are sold by banks rather than traded in a market.

Now take a different approach. Again, you want to take a bet on your belief that share prices will rise. You think that there is a good chance that the stockmarket index will rise by 10 per cent within three months. Suppose the present level of the index is 100. You bet somebody £1 that the index will rise above 104 within three months. For every percentage point that it rises above 104, he will pay you 50p. So if it rises to 110 as you expect, you will collect £3 (50p multiplied by 6) in return for your £1 stake: a £2 profit or a 200 per cent return on your £1 outlay. If you are wrong and the index does not rise above 104, you will have lost your £1 stake money. But that is all that you will have lost.

What we have just described is the principle behind an **option**. Again, the mechanics of a real options market are a little different and the sums involved are usually much larger. But there is an important difference to note between futures and options. In a futures market you can end up losing a great deal more than your original cash stake, as merchant bank Barings found out. But in an options market a buyer of options knows that his loss is limited to his original stake. In our example, the maximum loss is £1 (the potential losses for the person who creates or **writes** the option that you buy can, of course, be much larger).

The insurance aspect

We have also talked throughout in terms of a 'bet', and the options and futures markets can indeed be used for wild betting. But in many circumstances it would be more accurate to talk of our 'bet' as an 'insurance policy'. Suppose our investor is an institution that knows that it will have £5m to invest in shares in three months' time. It thinks that the market is going to rise and there is a risk that it will have to pay a lot more for the shares by the time it has the money available. For a relatively modest outlay today it could buy options on the stockmarket index. If share prices do rise, it will have to pay more for its shares when the £5m is available. But it will have made a profit on its options that it can offset against this higher cost. The stake money spent on buying the options has served as an **insurance premium**. The futures markets can be used to insure against future price movements in the same way.

How forward markets evolved

If the principles behind futures and options are relatively simple, the mechanics are inevitably more complex. Our best starting point is the **forward** commodity markets where the techniques evolved.

To focus on the essential elements rather than the detail of any particular derivative, we will invent a physical product – call it 'commoditum' – and imagine it is a relatively common metal used in many manufacturing processes.

There is a free market in which commoditum can be bought and sold. In the usual way, the price of commoditum will rise or fall depending on the balance between buyers and sellers in this market, and it can fluctuate quite widely. The mining companies that produce commoditum obviously want as high a price as possible for their product. Conversely, the manufacturers who use commoditum in their products want to buy it as cheaply as possible. But both producers and users of commoditum may have one clear interest in common: there are times when both of them will want to reduce the uncertainty as to price. The producer cannot plan his production of commoditum efficiently if he does not know whether he will get £500 or £1,500 per ton when he has stocks ready to sell in six months. The manufacturers who use commoditum in their products cannot budget efficiently if they do not know whether they will have to pay £500 or £1,500 per ton when they next need to restock on commoditum in six months.

So it could pay both sides to reduce or eliminate the uncertainty. How can they do this? One way would be for the producer and the manufacturer to agree today the price at which the one will supply and the other will buy commoditum in six months' time. Suppose today's price for commoditum for immediate delivery (technically, the **spot price**) is £1,000 per ton. Both sides think that the price is more likely to rise than to fall over the coming six months, though the possibility of a fall cannot be discounted. And after much haggling, they eventually compromise on a price of £1,100 per ton for the commoditum to be delivered in six months. The producer commits himself to selling 20 tons at £1,100 per ton in six months and the manufacturer commits himself to buying 20 tons at £1,100 per ton in six months.

Who wins and who loses from this arrangement depends on what actually happens to the price of commoditum in the market over this six months. If the price for immediate delivery has fallen to £900 per ton by the end of six months, the manufacturer will find himself paying £1,100 per ton for something he could have bought in the market at £900 and he will have lost. The producer, on the other hand will have gained. If the spot commoditum price is £1,400 per ton after six months, the producer will have lost by agreeing in advance to deliver at only £1,100 per ton and the manufacturer will have saved himself a lot of money.

However, both sides to the transaction will have removed uncertainty. They will have had a known price on which to base their planning. And it was to provide this certainty that the **forward** markets evolved. A forward market is one where buyers and sellers can establish a price for a product to be delivered at a specific date in the future. We took as our example a transaction in commoditum to be delivered in six months. But it could equally well have been commoditum for delivery in three months or nine months. Thus, in these forward markets, a range of prices will be quoted. We might talk of the price for 'three months' commoditum' (commoditum for delivery in three months), 'six months' commoditum', 'nine months' commoditum', and so on. And we also assumed a single transaction between one commoditum producer and one buyer. In practice, there will be a number of people prepared to offer commoditum for delivery in six months and a number of potential buyers of commoditum for delivery in six months. The price of 'six months' commoditum' will reflect the views of all these potential sellers and buyers.

Into the futures markets

This principle of buying and selling for future delivery has characterized the markets in physical commodities – mainly metals and staple foodstuffs – for generations. It has also been a feature of the foreign exchange market, where prices can be agreed today for foreign currencies that are to be delivered in the future (effectively the parties thus 'lock into' a known exchange rate). But all of this still seems some way removed from the forces that destroyed the Barings merchant bank in 1995.

To understand this, we have to follow the evolution of the markets a stage further. If **forward** markets are a very old concept, **futures** markets are a somewhat more recent one, though the underlying principles are very similar. In the forward markets, buyers and sellers can agree the price for a product to be delivered at any point in the future. It could be for delivery in two-and-a-half months or for delivery in 30 weeks. In futures markets, the agreements are standardized. Suppose we are looking at a market in commoditum futures from the standpoint of a date early in April. We might see that you can buy or sell a **contract** for delivery of commoditum in May, July, September, November or in January of the following year.

Not only the delivery dates are standardized; so are the terms and conditions of the contract. The standard contracts are, let us suppose, for delivery of ten tons of commoditum on one of the dates we have mentioned. The contracts relate to commoditum of a standard quality and purity. Thus, somebody who buys one commoditum contract for September delivery is, in theory, agreeing to take delivery of ten tons of commoditum on a specified date in September. The seller of a September commoditum contract is, again in theory, agreeing to deliver ten tons of the standard grade commoditum on the specified date in September.

How is the price established? Again, it is by the interplay of buyers and sellers in the market, but the mechanics are a little different from the simple forward market. In our hypothetical futures market, participants can buy and sell the September commoditum contract (and, of course, the May commoditum contract, the July contract and all the rest). The price of a September commoditum contract at any given time will thus reflect the balance between buyers and sellers of that particular contract at the time. If, subsequently, more buyers emerge, the price is likely to go up. If more sellers emerge, it will probably go down.

Let us suppose, as with our forward market example, that we are looking at the position from a standpoint at the beginning of April and that the spot price of commoditum at that point is again £1,000 per ton. A contract for immediate delivery of ten tons of commoditum would thus have a value of £10,000 at that point. And let us assume that a contract for delivery in September stands in the market at a price of £11,000. Anybody who buys the September commoditum contract is thus in theory agreeing a price of £11,000 for ten tons of commoditum to be delivered in September. Anybody who sells the September commoditum contract is in theory agreeing to supply ten tons of commoditum in September at a price of £11,000.

The important point to remember is that the September commoditum contract is itself a form of security that can be bought and sold in a market. It is not the same thing as the commoditum metal itself. But it is a **derivative** of commoditum whose market price at any given time will be largely influenced by buyers' and sellers' views of the outlook for the commoditum price. Once you grasp this fact, you can see how the principle can be extended to other types of product. Why not have a futures contract for delivery of a nominal £100,000-worth of a standard type of government bond in September? Or a basket of shares in companies? Or a standard amount of a foreign currency: US dollars, for example?

In practice, this is what has happened. **Financial futures** markets in a whole range of financial products have sprung up and expanded enormously in recent years. They are markets which the participants can use effectively to fix the price they will pay or receive for bonds, shares and currencies in the future. As such, they can be used to offset many of the financial risks that crop up inevitably in the course of business. But they can also be used for gambling on a massive scale. We are getting closer to the events that brought down the Barings merchant bank in 1995. But before turning to financial futures, there are a few further fundamental concepts that we can illustrate more easily with our example of commoditum futures.

Where the dangers begin

First, why should a market in derivatives be any more dangerous than a market in the underlying products? Why should it be more dangerous to buy commoditum futures than the commoditum metal itself? Or government bond futures rather than investing in government bonds? The answer is that it need not be more dangerous, but that it very often is. And the main reason is **gearing** (or **leverage** in the American terminology) built into futures markets.

Let us go back to our September commoditum futures contract. The contract, remember, is for ten tons of commoditum to be delivered in September. And, as of the beginning of April, the price of this contract in the market is £11,000. The vital point, however, is that a buyer of this contract does not have to put up £11,000 when he purchases it. At that stage he only has to put up a relatively small deposit or **margin**. It might be 10 per cent of the value of the contract. In financial futures markets it might be as low as 1 per cent (sellers of contracts, incidentally, will also have to provide a margin).

For our example we will stick with 10 per cent. The bulk of the contract price does not become due until the contract matures (in September, in our example). So our buyer of one contract has to put up £1,100 of initial margin. In return, he is exposed to the profit or loss on £11,000-worth of commoditum. Suppose by September the price of commoditum for immediate delivery has risen to £1,400 per ton. The contract for September delivery of ten tons of the metal is now worth £14,000. Our buyer of the contract has made a profit of £3,000 (the £14,000 current value of the contract less the £11,000 he originally agreed to pay for it). But the startling point is that he has made this profit on a cash outlay of only £1,100: the initial margin that he had to provide. His return on this cash outlay is thus about 273 per cent.

In this case everything went well. But what if the commoditum price began falling shortly after he bought the September contract for £11,000 in April? Suppose the price of the September contract was down to £9,900 by early June. On paper, he has a loss of £1,100. This has completely wiped out the initial £1,100 deposit or margin that he provided, and he will have been required to provide further margin – another £1,000, say – to top up his margin after the paper losses. If he could not or did not meet this **margin call** (provide the further cash margin), the exchange would simply have **closed him out**. In other words, his contract would effectively have been cancelled by the exchange and his paper losses would have become real ones. This is why exchanges always insist on a margin and insist that it is kept topped up. It is to ensure that the investor or speculator has always provided a sufficient safety cushion to cover any losses.

In our example, the purchaser of the September commoditum contract might have taken the view that the price fall in June was just a temporary blip and that the price would rise again by September to give him his expected profit. In this case he would have wanted to provide the further margin to 'stay in the game'. But note that futures markets have an element of a poker game. You may be pretty confident that you have a winning hand. But unless you have a big enough cash stake to be able to stay in the game, you could still lose.

Taking profits and losses

Now, our example so far has assumed that the buyer of the September commoditum contract had intended to hold it until it became due in September. But there is no reason why this should necessarily be the case. If the price of the commoditum contract for September delivery had risen to £13,000 by late July, he might well have decided to take his profit at this point. How would he take his profit? By selling an identical September commoditum contract for £13,000 in late July. His profit then (less expenses, of course) is the £13,000 he receives from selling a contract less the £11,000 he had agreed to pay originally to buy one. But in reality, as we saw, he had never had to put up the full price in cash. What happens in practice is that he simply receives a cheque for his profit and the return of his margin.

Thus, no commoditum has changed hands. There has been no transfer of the physical metal from a seller to a buyer. And this is an aspect that newcomers to the futures markets often find difficult to grasp. In practice, futures markets very rarely result in physical delivery of the underlying product (the **London Metal Exchange** is a little different in this respect). They are a mechanism for determining the price of a product at various delivery dates. They are a mechanism for allowing participants to benefit (or lose) from the rise or fall in the price of an underlying product. But they are not generally markets for distribution of a physical product. Gains or losses are settled in cash.

Betting on a market fall

And the markets can be used equally well to profit from a fall in the value of a product as from a rise. Somebody betting on a fall in the value of commoditum (or a rise less than the market was expecting) would sell a contract rather than buying one. Suppose that in April he sold a September commoditum contract at £11,000. And suppose that the price of this contract then duly fell to £9,000 by, say, July. He could then buy a contract at £9,000 and collect a profit of £2,000.

The point to remember is that the contract is the same, whether you are buying it or selling it. In theory, if you buy you are agreeing to take delivery of ten tons of commoditum in September. If you sell, you are agreeing in theory to deliver ten tons of commoditum in September. In practice, you realize your profit or loss by closing your position: doing the opposite of what you had done at the outset. If you had originally bought a contract, you close the position by selling an identical contract. Thus in theory you had originally agreed to take delivery of ten tons of commoditum and by selling a contract later you agree in theory to deliver ten tons of commoditum. The two obligations cancel each other, so no commoditum needs to change hands. Likewise, if you had sold a contract at the outset, you close the position later by buying a contract.

The move into financial futures

The extension of the futures principle to purely financial products was, perhaps, inevitable. It enables participants to take bets on (or protect themselves against) rises or falls in the value of the underlying products. These products might be government bonds, interest rates, currencies or shares. If the principle of an interest rate future sounds a bit odd, do not worry too much about the detail. In effect, a hypothetical futures contract is constructed, whose spot value rises or falls according to whether the interest rate in question moves down or up (the market price of a contract for future delivery is, of course, determined by buyers and sellers in the normal way).

You will often notice in the financial press that commentators report on what is happening in the futures market as a prelude to what might happen in the **cash** market. Suppose there is some news that might be judged good for gilt-edged stocks (UK government bonds). Speculators who want to profit from a rise in gilt-edged stocks might be inclined to buy gilt-edged futures in the first instance, because they will get a bigger percentage profit from any given price movement than they would by buying the gilt-edged stocks themselves in the stock market (the **cash** market). Thus the price of the gilt-edged futures contract might begin moving up and suggest that the prices of gilt-edged stocks themselves in the cash market might shortly follow suit.

How options work

The workings of **options** are probably easier to understand at the outset than those of futures, though in both cases the trading strategies followed by professionals in the market may be very complex. Start with a traditional option on shares. An option in this case is the right to buy or the right to sell a share within a stipulated time period at a price that is fixed when the option is bought. Technically, this is an **American option**, but it is the most common kind in Britain. The so-called **European option** is different in that it may only be exercised on a specific date, rather than at any point up to expiry.

Say that you decide at the beginning of April that the shares of XYZ Holdings are likely to rise sharply within the next month or so. The current price is 100p and you think it might well rise to 130p by the end of June. You could, of course, buy 10,000 of the shares for £10,000, and if you are right your 10,000 shares will be worth £13,000 within three months: a profit of £3,000, or 30 per cent on your outlay. But you need to have £10,000 to do it, and though the value of the XYZ shares is unlikely to fall to nothing, you are in theory putting the whole £10,000 at risk.

Instead, you might consider it was worth paying, say, 10p per share for an option that gave you the right to buy a share in XYZ for 105p at any time over the next three months. If the XYZ share price stays at 100p, the option has no value and you lose the 10p **premium** you paid. But this is the most you can lose. If the share price does rise to 130p, then your option clearly has a value and is worth **exercising**: you have the right to buy for 105p a share that you could resell for 130p.

Suppose you had bought options on 10,000 XYZ shares. The total cost at 10p per share would have been £1,000. If, once the price has risen, you exercise your option to buy the 10,000 shares at 105p and immediately resell them at 130p, your profit is £13,000 less £10,500. So you make £2,500 but against this you have to offset the £1,000 cost of your options. But this still leaves a profit of £1,500 (before expenses) on an outlay of only £1,000, or a profit of 150 per cent: considerably better than if you had simply bought the shares. The point to note is that options are a very **highly geared investment**. A comparatively small movement in the share price results in a proportionately far larger movement in the value of the option.

Writing options

But there is another side to the bargain. Who was prepared to agree to sell XYZ shares at 105p if you exercised your option? It was probably an owner of XYZ shares who took a different view from you of what the price was likely to do. He took the view that XYZ shares were pretty fully valued at 100p and that he would be prepared to sell at this price or a little above. But instead of selling at 100p today, he could create or **write** an option and charge 10p for it: the option you bought.

If the price of the shares failed to reach 105p, the option would not be exercised and he would hang on to his shares; but he would have an extra 10p per share in the kitty to set against any fall in the share price. If the price rose above 105p and the option was exercised, he would be obliged to part with his XYZ shares at 105p. But he would really be getting 115p, because he has the 10p premium as well. So by getting 10p for the option he has reduced by 10p his possible paper loss if the XYZ share price falls. He has also limited his possible profit if the XYZ price rises, because the maximum he gets is 115p: 105p for the share and 10p for the option. He has written options as a way of hedging his risk: limiting his possible loss but also restricting his possible profit.

Remember that in futures you *buy* a contract if you are betting on a price rise and you *sell* a contract if you are betting on a fall. The contract itself is the same in either case. With options, too, you can bet on rising or on falling prices. But in both cases you *buy* an option: it is the option itself that is different. If you are **bullish** you buy a **call option** (we assumed a call option in the example above) which gives you the right to buy shares at a pre-determined price. If you are **bearish**, you buy a **put option** which gives you the right to sell shares at a pre-determined price.

The traditional options to buy or sell shares that we have been describing so far are arranged with one of the stockbrokers specializing in this business. You can take out call or put options, or **double** options which give you the right to buy or sell.

The traded options market

More prominent today is the London market in **traded options**, now operated by **Liffe** (see below). The principle of traded options is clear enough if we go back to the example of XYZ Co. You paid 10p for the right to buy an XYZ share at 105p within the next three months. You exercised the option if the XYZ price rose above 105p. If it did not rise, the option **expired** valueless and you lost the whole of your money.

A traded option differs from the traditional type in that you can buy and sell the option itself, much as if it were a share. Again, it has become a tradable derivative product. Suppose after a month the XYZ share price rose from 100p to 110p. The call option for which you paid 10p now has **intrinsic value**, because it gives you the right to buy a share at a price (105p) below its current value (110p). So the option itself is now almost certainly worth more than the 10p you paid for it. Reflecting the rise in the share price, it might now be worth, say, 15p. So you could sell it at this point and take your profit without needing to exercise it. If the XYZ share price had fallen, the value of the option would also have fallen, but you would have had the chance of selling the option and recouping some of your outlay.

In and out of the money

The 10p you paid originally for your XYZ traded option was all hope value or **time value**. There was no intrinsic value initially in an option giving the right to buy a share at 105p (the **exercise price**)

LIFFE EQUITY OPTIONS

Option		Calls Jul	Oct	Jan	Puts Jul	Oct	Jan
Abbey Natl	750	41	71½	100½	18	51½	71½
(*770)	800	17	49	76½	44½	79½	98
Ald Dom ex	330	25½	40½	56½	6½	20	32
(*348½)	360	9½	26	42½	20½	35½	47½
Allied Zurich	750	34½	68½	93	9	33	48
(*773)	800	9½	43½	68	34	58½	73
AstraZeneca	2900	125½	269	360½	57½	184	228
(*2960)	3000	72½	220	311½	102½	234	278
BAA	500	18	42	54	14	31	41½
(*502½)	550	3	21½	33½	49	61	71
BAT	420	31	52½	69½	13	33	44
(*437)	460	12½	34½	51	34½	55	65½
Barclays	1600	62	136½	186½	40	111	140
(*1616)	1700	22	93½	141½	100½	168	195½
Bass	700	29½	63½	79½	21	45	65½
(*706½)	750	9½	41½	58	51½	73	94½
Boots	460	41	60½	70	3½	16½	27
(*496)	500	15	38	49	17	33½	44½
Br Airways	360	29	47½	62½	8	21½	31½
(*380)	390	13	33½	48½	21½	37	47
BP Amoco	600	30	57½	75	9½	31	41
(*619)	650	7	34½	51	36½	58	66½
Option		Jul	Oct	Dec	Jul	Oct	Dec
Cable & Wire	1100	62	135½	162	47½	109½	126½
(*1118)	1150	39	112	139	75½	136	153
Option		Jul	Oct	Jan	Jul	Oct	Jan
CGNU	1000	54½	91½	116	15	52	67
(*1036)	1050	26	66	91	37	76½	91½
Corus	90	9	13½	17½	1½	6½	9½
(*97½)	100	3½	8	12½	5½	11½	15
EMAP	1050	88	170½	207½	34½	103	131½
(*1100)	1100	60½	148	185½	57	129½	158
Glaxo	1900	75	156	220	53	132½	167
(*1912)	2000	34	111½	174	112	188	222½
HSBC 75p	700	52	80	105½	3½	30	47
(*746)	750	19	53½	80	20	53	70
Halifax	600	31½	53½	74½	15	37½	49½
(*615)	650	10	32	52	43½	66	76
ICI	500	20	46	62½	17½	48	59
(*501)	550	4	27½	44	51½	80	90
Land Secur	750	36	64	77	13½	31½	41
(*770)	800	12½	39½	52	40	57	66
Marks & S	220	20½	33	40	2½	12	15½
(*237)	240	8½	22	30	10½	21	26½

Option		Calls Jul	Oct	Dec	Puts Jul	Oct	Dec
Reed Intl	500	49½	75	88½	7½	29½	37½
(*540)	550	19½	49½	64	28	54	62½
Option		Jul	Oct	Jan	Jul	Oct	Jan
Reuters	1150	80½	162½	214	49	118½	155
(*1178)	1200	56½	140	192	74½	145½	182
Royal Bk Scot	1050	42	91	127½	32½	76½	99
(*1056)	1100	21	68½	103½	61½	104	125½
Royal/Sun Al	390	17	38½	54	12½	33	45
(*395½)	420	5½	26	41	30½	51	62
Safeway	240	17	28	35½	5	13½	20
(*251)	260	6½	18½	25½	15	23½	30
Sainsbury	300	13½	31	39	12½	26	33
(*300)	330	3½	19½	27	33	44	51
Sema	950	72½	146½	187	45½	107½	135½
(*974)	1000	46½	124	165	69½	134	162½
Shell Trans	550	21½	45	61½	11	32	42
(*558½)	600	3½	23½	40	43½	61	70
SmKl Bchm	850	39½	79½	108½	18½	50	69
(*868)	900	16	55	82	46	76	94½
Std Chartd	800	52	90½	123	16½	52½	73½
(*832)	850	25	66½	100	39½	78	100
Thames Wtr	800	34	51	73	16½	55	66
(*815)	850	12	30½	53	44½	87	96
Vodafone	280	16½	34	46	10	23½	32½
(*286)	300	8	24½	37	21	34	43
Woolwich	260	20½	31	41½	4	16½	22
(*275)	280	9	21½	32	13	27	32
Option		Aug	Nov	Feb	Aug	Nov	Feb
Allce & Leics	550	31½	52½	63½	22	45	47½
(*555)	600	12	32	43	53	75	77
Anglo Amer	3100	175½	288½	389	142½	239	298
(*3110)	3200	127½	239½	341	195	290	349
Blue Circle	420	20½	34	42	15	28½	31
(*422)	460	6	18	25½	41	52½	54½
BAE Systems	420	35	52	66	18½	32½	41
(*433)	460	17½	34	47½	41	54½	62
Brit Telecom	850	77½	114½	143½	44	77	102

Example 18.1 Traded options on shares of UK companies, traded on Liffe in London. Source: *Financial Times*.

when the share price was 100p. In the market jargon, the option was **out of the money**. If, on the other hand, it had been a call option to buy an XYZ share at 105p when the share price was 110p, it would have been **in the money** – it would already have had intrinsic value. An option to buy a share at 105p when the share price is 105p is **at the money** – exercise price and market price of the shares are the same. With put options this works the other way round; the option is in the money when the market price is below the exercise price.

The time value in an option erodes throughout its life. It may be worth paying 10p for the chance that a share price will rise by the required amount some time in the next three months. It would probably not be worth paying the same if the option only had a week to run. So the market price of an option will usually drop gradually with the passage of time unless the market price of the underlying share moves the right way (up for a call option and down for a put).

Naked option writing

While we have seen that the buyer of an option on shares – unlike the buyer of a futures contract – at least knows what his maximum loss will be, even this market can offer massive losses for the **writer** or creator of options. Again, selling options on shares that you own can be a conservative hedging strategy. But **naked option writing** – selling options when you do not have an existing position to hedge – is a very different matter. Perhaps the most dangerous technique of all is naked writing of put options.

Towards the end of London's stockmarket boom of the 1980s, many small investors were wrongly advised that they could make risk-free money by writing deep out-of-the-money put options on UK shares. In other words, for a premium of a few pence per share they contracted to buy, if required to do so, the underlying shares at a price fixed at a level 25 per cent or more below market prices at the time. The possibility that the market would fall that far was judged so remote as to be negligible. Then came the crash of October 1987 (see Chapter 7b) with shares in Britain falling more than 36 per cent from their peak. The option writers were thus obliged to buy shares at a price way above their market value, landing many of them with losses that far outran their total financial resources. Lesson: unless you are a financial institution with very deep pockets, do not write naked options.

Hedgers and speculators

There is little doubt that our naked option writers were speculating – though they may not have realized it until too late. However, the examples that are usually quoted of futures and options market techniques will tend to stress the **hedging** nature of the operation: using these markets to protect against an existing business risk. But where should we draw the dividing line between **hedgers** and **speculators**?

Let us look at the distinction in the context of the futures markets. In our example of commoditum futures, both parties to the transaction had a position to hedge. The producer was going to have

commoditum to sell and wanted to lock into a known price. The manufacturer was going to have to buy commoditum and wanted to lock
into a known price. Both were hedging a known risk. If the commoditum price rose, the manufacturer would pay more for his product but he would have a profit on the futures contract he had bought
to compensate him. If it fell, the producer would be offsetting a profit from the futures contract he had sold against the lower price he
received from selling his physical commoditum.

But our manufacturer could equally well have bought his commoditum futures contract from a speculator rather than a producer.
This speculator might never have handled commoditum in his life.
He might not even know what it looked like. No matter; he follows
the movements of the commoditum market and, because he thinks
the price is going to fall, he sells a contract. Since he has no commoditum to sell, his position is unhedged. If he loses on the futures
contract, he will not have profits on the physical metal to offset
against his losses. In practice, there are various ways he might hedge
his position to some degree in the futures market, but we will ignore
these. He is taking a very big risk.

If he sold the September contract at £11,000 and the price fell
to £9,000 by September, well and good. He has made £2,000 profit
on a small outlay. But what if an explosion puts the world's biggest
commoditum mine out of action and serious shortages of the metal
threaten? The price could rocket. Suppose the price of the September
contract more than doubles to £24,000. He will have to buy a contract at £24,000 to satisfy his obligation to deliver at £11,000: a
£13,000 loss. And he has no protection from ownership of stocks of
physical commoditum, which would have risen massively in value.

Straight bets of this kind – though in the financial futures market – appear to have been behind the collapse of the **Barings** merchant bank in early 1995. In this case the bank's trading operation in
Singapore was betting on a rise, not on a fall. So it was buying contracts rather than selling them. It was taking the bets on its own
account: so-called **proprietary** (or **own-account**) **trading**. And the
main 'product' on which it was betting was a Tokyo stockmarket
index. It bought futures contracts whose value would rise if the
Nikkei index of Japanese shares rose. Instead, pushed partly by the
Kobe earthquake, it dropped like a stone. The bets were not taken to
hedge an existing holding of Japanese shares. Since the value of the
shares represented by the futures contracts was many billions of
pounds, it was unlikely that they could have been. Estimates of the

bank's losses on futures contracts ranged from £800m upwards and Barings was wiped out as an independent entity.

Financial futures markets

Financial derivatives are traded in two main ways. There are the over-the-counter or OTC derivative products that are created and sold mainly by banks (see Chapter 14) and may be tailored to a client's individual requirements. And there are the standardized derivative products that are traded in specific futures markets. It is the latter that we are concerned with here and in the UK the **futures market** most closely related to the securities markets is the **London International Financial Futures and Options Exchange** or **Liffe** (pronounced 'life'). It is one of the largest in the world, though has always ranked after the Chicago Board of Trade and the Chicago Mercantile Exchange in the United States. Financial futures are a fast-moving business in every sense. New contracts are introduced quite frequently and dropped if they do not attract the requisite interest. Likewise, the different futures exchanges compete strongly with each other and swings in their relative status can take place rapidly. In the late 1990s Liffe found itself under competitive pressure from the European **Eurex** market, a joint venture of the German and Swiss stock exchanges but with trading links to other futures markets. This promoted a revamp of Liffe and a move from its traditional 'open outcry' trading system to a more modern electronic system (see below). At the end of the century Liffe's products spanned five different currencies and it offered derivative products based on bonds, short-term interest rates, swaps, equities and equity indices and commodities. It had taken over the **Traded Options Market** (offering options on shares in leading companies), which was originally part of the London Stock Exchange, and had also acquired the **London Commodity Exchange**, dealing in futures on **soft** (foodstuff) commodities such as cocoa, coffee, white sugar and others. Liffe also operated the **BIFFEX** market in **freight futures**, originally the province of the **Baltic Exchange**.

The members of Liffe are mainly subsidiaries of financial institutions – banks, discount houses, stockbrokers – but also include individual traders or **locals** who trade on their own account. Liffe now uses an electronic trading system called **Liffe Connect** for most of its financial products, which may have brought efficiency gains but has done away with one of the more colourful spectacles for visitors to London's financial markets. The old 'open outcry' system involved traders in garish jackets (the different colours and patterns identifying their parent firm) yelling and signalling to each across the various pitches on the trading floor. At busy periods the appearance was that of bedlam.

A financial futures contract

Just as commodity futures can be used to hedge an existing risk or to take a straightforward bet, so can financial futures. Each contract is structured differently from the others, but the **long gilt contract** on Liffe will illustrate the principle.

The size of this contract is a nominal £100,000 and the price is expressed in terms of a nominal £100-worth of a notional 7 per cent long-dated government stock. The minimum step by which the price can move (a **tick**) is 0.01 per cent and 0.01 per cent of £100,000 is £10. The buyer of a contract is theoretically buying a nominal £100,000 of gilt-edged stock for delivery in the future: let us say June.

If long-term interest rates fall, the market value of the June contract is likely to rise because gilt-edged stocks will rise in value. Suppose an investor had bought the contract at 110.31. If the price later rose to 113.22, he could sell a contract at 113.22 to close his position. He would have a profit of 291 ticks which, at £10 per tick, represents a gain of £2,910. The initial margin on the long gilt contract is – at the time of writing – £1,500, so anyone who had bought a contract would have a profit of 94 per cent. Financial futures contracts very rarely result in physical delivery. The purchaser of a contract simply closes his position by selling an identical contract and taking his profit or his loss.

The same principle applies to the contracts in interest rates or the FTSE equity index. By using futures it is possible to hedge against a rise in interest rates: the value of an interest rate contract falls if interest rates move up, much as with a gilts contract. So you buy a contract if you are betting on a fall in interest rates and sell if you expect a rise. The techniques available to the futures trader can be highly complex. But the most important point in terms of press comment is that price movements in the futures market will sometimes give advance warning of likely price trends in the stockmarket itself (the **cash** market) or in interest rates.

Options traded on Liffe

The market in traded options offers options on the shares of some 75 leading companies, including the major privatization stocks. It also

BOND FUTURES AND OPTIONS
France

■ **NOTIONAL EURO BOND FUTURES** (MATIF) €100,000

	Open	Sett price	Change	High	Low	Est. vol.	Open int.
Sep	86.40	86.47	-0.08	86.73	86.38	222,151	431,772
Dec	-	85.85	-0.14	-	-	-	-

Germany
■ **NOTIONAL EURO BUND FUTURES** (EUREX) €100,000 100ths of 100%

	Open	Sett price	Change	High	Low	Est. vol	Open int.
Sep	105.19	104.94	-0.22	105.29	104.91	565,590	526,402
Dec	104.75	104.59	-0.21	104.80	104.69	4,034	13,752

■ **NOTIONAL EURO BUND (BOBL) FUTURES**   (EUREX) €100,000 100ths of 100%

	Open	Sett price	Change	High	Low	Est. vol	Open int.
Jun	103.04	102.93	-0.11	103.10	102.90	188,956	278,608

Italy
■ **NOTIONAL ITALIAN GOVT. BOND (BTP) FUTURES** (LIFFE)* Lira 200m 100ths of 100%

	Open	Sett price	Change	High	Low	Est. vol	Open int.
Sep		102.56	+0.02			0	0

Spain
■ **NOTIONAL SPANISH BOND FUTURES** (MEFF) €100,000

	Open	Sett price	Change	High	Low	Est. vol.	Open int.
Sep	88.90	88.82	-	88.95	88.67	1,649	8,262

UK
■ **NOTIONAL 5 YEAR GILT FUTURES** (LIFFE) £100,000 100ths of 100%

	Open	Sett price	Change	High	Low	Est. vol	Open int.
Jun		104.20	-0.09			0	0
Sep		104.75	+0.01			0	0

■ **NOTIONAL UK GILT FUTURES** (LIFFE)* £100,000 100ths of 100%

	Open	Close	Change	High	Low	Est. vol	Open int.
Jun	113.61	113.40	-0.15		113.40	168	5075
Sep	113.35	113.33	+0.12	113.48	112.97	16559	58709

All Open interest figs. are for previous day.

■ **LONG GILT FUTURES OPTIONS** (LIFFE) £100,000 100ths of 100%

Strike	········· CALLS ·········			········· PUTS ·········		
Price	Aug	Sep	Oct	Aug	Sep	Oct
11250	1.23	1.55	1.77	0.40	0.72	0.95
11300	0.92	1.26	1.49	0.59	0.93	1.17
11350	0.66	1.00	1.24	0.83	1.17	1.42
11400	0.46	0.79	1.02	1.13	1.46	1.70
11450	0.30	0.60	0.82	1.47	1.77	2.00
11500	0.19	0.45	0.66	1.86	2.12	2.34

Est. vol. total, Calls 0 Puts 0. Previous day's open int., Calls 10 Puts 0

US
■ **US TREASURY BOND FUTURES** (CBT) $100,000 32nds of 100%

	Open	Sett price	Change	High	Low	Est. vol.	Open int.
Sep	96-26	96-15	-0.10	97-01	96-05	129,769	363,491
Dec	96-30	96-13	-0.11	96-30	96-05	32	4,072
Mar	-	96-12	-0.11	-	-	1	565

Example 18.2 Futures contracts and options on government bonds in various markets. Source: *Financial Times*.

offers options as well as futures on the **FTSE 100 Index** (the **Footsie** Index) and a range of other UK and international equity indices. The Footsie is the index of 100 leading UK shares and the option is thus a way of betting on the movement of the market as a whole.

For each individual company there are options with different **exercise prices**. The *Financial Times* carries a table of them headed **Liffe equity options**. The exercise price is shown in the column immediately following the company name, and prices are given for call and put options at each price. The idea is to have at least one **out of the money** and one **in the money option** for each company. And

SOFTS

■ COCOA LIFFE (10 tonnes; £/tonne)

	Sett price	Day's change	High	Low	Vol	Open Int
Jul	599	+2	599	595	573	14,284
Sep	622	+2	622	616	1,355	34,301
Dec	660	+3	660	656	1,050	41,070
Mar	679	+1	678	675	450	30,456
May	694	+1	694	690	170	19,222
Jul	709	+1	-	-	-	5,919
Total					3,737	174,963

■ COCOA CSCE (10 tonnes; $/tonnes)

Jul	812	+4	819	808	22	336
Sep	834	+5	844	830	6,526	42,008
Dec	869	+4	879	866	2,002	24,851
Mar	902	+4	913	900	294	9,277
May	925	+4	935	925	111	6,558
Jul	949	+4	955	955	101	7,674
Total					9,356	111,847

■ COCOA (ICCO) (SDR's/tonne)

Jun 27	Price	Prev. day
Daily	697.93	689.83

■ COFFEE LIFFE (5 tonnes; $/tonne)

Jul	850	-	861	849	4,323	10,192
Sep	878	-	891	878	2,799	35,659
Nov	898	-	909	899	635	11,852
Jan	918	-	929	920	75	3,674
Mar	937	-	952	942	64	1,065
May	956	-	-	-	-	855
Total					7,896	63,297

■ COFFEE 'C' CSCE (37,500lbs; cents/lbs)

Jul	87.65	-0.85	89.25	87.30	374	935
Sep	90.10	-0.70	92.00	89.50	4,918	34,765
Dec	94.30	-0.70	95.90	93.75	764	7,769
Mar	98.60	-0.90	100.00	98.50	246	3,255
May	100.80	-0.90	101.25	101.25	29	663
Jul	103.05	-0.90	-	-	15	171
Total					6,411	47,738

Example 18.3 Prices of 'soft' commodities for future delivery. Source: *Financial Times.*

at each price there are options with differing lives. They normally run initially for three, six or nine months. Once the life of the three-month option has expired, the six-month option will only have three months' life left, the previous nine-month option will only have six months' and a new nine-month option will be created. Options in British Telecom, say, have expiry dates in February, May, August and November – only three being available at one time. Others follow a different cycle to prevent all options having the same expiry dates.

The price quoted is the middle price for an option on a single share, but deals are in **contracts** which normally consist of options on 1,000 shares. Under the name of the company is shown the previous day's price for the shares themselves.

Because of the gearing, price swings in traded options can be very large and can happen very fast. There are theoretical models for calculating what the price of an option should be relative to the underlying share price, and professionals deal actively to take advantage of small anomalies. Activity is sometimes very heavy in options of companies in the news – particularly takeover candidates.

Commodity markets

London's main commodity markets divide between the **metals** and the **soft** commodities. Metals are traded on the **London Metal Exchange (LME)** and, as we saw, the soft commodities are now part of Liffe.

Copper, **lead**, **zinc**, **nickel**, **tin**, **silver**, **aluminium** and **aluminium alloy**, are traded on the LME, which is the centre of world trading in the non-ferrous metals. Trading is carried out by the **ring-dealing members** who transact their own or their clients' orders on an **open outcry** basis in trading sessions that last five minutes for each metal and take place four times a day. The official price for the metal for the day is the price ruling at the end of the morning session. After the metals have been traded individually, there is a **kerb** trading session in which any of the metals can be traded. But, as well as ring trading, there is also extensive dealing on the telephone by ring-dealing members and brokers before and after the official sessions, effectively giving 24-hour trading coverage.

In addition to the ring-dealing members, there are **commission houses** which offer a brokerage service to would-be investors or speculators in commodities. They channel their business through a

COMMODITIES PRICES

BASE METALS

LONDON METAL EXCHANGE
(Prices from Amalgamated Metal Trading)

■ ALUMINIUM, 99.7 PURITY ($ per tonne)

	Cash	3 mths
Close	1572.5-73.5	1593-94
Previous	1574.5-5.5	1593-4
High/low		1600/1567
AM Official	1574-5	1593-4
Kerb close		1597-98
Open int.	283,967	
Total daily turnover	94,472	

■ ALUMINIUM ALLOY ($ per tonne)

	Cash	3 mths
Close	1230-33	1269-70
Previous	1230-40	1270-80
High/low		1280/1276
AM Official	1236-8	1275-6
Kerb close		1277-79
Open int.	8,071	
Total daily turnover	2,702	

■ LEAD ($ per tonne)

	Cash	3 mths
Close	418-9	434.5-5
Previous	419-21	435-7
High/low		437/435
AM Official	418.5-9.0	435-5.5
Kerb close		437-8
Open int.	39,350	
Total daily turnover	9,454	

■ NICKEL ($ per tonne)

	Cash	3 mths
Close	8010-20	7830-40
Previous	8040-50	7840-50
High/low		7880/7720
AM Official	7990-8000	7840-50
Kerb close		7850-60
Open int.	56,842	
Total daily turnover	16,702	

■ TIN ($ per tonne)

	Cash	3 mths
Close	5490-500	5530-35
Previous	5495-500	5520-25
High/low		5540/5520
AM Official	5480-90	5525-30
Kerb close		5520-25
Open int.	19,995	

Example 18.4 Cash and three-months' prices for some of the metals traded on the London Metal Exchange. Source: *Financial Times.*

ring-dealing member.

Trading on the LME is a mix of **physical** and **forward** or **futures** business. A price is established for each metal for immediate delivery (the **cash** price or **spot** price) and also a price for delivery in three months. Prices may also be agreed for any period between, and nowadays it is also possible to deal up to 27 months ahead in some metals. The futures price is for a standard contract (25 tonnes in the case of copper) of metal of a defined grade. There are also official LME traded options on futures contracts, which have been a growth area in recent years. The *Financial Times* shows both the cash and three-months' prices for the LME metals and the movement on the day. Usually the three-months' price is higher than the cash price (**contango**) because the buyer is avoiding financing costs for three months. **Backwardation** is the situation where the cash price exceeds the three-months' price.

London also houses Europe's leading energy exchange. The **International Petroleum Exchange** (**IPE**) offers futures contracts and, in some cases, options on a range of petroleum products: **Brent crude**, **gas oil**, **natural gas** and **fuel oil**.

The **Baltic Exchange** is the traditional market for negotiation of shipping freight, though the freight futures contract has, as we saw, now moved to Liffe.

Internet pointers

Liffe has an informative website at www.liffe.com/ and Eurex, the European derivatives exchange, is at www.eurexchange.com/. The International Petroleum Exchange has a site at www.ipe.uk.com/. The Chicago Board of Trade is at www.cbot.com/ and Chicago Board Options Exchange at www.cboe.com/. Information on the London Metal Exchange may be found at www.lme.co.uk/, on the International Petroleum Exchange at www.ipe.uk.com and the world's largest commodity exchange, the New York Mercantile Exchange, is at www.nymex.com/. Many brokerages and similar firms use the Internet to offer their trading services in futures and options – on currencies, financial products and commodities – to the private investor. Remember that the gearing built into derivative products makes dealing a high-risk operation and commission charges can be very heavy.

19 Insurance, and Lloyd's after the troubles

Lloyd's of London, the international insurance market, is one of the oldest of the City's institutions. But in the last decade of the millennium it probably underwent more change than at any other period of its 300-year history. Traditionally a market supported by the capital of wealthy individuals, Lloyd's now derives most of the money it needs to operate from corporate members, though some of the wealthy individuals are still there. The changes follow a series of commercial disasters and scandals that rocked this august institution from the late 1970s to the early 1990s, wiping out the wealth of many of its 'investors'. A joke doing the rounds in the early 1990s sums up that era. Question: How do you make a small fortune at Lloyd's? Answer: Start with a large one.

Lloyd's now hopes that it has put those bad days behind it, though the commercial risks inherent in the insurance business are inevitably always present. Effectively, Lloyd's has devised a way of drawing a line under its pre-1992 financial troubles – we will come to the precise mechanisms later. But we cannot understand the Lloyd's of today without looking at the system under which it traditionally operated and which is still at the core of its structure.

Start with the business of insurance itself. In outline it is not unduly complicated. We're talking here about **general insurance** – **underwriting** the risk of damage or destruction to ships, aircraft, property, and so on – rather than **life assurance**, which is a different kind of business and more a part of the savings and personal finance world. The general insurer charges a **premium** commensurate with his view of the risk he is underwriting, and hopes that all the premiums he receives will exceed all the **claims** he has to pay out. If he is right, he makes an **underwriting profit**. But he does not rely on the **premium income** alone. The money he receives as premiums is earning interest until it has to be paid out in claims, so in addition he is receiving an **investment income** which can help to offset any losses he makes on the underwriting side. Insurance claims often take a number of years to finalize, so he may have use of the money for some considerable time (business where claims may arise a long time after the insurance was arranged is known as **long-tail business**).

Where an insurer is worried by the size of a risk he is underwriting, he can lay off part of his bet (rather like a bookie) by **reinsuring** it with another insurer. Thus the original insurer may say 'I'll bear the first £10m of any loss, the **reinsurer** will take the next £10m, and I'll accept any excess over that'. Part of the original premium obviously has to be handed over to the reinsurer. Many large risks will also be split with a number of insurers from the outset, each one taking a portion of the liability.

The principle is much the same whether the original insurer is a company or a Lloyd's **syndicate**. The greater part of insurance business in the UK is undertaken by insurance companies, particularly the more standard types of business such as household and car insurance. Lloyd's is best known for marine insurance and for insuring the more unusual types of risk.

Insurance goes in cycles. When the business looks profitable, competition hots up thus keeping premiums down and business gets less profitable until the industry swings into losses. The competition then abates, premiums are able to increase again and the new business becomes profitable. This **insurance cycle** applies to the general insurance companies as well as to Lloyd's, but the Lloyd's losses of the late 1980s and early 1990s were something quite outside the normal **underwriting cycle** (see Figure 19.1).

How capital is put to work at Lloyd's

An insurance company relies on the premiums plus the company's own funds to cover the risks it underwrites (though it may also reinsure part of its risk). Lloyd's, though its members also use reinsurance, traditionally worked on a different principle. As we saw, this principle has undergone some important changes, but these changes will be easier to appreciate if we deal with the traditional pattern first.

Lloyd's members were divided between working members who underwrote the business (accepted the insurance risks brought to them) and non-working members who pledged their personal wealth to meet possible losses. Confusingly, the non-working members were also 'underwriters' and both types of member who put their wealth at risk were known as **names**.

The names did not have to put up vast amounts of money. Instead, they stood surety for the risks that were underwritten at Lloyd's. In other words, they pledged the whole of their wealth to meet claims, should this be necessary. They hoped that premiums and investment income would outweigh claims and that they would never have to stump up. But if the worst came to the worst, they might have to sell virtually everything they owned to meet losses – though it was possible to insure against this risk, too.

The beauty of the system, when all went according to plan, was that wealth could be made to work twice over, and sometimes more. To become a name the individual had to be able to show a minimum amount of wealth (excluding his home and certain other assets): the figure was £350,000 in 1999. But the amounts he had to hand over in cash were very much smaller. So a fair portion of his £350,000 or more of wealth could be, say, invested in stocks and shares and earning a return for its owner. At the same time it provided the necessary back-up for the insurance risks that were being underwritten. When the syndicate's insurance business earned a profit, the name would receive his share.

There were substantial tax advantages in the past, too, which was one of the attractions for high earners and the rich. Some of the funds used in the insurance market could be compounding up interest after tax at a much lower rate than the individual might have to pay. The reduction in the top rate of income tax to 40 per cent in the 1988 Budget somewhat eroded the tax advantages of being a Lloyd's name.

The syndicate structure

In theory, all members of Lloyd's traded as individuals. In practice they were (and still are) grouped into **syndicates** and one name could spread his risk by belonging to a number of syndicates. A **working underwriter**, who was a Lloyd's professional, accepted insurance risks on behalf of the syndicate. The business was brought to him by a **Lloyd's broker**, who represented the client seeking insurance and whose duty was to arrange it on the best terms. The name was introduced to his syndicate or syndicates by a **members' agent** who was meant to look after his interests. A **managing agent** looked after the

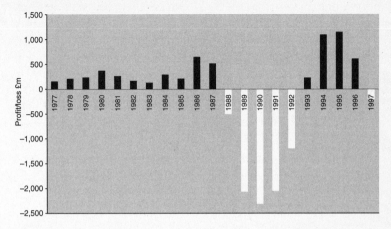

Figure 19.1 Pre-tax profit/loss to Lloyd's members The massive losses at
Lloyd's in the late 1980s and early 1990s wiped out many of the 'names' who
invested there. They were therefore not around to benefit when a more normal
insurance cycle reasserted itself from 1993 onwards. Source: *Lloyd's of London.*

organizational side of the syndicate's business. **Underwriting agencies** sometimes combined managing agents and members' agents in
one organization. Accounts were (and are) drawn up three years after
the year to which they relate, because of the length of time required
for claims to be assessed. Thus, the results for the 1997 underwriting
year were announced in May 2000.

Scandals and regulation

In the past Lloyd's has regulated its own affairs under an Act of
Parliament. The most recent legislation is the Lloyd's Act 1982,
introduced in response to scandals of the late 1970s and early 1980s.
But there has been pressure for a long time to bring Lloyd's under the
same regulatory regime as most of the rest of the City. Hence the
plans in 1999 to make the **Financial Services Authority** the ultimate
regulator for Lloyd's.

The 1982 Lloyd's Act was meant to deal with possible conflicts
of interest in the structure of the market as well as with scandals that
fell into several categories. At the heart of the problems was a strong
suspicion that some of the market's professionals were enriching
themselves at the expense of the passive investors: the outside names
whose wealth allowed the market to function. Brokers were accused of
excessive pressure on syndicates to settle dubious claims. Some

underwriting agents took on more business than the syndicate was entitled to underwrite, thus exposing it to excessive losses. Reinsurance was arranged with **offshore companies** in which working underwriters had interests they had not declared to the names and which could be highly profitable. There were suspicions of **baby syndicates**, whose members were Lloyd's professionals, to which the most profitable business might be channelled. And many underwriting agents managed **parallel syndicates** – two syndicates alongside each other, with a risk that one might be favoured at the expense of the other.

There were also cases of taking on business which was suspected to be fraudulent, and still worse cases of straightforward theft of names' money. The problem for names who lost heavily in some of these scandals was in establishing that they had suffered as a result of breaches of Lloyd's rules or fraud (in which case they might be entitled to compensation from Lloyd's) rather than poor underwriting alone (in which case they would have to bear the losses unless they successfully pursued a claim for negligence through the courts). In the biggest of these affairs of the time – the case of the PCW syndicates – names were faced with losses running into the hundreds of millions of pounds. But worse was to come.

For its underwriting years 1988 to 1992, Lloyd's syndicates clocked up losses of over £8 billion. These were not evenly spread throughout the market. Some syndicates continued profitable or made modest losses. But others clocked up losses running into the hundreds of millions of pounds. Far from receiving cheques from Lloyd's, many names found Lloyd's was demanding cheques to the value of everything they owned (and more) to meet the losses. Family fortunes were wiped out, homes that had been in the family for generations had to be sold (estate agents recognized this 'Lloyd's effect' at the top end of their business). There were suicides among names attributed to their Lloyd's losses. And some names decided that the time had come to band together and fight back through the courts. How had the debacle occurred?

Reinsurance to close

For the answer, we have to delve a little deeper into the syndicate system. Theoretically, a syndicate exists for one underwriting year. Names who are members can decide to drop out at the end of that year and new names can come in for the next underwriting year. But a name who drops out is not shot of the syndicate. No new business will be underwritten on his behalf after he has left. But he remains liable for his share of losses arising from the years for which he was a member until the books are closed for those years – and this, as we saw, is normally three years after the event.

Now, even after three years a syndicate cannot be sure that it has met all claims that might arise from business written three years earlier. Suppose we are now in 1999 and the syndicate wants to close its books for the 1996 year. How does it provide for claims that might still emerge from the 1996 underwriting year? The answer is that it uses a portion of its 1996 income as a premium to insure against any further residual losses that might arise in respect of the 1996 year. Once the responsibility for any residual risks has been passed on by this **reinsurance to close** process, a line can be drawn under the 1996 results and those who were members of the syndicate for that year will know how much they have made or lost.

With whom does a syndicate reinsure to close (reinsure its residual risk in respect of a particular year)? Usually it will be the same syndicate in a later year that picks up the risk in return for a premium. And this has led to the accusation that the membership of some syndicates was deliberately expanded by the recruitment of new names in order to provide cannon fodder to help bear the losses arising from the business of earlier years. Be that as it may, the system means that risk is perpetuated and that syndicate members can be hit by losses arising from business underwritten in earlier years when its membership may have been very different.

There is a further problem. If a syndicate still faces very large or unquantifiable losses in respect of an earlier year, it may prove impossible to reinsure to close. In that case the year in question – 1996 in our example – remains 'open' well after the normal three years are up and for many years the names who were members of the syndicate in 1996 do not know the full extent of their losses. We have taken our example from recent years, but the problem was at its most acute in the early 1990s when the number of **open years** had grown rapidly and a significant proportion of them related back to the early 1980s.

The excess of loss spiral

To compound Lloyd's difficulties, another form of reinsurance spelled doom for a number of syndicates: **excess of loss** insurance. As a backstop against **catastrophes**, a syndicate would reinsure with another syndicate against the possibility of losses exceeding a certain unlikely amount. Part of the risk might then be reinsured with a third syndicate, and so on. In this so-called **LMX (London Market Excess of Loss) spiral**, a game of pass-the-parcel was taking place round the market, with the possibility that the original syndicate might even end up taking back part of the risk that it had laid off in the first place. Given the rarity of major catastrophes, this excess of loss insurance was regarded as good business by those who took it on at the time.

But the late 1980s and early 1990s proved a bad time for insurers. Costly catastrophes included the Piper Alpha oil rig explosion in 1988, hurricane Hugo in the following year and the storms of early 1990 in Europe. Since many of the risks had simply been reshuffled round the market, a domino effect resulted, with the problems of one syndicate affecting the next one.

In addition, Lloyd's had suffered in another quarter. There were enormous claims, mainly from the United States, in respect of employers' liability for asbestosis claims and for the costs of cleaning up earlier industrial pollution. Prior to 1986, the wording of Lloyd's policies did not restrict claims to those arising in the year for which insurance had been bought. The effects of pollution or of asbestos-related illness may take many years to surface. Thus claims were emerging in, say, 1985 in respect of insurance policies in force 20 years earlier when the pollution or the exposure to asbestos actually occurred.

Into the litigation era

Faced with massive losses from this variety of causes, some names on the worst-hit syndicates were cleaned out entirely. Others refused to pay, **names' action groups** sprang up and the litigation got under way. The names' action groups sued managing agents for negligent underwriting. The agents themselves were insured up to a point under errors and omissions policies, but usually did not have enough cover to meet all claims. In any event, they were probably insured with Lloyd's syndicates, so anything they had to pay out simply increased the pressure on other syndicates in the market. The pot of money available within Lloyd's was simply insufficient to meet all justifiable claims from names. The Lloyd's authorities had attempted to head off litigation, which generally showed the institution in a poor light, and to broker out-of-court settlements between the names and those whom the names held to be negligent. But until it could draw a line under its historical problems, Lloyd's was going to find it very difficult to restructure and adapt its market for profitable business in the future. Its solution took two main forms.

First, a settlement of £3.2 billion in total was agreed with names who had justifiable claims against Lloyd's members in respect of past losses caused by negligence or other factors aside from normal commercial risk. This included names who had already won compensation claims in the courts. In return for this settlement, names had to abandon litigation (strictly, to hand over their litigation rights to Lloyd's itself) and relinquish the rights to compensation that they might already have been awarded in the courts. The £3.2 billion came from a variety of sources: the Lloyd's central fund, the errors and omissions insurers and from a levy on all members.

The second arm of the solution was to find a way of 'ring-fencing' liabilities that could still arise in respect of business written in earlier (often much earlier) years. This was to be achieved by setting up a company called **Equitas** into which the residual risks of those earlier years could be reinsured, thus drawing a line under names' possible losses. Originally the plan was to ring-fence losses up to 1986 but in 1995 the scope of the proposed Equitas company was extended to ring-fence losses up to 1992. Needless to say, this solution came with a cost. The total funding required for Equitas to assume these liabilities was in the order of £13 billion. Some £1 billion of this came from additional premiums from names who were at risk and the remaining £12 billion came from syndicates' existing reserve funds.

Once set up, Equitas took the form of a company separate from Lloyd's and was registered and approved by the Department of Trade and Industry (now by the Treasury). So far the run-off of liabilities appears to be going according to plan. There is, of course, no absolute guarantee that the funds in Equitas will be sufficient to meet all claims that might arise in the future. But the Lloyd's market itself is off the hook, even if names and former names have no total guarantee. Should claims arise that Equitas is unable to meet in full, the claimant would have to pursue the names who underwrote the business, not Equitas or the Lloyd's market as a whole. If, of course, the claimant thought this was worth while.

With the decks cleared in this way, Lloyd's was able to pursue its development plans, in which **corporate capital** played a central role. The number of individual names was, in any case, declining

dramatically. Some got out because of their experiences in the 1980s
and early 1990s. Some were simply wiped out – their losses did not
leave them with sufficient wealth to remain in membership, even had
they wanted to. From a peak of 32,000, the number of names had
dropped to some 4,700 by 1999, of whom about 900 were working
members of the market.

Replacing the insurance capacity of these vanishing names
were the new **corporate members** of Lloyd's: close to 700 of them
by 1999. And of Lloyd's total capacity of £9.94 billion, they provided the bulk: £6.48 billion against £2.73 billion from individual
names, with their contribution rising to 80 per cent the following
year. Capacity, incidentally, is measured in terms of the amount of
premium income that the market has the resources to generate.
Capacity of £9.94 billion means that risks can be underwritten that
bring in premiums of £9.94 billion. Corporate members operate
through syndicates in the same way as individual names.

The new corporate members include major insurance companies and also Lloyd's investment trusts. The latter operate on similar
lines to a conventional investment trust (see Chapter 21) but the
investments they own can be used as backing for underwriting insurance business at Lloyd's. The corporate members also include some
individuals – almost 1,000 of them by the year 2000 – who previously operated as names, but who have now turned themselves into
companies, known as **namecos**, for the purposes of underwriting
risks at Lloyd's.

Does the arrival of corporate members mean an end to the principle of **unlimited liability** at Lloyd's? It depends how you look at
it. An individual name still puts everything he owns at risk. A company member also puts everything it owns at risk to cover losses if
necessary. But since the company has limited liability, it cannot be
forced to pay up more than it owns – the liability does not extend to
the directors and shareholders as individuals. Both individual names
and corporate members have to deposit a certain level of funds at
Lloyd's, which can be in the form of cash or investments. This is normally expressed as a percentage of the amount of premium income
they are entitled to underwrite. The normal minimum is 45 per cent,
but there is a system of varying the percentage according to the perceived riskiness of the type of insurance business underwritten. It can
be as high as 100 per cent for the riskiest classes of business. Usually,
however, anyone intending to underwrite premium income of £1m
would have to deposit £450,000.

With the concentration of underwriting capacity into fewer hands has come a concentration of the market's organizations. There are now around 140 syndicates (once there were over 400), 63 managing agents and only 12 members' agents. The old system of a market run by professionals with wealth largely provided by passive investors has been greatly watered down. The new breed of corporate investor is likely to want a part in the management of the business where his money is at risk. And no longer can you become a member of Lloyd's simply by having the requisite wealth and the right introductions. You have to buy your way in. There are regular auctions of capacity at Lloyd's, where those wanting to enter the market bid for the right to underwrite business: so many pence per pound of premium income that may be written. At least it means that those who are leaving the market may expect a windfall from selling their capacity to somebody else.

Internet pointers

Insurance is closely connected with the business of selling, and the industry's websites reflect this. In general they are better at promoting insurance products and services than at providing useful background on the industry. The Chartered Insurance Institute site at www.cii.co.uk/ is a possible exception. Lloyd's of London has a site at www.lloyds.com/ and the Association of British Insurers – the industry body for UK insurance companies – is at abi.org.uk/. There is also a corporate governance site where the insurance companies' and pension funds' rules on share issues, etc. are set out at www.ivis.computasoft.com/. There are innumerable sites for individual insurance companies and insurance brokers.

20 Commercial property and market crashes

Commercial property – office buildings, shops, factories and warehouses – has been one of the major avenues for investment by the **insurance companies** and **pension funds**. It was less popular at the end of the millennium than it once was. But together, these two types of institution still hold properties valued at around £66 billion. There is, however, no central marketplace in commercial property. The 'market' is largely organized by the major firms of **chartered surveyors** or **estate agents**. These firms provide a range of property investment services. They advise on property portfolios, often manage portfolios on behalf of institutions, provide valuations, negotiate lettings, purchases and sales and assist in arranging finance for developments.

But the estate agency firms themselves have undergone recent change. Among the traditional big names of the business in the UK – Jones Lang Wootton, Richard Ellis, Healey & Baker and Hillier Parker – merger or takeover has proved irresistible, often in the quest for a more international financial flavour. Thus Jones Lang Wootton has teamed up with an American group to become Jones Lang LaSalle and the others have similarly joined new groupings. Accompanying the growing American involvement in the UK business, the term '**real estate**' is beginning to replace 'property' in some contexts. We will stick with the traditional term.

There are really two **commercial property markets** which centre round the estate agency firms. There is the **letting market** in which landlords let buildings to tenants. And there is the **investment market** where completed and revenue-producing buildings are acquired by **financial institutions** as long-term investments. The two markets overlap and the larger institutions may be involved in both aspects. They create investments by undertaking **property developments**, letting the completed buildings and holding on to them for the rent they provide.

Property journalists write about both markets: how rents are moving for particular kinds of property, and the prices investors are prepared to pay for revenue-producing properties.

Property as an investment

The commercial property market has always followed a cyclical pattern, but the 1990s provided more drama than most earlier decades. The decade started with the most dramatic **property market bust** following an over-heated boom in the late 1980s. The values of some City of London offices halved, rental levels and values for most classes of property across the country fell significantly and many of the cherished assumptions of the post-war period were overturned. The second half of the 1990s saw some recovery, but the confidence that commercial property would rise in value almost automatically was gone. Particularly in contrast with a booming equity market, property had often proved a lack-lustre investment in recent years. And, sparked partly by much lower inflation, some structural changes in the market were under way. We will examine these later, but they need to be seen in the context of what had gone before.

For most of the post-war period a commercial property tended to be regarded as a growth investment rather like an ordinary share, though the income comes in the form of **rent** rather than dividend and it requires more management by the investor. However, properties in Britain are often let on **full repairing and insuring leases** which put much of the responsibility for maintenance on the tenant.

Commercial properties are often let on very long **leases** – 99 years used to be common – but by the 1980s 25 years or less would have been the norm. A long lease on full repairing and insuring terms is often described as an institutional lease because it is the type that institutional property investors try to insist on. The market collapse of the early 1990s saw some swing in the balance of power from landlord to tenant and tenants were less ready than in the past to enter into very long commitments, so the length of the typical lease tended to drop still further, perhaps to 10 or 15 years. Proposals from the **Accounting Standards Board** at the end of 1999, which could require tenants to show leases as assets and liabilities on their balance sheets, suggested that tenants might insist on even shorter leases in the future.

The rent that the tenant pays is usually reviewed every five (or even three) years. The owner of the building obviously hopes that the **rental value** of the building (the rent it would fetch if let today in the open market) will rise consistently, but he only collects these increases at three- or five-year intervals when **rent reviews** occur or when the lease comes to an end and is renegotiated.

Properties are traditionally **valued** as a **multiple** of the rent they produce. Take an office building in London with 10,000 square feet (sq. ft.) of lettable area and recently let at a rent of, say, £30 per sq. ft. (psf) per year. The total annual income will be £300,000. An investor might be prepared to buy the building at a price which showed him a return of five per cent on his outlay. He is prepared to accept a fairly low initial return because he expects the income to increase in the future, as with an ordinary share.

He is therefore prepared to buy the investment at £6m, which is the price that would show him a five per cent return and is 20 times the rent it produces. This is effectively the 'PE ratio' of the investment, though the property world would talk of buying the building at 20 **years' purchase** of the rent, which means the same thing. The only real difference is that PE ratios are calculated on a company's income after corporation tax whereas the year's purchase for a property is calculated on the rental income before tax (if any).

Suppose the first **rent review** on our investment property is due in five years, and as this point approaches the rental value has risen to £40 psf. The income from the building if let at its market rent would now be £400,000, though the tenant is still only paying £300,000. But once the rent is reviewed at the end of the fifth year, it jumps to £400,000, which then holds good for the next five years.

Because rent reviews only come at intervals, it is clear that for much of the time the tenant may be paying a rent below the current market value. The rent will **revert** to its market value when the lease runs out and a new one is negotiated or when the rent review in the existing lease occurs. At a time of rising rental levels property journalists thus talk of a landlord expecting large increases in revenue as 'rent reviews and **reversions** occur over the next few years'.

Freeholds and leaseholds

The pattern of property ownership in Britain is complex. The example above is of a **freehold** building, which for most purposes is owned outright by the landlord. But often the interests in the building are split. The original owner of the land may only have granted a lease – for 99 years, say – to the developer who put up the building and who now

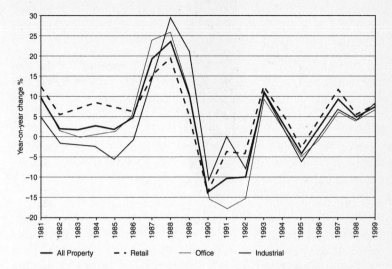

Figure 20.1 Commercial property values: year-on-year change The boom in commercial property values in the late 1980s was followed by a horrendous crash at the beginning of the 1990s. Our graph shows the average performance of all commercial property and the performance of the three main categories. Offices fared worst in the crash, and offices in the City of London fared even worse than shown here. The recovery around 1993 proved something of a false dawn – it was driven mainly by interest rate factors – but later in the decade some real growth began to reassert itself. Source: *Investment Property Databank*.

'owns' it. In this case the freeholder is the owner of the land, and he charges the developer an annual **ground rent** which used to be a fixed amount but nowadays will probably be adjusted upwards at intervals. The developer becomes the **leaseholder** and his building is **leasehold**. He lets the building to a tenant at a market rent or **rack rent**, and from this he has to pay the ground rent to the freeholder. In practice, ownership of property can be considerably more complex than this with several layers of lease before you get to the tenant who pays the market rent.

Valuation

Valuation of properties – but particularly of leasehold buildings or of **reversionary properties** (properties currently let below the market rent) – can be very complex and is usually undertaken by a chartered surveyor. Since no one property is quite like any other property, he has to work from recent precedents. Suppose investors seem to expect a five per cent return from standard office buildings of the type he is valuing; he adjusts for the different special factors that apply to this particular building and works out what price would provide a comparable return.

If a property is reversionary – the rent it currently produces is, say, £300,000 but this will jump to £400,000 in a year's time when the rent review occurs – the forthcoming increase in rent will be reflected in the value put on the building. Thus the yield based on the current rent may be very low. However, this yield is often adjusted to produce an **equivalent yield**, which shows what yield the valuer would be working on if the building were let at the market rent.

Finance for developers

We have talked about both investors and **developers** in the property business, though the financial institutions may now fulfil both functions. But long before they got into the development business on their own account, they were the traditional source of long-term finance for property developers because they had large-scale funds looking for a long-term home. The 'developer' was usually an entrepreneur with an eye for a good site who would carry out the development but mainly use other people's money to finance it.

In the immediate post-war years, developers of commercial buildings (mainly property companies) normally obtained their long-term finance by **mortgaging** the development to a financial institution when it was completed and let. Insurance companies and pension funds would, typically, provide a loan of two-thirds of the value for 25 years or more at a fixed rate of interest.

As interest rates rose, this became less practicable and various forms of partnership between institution and developer evolved. The most common was the **leaseback** or **sale and leaseback**. The developer identified the site and the possibility of putting up a building. The institution bought the land and provided finance for the development, which was managed by the developer. On completion, the institution granted a lease to the developer, who in turn granted a lease to the tenant at a rack rent. The developer paid a ground rent of, say, 70 per cent of the rental value of the building to the institution. The remaining 30 per cent **top slice** belonged to him. There were numerous variations on this theme, and the developer's rent to the institution would normally rise as the rental income of the building rose. Clearly, if the developer was unable to let the last 30 per cent of space in the building, he had no profit.

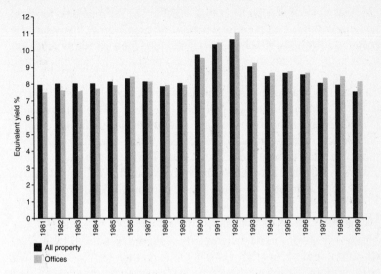

Figure 20.2 Average yields on property: all property and offices The yields on which investors are prepared to buy commercial property reflect expectations of future growth. When yields rise, all else being equal, values fall. The chart shows the average for all property and the yield on offices (which are often particularly volatile). Note the very sharp rise in yields in the property market crash of the early 1990s. Even in the latter part of the decade, yields remained fairly high on historical criteria. With relatively low interest rates on borrowed money, property again appeared to offer value for money. Source: *Investment Property Databank.*

Subsequently, various other forms of partnership financing arrangement evolved which split the risk more equitably between the provider of finance and the developer – these may be referred to as **side-by-side** or **partnership** arrangements. But increasingly the bigger institutions began to cut out the developer altogether by undertaking their own projects, possibly with the help of one of the large firms of surveyors.

The **sale and leaseback**, incidentally, has also been widely used as a financing method for commercial companies, particularly retailers. Company A might take over Company B, which owns the shops from which it carries out its trade. The shops can then be sold for a lump sum to an institution but Company B continues to occupy them, now paying a commercial rent as a tenant.

The second half of the 1980s saw a big change in financing techniques for property development. The insurance companies and pension funds became relatively less important and far more of the development finance came from the banking system. Bank loans to property companies (not all for development) rose by over 1,500 per cent between 1981 and 1991. Much of this lending took the form of **project loans** to the fast-growing property development and trading companies. The loan was secured on the individual development project. A loan such as this was often made on **limited-recourse** or **non-recourse** terms. This meant that the property company itself was only responsible to a limited extent or not responsible at all for the loan. The banks could only look to the individual development project itself to provide the money to repay them at the end of the day. The larger loans were almost always **syndicated** between groups of banks, each putting up a part of the money. Ultimately, the banks lost heavily on this kind of lending.

The property companies

Apart from the institutions, **property companies** are also significant property owners. These are often stockmarket-quoted companies that either simply hold properties as an investment (**property investment company**) or undertake developments (**property development company**). Many of them do both. An investment and development company (one which hangs on to the new buildings it has developed) usually provides a very secure income, since its revenue comes mainly from recurring rents. A development company whose profits come from selling buildings on completion (a **property trading company**, sometimes known as a **merchant developer**) can be more erratic, since profits can fluctuate widely. It was mainly companies of this kind that boomed in the late 1980s but got into trouble (and frequently went bust) in the crash of the early 1990s.

Many of the longer-established investment or investment and development companies were originally built up by entrepreneurial developers after the war. Property investment companies tend to be valued on the stockmarket by reference to the **asset backing** for their shares. As with single-tiered investment trusts, the shares usually stand at a discount to the net asset value, except at times of temporary market euphoria. Trading companies that make their profit from selling properties are more likely to be rated on a PE ratio basis and the shares often stand above the asset value when conditions are 'normal' in the property market.

Unitized property

Apart from the shares of property companies, there are a few other avenues for investment in commercial property. There are specialist

property unit trusts which own a range of properties. Pension funds or charities can invest in these units to obtain a stake in a portfolio of commercial property as an alternative to owning properties outright. But these vehicles are not open to the public.

The public can, however, acquire a stake in commercial property by investing in **property bonds**. These are unit-linked life assurance contracts (see Chapter 21) where the link is to the value of a portfolio of commercial properties rather than shares. **Authorized unit trusts** (those in which the general public may buy units) used to be prohibited from owning property direct. That has now changed. But while property-owning authorized unit trusts in theory provide another avenue for the public to invest in commercial property, they have not as yet caught on in any significant way.

For some time there have been plans to extend the principle of **unitization** – dividing the ownership of properties among a number of investors – to single properties. The reason is that some individual buildings are now so valuable that it is difficult to find even an institution that will buy or finance one by itself. If the ownership can be divided, however, the problem is eased. The ownership of the £100m building could be divided, say, into 100,000 units of £1,000 each, and both institutions and private investors could take a stake.

Most schemes of this type that were researched in the 1980s subsequently stumbled on legal or tax problems or were simply abandoned in the crash of the early 1990s. But you will still sometimes hear references to **PINCs** (**Property Income Certificates**), **SAPCOs** (**Single Asset Property Companies**) or **SPOTs** (**Single Property Ownership Trusts**). Further attempts to find a viable structure for unitizing single properties are constantly being made. A development on these lines in the 1990s (though not strictly a unitization) was the **property limited partnership**, which allowed two or more investors to share in property investments or developments.

There have also been attempts to market property-based **derivatives**. The former **London Commodity Exchange** (which is now part of Liffe) introduced **property futures** in 1991 – its name in those days was the **London Futures and Options Exchange** or **London FOX**. These worked in much the same way as futures based on a stockmarket index (see Chapter 18) but used indices of property rents and values instead. They allowed bets on commercial property rents, commercial property values, house prices and building society mortgage rates. But the venture very shortly collapsed in scandal when evidence of fabricated deals emerged.

More successful was the launch in 1994 of **Property Index Certificates** or **PICs** by Barclay's Bank. These were bonds issued for two, three, four or five years where the return to the investor was linked to indices of property rents and values. However, PICs were issued in large denominations and aimed at the financial institutions, not at private investors. Property index forward contracts were introduced later. There have also been a number of cases of securitizing the rents from property by issuing bonds or other forms of debt backed by the property's income flow, but this is different from offering a share in the growth of the property.

Property indices

In writing about property there are several yardsticks that journalists and others use. For **property company shares** there is a real estate sub-index of the FTSE Actuaries indices. And a number of firms of estate agents produce **indices of rental values** of different types of property, of **movement in capital values** and of the yields on which **prime properties** (the best property investments in their category) or average investment-grade properties are changing hands. But the most widely used property indices today are those produced by **Investment Property Databank** or **IPD**, an organization that monitors and analyses the performance of many billions of pounds' worth of commercial property owned by the investing institutions (and to a lesser extent by property companies).

Of the three main classes of property, normally **shops** show the lowest yield (are the most highly valued), **offices** come next and **industrial properties** which covers factories and warehouses are valued on the highest yields. There are markets in virtually every type of property, but institutional investment activity concentrates on the quality end of the market. Further down the scale from prime property is **secondary property** which may not be of investment grade for the institutions.

Property performance

Commercial property values tend to follow a pronounced cyclical pattern, and often move counter-cyclically to shares (and also sometimes to residential property). The period 1982 to 1986 (while the stockmarket was booming) was very dull in the commercial property market with values showing comparatively little growth. Then in 1987 and 1988 rents and values rose very sharply and were virtually untouched by the October 1987 crash on the stockmarket. By 1989 some worries over the level of bank lending to property companies were beginning to surface: it had reached £22 billion. It subsequently rose to an all-time peak of over £40 billion in 1991. But by then a major crash in the property market was well and truly under way.

The crash of the early 1990s

Between 1985 and 1989, the average value of shop property in the UK had risen by 85 per cent. **City of London office property** had more than doubled in value. The boom attracted enormous amounts of new development, particularly in London offices. When recession struck, the commercial property world thus faced a surplus of space just at the time that prospective tenants were cutting back on their own businesses and their space requirements. With too much space and too few tenants, rental values began to fall. Completing the picture of disaster were very high interest rates which had two effects. Developers faced vastly higher interest bills on their loans from the banks. And the higher returns from bank loans and other investments also meant that investors demanded higher initial yields from property – at a time when yields would have been rising anyway because of the worsened growth prospects for property. In other words, commercial property values had to fall very sharply.

Fall they did. The value of City of London offices dropped on average by over 60 per cent between 1989 and 1992. Shops suffered less badly but on average still lost roughly a quarter of their value. Average yields on all classes of property rose from 7.2 per cent in 1989 to 9.4 per cent in 1991. Rental levels for all classes of property across the country fell on average by 28 per cent from their peak and for City of London offices by half.

The property development and trading companies were faced with buildings that they could not let and therefore could not sell as investments. They had no way of repaying their bank loans, which were clocking up interest charges at a terrifying rate. Even if they could have sold the buildings, values had fallen so far that they would not have produced enough to repay the loans. Many companies of this type, including some of the biggest, went bust. The British clearing banks alone wrote off several billion pounds on their property loans. But the property development and investment companies generally survived because they had the income from completed and tenanted properties to pay the interest on their loans.

The market crash threw up several novel phenomena. The rent review clauses in most leases had long included an **upwards-only** provision. The rent could rise to the market level at the review point but never fall. So an office tenant who agreed a rent of £60 psf in 1989 had to continue to pay £60 psf after the rent review in 1994, even though the real rental value of the building had dropped to £30 psf. This gave rise to the phenomenon of **over-rented properties** – those bringing in a rent above the market rate – which were very difficult to value. The old post-war assumption that rents would always be higher at the review point than five years earlier had, needless to say, gone by the board.

Valuation was made doubly difficult because many parts of the commercial property market virtually dried up and there were few transactions to take as a guideline. Compounding the problem were the very large **inducements** that owners of new buildings were obliged to offer prospective tenants to persuade them to sign a lease. It was not uncommon for the landlord to offer an incoming tenant a three-year **rent-free period** or a large **lump sum inducement** to take a long lease at, say, £35 psf. That posed the problem of what the real rental value of the building would be without the inducement. And **confidentiality clauses** often prohibited landlord and tenant from disclosing the terms of the lease.

By late 1993 or early 1994 the worst was past in the commercial property market. Values had staged a recovery as investors turned to property for higher yields than they could get at the time on bonds, and the buying pushed values up. But we were into 1995 before there was much evidence that rental values were rising again.

And the crash and subsequent financial events were prompting important changes in the commercial property market as the millennium approached. Leases, as we have seen, were getting shorter and there was pressure to introduce totally new forms of lease which did not require such long-term commitment from the tenant. Investors could no longer rely on high inflation to help property values upwards. Because of their lower growth expectations they demanded higher yields – the average for all classes of investment-grade property at the end of 1999 was around 7.5 per cent. And this, combined with dramatic falls in both short- and long-term interest rates, brought another significant structural change. For most of the post-war period, the interest on the money borrowed to buy a property had been higher than the income the property produced. You had to borrow at, say, 10 per cent to buy properties yielding 5 per cent, which implied severe cash flow problems for the property investor. But at times in 1999 government bonds were showing yields as low as 4.5 per cent and good-quality bonds issued by property companies were yielding around 6 per cent. Whatever the growth prospects, it made good-quality property that yielded 7.5 per cent or more look quite attractive on simple income grounds.

Internet pointers

Marketing of residental property over the Internet is beginning to take off in the UK and there are ambitious plans for marketing of business accommodation. But if you want to find out about the structure of the commercial property market in the UK, the websites of the major firms of surveyors and agents are, at the time of writing, generally disappointing and are not therefore included here. However, there are very useful statistics on property performance available free from Investment Property Databank at www.propertymall.com/ipd/. The weekly magazine *Estates Gazette* (the bible of the UK property business) has a paid-for electronic property news and information service at www.egi.co.uk/ which currently offers a week or so's free trial use. Major property companies have their own websites. The Royal Institution of Chartered Surveyors, the professional body for chartered surveyors in the UK, has a site at www.rics.org.uk/, but this is likely to be of more interest to members than to the public and would-be clients. However, an RICS-associated organization, the Investment Property Forum, covers topics of interest to investors at www.ipf.org.uk/ though again it is aimed at real estate practitioners rather than the general public.

21 Savings, pooled investment and tax shelters

The public flotations of British Telecom, Trustee Savings Bank, British Gas, the water companies and the electricity companies attracted millions of first-time investors to the stockmarket. The flotation of former building societies such as Abbey National brought many more. But these issues could give a misleading impression of the way the bulk of the British public invests its money. Direct holdings of shares represent only a small proportion of the public's savings. Most of it is tied up in a range of managed-savings products whose features and virtues are examined and discussed at great length in the personal finances pages of the national press, in specialist personal finance magazines and on a variety of personal finance websites on the Internet.

Personal-finance advice homes in on questions of performance, security and tax efficiency, with much attention devoted to tax shelters such as **Individual Savings Accounts** or **ISAs** (we will come to these later). So the advice you get from the press and elsewhere is likely to include the following elements:

- Start buying your own **house** as soon as you are able to do so. The interest payments on your mortgage are no longer tax-favoured as they were in the past. But capital gains on the sale of your main home are still tax-free.

- Make adequate **life-assurance** arrangements, both as protection for your family and as a means of saving. Here, too, former tax reliefs have gone, though there is partial relief on premiums for people with pre-1984 policies.

- Make sure you have adequate **pension** arrangements. Even if you are a member of an occupational pension scheme (a scheme run by your employer) there may be scope for making additional payments to secure additional benefits.

- Spare cash may be invested for safety and convenience with your **bank** or **building society** (and look carefully at the range of accounts on offer and the rates of interest that they pay).

- Only once you have taken care of the basics should you dip a toe in the stockmarket. And in the first instance this should be via some form of **pooled investment** vehicle where you have the benefit of a spread of risk and of (supposedly) professional investment management.

- Direct ownership of shares, in the traditional wisdom, is for those with enough spare cash to afford holdings in a spread of companies, thus reducing the risk if any one of them falls on hard times.

- Above all, take advantage of whatever tax shelters the government of the day offers. In the case of the previous Conservative government it was **Personal Equity Plans** (**PEPs**) and **Tax Exempt Special Savings Accounts** (**TESSAs**). With New Labour it is **Individual Savings Accounts** (**ISAs**). Various of the types of investment already mentioned may be held within the ISA tax shelter. Pension savings used to offer the best tax breaks of all, and still do to the extent that contributions (up to approved levels) are offsettable against income tax, while income and capital gains on the investments held in the pension fund are tax free. But the abolition of the reclaimable dividend tax credit under New Labour reduced the returns that pension funds can derive from their equity investments.

A quick glance at the **investments and savings** held by the British public mid-way through 1999 underlines the pattern suggested by the advice above (see Table 21.1).

Investments and savings held by the British public at mid-1999

	£bn
Equity in life assurance and pensions	1,576
Sterling bank deposits	367
Sterling building society deposits	105
Quoted UK shares	231
Unquoted UK shares	214
UK mutual funds	136
UK government bonds (gilts)	31

Table 21.1

Savings via **financial institutions** (life assurance companies and pension funds) account for the vast bulk of the British public's savings. Deposits with banks and building societies come next; bank deposits have grown and building society deposits declined as more building societies have transmuted into banks. Direct holdings of quoted UK shares come a very poor third. These direct holdings of shares have actually been rising in value terms in recent years because of a buoyant UK stockmarket in the later 1990s and the coming to market of previously mutual concerns such as building societies. But private individuals still regularly sell more shares than they buy each year. Indirect holdings of shares via mutual funds (essentially, unit trusts) are smaller still, though have grown a lot in recent years.

From these bare figures it is clear already that provision of personal finance services is big business. A walk down any high street suggests that Britain, once characterized as a nation of shopkeepers, has become a nation of money-lenders as bank and building society branches often outnumber conventional retailers. But this is only the tip of the iceberg. Less visible than the high-street deposit-takers and money-lenders is the vast fund-management business that makes its very comfortable living from the fees it charges for investing other people's money. There are little more than 2,000 stockmarket-listed British companies that actually put money to work to earn a profit by providing goods or services. There are almost as many funds offering, for a fee, to invest the public's money in the shares of these companies or, in some cases, their overseas counterparts. Have a look at the 'Companies & Markets' section of the *Financial Times*. London share prices occupy, at the time of writing, two pages. Listings of **managed funds** occupy seven pages, of which three relate to UK-regulated funds.

Much of the comment in the personal finance pages of the press concerns the relative performance of these managers of other people's money. To see why performance – in terms of the overall return achieved – over a period of years is so important, just consider a few figures. If you invest £1,000 today at a compound annual rate of return of 6 per cent, in 40 years it would have grown to about £10,286. At a compound rate of 6.5 per cent it would have grown to £12,416. At 7 per cent, to £14,974. And so on. At 12 per cent it would have grown to the massive sum of £93,051. In other words, even quite a small difference in the annual return achieved can, over a long period, make an enormous difference to the outcome. These are the sort of sums that pension-fund managers, who may indeed be investing for 40 years, have to do. And they serve to emphasize the importance of tax in the investment figuring. If your £1,000 is compounding up at 6 per cent a year free of tax (as it could do in a tax-free pension fund), it will indeed be worth £10,286 after 40 years. If you have to pay 20 per cent tax on each year's income, your net annual rate of return reduces to 4.8 per cent. At 4.8 per cent a year, £1,000 grows to only £6,523 after 40 years.

So we will need to look at tax shelters. But first the broad investment choices need to be put into context. With money left over after they have met their basic financial needs (life assurance, pension, etc.) savers may:

- make their own investment decisions direct (by buying shares in individual companies, buying government bonds, or whatever)

- put themselves in the hands of professional managers and achieve a spread of risk by buying into different kinds of pooled investment vehicle. But even here they have to make the choice of which manager or investment vehicle to select. There are, of course, managers who offer to select among the investment vehicles run by other managers. But even these managers of managers have to be selected!

Personal-finance advice in the press and the broadcast media concentrates very much on the pooled investment route. But remember that the performance of pooled investment vehicles depends ultimately on the performance of the underlying investments that they pick. Don't rely too heavily on advice you read or hear from representatives of the fund-management industry. They make no money from people who decide not to invest, and even when the stockmarket is looking dangerously high they very rarely advise investors to hold off for the moment. Their usual argument is that, in the very long term, an investment will pay off even if it is bought close to the peak. It would, of course, pay off very much better if bought at a time when prices were more rational. For investors who are not confident that they can predict the peaks and troughs of the market, **averaging** is often a sensible policy. Invest a certain amount each quarter or each year. This way you will sometimes buy when the market is high, but these purchases should be offset by others that are made when the market is lower.

Whether investors choose direct stockmarket investment or the pooled funds route, they still have to decide on how to make best use of the tax shelter available. But choosing the tax shelter is not necessarily the same decision as choosing the underlying investments. First, what are the main savings products and from whom are they bought?

Financial intermediaries in the savings market

Much life assurance and related savings products is sold through **financial intermediaries**. In practice this often means **insurance brokers** who frequently (and often misleadingly) also operate under the title of **investment advisers** or **financial consultants**. These are one type of middle-man between the public and the insurance companies or savings institutions. Since most of them live from the commission on the products they sell, there is an inevitable temptation for them to be swayed in favour of the product paying the highest commission, and the independence of their advice is frequently called into question. Along with the insurance companies' own sales forces, they have met considerable criticism over the mis-selling of personal pensions (see below).

As an indirect result of the City's regulatory system, an increasing number of these financial intermediaries have in any case tied themselves to one particular insurance company or provider of investment products. Under a process known as **polarization**, investment product advisers have to decide whether they confine themselves to marketing the products of a particular group or whether they want to operate as **Independent Financial Advisers** or **IFAs,** marketing products from a range of providers. Nowadays the banks and building societies are also important middlemen in the savings market, selling their own or other people's insurance and savings products. Professionals such as accountants and lawyers may also act as middlemen for savings products.

You will also come across the term **discount brokers**. These are vendors of investment products who, where the client does not require advice, may be prepared to remit to the buyer part of the commission that they earn on the sale.

Traditional life assurance

The basic life assurance theme has an infinite number of variations. **Term insurance** is a straight bet with the insurance company: you pay premiums for an agreed period, and if you die during that time the insurance company pays the sum for which your life was insured. If you survive, you've lost the bet (or won it, depending on your outlook!) and you get nothing at the end of the period. **Whole-life** insurance pays a lump sum when you die, at any age. So your family gets something even if you live to 100.

Endowment asssurance is a savings vehicle for you as well as a protection for your dependants. You pay the premiums, and at the end of the term of the insurance you get a lump sum. If you die earlier, your dependants get a lump sum, as with whole life. The life assurance aspect of the contract is not too complicated: insurance company actuaries can calculate pretty accurately from mortality tables the risk of death before such-and-such an age (though new dangers such as AIDS cause problems) and provide for it in the premium they charge. The premium income goes into the **life funds** of the insurance company, where it is invested and this is where the main uncertainty arises: the return the insurance company will earn on its investments. In the case of a **with-profits policy** the policyholder is entitled to a share of the profits from the growth of the fund.

Two points are worth noting on life assurance investment. First, returns on (particularly equity) investment may turn out to be considerably lower in the new century than they were in earlier boom days and the with-profits element for policyholders looks less attractive than in the past. This has worried people who bought life assurance to pay off their mortgage (see below). Second, many investors who enter into a life assurance contract subsequently find themselves unable to maintain their payments and need to take their money out early. What they receive – the **surrender value** – is usually very low in the early years compared with what they have paid in, partly because the salesman's commission comes mainly out of the early payments (**front-end loading**). Insurance companies are now required to give prospective clients more information than in the past on commissions and costs.

Company and individual pensions

Personal pensions are best viewed as being part of the same general business as life assurance, and the major insurance companies provide them. They also run a lot of company pension schemes for smaller and medium-sized groups. Take the company schemes first. These may be **insured schemes**, where the insurance group tells the company what premium it needs each year to provide the eventual level of benefit required for the employees. Or the company may hand over the contributions to be invested in a **managed fund** run by the insurance group; the pension scheme is allocated units in the fund *pro rata* with its contribution, and the value of the units depends on the investment performance of the fund. Or the pension fund may simply employ the insurance company as an **investment manager**, to manage its assets as a separate fund: a field in which merchant banks, brokers and other fund management groups also compete fiercely.

Alternatively, the pension fund can, of course, manage its own investments, as some of the larger ones do, or it can manage part of the funds itself and contract out management of the rest. With a buoyant stockmarket and high real returns on investment, many pension funds showed **surpluses** in the second half of the 1980s and the earlier 1990s. The value of their investments exceeded what was needed to meet expected liabilities. These surpluses were reduced in a number of ways – many companies took a **contributions holiday** – and were also being 'raided' by the sponsoring company and by takeover practitioners.

For much of the post-war period, employees of a company which ran its own pension scheme were normally forced to join that scheme. From 1988 they have been free to make their own arrangements, sometimes known as **personal portable pensions** because they can be taken from job to job. The self-employed already do this if they do not wish to rely on the fairly meagre benefits of the **state pension schemes**. To build up bigger pensions, those in occupational pension schemes may make **additional voluntary contributions** or **AVCs**.

Private-sector pension arrangements fall into two main types. Traditionally, company schemes have been mainly **defined benefit** (otherwise known as **final salary**) schemes. An employee builds up his entitlement each year he works for the company and, typically, might receive a pension of two-thirds of his final salary if he has worked for 40 years for the same company by the time he retires. The problem with this type of scheme for the sponsoring company is that it does not know in advance what the pension liabilities will be. This is because it does not know what salaries will be at retirement age or what investment returns will be earned on the contributions over 40 years.

This problem does not crop up with the other type of scheme: the **defined contribution** or **money-purchase** scheme. With these schemes a certain amount of money is contributed each year and invested. When the member retires, his 'pot' of accumulated money is used to buy an annuity to provide him with an income for the rest of his life. But the income does not necessarily bear any particular relationship to his salary in employment. Its size depends on the investment returns earned on his money over the years and the levels of investment yields at the time that the annuity must be bought. **Personal portable pensions** are of the money-purchase type.

For prospective pensioners in money-purchase schemes, the big fall in long-term bond yields that took place in the later 1990s has come as bad news. If money earns lower long-term returns – which is the effect of a fall in bond yields – then a given pot of money buys only a reduced income on retirement. Those in a company scheme with the promise of a pension linked to final salary are more fortunate.

Pensions have, in general, been under something of a cloud in recent years. The plundering of his company pensions schemes for many hundreds of millions of pounds by the late Robert Maxwell sent a shiver through the pensions business. And the mis-selling of personal pensions brought further unfavourable publicity for parts of the pensions industry (see Chapter 22). Pensions are an exceedingly complex area and it is often difficult if not impossible to get competent impartial advice. Walk with extreme care.

Repayment and endowment mortgages

Buying a house with the help of a **mortgage** is usually regarded as a form of savings and mortgages, too, can have a life assurance element. The homebuyer can take out either a **repayment mortgage** or an **endowment mortgage**. With the **repayment mortgage** the amount borrowed is repaid via monthly instalments of interest and capital (more interest and less capital in the early stages and more capital and less interest in the later ones). Repayments are calculated so that the whole of the sum will have been repaid by the end of the term: usually 25 years though, because people move house, the average life of a mortgage in practice is much shorter. The interest rate on mortgages is traditionally variable, so payments have to be adjusted up and down as interest rates change. Changes in the rates are always hot news. But the shock of very high interest rates in the late 1980s and early 1990s encouraged many home-buyers to require (and mortgage-providers to supply) mortgages where the interest rate was fixed, at least for the first few years, or where there was a **cap** on the maximum interest that could be charged. Homebuyers taking out a mortgage need to check the fine print very carefully. Are there penalties for early repayment, for example?

The **endowment mortgage** introduced the life assurance. The money to buy the house was borrowed, usually from a **building society or bank**, and interest was paid to the lender in the normal way. But no capital was repaid. Instead, the borrower took out an endowment life assurance policy which, when it matured, was intended to provide a lump sum large enough to repay the loan from the building society or bank and – with any luck – provide a surplus on top. But in recent years there have been fears that these lump sums might not turn out to be large enough to repay the mortgage and the popularity of the endowment mortgage has evaporated. There is no doubt that many homebuyers were persuaded into endowment mortgages when a repayment mortgage would have been a better bet. You don't need to look far for the reason. There was a commission to be earned from the sale of the endowment policy.

Unit-linked investment vehicles

Move beyond the basic insurance and loan products, and you are next likely to meet the **unit-linked** investment vehicles, a form of **pooled investment** scheme. These give some of the benefits of stockmarket investment while spreading the risks.

It is inappropriate, as we have seen, for an individual with modest savings to risk them all on the vagaries of one share price – although we were asked to believe that this did not matter when the Government was off-loading previously nationalized industries. It makes sense for those with small amounts of capital or no knowledge of the stockmarket to invest in a spread of shares rather than the shares of a single company. Hence **unit trusts** and **unit-linked assurance**. Look at the pages of tables at the back of the *Financial Times*, before the stockmarket prices and at the beginning of the section headed **FT managed funds service**, with the main sub-headings **authorized investment funds** and **insurances**.

Principles of pooled investment

Despite the variety on offer, the principle of **unitized**, **pooled** or **collective** investment is simple. Suppose you and 99 other people each stump up £1 for investment in a new **unit trust**. The managers thus

collect £100 in total and use it to buy shares in a variety of companies. Over a period the value of the trust's investments rises by, say,
20 per cent. The original £100 of investments is now worth £120. You
own one of the 100 units in issue, so the value of your unit is one
hundredth of the total value of the fund. In other words, its value has
risen from £1 to £1.20 (the actual calculations, allowing for costs, are
of course more complex). How would you sell your unit if you wanted to cash in? You would sell it back to the managers of the unit trust,
who will then try to sell it to somebody else. If they cannot do so,
they may have to sell some of the trust's investments to raise the
money to pay you.

Unit-linked insurance incorporates a similar collective-invest-
ment mechanism, where the value of the unit is linked to the value of
a specific fund or sub-fund of investments, but technically it is a life
assurance contract. You hand over your money to the managers. A
small proportion of it goes to provide a minimal amount of life assurance cover. The remainder is invested in units of what is technically
a **life fund**. If the value of the fund rises, the value of your investment
rises, too. What is the point of unit-linked insurance, when you can
invest in unit trusts? In the past, there were tax advantages in investing in a life assurance contract. Also, a life fund could invest direct
in property (unit-linked schemes invested in property are called
property bonds) and the scheme could be sold door to door, which
was not then allowed in the case of unit trusts. The treatment of the
two types of investment is now closer in line and property-owning
unit trusts are now permitted.

Pricing of unit trusts

The operations of a unit trust are not, of course, quite as simple as in
the example. There are charges for the service: typically, an initial
charge of 5 per cent or 6 per cent of the value of your investment and
an on-going annual charge of 1 per cent or more. Both initial and
annual charges have risen over the years, notably the annual rate.
And, as with shares, there is not a single price for the units. There is
a buying price and a selling price: you buy the units from the managers at the higher 'offer' price and receive the lower 'bid' price
when you sell them back. The price spread partially reflects the fact
that the unit trust itself has to pay a higher price when it buys shares,
gets a lower price when it sells them and will incur dealing expenses. If a unit trust suffers a large outflow of funds it has some leeway
to move bid and offer price down to a lower pricing basis, sometimes

known as a **bid basis** or **liquidation basis**. Some unit trusts are now structured with no initial charge, but with an 'exit' charge diminishing over a period of years. A few may make an exit charge anyway when the investor sells within a given number of years.

Note that performance figures for unit trusts should always allow for the spread. So if the quotation for a particular trust has moved up from 100p–107p to 120p–128p over the year the calculation should allow for the fact that the investor would have bought at 107p and sold at 120p: a gain of 13p or 12.1 per cent, not 20p.

Open-ended investment companies

Open-ended investment companies or **OEICs** operate much like unit trusts, and some unit trusts have turned themselves into OEICs. But there are technical differences. OEICs are companies, not trusts, and they therefore issue shares, not units. But the share price is not determined by the interplay of buyers and sellers in the market. As with a unit trust, it is calculated from the value of the assets that the OEIC owns. Unlike a unit trust, however, the OEIC quotes a single price rather than a buying and selling price. Management charges are levied separately. The OEIC is open-ended (like a unit trust) because it can create further shares when required by investor demand. The OEIC was introduced because its operation may be simpler to understand than that of the unit trust and its structure conforms more closely with the structure of mutual funds in the rest of Europe.

Features of unit trust operation

A unit trust which is marketed to the public needed in the past to be **authorized** by the **Department of Trade and Industry**, though responsibility for authorization has passed to the **Financial Services Authority**. There are also **unauthorized** trusts which some stockbrokers run for their clients or which may be located offshore. Advertisements for unit trusts are fairly closely monitored and must contain a **health warning** – a reminder that the unit price can go down as well as up.

When they first launch, unit trusts may make a **fixed price offer** for a limited period – you will see the advertisements in the financial pages of the national papers, usually on a Saturday or Sunday. At this time you can apply for units at a known price. The rest of the time you normally pay the price ruling around the time your application is received. Fund management groups also frequently provide the opportunity for regular savings plans: you arrange to pay so much a month, the money being invested in units when it is received.

Unit trusts must pay out the income they receive on their investments to their unitholders, *pro rata* with their holdings. But sometimes the investor has a choice between **income units** (where he receives his share of the dividends in cash) and **accumulation units** (where his share of the income is added to the value of each unit). This second option is a convenience but does not offer any tax saving: the income is reinvested net of basic rate tax and any higher rate tax due has to be paid. However, accumulation units are not charged with the cost of reinvestment and the investor also has a better record of his total return when he keeps the same number of units. An alternative is for the investor to be credited with additional units representing the reinvested net income. This may involve paying preliminary charges on the new units.

Who offers unit-linked investment?

The *Financial Times* lists over 150 fund-management groups offering authorized unit trusts or OEICs and not far short of 100 offering unit-linked assurance. Variations of the same name frequently crop up in both categories: most of the larger fund management groups offer the whole range of unit-linked products.

Computers make it easy to calculate the value of a trust's investments each day, and hence the unit price. The *Financial Times* listings show, for unit trusts, both the lower **bid price** (price at which an investor may sell) and the higher **offer price** (price at which an investor may buy) and the price movement over the previous day, plus the **yield**. In many cases separate prices are shown for income units and accumulation units: the latter will be higher, because of the reinvested income.

Specialist investment policies

The original idea of unit trusts was to offer a spread of investments across most areas of the stockmarket. Then came more specialist funds, investing according to particular philosophies or in particular areas. Have a look at the trusts run by the major management groups. There will probably be a **general fund**. Then there may be funds investing for **high income**, in **smaller companies**, in **recovery stocks** (companies down on their luck whose share price should improve dramatically if they pull round) in **technology stocks**, and so on. There may be unit trusts investing only in investment trust shares. And there is probably a **tracker fund**, simply seeking to mirror the performance of a particular stockmarket index. There will also be trusts investing in specific geographical areas or types of market: America, Australasia, Japan and Europe, emerging markets and the rest. There are also unit trusts which do not invest in shares at all but invest in the money market or in government or company bonds.

A similar range of investment policies is evident in the unit-linked assurance funds, normally known as **bonds** (though not to be confused with government or company bonds). In fact, many unit trusts have a **bondized** equivalent: an insurance fund that invests in the relevant unit trust. The prices for the bonds, under the heading of **insurances**, follow the same pattern as those for unit trusts, except that no yield is shown since no income is distributed. With unit-linked assurance, the income from the fund's investments is automatically reinvested in the fund after deduction of tax at the life assurance rate. A life fund is also taxed on capital gains (unlike unit trust funds, which are exempt from gains tax) and this is reflected in the price of units.

Offshore and overseas funds

After the **insurances** in the *Financial Times* come the prices for **offshore and overseas funds**. These are not authorized unit trusts, though they operate on the unit principle and many operate under the umbrella of one of the fund management groups that offers authorized unit trusts in the UK. Many of the offshore funds are technically located in the Channel Islands and managed from there, the UK parent group being described as 'adviser' to the fund. Hence management group names with 'C.I.' in the title.

The **offshore funds** operate under the tax regime of the country where they are located: usually more liberal than in Britain. But for a British investor living in Britain there is no tax advantage in investing in them. He will be treated for tax according to the UK rules. Expatriate Britons working, say, in the Middle East and paying little if any UK tax may do better in an offshore fund than in one registered in the UK.

Monitoring performance

Performance statistics for unit trusts and bonds are closely followed. The monthly magazine *Money Management* provides a comprehensive list showing the value of £1,000 invested over periods ranging from six months to seven or ten years, and various Internet websites also provide performance information (see end of this chapter). Performance can vary very markedly, particularly over the shorter periods, and for the intrinsically more speculative funds invested in foreign markets, picking the right country is often more important for the managers than picking the right share, especially at times of wild currency swings. Needless to say, around the turn of the millennium, trusts specializing in technology companies had done particularly well over the previous year. The problem is that an investment policy that was precisely right one year, in terms of market sector or geographical area, could equally well be precisely wrong the next. More cautious investors will look for consistent outperformance over longer periods as evidence of management quality.

In fact, unit trust investors should be aware that many trusts are marketing-led rather than investment-led. The managers find it easy to market a new trust investing in an area that has recently become fashionable and attracted widespread press comment. But by the time the trust is launched, the best of the growth may be past. For investors the trick is, as always, to get into the areas that will become fashionable before they have done so. Likewise, unit trust sales and the volume of unit trust marketing tend to rise when the stockmarket has been on a rising trend for a long time and everybody has noticed the profits being made. In practice, the market may be near its peak and it could be the worst possible time to buy. Cynical unit trust investors tend to invest **counter-cyclically**. They may buy the previous year's worst-performing trust on the basis that its policy could turn out right the next year – and buy unit trusts in general when the market is low and marketing hype is minimal.

Investment trusts

There is one other – and much older – form of collective investment vehicle that crops up frequently in the personal finance pages: the **investment trust**. An investment trust is a company whose business – rather than making widgets or running laundries – is simply to invest in other companies. It holds a portfolio of investments in the same way as a unit trust or a life fund, thus providing professional

M & G Securities (1330)F
M & G House, Victoria Road, Chelmsford CM1 1FB
www.mandg.co.uk Enq: 0800 390 390   UT Deal: 0800 328 3196

American	5	1013.0	1063.7	−13.7	0.00
(Accum Units)	5	1280.9	1345.1	−17.3	0.00
Amer Recovery	5	1176.0	1234.8	−12.6	0.00
(Accum Units)	5	1368.4	1436.8	−14.6	0.00
Amer Smlr Cos	5	321.0	337.1	−5.9	0.00
(Accum Units)	5	328.0	344.4	−6.1	0.00
Australasian	5	220.4	231.4	+0.2	1.8
(Accum Units)	5	299.0	313.9	+0.3	1.8
Blue Chip	0 C	102.90xd	103.16	−0.3	2.28
(Accum Units)	0 C	337.8xd	338.61	−0.99	2.28
British Opps	5	96.70	101.5	−0.5	1.39
(Accum Units)	5	365.2	383.5	−1.7	1.39
Capital	5	1250.6	1313.1	−9.1	0.39
(Accum Units)	5	1596.3	1676.0	−11.7	0.39
Charifund**	0 C	1056.0	1058.73	+0.15	4.95
(Accum Units)**	0 C	6576.6	6593.13	+0.93	4.95
Commodity	5	387.5	406.9	+1.5	1.3
(Accum Units)	5	590.3	619.9	+2.3	1.3
Corporate Bond	0	28.50xd	28.66	−0.21	6.0
Dividend	5 C	55.70xd	58.50	−0.1	3.66
(Accum Units)	5 C	286.5xd	301.2	−0.5	3.66
Emerging Markets Bond	0 E	58.42xd	58.92	−0.09	9.4
(Accum Units)	0 E	60.70xd	61.22	−0.09	9.4
European	5	1328.6xd	1395.0	+4.2	0.00
(Accum Units)	5	1731.4xd	1818.0	+5.5	0.00
European Dividend	5 C	141.0	148.1	+0.4	2.14
(Accum Units)	5 C	195.7	205.5	+0.5	2.14
European High Yield Bond	0 E	49.54	49.95	−0.2	7.9
(Accum Units)	0 E	51.38	51.81	−0.21	7.9
European Index Tracker Inc ♦	0	56.40xd	56.43	−0.17	0.74
(Accum Units) ♦	0	56.40xd	56.43	−0.17	0.74
ISA CAT ♦	0		56.43xd	−0.17	0.74
European Smaller Cos.	5	185.8xd	195.1	−1.3	0.00
(Accum Units)	5	186.4xd	195.8	−1.3	0.00
Extra Income	5 C	604.7	634.9	−2.7	3.87
(Accum Units)	5 C	2348.6	2465.9	−10.3	3.87
Fund of Inv Tsts	5	1173.7xd	1232.4	+1.8	0.00
(Accum Units)	5	2341.1xd	2458.2	+3.6	0.00
Gilt Income	0	71.29	71.42	−0.06	4.7
(Accum Units)	0	259.39	259.87	−0.22	4.7
ISA CAT	0		71.42	−0.06	4.7
Global Managed Bond	3	50.50xd	52.00	−0.2	5.8
(Accum Units)	3	51.50xd	52.90	−0.2	5.8
Global Technology	5	104.6	109.8	−1.2	0.00
(Accum Units)	5	104.6	109.8	−1.2	0.00
Gold	5	38.60	40.50	+0.1	0.76
(Accum Units)	5	47.40	49.70	+0.1	0.76
High Interest	0	25.00xd	25.00		5.9
High Yield Corporate Bond*	0 E	51.80xd	52.33	−0.14	8.3

Example 21.1 Some of the unit trusts offered by one of the UK's major fund management groups. Source: *Financial Times*.

management and a spread of risk. But you cannot buy 'units' in an investment trust. You buy its shares, in the same way as you would buy the shares of an industrial company. Investment trust share prices are thus listed in the share price pages of the *Financial Times* rather than on the unit trust or insurance fund pages.

The value of shares in an investment trust is determined in exactly the same way as the value of the shares in any other company, by the balance of buyers and sellers in the stockmarket. But in making their buying and selling decisions, investors naturally look at the value of the investments the trust owns, usually expressed as a **net asset value per share**, or **NAV** (see Chapter 4) and for technical reasons the share price of an investment trust nowadays is normally below the value of the assets backing the shares. In other words, it stands at a **discount** to the NAV. The size of the typical discount varies with stockmarket conditions.

This poses a considerable problem for anyone wanting to launch a new investment trust. Say he proposed to offer 100 shares to the public at £1 each and invest the £100 he received across a range of companies. The investment trust would have a portfolio of investments worth £100 and the NAV of each of its own shares would thus be £1. But the chances are that the shares would trade in the stockmarket at less than £1: say, at only 80p (a discount of 20 per cent to the NAV). Few investors want to put up £1 for something which shortly afterwards will be worth less.

Geared and split-level trusts

There are various ways an investment trust can try to reduce or elim-inate the discount to the asset value. It may offer special investment expertise in a particular area, which encourages investors to rate its shares more highly, or may attempt to cash in on a current stockmar-ket fashion. It might have considerable **gearing** – investment trusts can use borrowed money as well as shareholders' money – which means the asset backing for the shares would rise faster than the value of the investment portfolio in a rising market. Or it might organize itself as a **split-level trust**. The principle is that the investment trust's own share capital consists of **income shares** and **capital shares**, the income shares being entitled to all the income from its investment portfolio and the capital shares being entitled to the whole of the rise in capital value of the portfolio over the life of the company, which is limited to a specific period. There are a number of variations on this theme, some of them considerably more complex and involving the issue of several classes of capital. In one version the trust also issues **zero-dividend preference shares**. Except for the fact that these are share capital rather than debt, they work rather like zero-coupon bonds (see Chapter 13). They pay no income, but are eventually redeemed at a premium, which therefore provides the equivalent of an annual rate of return over their life. The idea of these complex capital structures is that, by tailoring different securities to the needs of dif-ferent investors, their value will be enhanced and the sum of the parts will be worth more than the whole would be if marketed as a single entity. Thus the discount problem can be alleviated.

Unitizing investment trusts

But the surest way for an existing investment trust to increase its total worth is to be taken over or to **unitize** itself. **Unitization** simply means that the investment trust turns itself into a unit trust, substitut-ing units for shares. The unit price is then calculated directly from the value of its investments (and fully reflects this value, which the share price did not). An investment trust is a **close-ended** investment vehicle, because it has a finite share capital. A unit trust is **open-ended** because the managers can create new units or cancel existing ones as demand and supply dictate.

The tax shelters

However you choose to invest your money, you also have to think how you can best shield your savings from the taxman. Under the Conservative government there were two main forms of tax shelter available: **Personal Equity Plans** or **PEPs** (for holding shares or pooled investments) and **Tax Exempt Special Savings Accounts** or **TESSAs** (for holding money on deposit). Up to the stipulated limits, investments held within these shelters would be exempt from income tax and capital gains tax. The New Labour government has abolished these shelters for the future (though existing PEPs and Tessas may continue) and put in their place an even more complex tax shelter called the **Individual Savings Account** or **ISA**, which also protects from income tax and capital gains tax.

You read and hear a great deal about 'buying' an ISA, as if an ISA in itself were an investment vehicle. It isn't. It is merely a form of wrapper in which your investments may be held. Unfortunately, you have to acquire this wrapper from an established financial organization and it is usually marketed complete with its content of investments. So in this sense you are 'buying' the wrapper and the contents at the same time. There are also what are known as **self-select ISAs** where you pay for the wrapper and decide yourself what shares you want to put into it, but these are rarer.

ISAs can be used to shelter a range of investments from tax, up to an overall limit of (in 2000-01) £7,000 a year. The three main categories are:

- cash (bank and building society accounts, and similar forms of deposit)

- shares and bonds (or pooled investments like unit trusts and investment trust shares)

- life insurance policies (or those designed for use in ISAs).

But to complicate matters there are two different types of ISA: **mini ISAs** and **maxi ISAs**. In any single tax year you have to opt for one type or the other. You cannot have both. But you may have up to three mini ISAs each year (one for cash, one for shares and one for life assurance) and you could 'buy' each from a different manager. You may have only one maxi ISA per year, into which you can put the same range of investments but the proportions may be different. For the 2000–01 tax year, the rules were that you could put into a mini ISA a maximum of £3,000 cash, £3,000 in stocks and shares or pooled investments and £1,000 of life assurance (there would, of course, be a separate mini-ISA for each element). The total amount that could be sheltered was thus £7,000. This same £7,000 overall limit also applies to a maxi ISA, but the difference is that you could put the whole £7,000 into shares, pooled investments or bonds, though you could also split your £7,000 between shares, cash and insurance as with a mini ISA if you wanted to. These maximum limits were likely to reduce in future years. Investors wanting the maximum possible tax shelter for direct or indirect stockmarket investment would obviously tend to opt for a maxi ISA with the whole £7,000 in shares, pooled investments or bonds.

Apart from their complexity, ISAs are far from ideal. They do provide protection against income tax and capital gains, but are obviously of limited interest to those who are not liable to tax and unlikely to become liable in the future. You have to go through a stockbroker or financial institution and the initial and annual charges from the manager may soak up a fair bit of any tax benefit that you get. But it does still make sense for most investors to use an ISA to shelter as much as possible of their investments from tax each year. For more information on how ISAs work, and the residual arrangements applying to PEPs and TESSAs, ignore the marketing hype from the ISA vendors and look instead at the independent *FSA guide to ISAs*. You may download it free from the Financial Services Authority website at www.fsa.gov.uk.

The government CAT mark

How do you know if you are paying too much in charges when you buy investment products? This is a problem area because performance is often more important than the fees levied by the provider. An investment manager making an initial charge of 6 per cent but delivering 20 per cent growth will be a better bet than a manager who charges only 4 per cent but manages to achieve only 10 per cent growth. Unfortunately, there is no guarantee that higher charges mean better performance and managers prepared to be paid according to performance are conspicuous by their absence.

The government has tried to address this issue by introducing a **CAT standard** for certain financial products such as ISAs, pensions and mortgages. CAT stands for 'charges', 'access' and 'terms', and products which comply must meet fairly stringent conditions on all these points. You thus know that you are not being ripped off on charges if you buy a product that conforms to the CAT standard, but this does not necessarily mean that it is the best product for you or the one that will show the best return. Because of the limit on charges, the CAT-compliant version of a product is likely to be the most basic model, and another version which does not comply with the CAT standard might provide more of the features that you want.

Internet pointers

Far more people buy personal finance products than would ever deal actively in the stockmarket. So this is where much of the money is for the financial services industry, which has not been slow to wake up to the opportunities offered by the Internet. Most of the larger providers of pensions, mortgages, unit trusts, ISAs, etc. have their own websites, which promote their products and vary considerably in quality. Many of the brokers who act as a selling conduit also maintain websites. But there are also a host of more independent sites providing both background information and latest price and interest-rate information on the whole range of savings products, often including performance comparisons. More detail on these personal finance sites is given in Chapter 23, but a good starting point is Moneyextra (which now incorporates Moneyworld) at www.moneyextra.com or Interactive Investor at www.iii.co.uk/. These sites cover the whole range of personal finance products and also provide educational and explanatory material, as do Moneyweb at www.moneyweb.co.uk/ and AAA Investment Guide at www.wisebuy.co.uk/. More detailed background information on unit trusts is obtainable from the Association of Unit Trusts and Investment Funds at www.investmentfunds.org.uk/ and on investment trusts from the Association of Investment Trust Companies at www.aitc.co.uk/. TrustNet at www.trustnet.co.uk/ provides performance information on pooled investment funds and two sites offering global funds performance information are Lipper at www.lipperweb.com/ and Micropal at www.micropal.com/. The Financial Services Authority site at www.fsa.gov.uk/ is worth a visit for the information it provides on some personal finance products, particularly ISAs, as well as for background on safeguards for investors and on the precautions they should observe.

22 Supervising the City

Users of financial products need protection against unscrupulous traders and shoddy products, just like any other kind of consumer. More so, in fact, since you cannot judge a financial product from the look and the feel. Thus, there are rules regarding the nature of the products on offer. And there are rules to govern the operations of the markets themselves, the professionals who trade in them and the vendors of investment products. But remember that there is a limit to the protection that can be offered. At the end of the day, the principle of 'buyer, beware' prevails.

The City's **supervisory systems** feature frequently in press reports and they have been in a state of almost constant flux over the past two decades. A new supervisory system for investment products, investment advisers and the markets was introduced in the period 1986–88 and was never long out of the news. It replaced a ramshackle regime that frequently left investors at the mercy of con-men such as unscrupulous investment advisers and promoters of dubious commodity investment schemes. But it laboured under the same disadvantages as all regulatory systems. The abuses that it prevented were not news. When it was forced to move publicly against investment operators, it risked the criticism that it should have prevented the abuse from taking place at all. It is now being replaced in its turn by a more unified system under a single regulatory body, the **Financial Services Authority** or **FSA**.

Statutory versus non-statutory supervision

There are two main approaches to regulating financial markets: **statutory regulation** and **self-regulation**. Most financial systems have some elements of both. The American system leans towards statutory regulation. A statutory body, the **Securities and Exchange Commission** (**SEC**), monitors the issue of securities to the public and the securities markets in which they are traded and reinforces the work of self-regulating bodies such as the New York Stock Exchange.

The British regulatory system

In Britain the regulation of the financial system has traditionally been a mixture of statutory and non-statutory measures, but until recently with a strong bias in favour of self-regulation. That is now changing, with the pendulum swinging in favour of statutory regulation. But the edges have always been blurred. In the system that prevailed from the second half of the 1980s to the late 1990s, the apex of the regulatory system was occupied by a body called the **Securities and Investments Board (SIB)**. The SIB was not a part of government or a government agency, but rather a private-sector organization. However, it drew its authority from legislation – the **Financial Services Act** of 1986 – under which regulatory powers were delegated to the SIB. The scope of the SIB or its subsidiary **Self Regulating Organizations (SROs)** covered, *inter alia*, the operations of brokers, marketmakers, investment managers, sellers of investment products, financial intermediaries of various kinds, commodity scheme operators (a previously glaring gap) and even publishers of investment newsletters and tip sheets. But a number of areas remained outside the scheme. Banks were regulated by the Bank of England, for example, and building societies had their own separate regulator.

By the end of the second millennium the operations of the SIB had effectively been subsumed into the new body, the **Financial Services Authority**. But this new monolith also took under its wing most of the regulatory functions that had previous remained outside the SIB system. It acquired responsibility for supervising banks, the wholesale financial markets of the City, building societies and friendly societies and was even acquiring regulatory powers over Lloyd's of London (see below and Chapter 19). But the FSA was not technically an arm of government, any more than the SIB. In terms of structure it was a company limited by guarantee and it was to be financed by the industries it regulated, rather than from the public purse. But the FSA, too, would derive its powers from legislation, which was going through the parliamentary process at the turn of the century. The **Financial Services and Markets Bill**, which would delegate its regulatory powers to the FSA, was expected to become law in the first half of the year 2000.

The basic principle underlying both the new legislation and its predecessor Act is that virtually anyone wishing to carry on a 'regulated activity' (a broad definition that embraces most types of investment or financial business) in the UK must be authorized to do so. The maximum penalty for undertaking a regulated activity without authorization is two years in jail plus a fine. Whether you are a bank, a stockbroker, a fund manager or an insurance salesman, you need authorization. The only major gap – and this was still being debated at the turn of the millennium – was the supply of various forms of loan and mortgage. Technically, loans are not investments. So the man or woman who tries to sell you a pension must be authorized, but the person who tries to sell you a mortgage does not need authorization for this activity (though the bank or building society he represents would, as an organization, be regulated by the FSA). It looked, however, as if some aspects of the mortgage business were likely to be subject to FSA scrutiny in the future.

With whom do you register for authorization? Under the old SIB regime, you registered with the appropriate Self-Regulating Organization or with the SIB direct. Authorizations granted in this way will be carried over to the FSA once it acquires its full powers. But in future new authorizations will be granted (or refused!) by the FSA itself. Likewise, under the old regime each SRO had its own rulebook, which it was required to enforce. The FSA is developing its own single rulebook which will seek to apply a consistent approach to all those who are registered with it.

At the start of the SIB regime there were five Self-Regulating Organizations. These later boiled down to three, whose activities are being incorporated within the FSA. They are (or were):

- The **Securities and Futures Authority (SFA)**. This body covered three main activities: dealing in securities, dealing in the financial and commodities futures markets and dealing in international bonds from London. It therefore embraced members of the London Stock Exchange, of the Liffe financial futures market and the commodities markets as well as London eurobond dealers. Prior to their amalgamation in the SFA, there were initially separate bodies for members of the London Stock Exchange and of the futures markets.

- The **Investment Management Regulatory Organization (IMRO)** brought together those managing the main forms of pooled investment: investment trusts, unit trusts and pension funds.

- The **Personal Investment Authority** or **PIA** emerged from the amalgamation of two previous SROs. One of these was the

Financial Intermediaries, Managers and Brokers Regulatory Association (FIMBRA) which covered insurance brokers and independent investment advisers. The other was the **Life Assurance and Unit Trust Regulatory Organization** or **LAUTRO**. This covered the marketing of pooled investment products by the companies that provided them – an activity that was regulated separately from the investment management side. It therefore embraced the retail marketing of life assurance and unit trusts. The PIA thus covered the retailing aspect of investment products, whatever the distribution channel, and was the body of most relevance to the general public.

In addition to the SROs, there were several other types of body that existed under the SIB regime and which therefore become part of the FSA framework. Certain professional bodies whose members undertake investment business that is incidental to their main activities – accountants or lawyers, for example – could apply to be **Recognized Professional Bodies (RPBs)** to avoid the need for their personnel to seek authorization individually. The markets in which investments are traded did not need recognition as investment businesses if they obtained recognition from the SIB as **Recognized Investment Exchanges (RIEs)**, though their members still needed to be authorized to carry on investment business. The London Stock Exchange is, of course, a Recognized Investment Exchange, as is the Liffe financial futures market.

The **Financial Services and Markets Bill** sets out four statutory objectives that the FSA would be responsible for implementing:

- maintaining market confidence in the financial system
- promoting public awareness of the financial system
- securing the appropriate degree of protection for consumers
- reducing financial crime.

It will be interesting to see how, in the long run, the FSA approaches these different remits. Regulators tread a tightrope. If you over-regulate, the business may find operating conditions too difficult and will go elsewhere. If you under-regulate, scandals erupt which destroy confidence in the financial system and may also have the effect of driving respectable business away. The FSA, like its predecessor bodies, will almost certainly regulate with a lighter touch in the wholesale markets (money markets, foreign exchange, etc.) than in markets that impinge directly on the public. The wholesale markets are the province of professionals, who should be able to look after themselves to a reasonable degree. Markets and products that are open to the public are a different matter. And even in the early days of its life it is clear that the FSA is taking its 'public awareness' brief seriously. As well as guidance for financial businesses, it produces a fair volume of information for the general public, ranging from the pitfalls of transferring a pension to the technicalities of ISAs. It also publishes 'investor alerts' when practices surface that call for a cautionary comment.

The educational role is new, but the FSA inherits a series of standards to apply from the SIB regime. Some are self-evident. Those authorized to carry on a regulated business must be fit and proper – and of adequate financial standing – to do so. Spot checks on a firm's records can be carried out where necessary and a range of sanctions ranging from a rap on the knuckles, through fines, to removal of authorization can be meted out.

The basis of an investment business's relationship with its customer normally needs to be set out in writing. The investment business has to deal fairly with its client. There has to be a complaints procedure. Unsolicited calls to sell investments (**cold calling**) are normally prohibited except for insurance and unit trusts.

Adequate arrangements for segregating clients' money from that of an investment business are required, though in practice this has sometimes been one of the shakier areas. Much pain in the past had been caused by investment managers who collapsed, taking clients' money down with their own. And – an interesting provision for brokers and tipsheet writers, though one that is difficult to enforce – published investment recommendations must be researched and be able to be substantiated.

Compensation arrangements

In the past, different City businesses – the stock exchange, the banking system, etc. – had their own arrangements for compensating (up to certain limits) clients who suffered from the default or misdeeds of a member business. That is set to change, with the FSA establishing a new single **compensation scheme**, to be operated by a separate company, not by the FSA itself. The idea is that the new scheme will divide into three sub-schemes, for deposits, investments and insurance. It is intended to be simpler than the old arrangements and will replace five existing schemes.

Where legislation takes a hand

The new regulatory structure is designed mainly to supervise those who operate in the investment business. The nature of many of the investments in which they deal is still shaped by legislation.

The affairs of **companies** (both private companies and those whose shares are traded on a market) are largely governed by the **Companies Acts**, of which the latest comprehensive revision is the **Companies Act 1985**. The **Department of Trade and Industry (DTI)** is the ministry responsible for enforcing companies legislation. Companies Acts cover matters such as preparation and submission of accounts, requirements for prospectuses, duties and rights of auditors, safeguards for creditors and shareholders, duties of directors, powers to appoint inspectors into the affairs of a company, and the like. But they also touch on some aspects of securities markets and share trading. **Disclosure** of **3 per cent shareholdings** in a public company (it used to be **5 per cent shareholdings**) is a Companies Act provision. So is a provision which gives a company the power to require disclosure of the investors who lie behind **nominee shareholdings**. The prohibition of **insider trading** (dealing in shares on the basis of privileged **price-sensitive information**) is now covered by the 1993 Criminal Justice Act, but the DTI has powers of investigation. The Companies Acts prohibit a company from giving **financial assistance for the purchase of its own shares** except with a lengthy process of shareholder approval: one of the key issues in the **Guinness affair** which surfaced in 1986.

Companies, public or private, are required to file accounts, annual returns and a variety of other information, including information on the directors, with the **Registrar of Companies**. The public may access this information via **Companies House** (headquartered in Cardiff) or various other offices in the UK including one in Bloomsbury, London. Basic information, including a company's registered office, can be accessed via the Internet (see end of chapter). The Registrar is not exactly a regulator, except to the extent that he ensures that companies file the legally required information.

The new accountancy regime established at the beginning of the 1990s under the aegis of the **Financial Reporting Council (FRC)** also has a part to play in companies regulation. In the late 1980s, accounting standards in Britain threatened to come into disrepute as lax interpretation of the rules frequently allowed company managements to present the picture they wanted, and to mislead shareholders and others in the process. Not only has one of the FRC's arms, the **Accounting Standards Board (ASB)**, considerably tightened up on the rules under which accounts are prepared. Another arm, the **Financial Reporting Review Panel**, can take to task companies which it considers are breaking the financial reporting rules, requiring them to amend their presentation. If they refuse to do so, it can apply to the courts. A sub-committee of the ASB, the **Urgent Issues Task Force**, can give rapid interpretations of disputed issues in the accounting rulebook, again with the threat of court action from the Financial Reporting Review Panel should companies refuse to comply.

The new accounting regime is not statutory. But by a typically British process its decisions have virtually the force of law. Companies are required under the Companies Act to prepare accounts which give a '**true and fair view**'. Giving a true and fair view normally implies conforming to the relevant accounting standard, or justifying any departure. Thus, companies that unjustifiably depart from accounting standards in their presentation can be accused of a breach of the Companies Act and the accounting authorities have the power to test the issue in the courts.

The new accounting regime has sometimes been accused of inflexibility – imposing tight rules rather than allowing room for interpretation in the light of individual circumstances – and the issue sometimes surfaces in press comment. After the laxity of the 1980s, some rigidity was probably inevitable. But the proof of the pudding is in the eating. The reliability and usefulness of company accounts improved enormously in the 1990s.

Unit trusts had been regulated for many years under the **Prevention of Fraud (Investments) Act**. Now they are authorized and supervised under the FSA regulatory structure.

Other Acts govern the affairs of specific types of business. **Insurance companies** are governed by the **Insurance Companies Acts** as far as the running of the corporate insurance business is concerned – investment management and selling would come under the FSA structure. **Building societies** come under the **Building Societies Act** though nowadays the regulator is again the FSA.

Banks are regulated under the **Banking Act** – a revised Act reached the Statute Book in 1987 – and supervision, as noted, has moved from the Bank of England to the FSA. A problem in banking supervision is the international nature of the operations of major banks: a key factor in the **Barings** debacle and in the earlier collapse of the **Bank of Credit and Commerce International (BCCI)** where the head company was registered in Luxembourg. Though losing its responsibility for prudential supervision of the banking system, the Bank of England retains responsibility for the overall stability of the banking system as a whole.

The **Lloyd's insurance market** used to govern itself within the powers granted by a specific Act of Parliament. The latest **Lloyd's Act**, which came into force in 1983, tightened up the self-regulatory requirements in response to a variety of scandals. But Lloyd's has lost its fight to retain complete independence. Its exercise of its self-regulatory powers will now be directed in some respects by the FSA, which will also be involved directly in the authorization and approval processes and regulation of advice given by members' agents.

Traditional self-regulating bodies

The London Stock Exchange used traditionally to regulate its own members who, in the past, could be disciplined by the representative **Stock Exchange Council**. Though the Council has gone, in some respects the LSE probably changed least under the SIB (and now the FSA) regime. The difference is that the job of regulation is now split between the stock exchange and the FSA structure. Broadly, the stock exchange is responsible for matters relating to the running of the market and the FSA for policing the financial health of the market's members. If a stockbroker was unable to meet his commitments (in other words, went bust), he used to be **hammered** on the stock exchange floor. More financially than physically painful, this meant the market was told of his default and that he had ceased to trade. Prosaically, the message would now go out on the screens.

The **City Panel on Takeovers and Mergers** (the **Takeover Panel**) was established by City institutions (including the stock exchange) in 1968 to police the takeover jungle where most abuses occurred (see Chapter 10). It is not directly part of the FSA regulatory framework, though nowadays its decisions have the backing of the FSA's range of sanctions, if required, and its decisions may possibly carry a right of appeal to the FSA (see Chapter 10).

Regulatory problems across frontiers

The internationalization of securities markets poses various problems for regulators. First, it is difficult for the supervisors of any one country to monitor effectively the activities of an international securities house, which can switch its 'book' between Tokyo, London and New York in the course of a day.

Second, some markets such as the euromarket are truly international in that they are not attached to any one country. There is no official supranational body with the power to enforce rules on all participants: a cause for concern which crops up periodically in press reports of discussions among leading bankers.

Finally, the international nature of today's securities business can frustrate the efforts of the best-intentioned domestic supervisory authorities. The removal of **exchange controls** in Britain, combined with the use of **nominee names**, means that the British as well as foreigners can deal anonymously in British markets via the medium of a Swiss bank and run little risk of detection if they flaunt the rules. It is also very difficult to clamp down on dubious investment schemes selling from overseas to investors in Britain – a problem which is unlikely to be eased by the coming of the Internet.

The regulatory system in practice

Britain has a tradition of fairly light regulation in many areas, which has been a significant factor in attracting international business to Britain and maintaining the City as an international financial centre.

And there have been loopholes in the regulatory defences. The SIB regulatory structure did not prevent the theft of many hundreds of millions of pounds from the pension funds of companies run by the late **Robert Maxwell** in the early 1990s, though many City institutions must share responsibility for this disaster and pensions legislation has subsequently been somewhat tightened. The SROs have, however, been active in fining or closing down investment advisers who failed to obey the rules.

The highest-profile action of the SIB concerned the **mis-selling of personal pensions**. An investigation suggested that hundreds of thousands of individuals had been persuaded by salesmen and saleswomen to opt out of perfectly good occupational pension schemes in favour of taking out personal pensions that were likely to deliver far lower benefits. The government must shoulder a fair degree of responsibility for this situation, having encouraged individuals to make personal pension provision without ensuring that adequate safeguards were in force. But the SIB, if it did not prevent this debacle, showed itself reasonably tough in addressing the consequences.

Major insurance companies were fined and forced to send their salesforces back to the classroom for retraining. Moreover, those responsible for giving incorrect advice (or their employers) have had to compensate their victims for the financial loss they were likely to suffer – a process that is not complete yet and involves sums running into billions of pounds. But the directors of the culprit companies escaped virtually unscathed.

The 1990s were a troubled period for the vendors of life assurance and savings products in other ways. A major bone of contention was been the question of **polarization** (see glossary) under which financial intermediaries had to decide whether they were independent investment advisers or whether they simply marketed the investment products of one group. The system encouraged many one-time independents to link with a particular provider of savings products and raised fears that genuinely independent advice had become even more scarce. Moreover, the 'independence' of supposedly independent advice is itself open to question when the advisers are paid in the form of commission on the products they sell (see Chapter 21). The regulatory system did, however, ensure that buyers of life assurance and investment products received rather more information than in the past on the commission the salesperson would receive. But given the enormous complexity of many savings products, it must still be open to question whether most buyers are likely to be directed towards the most appropriate product. And promotional literature is often at best complex and at worst deeply confusing. It remains to be seen whether the FSA can bring radical improvements in this area.

When the system is breached

Ideally, a regulatory system prevents misdeeds rather than detecting and prosecuting wrongdoers once abuses have occurred. The fallback for serious cases of financial crime is the state's powers of criminal prosecution. But the British legal system has often proved ineffective in delivering convictions in high-profile cases of alleged financial crime.

Frequently (and often unfairly) blamed for this state of affairs is the **Serious Fraud Office**, though overall it has a conviction rate of over two-thirds in the cases it brings. The SFO has the brief of investigating and prosecuting cases involving serious and complex fraud, particularly where there is a public interest aspect. This would include most of the major cases that are likely to hit the newspaper headlines. It used to deal only in cases involving £5m or more, but the threshold is now down to £1m for cases that satisfy its other criteria.

The real problem is that major frauds are often of a complexity that tax the trained accountant, let alone the understanding of a lay jury, and alleged fraudsters usually seem able to obtain the best legal representation however low their fortunes are said to have sunk. There have been suggestions that cases of complex fraud should be dealt with by a judge and expert assessors rather than by a judge and jury, but they have so far been resisted. An added complication is the number of different individuals and bodies that may be picking over the carcass when fraud is alleged in connection with the demise of a company. Liquidators attempting to salvage something for shareholders and creditors may not find it easy to get information when some of those involved face criminal charges. And the existence of criminal charges can hamper the press's own investigative efforts.

You will also frequently read references to the **Fraud Squad**. In practice, most police forces have their experts in financial crime, and London's Metropolitan Police has a large fraud section. But in the context of City crime the body probably referred to is a branch of the Criminal Investigation Department of the City of London Police. With – in 1999 – around ten officers seconded at any one time to the SFO and 55-odd at its own Wood Street headquarters in the City, it both investigates Square-Mile crimes itself and passes on high-profile cases to the SFO. The Maxwell investigation started with the City Fraud Squad and moved to the SFO when the scale of the debacle emerged.

Internet pointers

The chief website for matters of a regulatory nature is, of course, that of the Financial Services Authority at www.fsa.gov.uk/. Note in particular the growing range of publications for consumers, most of which can be downloaded free. Note also the Central Register, where you can check whether a vendor of financial products has the relevant authorization. There are details on the pensions mis-selling affair and there are up-to-the-minute 'investor alerts' about matters of current concern (the dangers of 'day trading' featured strongly when the stockmarket was roaring away at the end of 1999). For professionals there is also a section on wholesale market supervision. The Department of Trade and Industry site at www.dti.gov.uk/ contains information on the DTI's regulatory and investigation role. The Companies House website is at www.companieshouse.gov.uk/; as noted, you can get very basic information on a limited company (address, date of registration, etc.) free over the net and there is guidance on where and how to get more detailed information. If you want to know what sort of information on members of the public is being stored by various organizations in their computer databases, look at the Data Protection Registrar's site at www.dataprotection.gov.uk/. The Accounting Standards Board has a very useful site at www.asb.org.uk/ with links to the other constituents of the UK accounting authority. If your interests extend to regulation in the United States, the Securities and Exchange Commission site at www.sec.gov/ is well worth a visit. Again, there is useful educational material but there is also a facility to examine company filings with the SEC on the EDGAR database.

23 Print and Internet: the financial pages

If you talked about 'financial pages' when the first edition of this book appeared in 1987, nobody was in much doubt as to what you meant. Slabs of financial text interspersed with the odd picture or table and printed on pink or white paper. Today, all of that has changed. The 'pages' referred to are as likely to be electronic pages on the **Internet**, accessed via computer, modem and telephone line. So this chapter now divides into two separate, though overlapping, parts. First, we will deal with the traditional print media. The second half of the chapter then turns to the newer electronic pages, many of them spin-offs from these established publications.

The British have traditionally had access to a very wide range of financial reading matter. Much of it comes as an adjunct to more general daily reading: the business and City sections of the national daily and Sunday newspapers. At times of boom in the financial markets the national newspapers derive a large portion of their revenue from financial advertising and the editorial pages of the financial sections expand to reflect the heightened interest.

But any review of the financial press has to start with London's *Financial Times*: the '*FT*'. It sells around 440,000 copies a day of which some 240,000 is overseas circulation. It prints in two locations in the UK, five in the United States, and in France, Germany, Sweden, Italy, Spain, Japan and Hong Kong. The overseas editions contain a greater amount of information relevant to the local markets. Back home, it is the City's bible, and on the rare days in the past when the *FT*'s pink pages have failed to appear the City has had a rudderless feel. It is international in outlook with a range of overseas correspondents that much of the British press lacks. The UK edition covers as a matter of course all the major financial markets of the UK and the more important ones overseas. It is a journal of record for news of UK companies. Its news reporting covers the major political, economic, business and financial events worldwide, and its interests extend to the arts, sport and leisure activities. News is put into perspective with the help of background analysis and feature articles. And its statistical information and price coverage of all major financial markets is far more comprehensive than can be found elsewhere. On working days it is now divided into two sections, with the more general domestic and international business and political news in the first part and the specific news of companies and financial markets in the second. On Saturday it is divided into three main sections, plus magazines and supplements.

In fact, the FT is easier to define by what it does not cover than by what it does. First, it does not make investment recommendations as such, though you can read between the lines in the Lex investment comment column and some of the company comment. Second, it normally deals in fact rather than speculation. Though its market reporting duly records the rumours that move share prices, it does not always fully mirror the gossipy nature of much City activity. Its nearest American counterpart, the *Wall Street Journal*, is also read in the City: primarily for its coverage of North American business. It has not seriously challenged the *FT* on its home beat. The *FT* has, needless to say, embraced the Internet with a number of websites including www.ft.com/ for mainstream finance and business news and www.ftyourmoney.com/ for personal finance coverage.

Not everybody has the time to read a newspaper of the *FT*'s scope each day. The financial pages of the quality press – the *Guardian*, the *Independent*, the *Daily Telegraph* and *The Times* – offer an alternative, covering the main items of business and financial news and dealing briefly with many of the minor ones. A similar formula – news stories, company results coverage, editorial comment and feature articles – surfaces in different guises. While the *Guardian* has sometimes had a rather ambivalent attitude to specific share recommendations, the other three carry regular investment comment.

On Saturdays these quality dailies – like the *FT* – change their spots and devote much of the available space to personal finance coverage: questions of tax, insurance, pooled investments such as unit trusts and family finance-planning in general.

A number of Britain's major regional papers – the *Birmingham Post*, the *Yorkshire Post* and *The Scotsman* – follow a similar pattern to the national dailies, though with a bias towards news of local businesses and events.

Below the level of the 'heavy' dailies, the *Daily Mail* and the *Daily Express* have less space to devote to financial coverage, though the *Mail* in particular has at times had significant influence on the stockmarket. The result is a greater emphasis on one or two major financial 'stories'. Both also provide stockmarket reports and both have regular personal finance sections. The attention to financial news in the London's *Evening Standard* shows that this is regarded as a significant selling point in the battle for readers in the capital. The *Standard*'s financial pages are printed on pink paper – a compliment to the *Financial Times*, though the *FT* has not always regarded it as such.

The heavyweight Sunday papers – the *Sunday Times*, the *Observer*, the *Sunday Telegraph* and the *Independent on Sunday* – start with the assumption that their readers will have picked up the main items of the week's financial news elsewhere. Thus the emphasis is on background analysis of current stories and attempts to get in first with the stories that will hit the financial headlines in the coming week. In this some of them are often helped by financiers (or their public relations advisers) who find it convenient to float a story before the new week's dealings begin in the markets. Not every 'story' necessarily results from journalistic legwork, nor is a partisan approach always entirely absent. All provide personal finance coverage and all at one time or another are active with share tips, often of the 'close to the market gossip' variety. In addition to the 'general' Sunday papers, *Sunday Business* aims fair and square at finance and business stories.

Because of the extensive financial coverage in the national press, Britain supports relatively few stockmarket magazines. The largest and by far the longest established is the *Investors Chronicle*, now under the same ownership as the *Financial Times*. Its strength has traditionally been its very detailed analysis of company profits and company prospects, useful for those who want to monitor their existing investments as well as pick up ideas for new ones. It does make specific share recommendations, but the bulk of its coverage also contains an element of evaluation or advice. Its feature material contains much that is aimed at helping the newcomer to the stockmarkets. It also carries a regular personal finance coverage. Considerably larger in terms of circulation is *The Economist*, but domestic financial markets now occupy a relatively small amount of space in its pages, though its selective coverage of international business issues is strong.

Mirroring the decline in direct stockmarket investment by the individual and the growth of pooled investment schemes, publications on personal financial planning for the individual have blossomed. New magazines spring up and older ones change their names or their owners. A glance at any major newsagent's magazine rack reveals a fair selection, probably including *Money Observer* (an offshoot of the newspaper). For subscribers, *Money Which* provides advice on financial services and products. There are also specialist magazines advising on what mortgage to go for and the like.

These personal finance magazines for the individual should not be confused with the publications aimed primarily at financial intermediaries – insurance brokers and so-called financial advisers – who market investment products to the public. The leaders here include the monthly *Money Management* and *Planned Savings*, both of which provide detailed coverage of the performance of unit trusts, insurance funds and other investment products. *Money Marketing* is a news-oriented weekly paper that aims for something of the same market and has attracted several competitors. These papers for the personal finance business overlap with trade magazines for the insurance and pensions industries (insurance magazines are legion).

Banking is served by the *Banker*, a monthly magazine under the same ownership as the *Financial Times*, and the eurocurrency market by the monthly *Euromoney* and allied publications from the same stable. The weekly *International Financing Review* is aimed primarily at the banks and bankers that put together the big financing packages in the international market, which it records.

Britain has a highly developed trade press. The property world is served mainly by the long-established weekly *Estates Gazette* and by *Property Week* (formerly *Chartered Surveyor Weekly*). Accountancy spawns numerous publications, of which the monthly magazine *Accountancy* and the weekly free newspaper *Accountancy Age* are prominent.

Newsletters are a publishing market in themselves. Many sectors of the financial community are served by a range of specialist newsletters: taxation, accountancy and eurobond newsletters in particular. But in addition there is a range of stockmarket newsletters – **tip sheets** – promoting themselves directly to the general public.

Some stockmarket newsletters are established, well researched and reputable. But some are distinctly dubious, backed by claims of successful recommendations in the past which may fall down on detailed scrutiny. Promotional costs aside, the newsletter publishing business is cheap to get into – little more than a wordprocessor and a telephone is required – and it attracts its fair share of get-rich-quick merchants. You have been warned!

The electronic pages

The warning we sounded on hard-copy newsletters applies with double force when we turn to the electronic pages. Nobody enforces editorial standards of truth or accuracy on the **Internet** as a whole, and there is a great deal of dangerous rubbish out there, particularly in the share-tipping department and among newsgroups and discussion groups. There are, however, some wonderful information resources as well. The Internet is, inevitably, heavily biased towards United States sources, but we are focusing here on sites with a particular UK relevance and generally concentrating on those that provide information free.

First, however, we should underline the warnings we sounded in the introduction to this book. Be a little cautious of sites that do not give the name and physical address of the organization that provides them. You may need this to assess the likely quality and reliability of the information on the site. Be doubly cautious, of course, in the case of a site offering a service such as broking or banking.

Always check the date on a document that you access and be careful when a date is not provided. Many organizations that have been keen to establish an Internet presence are a lot less punctilious about maintaining the site and updating or removing old material or publications. You may come across tax guides that refer to long-outdated tax rates and the like (even government departments do not always get this right!).

Finally, avoid being seduced by the speed and power of the Internet. Yes, it allows you to trade shares, commodities and the like with great ease. But the danger is that the whole thing comes to be regarded as some sort of computer game – it is all to easy to forget that you can lose real money, and very rapidly. This applies with particular force to practices such as 'day trading' – buying and selling stocks within a short space of time to take advantage of short-term price movements. If you are tempted, have a look at the warning from the Financial Services Authority first.

There are any number of headings under which you may classify the financial information available on the Internet. In addition, you may look at it from the point of view of the type of material or the type of provider. We have approached it initially from the point of view of the material itself. But before getting into the detail, there is a general point to be made. Chasing links round the World Wide Web for the information you want can be enormously time-consuming and frustrating. So there is a high premium on sites that, rather than providing a great deal of information themselves, offer links to the most useful sources.

There are a great number of these in the financial area. For a start, the main 'portals' such as Yahoo have financial and business sections that offer such links. But two sites that we have found particularly useful as jumping-off points in the context of UK finance and business are the site maintained by Sheila Webber at the University of Strathclyde and the site maintained by Peter Temple. The first may be found at www.dis.strath.ac.uk/business/ and the second at www.cix.co.uk/~ptemple/. The Strathclyde site has its own search facilities to find the kind of links you want, plus a certain amount of basic information on each of the sites to which it provides a link. However, it is concerned with business information, not with details of on-line banks or brokers, though it might point you to other sites that would have this information.

The Peter Temple site consists of a series of listings of websites under different categories, such as listed UK companies, major European companies, stockmarket price providers, markets themselves, brokers, personal finance sites and the like. It provides the link, but generally without further information. If you are not exactly sure what you are looking for, the Strathclyde site might be the best. If you know what you want, like the web address of a company or a broker, the Peter Temple site is probably the quickest way in. Both sites also have the virtue (at least at the time of writing) of freedom from the superfluous graphics, flashing advertisements and general clutter that make accessing many websites such a painful experience. Incidentally, if you want to get deeper into the question of investing or seeking business information via the web, Peter Temple is also the author of a comprehensive guide: *The new online investor*. Details of this book can be found on his website.

Information about listed companies

This comes in a number of forms. Most of the larger companies have their own websites (you can access them easily via the Peter Temple linksite). The quality varies quite a lot, but the better ones will provide you with a fair volume of background information and allow you to view or download recent profit or other announcements and press releases. You may also be able to download a full version of the latest report and accounts in Adobe Acrobat (PDF) format, though this takes a fair time and can be heavy on telephone bills. If you are not in a rush, there is probably a cheaper way of getting hold of it. The CAROL site at www.carol.co.uk/ allows viewing of many company reports on-line while there is a *Financial Times*-linked service, accessible at www.annualreports.ft.com, where you may order a wide range of company reports for delivery free by post within a few days. Most individual company sites also provide an e-mail address which you could use to request a report by post. On the better company sites you will also find the latest share price and a recent share price history and the company may provide reports of functions such as recent briefings for stockbrokers' analysts. These may come in a specific 'investors' section of the site which may also give a financial calendar – likely dates of the main profit announcements, dividend payment dates, date of the AGM, etc. – and details of the company's main professional advisers. There may also be links to the websites of individual group businesses.

As well as information from the companies themselves there is the information about listed companies from other investment sites. Much of this is merely share price-related, but for people wanting to do more fundamental analysis, the Hemmington Scott site at www.hemscott.net/ is the essential starting point. It does, incidentally, have share prices as well. A great deal of free and reliable information on listed and AIM companies is available here, including key statistics, share price histories (you can get a share price chart going back as much as ten years), brokers' forecasts of earnings and the like. Hemmington Scott now operates as a free Internet service provider (ISP) as well, and those who use it as their Internet access point are entitled to a range of additional information without payment. Others can access this additional information in return for a fee.

Price and performance information

There is a whole range of sites providing information on latest share prices, and movements in stockmarket indices, currencies, etc. At the time of writing the usual pattern is that share prices that you may access free are delayed by a quarter of an hour or 20 minutes and you need to pay a subscription to access real-time prices. The delayed prices are usually adequate for most sensible private-investor needs

– they are certainly a big advance on the previous day's closing prices available in the morning newspaper. The Market-Eye Internet site at www.market-eye.co.uk/ is particularly worth a visit because you have the option of downloading a five-year run of company share prices or of a particular market index. You can then feed this information into a spreadsheet and manipulate it at will. Some sites, including personal finance sites, allow you to store details of your own portfolio and revalue it automatically when you want to.

Prices for personal savings products such as unit trusts or insurance bonds are available from a number of personal finance sites and in some cases comparative performance tables are also provided. Two 'comprehensive' sites which cover the stockmarket as well as personal finance are Interactive Investor International at www.iii.co.uk/ and Moneyextra (now incorporating Moneyworld) at www.moneyextra.com/. They offer a useful starting point for newcomers to the net as well as services for more seasoned users.

Markets

Stock exchanges and other types of financial market, at home and overseas, usually have their own websites. Some of these provide prices (the London Stock Exchange does not). They are usually designed more to provide information on the functioning of the market, its dealing methods, the types of company listed, how to contact a broker, and so on. The London Stock Exchange site is at www. londonstockexchange.com/, and other major exchanges are listed at the end of this chapter.

Financial news

The main newspapers have websites with electronic versions of the news, including financial news sections. The *Financial Times* website at www.ft.com/ is, of course, almost exclusively devoted to financial and business news; most of the current and recent information is free, though at the time of writing you have to pay to view past articles more than a few months old. The *FT*'s separate personal finance website is at www.ftyourmoney.com/. The *Daily Mail/Evening Standard* newspaper group has a specific financial site at www.thisismoney.com/, which is devoted mainly to personal finance information, and the *Guardian/Observer/Money Observer* grouping also has a personal finance site at www.moneyunlimited.co.uk/. The main financial magazines also have a web presence. The

Investors Chronicle's site at www.investorschronicle.co.uk/ is useful primarily for a very detailed listing of stockbrokers and their charges and services, though at the time of writing the site is being extended. The major news agencies also provide financial news on-line as it breaks. Reuters is at www.reuters.com/news/ (select the 'business' option for international financial news). For coverage geared to the UK, Reuters stories can be found at http://uk.finance.yahoo.com/, along with a lot of other finance and business information. An alternative source of UK financial news is Bloomberg at www.bloomberg.com/uk/. Many other finance and investment sites, plus the 'portal' sites, have regular feeds of business news from one source or another.

Personal savings products

There are two main types of information source on personal savings and loan products (in which we would include unit trusts, insurance bonds, ISAs, mortgages, pensions and the like, down to deposit rates available). There are the general personal-finance websites and there are the sites of individual vendors of savings products, such a insurance companies, fund managers and banks. If you go to the site of an individual vendor, remember that the vendor is pushing the merits of his own product. Check as well with one of the general personal finance sites that provides comparative information. The Association of Investment Trust Companies has its own site at www.aitc.co.uk/ where there is useful background material on investment trusts as a whole. Unit trusts are likewise catered for at the Association of Unit Trusts and Investment Funds' site at www.investmentfunds.org.uk/ and there is useful and user-friendly performance information on unit trusts and investment trusts at www.trustnet.co.uk/.

Broking and banking on-line

We have deliberately not included the web addresses of individual on-line stockbrokers or banks. Newcomers are joining their ranks so rapidly that it would quickly become out of date, and we would also be reluctant to seem to recommend particular firms or services. You may find lists and links on the Peter Temple website, as well as on personal finance and other sites such as those of Moneyextra or Interactive Investor International. And, as noted, the *Investors Chronicle* website provides details of brokers with information on the commission that they charge. Note that 'on-line' broking can mean different things to different firms – sending buy or sell orders by e-mail is not the same thing as being able to enter buy or sell orders direct over the Internet, for immediate execution.

Background and educational material

Except for in-and-out market dealers, this is arguably the most valuable resource on the Internet. First, the general public can now access a whole range of information – press releases, background briefings, etc. – that was formerly available only to journalists and the like. Most organizations that run a press or information service now make their news items and press releases available to all at their website. These organizations include individual companies, markets and exchanges, professional firms such as accountants and surveyors (as well as their professional associations), regulatory bodies and government departments. In addition to news releases, many organizations offer a range of weightier publications that may be downloaded on the spot or ordered via e-mail. The range is much too vast to cover in detail here, but it falls into a number of categories.

First, there is educational material. Very basic guides to investment and to individual investment products are available from a range of sources: the personal finance websites, the unit trust and investment trust associations, the ProShare organization, the 'Share-Aware' section of the London Stock Exchange's site, the Financial Services Authority and many others. The quality of the material varies and it is not always easy to find, but a little digging usually pays off. For example, there is a useful introduction to the gilt-edged market published as *Gilts: An Investors Guide* on the website of the UK Debt Management Office at www.dmo.gov.uk/. But you have to select 'publications' and then 'other publications' and trawl through a fairly long list to find it. And for an impartial description of ISAs you would not necessarily think of going to the website of the Treasury at www.hm-treasury.gov.uk/ or that of the Financial Services Authority at www.fsa.gov.uk/. But both provide factual information on the structure of ISAs which may be a useful antidote to the more hyped-up approach of the ISA vendors. The Inland Revenue site at www.inlandrevenue.gov.uk/ includes many brochures and other publications giving information or guidance on different aspects of the tax system, though be sure that anything you download reflects any recent changes.

Second, a great deal of statistical information is available, though again the range is too great to cover in detail here. You can download from the London Stock Exchange, for example, the monthly fact sheets on market activity, new issues, etc. And a range of financial and economic statistics is available from various government sites, though not quite as much as one might sometimes like (since long-run statistical information is sold commercially in a variety of publications, what you can get free may be limited to the data for recent months). There are, incidentally, two main routes into UK government sites. The CCTA Government Information Service at www.open.gov.uk/ provides an entry point into all other sites such as the Inland Revenue, the Treasury and the Department of Trade and Industry. Or each department has its individual address, which you can access direct.

Third, a great deal of technical information is available. This is more likely to be of interest to the professional or the serious student, though some has a wider application to business in general. The information on preparations for the euro on the Bank of England website at www.bankofengland.co.uk/ is a case in point. The precise details of the stock exchange's regulatory arrangements, on the other hand, are clearly of importance to stock exchange firms but may be of limited interest to a wider public. However, they are on the website if you want them. Likewise, if you want precise details of the construction of the FTSE stockmarket indices, you can find them at the FTSE International site at www.ftse.com/. But they are not exactly bed-time reading.

Below is a listing of websites under different headings. Where a single site provides a range of different services, it may appear more than once. The list is in no way intended to be comprehensive, nor does inclusion imply a recommendation of the particular site. But by and large the sites listed are among those which have been accessed in the course of preparing this book for the fifth edition and which have appeared to offer something of interest or use.

Websites

Pointers to information sources

There are any number of these, but for links to useful websites you should try one of the two linksites that we have already mentioned.

Peter Temple Linksite	www.cix.co.uk/~ptemple/
University of Strathclyde	www.dis.strath.ac.uk/business/

Share prices, indices, currencies

There are any number of sites offering delayed share prices (or real-time prices for a fee), including stockbroker sites and some portal sites. See the Peter Temple website for a more comprehensive list.

Freequotes	www.freequotes.co.uk/
Hemmington Scott	www.hemscott.net/
Interactive Investor	www.iii.co.uk/
Market-Eye	www.market-eye.co.uk/
Moneyextra	www.moneyextra.com/

Brokers and banks (links to)

It is not difficult to find links to brokers and banks – the brokers' 'Trade now!' advertisements are flashing up on many of the financial websites that you visit. You can get a list of Internet brokers from the Peter Temple website or the personal finance sites, and the *Investors Chronicle* site has comprehensive information on brokers.

Exchanges, markets and related sites

This includes the main UK financial markets with websites and a selection of principal overseas sites. The main UK and US regulators are also included.

American Stock Exchange	www.amex.com/
Chicago Board of Trade	www.cbot.com/
Chicago Board Options Exchange	www.cboe.com/
CREST settlement system	www.crestco.co.uk/
EASDAQ	www.easdaq.be/
EUREX	www.eurexchange.com/
Financial Services Authority	www.fsa.gov.uk/
FTSE International (indices)	www.ftse.com/
German Stock Exchanges (Frankfurt)	www.exchange.de/
International Petroleum Exchange	www.ipe.uk.com/
LIFFE	www.liffe.com/
Lloyd's of London	www.lloydsoflondon.co.uk/
London Metal Exchange	www.lme.co.uk/
London Stock Exchange	www.londonstockexchange.com/
NASDAQ	www.nasdaq.com/
New York Mercantile Exchange	www.nymex.com/
New York Stock Exchange	www.nyse.com/
OFEX	www.ofex.co.uk/
Paris Stock Exchange	www.bourse-de-paris.fr/
Securities and Exchange Commission	www.sec.gov/
SETS (London trading system)	www.sets.co.uk/
Tokyo Stock Exchange	www.tse.or.jp/

Company and investment information

Fundamental information on companies is not as easy to find as share-price information. Aside from companies' own websites, the Hemmington Scott site is the essential starting point. Some company research is available on other sites, though not always free, and stockbroker sites may provide research for their clients. Commercial property performance information is available on the Investment Property Databank site.

Carol (company reports on-line)	www.carol.co.uk/
Companies House	www.companieshouse.gov.uk/
Extel Survey of Brokers' Analysts	www.primarkextelsurvey.com/results
Financial Times	www.ft.com/
FT reports service	www.annualreports.ft.com/
Hemmington Scott	www.hemscott.net
IPD (commercial property performance)	www.propertymall.com/ipd/

Personal finance and pooled investment

There are many sites in this area, ranging from sites that cover all aspects of savings and personal finance (probably including shares) to those specializing in fund performance like Trustnet, Lipper and Micropal. The addresses below are just a selection.

AAA Investment Guide	www.wisebuy.co.uk/
Association of Investment Trust Companies	www.aitc.co.uk/
Association of Unit Trusts and Investment Funds	www.investmentfunds.org.uk/
FT Your Money	www.ftyourmoney.com/
Guardian/Observer/Money Observer	www.moneyunlimited.co.uk/
Interactive Investor	www.iii.co.uk/
Lipper (Reuters)	www.lipperweb.com/
Micropal (Standard & Poor's)	www.micropal.com/
Moneynet	www.moneynet.co.uk/
Moneyweb	www.moneyweb.co.uk/
Moneyextra	www.moneyextra.com/
This is Money	www.thisismoney.com/
TrustNet	www.trustnet.co.uk/

Newspapers, magazines and news

Basic news supplied by the electronic versions of the main newspaper sites is usually free, though you may need to register to gain access

BBC	www.bbc.co.uk/
Bloomberg	www.bloomberg.com/uk/
Daily Express	www.express.co.uk/
Economist	www.economist.com/

Estates Gazette	www.egi.co.uk/
Euromoney	www.euromoney.com/
Financial Times	www.ft.com/
FT personal finance	www.ftyourmoney.com/
Guardian and Observer	www.newsunlimited.co.uk/
Guardian/Observer personal finance	www.moneyunlimited.co.uk/
Independent	www.independent.co.uk/
Investors Chronicle	www.investorschronicle.co.uk/
Mail/Standard personal finance site	www.thisismoney.com/
Reuters	www.reuters.com/
Sunday Times	www.sunday-times.co.uk/
Telegraph	www.telegraph.co.uk/
Times	www.the-times.co.uk/

Educational and explanatory material

For the absolute basics of investment, start with the ProShare site and
for a few timely cautions, plus other educational material, look at the
Financial Services Authority's offering. There's information on personal-finance products from a variety of sites including the unit trust
and investment trust association sites and the general personal
finance sites. For booklets on different aspects of taxation, go to the
Inland Revenue site.

AAA Investment Guide	www.wisebuy.co.uk/
Association of Investment Trust Companies	www.aitc.co.uk/
Association of Unit Trusts and Investment Funds	www.investmentfunds.org.uk/
Bank of England	www.bankofengland.co.uk/
Debt Management Office (on gilts)	www.dmo.gov.uk/
Department of Trade and Industry	www.dti.gov.uk/
Financial Services Authority	www.fsa.gov.uk/
FT annual reports service	www.annualreports.ft.com/
FT Your Money	www.ftyourmoney.com/
Inland Revenue	www.inlandrevenue.gov.uk/
Interactive Investor	www.iii.co.uk/
Kauders Portfolio Management (on gilts)	www.gilt.co.uk/
London Stock Exchange	www.londonstockexchange.com/
London Stock Exchange (investors)	www.share-aware.co.uk/
Moneyweb	www.moneyweb.co.uk/
MoneyWorld	www.moneyworld.co.uk/
ProShare	www.proshare.org.uk/
Securities and Exchange Commission (USA)	www.sec.gov/
Treasury	www.hm-treasury.gov.uk/

Government departments, regulators, standard-setters, etc.

UK government departments may be accessed via the CCTA Government Information Service site or you may use the web address of the individual department. Also included here are addresses of a few major European and international bodies.

Accounting Standards Board	www.asb.org.uk/
Bank of England	www.bankofengland.co.uk/
British Invisibles	www.bi.org.uk/
Business Link	www.businesslink.co.uk/
Central Office of Information	www.coi.gov.uk/
City of London	www.cityoflondon.gov.uk/
Companies House	www.companieshouse.gov.uk/
Competition Commission	www.mmc.gov.uk/
Data Protection Registry	www.dataprotection.gov.uk/
Debt Management Office	www.dmo.gov.uk/
Department of Trade and Industry	www.dti.gov.uk/
Enterprise Zone	www.enterprisezone.org.uk/
Euro (get ready for)	www.euro.gov.uk/
European Bank for Reconstruction and Development	www.ebrd.com/
European Business Register	www.ebr.org/
European Central Bank	www.ecb.int/
European Commission	europa.eu.int/
European Commission euro information	europa.eu.int/euro/
Eurostat	europa.eu.int/en/comm/eurostat/
Financial Reporting Council	www.frc.org.uk/
Financial Reporting Review Panel	www.frrp.org.uk/
Financial Services Authority	www.fsa.gov.uk/
Inland Revenue	www.inlandrevenue.gov.uk/
International Monetary Fund	www.imf.org/
Office of Fair Trading	www.oft.gov.uk/
Organisation for Economic Co-operation and Development	www.oecd.org/
Serious Fraud Office	www.sfo.gov.uk/
Treasury	www.hm-treasury.gov.uk/
UK official statistics	www.statistics.gov.uk/
World Bank	www.worldbank.org/
World Trade Organization	www.wto.org/

Professional and trade bodies

Some of the professional association sites are geared more to members than to the public, but may still provide useful information

Association of British Insurers	www.abi.org.uk/
Association of Consulting Actuaries	www.aca.org.uk/

Association of Investment Trust Companies	www.aitc.co.uk/
Association of Unit Trusts and Investment Funds	www.investmentfunds.org.uk/
British Bankers Association	www.bankfacts.org.uk/
British Venture Capital Association	www.bvca.co.uk/
Building Societies Association	www.bsa.org.uk/
Chartered Institute of Bankers	www.cib.org.uk/
Chartered Insurance Institute	www.cii.co.uk/
Confederation of British Industry	www.cbi.org.uk/
Corporate governance (institutions' site)	www.ivis.computasoft.com/
Institute of Chartered Accountants (ICAEW)	www.icaew.co.uk/
Institute of Directors	www.iod.co.uk/
International Securities Market Association	www.isma.co.uk/
National Association of Pension Funds	www.napf.co.uk/
RICS Investment Property Forum	www.ipf.org.uk/
Royal Institution of Chartered Surveyors	www.rics.org.uk/
Trades Union Congress	www.tuc.org.uk/

How to read between the lines

Reading the financial pages is one thing. Reading between the lines of the financial pages is a different art. Financial journalists do not always say exactly what they think – often because Britain's very strict libel regime prevents them from doing so. Moreover, they are reporting on a world – the world of finance – that has its own layers of jargon and pseudo-scientific gobbledegook, often disguising the banal nature of what is going on.

To round off our examination of the financial markets, here's a less serious guide to some of the more confusing turns of phrase you might come across in financial reports and the financial press. The interpretations are purely personal and in no way imply that the words and phrases are used in any particular paper or report in the sense suggested here.

The first problem the financial journalist hits is when he wants to put across a warning or express disbelief. Remember, we're talking about money and a surprising number of people take money very seriously: particularly those who hope to make a lot of it or already have a lot of it to lose. Since this definition embraces a high proportion of people in the City, the journalist attacks them at his peril. A casual aside suggesting that the directors of Muggitt Finance put in a bulk order for rose-tinted spectacles before preparing their prospectus profit forecast is enough to have Muggitt's lawyers baying at the gate.

In fact, can a journalist safely suggest that a share is vastly overpriced, even if he is not implying skulduggery on the part of the directors? It's a moot point and he'll often try to find a way round it. 'Muggitt's shares have fallen from 300p to 100p so far this year, and holders should consider taking their profits' is one approach. If he simply thinks they're far too high, without the company necessarily being on the skids, he might say 'On a PE ratio of 35, Muggitt

Finance is rated well above the sector average; this anomaly is likely to be ironed out in the near future'. He doesn't mean that shares of the other companies in the sector are due for a rise. He means that Muggitt is heading for a fall. 'With the PE ratio at 35, investors should not ignore Muggitt's downside potential' is another way of saying the same thing. 'Not for widows and orphans' simply means 'highly speculative' and occasionally 'not for anyone in his right mind'. It is rather like the definition of a 'recovery stock'. It can mean a share that is going to rise as the company recovers or a company that won't be around very long if it doesn't recover.

When a journalist suggests shares are 'fully valued' he is almost certainly trying to say 'overvalued' without offending the company too deeply. This is not the same thing as describing them as 'fairly valued', which probably means the writer hasn't a clue one way or the other ('a sound long-term hold' also implies that he is sitting firmly on the fence).

There was a journalist in the pre-decimalization days who spoke his mind and suggested that one company's shares 'standing at 2s 6d' were 'about half-a-crown too high'. His fate is lost in the mists of history.

Comment on individuals is more perilous. For the financial journalist there can be no such thing as a crook, at least until he is safely convicted and behind bars (which, in Britain, he rarely is provided his crime is big enough). The paper's lawyer might just let him get away with 'controversial City financier'. Hence you'll occasionally read pieces like this: 'Speaking from Panama City, Mr Cyril Buck, the controversial financier at the head of the troubled Muggitt Finance group, today strongly criticized the decision by the company's auditors to state that the accounts were prepared on a going concern basis and did not reflect a true and fair view of the company's affairs'. In the vernacular this might be translated as 'Cyril Buck, the spiv at the head of Muggitt, has done a bunk. He's annoyed because the auditors say that the company is bust and the accounts are fiddled.'

Even journalism has had characters of questionable judgement, probably operating at the fringes of the share-tipping end of the market and almost certainly writing for a stockmarket 'newsletter' of the kind that claims divine insight into the future movement of share prices. Be a little careful when you read the following: 'Since Rudyard Sharpe took the helm at the end of last year and injected his private business into Salter Way Holdings it is recognized as one of the most dynamic groups in the financial services sector. The shares are a narrow market, but should be bought at prices up to 200p'.

It may be a well researched and genuine tip. It could equally well mean: 'Ruddy Sharpe flogged his private company to Salter Way at an exhorbitant price and is now ramping the shares for all he's worth. That's why he had me to lunch last week. The company's a load of junk but there aren't many shares around so the price will rocket if a few mugs jump in and buy them on my advice. That's why I bought 20,000 myself at 140p last week. I'll sell the moment my readers have pushed the price up to 190p.'

Crooked writers are rare. Two other types of financial commentator can be dangerous to your financial health: the excessively vague and the excessively precise. How many times have you seen a share described in terms like these: 'The shares stand on a PE ratio of 12, which is generous in today's markets'. What does it mean? That the rating is generous to the investor (the shares are priced below their true worth and should be bought)? Or the rating flatters the company (the shares are over-rated and should be sold)? Take your pick.

Then the over-precise, which is most likely to crop up in the research circulars produced by Porsche-powered stockbrokers' analysts but may well be repeated in the financial press: 'The acquisition of Nuggins should contribute around £2.735m to the pre-tax profits of Bloggins Plc next year. Assuming internally generated sales growth in the range of 11.7 to 11.8 per cent and a 2.34 per cent improvement in the margins of the timber business, the shares at 393p are on a prospective PE ratio of 14.27 and are a medium to strong buy on a seven-month view'. Roughly translated, this might mean: 'Your guess as to Bloggins's profits is as good as mine. But our marketmaking arm has a whole load of Bloggins's shares on its books and told me to help shift them. And it's for writing this sort of junk that they pay me £80,000 a year.'

The big institutional investors know which stockbrokers' analysts are worth reading. Most 'research' material goes straight in the bin, and one very large financial institution has a gigantic wheeled tub that goes round the investment department once a week to collect brokers' circulars for the bonfire.

Much of what you read about the City falls into place if you bear in mind a few simple facts. Most financial people the private individual is likely to meet are salesmen of one kind or another. Like salesmen in other fields they'll be tempted to sell you the product that pays them the highest commission or which they happen to have in stock. Like any salesmen, they are not always the best people to advise on the merits of the product.

They have a particular problem when markets are going down or likely to go down. 'Put your money into Bloggins – you won't lose more than half of it' is not an appealing sales message. They have to convince themselves and their clients that markets are going up for ever. Or they devise strategies like 'switching' that generate commission income but fall short of a straight 'buy' recommendation. In either case the message is likely to be wrapped up in further layers of gobbledegook.

Hence: 'Mike Puff, manager of the Duffer group of unit trusts expects to see the equity market rise by 20 to 25 per cent over the year after a weak start, given the relative strength of the UK corporate sector'. This might translate as: 'Mike Puff has as little clue as the rest of us, but he's in the game of flogging investments'.

Or the message from a broker to clients: 'We therefore recommend a switch from Sainsbury to Tesco on income growth grounds. Our charts show that ...'. The meaning here could be: 'There's damn all to choose between the two shares, but we rake in the commission each time you sell one and buy the other. We'll recommend you switch back next year.'

Finally, no review of moneyspeak is complete without a glance at that bastion of City tradition: the daily stockmarket report. How often have you seen that shares 'closed narrowly mixed in nervous trading'? The beauty of phrases of this kind is that the words can be used in almost any order with little if any change to the sense: 'closed nervously in mixed narrow trading', 'traded nervously in a narrow mixed close', and so on. Perhaps it means something to somebody. At least it fills column inches and helps to preserve the mystique of the financial markets.

Quick guide to moneyspeak

Here's a quick glossary of some common current terms and phrases you'll meet, with possible meanings.

Overdue market correction A near meltdown of the financial system.

Free market A market in which share prices can be manipulated with relative freedom from official supervision.

Self-regulation Regulation of financial markets by the practitioners, for the benefit of the practitioners.

International (or **global**) **market in securities** A system for ensuring that a panic in New York or Tokyo spreads rapidly to London – or *vice-versa*.

Popular capitalism A device for selling shares in state monopolies to some of the people who already own them.

Insider dealer Investors who do not work in the City are 'outsider dealers'.

The shares are acquiring strong institutional backing This is one the boys have decided to ramp up.

Our research report suggests ... In a broker's report on a new issue this may mean that what follows is a few unchecked facts gleaned from the company's own prospectus.

Following the acquisition of Muggitt a phased programme of asset disposals was put in train We got control then asset-stripped it like crazy.

Acquisitive stockmarket-oriented financial conglomerate Paper-shuffling asset stripper.

Acquisitive Antipodean financial entrepreneur Aussie or Kiwi market raider.

Colourful usually linked with the word **entrepreneur**. It is not racist, neither does it usually imply blue blood. **Colourful entrepreneurs** are probably active stockmarket operators. While their tactics pay off they are in the pink. They attract acres of purple prose from the spivvier share tipsters and their competitors go green with envy or white with rage. All too often they overstretch themselves and end deep in the red.

Mr Rudyard Sharpe regards his 18 per cent holding in Nuggins as a long-term investment Ruddy Sharpe is bidding for Nuggins next week.

On a long-term view ... Looking beyond the next five minutes.

We are responding vigorously to recent consumer complaint In a company report this may mean they are stepping up their public relations budget and running an image-building TV campaign – otherwise carrying on as before.

The accounts give a true and fair view ... In the auditors' report on a major bank this possibly means that the accounts give a true and fair view except that the £5 billion of loans to Latin America are worthless but can't be written off because the bank hasn't the resources.

... has been freed from day-to-day responsibility so that he can concentrate on long-term development of the company Has been fired. Employees are sacked; directors leave in a company Mercedes and a flood of euphemisms. When a director resigns for reasons of health, it is not necessarily his current health that is at issue. It is what will happen to his health if he tries to stay.

*   *   *

'How to read between the lines' is reproduced by kind permission of The Independent, *in which a version of this section first appeared.*

Glossary and index

Advance Corporation Tax (ACT) (*see also* **unrelieved ACT**) 6, 51, 162

AFBD (*see* **Association of Futures Brokers and Dealers**)

aftermarket (*see also* **secondary market**) 142

agency broker 35, 97, 98, 103-104, 106, 111, 215

AGM (*see* **annual general meeting**)

agreed (takeover bid) 167

AIM (*see* **Alternative Investment Market**)

All-Share Index (*see* **FTSE Actuaries All-Share Index**)

allotment letters 146

allotment, allocation (of shares, etc.) 143-144, 146

Alternative Investment Market 100-101, 138, 141

alternative investments. Refers to objects owned at least partly as investments, which would not normally count as financial assets. Examples are: works of art; Georgian silver; antique coins; **busted bonds** (q.v.), etc. Sometimes also referred to as **collectibles**. Alternative investments in this sense have nothing to do with the **Alternative Investment Market** in small company shares.

aluminium 307

American Depositary Receipts (**ADRs**). Instead of trading in shares of British companies as such, Americans may buy and sell ADRs, which confer ownership rights to the shares. The shares themselves are held on deposit with a bank. Trading in ADRs rather than the shares cuts the administrative hassle of registering changes in share ownership and avoids the need to pay stamp duty on each transaction.

American option 297

American Stock Exchange. The smaller of the two Stock Exchanges in New York, now merged with Nasdaq. The larger, on which the shares of most of the biggest corporations are traded, is the New York Stock Exchange (q.v.).

amortization (*see* **depreciation**)

amount paid up 146

AMPS (*see* **auction market preferred stock**)

analyst (*see* **investment analyst**)

angel (*see* **business angel**)

Annual General Meeting (AGM). General meeting of a company at which normally routine matters are put to the vote of shareholders: acceptance of the accounts, remuneration of auditors, re-election of directors, etc. 40, 47

annual percentage rate (APR). Organizations granting credit in the UK are required to state the true cost in terms of interest as an annual percentage rate. This is because many of the ways in which interest is expressed in advertisements can be misleading without an APR. An individual who borrows £100 and pays it back in instalments over a year may be quoted a **flat rate** of, say, 12 per cent. But this means he is paying 12 per cent on the full amount for the whole year, whereas after 6 months only £50 will actually be outstanding. The true rate of interest or APR is close to double the flat rate.

annuity. A form of pension bought from an insurance company. In the simplest form the buyer pays over a lump sum in return for which they receive a stipulated income for life, consisting part of income on the money paid and part of return of the capital. Whether or not it turns out to be good value depends on how long they live.

application form (in share issue) 147

APR (*see* **annual percentage rate**)

arbitrage. Taking advantage of differentials in the price of a security, currency, etc., usually in two different markets. If Fastbuck Finance shares are quoted at 200p in London but at the equivalent of 205p in Amsterdam, the arbitrageur would make a profit by selling in Amsterdam and buying in London. This would tend to make the Amsterdam price fall and the London price rise, and the anomaly would be ironed out. Arbitrage in this sense is an example of the way speculators assist in the smooth running of markets. In the United States arbitrage is often associated with risk arbitrage, which has come to mean taking positions in takeover stocks. (*See* **arbitrageur** or **arb**.) 132, 274

arbitrageurs (arbs) 173, 175

Articles of Association. A form of written constitution (technically a contract between the shareholders and the company), required of UK companies. Covers a number of (often standard) items such as borrowing powers, issue of shares, etc. Usually referred to in conjunction with the **Memorandum of Association** which contains information on the company's objects, share capital, etc. (*See also* **Companies House**.)

ASB (*see* **Accounting Standards Board**)

asset 45 *et seq*

asset backing (*see also* **net asset value**) 77-79, 326, 345-347

asset stripping. Gaining control of a company with a view to selling its assets (often properties) at a profit rather than developing the business as such. Very common among take-over practitioners in the early 1970s. 127

asset-backed securities. The result of securitizing various forms of loan. A company which provides loans via credit cards might issue floating rate notes or other forms of security to investors in the securities markets, the interest and capital repayment being provided by the payments from the credit card borrowers. The most common form of asset-backed security in the UK is **mortgage-backed securities** (q.v.).

asset-rich companies 78-80

associated company, associate, related company 52, 82

associates (of companies involved in takeover) 173

at a premium, a discount 78, 204-205, 273, 326, 346

at best 107

at call 245

at the money (of options) 300

auction market preferred stock (AMPS). A form of preference share issued by UK companies or their subsidiaries in the US. Though techically share capital, the preference shares have some of the characteristics of a floating rate debt since the 'dividend' is not fixed but varies with money-market rates.

auctions (in gilt-edged market) 214

audit 36, 41

audit committee. Already common in different forms in various overseas countries, the audit committee is a committee of non-executive directors that acts as a check on various aspects of the financial governance of a company by the executives. The establishment of audit committees was recommended by the **Cadbury Committee** (q.v.).

auditors' fees 41, 50

auditors' report 41

auditors 41

authority to issue shares 90

authorization (for investment business) 353

basket (of currencies) 260
Basle Accord 232
BCCI (*see* **Bank of Credit and Commerce International**)
bear (*see also* **short**) 111 *et seq*, 122
bear covering 122
bear market 112, 116
bear raid 123
bear sale, short sale 111, 122
bear squeeze 122
bearer bond 278
bearer security 109, 278
bearish 112, 299
beat the index 73
bed and breakfast. Stock exchange technique whereby an investor sells particular shares on one day and buys them back the next morning. The purpose is normally to establish a loss for capital gains tax purposes – the investor may have capital profits in that year against which the losses can be offset to reduce tax liability.
below the line 53
benchmark gilt, bond. A government stock whose redemption yield is taken as the yardstick by which redemption yields on company bonds are set at the outset and measured subsequently. There will be a different benchmark gilt for short, medium and long-dated stocks. 223
beneficial owner 109
benefits in kind (for directors) (*see also* **directors' pay and perks**) 189
BES (*see* **Business Expansion Scheme**)
beta. A measure of the volatility of a share. A high beta share is likely to respond to stockmarket movements by rising or falling in value by more than the market average.
bi-lateral facility, credit line. A loan arrangement negotiated by a borrower with a single bank rather than with a syndicate of banks. The borrower could, however, negotiate separate bi-lateral lines with a number of individual banks.
bid (*see* **takeover**)
bid basis (liquidation basis) 342
bid price 103, 112, 343
bid rate 253
bid timetable 173-175
Biffex 303
Big Bang (27 October 1986) 97 *et seq*, 105
Big Board. (*See* **New York Stock Exchange**)
bill of exchange 245, 246 *et seq*
BIMBO (**buy-in management buy-out**) 179
black economy (cash economy). Areas of the economy where transactions go unrecorded (and therefore untaxed). If your local plumber quotes you two prices for a job – one which will include VAT if you want a receipt and a lower one if you pay cash and forego the paperwork – you are almost certainly contributing to the black economy if you pay cash.
Blue Arrow affair. More accurately described as the National Westminster Bank or County NatWest affair. A major scandal which led in July 1989 to the resignation of the chairman of the National Westminster Bank, several senior executives and various employees of County NatWest, its investment banking subsidiary, and of securities house UBS Phillips & Drew. The scandal concerned a £837m rights issue by employment agency group Blue Arrow, and the various stratagems used by its bankers and brokers to disguise the relatively-low take-up of shares by investors.
blue chip 70
board of directors. The men and women legally responsible for

running a company. The structure of the board varies greatly between companies. Directors who are also employees of the company and have management responsibility are **executive directors**. Directors who simply provide experience and advice in board deliberations, are not employees and possibly have jobs elsewhere, are **non-executive directors**. The **chairman** presides at board meetings, but is not necessarily top dog in practice unless he combines his role with that of **chief executive**. The chief executive is responsible for the management of the company as a whole and is often the same person as **managing director**; but some companies have both, with the managing director in the subordinate role (Americans talk of the chief executive as **Chief Executive Officer** or **CEO**). Other directors may be distinguished according to their area of responsibility: **finance director**, etc. Each company also needs a **company secretary**, responsible for administration of the legally required paperwork involved in running the company. He or she may or may not also be a director. You need to know your company to know who really counts among the directors – titles can be misleading.

boardroom pay and perks (*see* **directors' pay and perks**)

boiler room. Room with numerous telephones, usually in overseas country where British regulations cannot be enforced, from which high-pressure salesmen attempt to sell securities direct to the public. Pejorative term. (*See also* **bucket shop**.)

bond (insurance) 344

bond-rating services (Moody's, Standard & Poor's and Fitch IBCA) (*see* **credit rating**)

bond. Form of medium- or long-term 'IOU' issued by companies, governments, etc., usually paying interest and usually traded in a market. May be secured or unsecured. Interest may be fixed rate or floating rate (*see also* **gilt-edged stocks**, **government securities** and **corporate bonds**, **industrial debentures**, **loans**, **floating rate notes**). Bonds in the UK normally have a face value of £100. Fixed-interest bonds pay a fixed rate of interest on the £100 face value. But the yield or return to the investor depends on the price he pays for the bond in the market. A fixed-interest bond paying 5 per cent interest (carrying a 5 per cent **coupon**) gives an income yield of around 5.7 per cent to someone who buys it in the market at a price of £88. But **redemption yields** (q.v.) are the measure used for the total return from bonds. 18-19, 25-26, 83-84, 99, 198-227, 275-287

bondized (insurance) 344

bonus issue (*see* **scrip issue**)

bonuses (directors'). (*See* **directors' pay and perks**)

bonuses (in City). In good years employees in City firms may get very large additions to their salary in the form of bonuses related to the firm's performance.

book (in shares) 20

book value 43, 45

book-keeping transaction 158

bookbuilding. An exercise sometimes undertaken by financial advisers when a new issue or a secondary issue of shares is to be made. They canvas major institutional investors to establish how many shares each would be likely to take at what price. It may assist in establishing the price for the issue and judging its likely success. 142

clearing house. Particularly in a futures market, the body which reconciles sales and purchases, organizes margins and settlement and provides guarantees against default to users of the market.

Clearstream 280

close a position. The buyer of, say, a contract for a ton of metal for May delivery closes (cancels out) his position if he later sells an identical contract. He no longer has an outstanding liability to take delivery or to deliver. If the user of a futures market fails to maintain his margin, he will automatically be **closed out** by the market authorities who will buy or sell contracts on his behalf to close his original position. 295

close-ended 347

cocoa 303

coffee 303

cold calling 355

collar, cylinder. A combination of an interest rate **cap** and an interest rate **floor**, limiting exposure to changing interest rates within a defined range. 251

collateral. Assets pledged as security for a loan.

collateralized mortgage obligations (CMOs) (*see* **mortgage-backed security**)

collectibles (*see* **alternative investments**)

Combined Code (corporate governance) 192

coming to the market (*see also* **new issues**) 138

commercial lawyers 36

commercial paper. A form of short-term IOU issued to investors by a company or other major borrower, usually at a discount to its face value. Britain now has a commercial paper market, which was opened to a wider range of companies in the 1989 Budget. 249-250, 281-282

commercial property (*see* **property**)

commission (stockbroker's, etc.) 102, 103, 215, 360

commission houses 307

commitment fee. Fee paid by a borrower to a lender for arranging a loan or agreeing to hold funds available for a loan.

committed facility 250

commodities 15, 288-309

commodities futures markets 32, 307 *et seq*

common stock (American term for **ordinary shares**) 89, 157

companies (regulation of) 356 *et seq*

companies 38-94

Companies Act 1985 356

Companies Acts 89, 90, 169, 172, 173, 356

Companies House. Name for the Companies Registry where legally required information on public and private companies must be filed with the Registrar of Companies. It is based in Cardiff, but has a building in London and in various other cities. Members of the public can consult the records of any company (in microfiche form) on payment of a fee. Useful source of information for investigation-minded financial journalists and those checking on a company's credit standing. 356

company secretary (*see* **board of directors**)

compensation fund (*see also* **deposit protection**) 355

Competition Commission 172

compliance department, officer. Department or person responsible for preventing improper cross-fertilization between the different businesses grouped in a securities house. The system has been likened to putting a dozen rabbits in a hutch and giving one of them a red flag to wave if the others show signs of breeding. 111

compound interest, simple interest.
The difference between compound interest and simple interest is vital, and most investment calculations will be concerned with compound interest. A compound interest calculation assumes that the interest earned on a sum of money will be added to that sum of money (will be reinvested) when received, so that there is then a larger sum of money to earn interest, and so on. In other words, you are earning interest on interest, and money can build up rapidly this way. A simple interest calculation, on the other hand, assumes that any interest received is taken out and spent, so that the capital sum you end up with is the same as the one you started with. To see the difference, assume that £100 is invested for ten years at an interest rate of 7 per cent. Using a simple interest calculation, the investor will receive ten annual payments of £7, totalling £70, and get back his original £100 after ten years. With a compound interest calculation the investor will get the same £7 of interest in the first year, then in the second year he will get interest of 7 per cent on £107, which is £7.49, and so on. By the end of the ten years the original sum will have grown to £196.72, of which £100 is the original capital and £96.72 is the accumulated interest.

compulsory acquisition 172

computerized systems 105-107, 131-132

concert party 172

conditional (of takeover offer) 171-172

confidentiality clause (in property lease) 330

conflicts of interest 111, 313-314

conglomerate. Diversified and usually large company with a range of different and often unrelated businesses.

consideration. The price paid for something, not necessarily in cash. If Company A issues a million of its shares to Company B to acquire a business from Company B, the shares are the consideration for the purchase.

consolidated balance sheet 43

consolidated profit and loss account 44

consolidating 123

consulting actuaries 36

contango (futures markets) 309

contested takeover 167

contingent liabilities 87

contract (futures, options) 293, 304, 307

contract note (stock exchange) 108

contracts of employment (directors') 190, 193

contractual savings 32, 333-334

contributions holiday (pension fund). A company running a final-salary pensions scheme for its employees may be able to take a holiday for a few years from contributing to the scheme if the scheme has more assets than are currently needed to cover estimated liabilities. This may significantly boost the company's profits in the short run. 338

control of company 40, 166 *et seq*

convergence 264

conversion period 85

conversion premium 85

conversion terms 85

conversion value 85

convertible 83 *et seq*, 225, 281

convertible bond, loan stock 83, 99, 156, 202, 282

convertible capital bond 86

convertible preference 87, 89, 282

copper 307

corporate bonds, loans 99, 202, 221-227

depositors 229

deposits (*see* **retail deposits, wholesale deposits**)

depreciation (amortization) 45, 50, 63, 82

deregulation 10, 276

derivatives. Financial instruments that are a spin-off from the basic products and markets. Thus **options** and **futures** are derivatives, as they are a spin-off from shares, bonds, etc. (*See also* **forward market, forward rate agreement, future, option, cap, floor, swap**) 11, 31, 232, 234 *et seq*, 288-309, 327

Deutsche Börse 96

development finance 35, 179, 181

development of property 36, 324

dilute, diluted, dilution (of earnings, assets, etc.) 86 *et seq*, 93-94

direct shareholdings, ownership of shares 30, 32-33, 102, 333-334

directors' pay and perks 50, 187-197

directors' report 41

directors (*see* **board of directors**)

dirty, managed float 256

disclosure of shareholdings (*see also* **3 per cent rule**, etc.) 172, 356

discount houses 245

discount market 245

discount market deposits 252

discount rate 18, 216-219

discount. Used in many contexts. Stockmarkets discount future events by reacting to them before they happen. To buy or sell securities at a discount is to buy or sell them at a price below some standard measure of value, which depends on the context: their par value; their offer-for-sale price; their net asset value, etc. In this sense it is the opposite of a premium. To discount a financial instrument is to buy it below its face value, earning a return from the capital gain when it is repaid (*see*

bills of exchange). A **discount broker** is a broker offering a cut-price service (*see also* **at a discount**) 20, 78, 120, 204, 246, 273, 336, 346

discretionary. When an investment manager looks after investments for clients on a discretionary basis, the decisions are made at his discretion, not the client's.

discretionary clients of a broker are clients whose investments he manages in this way at his discretion.

disintermediation. Cutting out the middle-man: the intermediary. The person with spare cash, instead of depositing it with a bank, lends it direct to the end-user. 11, 233

distribution. Usually a distribution of income by a company and often used as a synonym for dividend.

diversification. A company diversifies when it extends its activities from its original business or businesses (which it presumably understands) to other business areas (which it may not understand so well). Not always a sure-fire recipe for success (*see also* **conglomerate**)

dividend 13, 26, 47, 51-52, 117, 132-133, 153, 162

dividend cover 62

dividend per share 62, 153

dividend stripping 211

dividend yield 14, 64-65, 153

DMO (*see* **Debt Management Office**)

domestic interest rates (*see also* **interest rates**) 257

dotcom companies 139, 142

double option 299

Dow Jones Industrial Average. Most frequently quoted index of the New York Stock Exchange. Covers thirty stocks, mainly industrial companies. 73

(**EGM**). General meeting of a company at which non-routine proposals are voted on by shareholders. Examples of matters requiring an EGM would be an increase in authorized capital or changes to the company's aims and objects.

extraordinary items (*see also* **exceptional items**) 53

face value. **Nominal** or **par value** of a security, rather than its market value. 25, 89

factoring. A form of off balance sheet finance which can have the same effect as a loan. A factor will undertake to collect debts owing to a company on the company's behalf and meantime make an advance to the company of a proportion of the money it is due to receive.

fan club 173

fees (in eurobond market) 279

fill or kill 107

FIMBRA (*see* **Financial Intermediaries, Managers and Brokers Regulating Association**)

final closing date 174

final dividend 47

final salary scheme (*see also* **pensions**) 338

Finance Bill, Act. The legislation which implements the Budget proposals each year in the UK. The detailed provisions of the Finance Bill are normally debated for some months after the Chancellor has delivered his Budget statement.

finance director (*see* **board of directors**)

finance houses. Quasi-banks, often owned by the major clearing banks. The finance houses specialize in hire purchase and other instalment credit, leasing, debt factoring, etc.

financial advisers, consultants 12, 336

financial assets of individuals 333-334

financial assistance for purchase of own shares 161-162, 173, 356

financial crisis (1973-75) 116, 231

financial engineering. Transforming one type of financial product into a different one to suit the needs of a particular type of borrower, lender or investor. The simplest example is an **interest rate swap** (q.v.) where a borrower may raise, say, fixed interest funds but swap them so that he has the use of floating rate money. 216

financial futures (*see also* **LIFFE**) 32, 201, 294 *et seq*, 303 *et seq*

financial health 43

financial institutions 30, 102, 156, 194, 320, 334

financial instrument. A term covering most forms of short- and long-term investment traded in the money markets or the stockmarket: bank bills, certificates of deposit, shares, bonds, etc. 243 *et seq*

financial intermediaries 33, 336

Financial Intermediaries, Managers and Brokers Regulatory Association (FIMBRA) 353-354

financial public relations 37

financial ratios 56 *et seq*

Financial Reporting Council (FRC) 356

Financial Reporting Review Panel 357

Financial Services Act 101, 352

Financial Services and Markets Bill 352 *et seq*

Financial Services Authority (FSA) 37, 100, 239, 241, 313, 342, 352 *et seq*

Financial Times (*see* **FT**)

financing gap 178

financing proposal (venture capital) 181

firm hands 144

firm, **firmer**. When a market firms it means that prices are moving up rather than down, though the motion described is probably gentle. If interest rates firm they are also moving up rather than down, but in bond markets this means that prices of securities will be moving down. (*See also* **easier**.)

first closing date 174

fiscal year. Year adopted for accounting and tax purposes. In the UK the government's fiscal year runs to 5 April. Companies can choose the year-end they wish, though end-December and end-March are common.

Fitch IBCA (bond rating service) (*see* **credit rating**)

fixed assets 45, 81

fixed charge (on assets) 76

fixed rate (*see also* **variable rate**, **floating rate**) 25, 59

fixed-interest market 99, 201

fixed-interest securities, bonds (*see also* **government bonds**) 19, 24, 198-227, 278-282

fixed-price offer (stockmarket) 141

fixed-price offer (unit trust) 342

flat rate. Rate of interest, expressed in a way that often disguises the true interest rate (*see* **annual percentage rate**)

flat yield (*see* **income yield**)

float 138

floating charge 76

floating exchange rates 255-256

floating rate of interest (*see also* **variable rate, fixed rate**) 25, 59

floating-rate bonds, notes (FRNs) 225, 253, 281

floor (interest rate) 251, 281

flotation (*see* **new issue**)

flowback 154

Footsie Index (*see* **FTSE 100 Index**)

forecast (prospectus) (*see also*

forecast profit, forecast dividend) 141

forecast dividend 67, 141

forecast profit 141

foreign banks 34

foreign exchange 15, 22, 31, 32, 125, 255-274

foreign exchange brokers 273

foreign exchange reserves 256, 260

foreign income dividend. Companies with much of their earnings from abroad and therefore an **unrelieved ACT** (q.v.) problem in the UK used to be able to reduce their overall tax liability by paying a dividend out of their foreign earnings which had not borne UK tax. They did not have to pay (or could reclaim) the **Advance Corporation Tax** (q.v.) on the **foreign income dividend**. Correspondingly, the shareholder who received the foreign income dividend did not receive any tax credit.

foreign investors 102

forex (*see* **foreign exchange**)

formal documents (in bid) 173

forward exchange rate 272-273

forward market 272-273, 290 *et seq*, 308

forward rate agreement (FRA). A form of interest rate hedge which allows a prospective borrower to fix the cost of money he knows he will need to borrow in, say, three months' time. He is thus protected from adverse interest rate movements in the interim, which could otherwise have made the money more expensive when he needed it.

FRA (*see* **forward rate agreement**)

Fraud Squad. Usually refers to an overworked branch of the City of London police specializing in the investigation of suspected fraud (*see also* **Serious Fraud Office**). 361

go-go fund. A fund which invests in special situations and highly speculative stocks and probably deals very actively in its investments.

going concern basis. The basis on which accounts of a company are normally produced and audited. It assumes the company is viable and is continuing in business. Lower values would normally be put on a company's assets if accounts were produced instead on the assumption the company was going to be broken up (**liquidation** or **break-up** basis). If an auditor feels obliged to point out that he has approved the accounts on a going concern basis, it normally means there is some doubt as to whether the company is, in fact, viable.

gold. Is bought as an investment particularly at times of financial uncertainty. The London Gold Market was traditionally operated by five merchant banks and bullion dealers who twice a day 'fix' a gold price in the light of supply and demand for the metal; but dealing has now been opened up to a wider range of marketmakers.

golden hallo. Lump-sum payment to persuade someone to join your staff, particularly in the investment world.

golden handcuffs. Arrangements to lock employee into his job, with guaranteed bonuses if he stays a certain period, etc.

golden handshake. Lump sum payment made to compensate sacked or redundant employee for loss of office. The more exhorbitant payments normally apply in the case of company directors, who generally 'resign' rather than being dismissed. 167, 190

golden parachute. Arrangements made in advance by directors of a company to provide themselves with a happy financial landing if ousted in the course of a takeover, etc. Would include long service contracts with big in-built payments on loss of office, etc.

government bonds (*see also* **gilt-edged securities**) 13, 15, 19, 24, 27, 198-220

government borrowing (*see* **PSBR, PSDR**)

government guarantee (Loan Guarantee Scheme) 185

government securities (*see* **gilt-edged securities**)

gross fund. An investment fund such as a pension fund which is not liable to tax and may therefore enjoy its income gross (untaxed).

gross up, grossed up. Grossing up is the process of calculating the gross (pre-tax) equivalent of a given net (after tax) return. For example, a dividend received by an individual is deemed to have had basic rate tax already paid. So, for a basic rate taxpayer, a 10p dividend is worth 12.82p of income from another source, on which 22 per cent tax would have to be paid. This is because 12.82p is (roughly) the pre-tax figure that would provide 10p after 22 per cent income tax. So – for a basic rate taxpayer – 12.82p could be described as the grossed-up equivalent of 10p net.

gross. Normally used in the sense of 'before tax' or 'before deductions'. 50-51, 74, 207, 208

ground rent 323

group balance sheet (*see* **consolidated balance sheet**)

Group of Five, Seven, Eight (G5, G7, G8) 262

growth by acquisition (*see* **external growth**)

growth prospects 142

guarantee 88, 185, 232

Guinness affair 176-177, 356

half-year 40

hammered (of broker) 358

Hampel Committee 192

Hang Seng index. The most commonly quoted index of share prices in the volatile Hongkong stockmarket.

head company (*see* **parent company**)

headline earnings 54

health warning 342

heavily-stagged 147

heavy (of share price) 158

hedge (*see* **management of risk**)

hedge funds. Very inappropriately-named investment vehicles: they rarely have anything to do with hedging. They are international funds, subscribed to by wealthy individuals and usually run by go-go managers, which attempt to achieve above-average returns by betting heavily on currencies and special situations in any of the world's markets. They frequently gear-up their bets with borrowed money, and can be a very destabilising influence in the internatonal markets, particularly in currencies. The near collapse in 1998 of the Long Term Capital Management (LTCM) hedge fund in the United States contributed to the severe but temporary stockmarket setback of that year. 271

high income fund 344

high income gearing 60

high PE ratio 66

high yield, yielding 65

high-tech. A 'high-tech business' should describe a company operating at the frontiers of technology – and sometimes does. Many more mundane businesses try to acquire a high-tech label in the hope of a improvement in their share ratings; this can misfire, as the stockmarket is weak on understanding of technology and when one high-tech company gets into trouble, all those with the same label may see their share prices suffer.

highly geared 49, 146, 229, 298

highs and lows. Prices of securities quoted in the newspapers, showing the highest and lowest prices reached, probably over the past year. These highs and lows will have been adjusted for scrip issues, etc. 72

historical cost convention 54

historical cost profits (*see* **note of historical cost profits and losses**)

historical dividend 66-67

historical dividend yield 67

historical PE ratio 67

holding company 43

hostile (of takeover) 163, 167

housing (value of) 6, 8

hybrid financial instruments. Financial instruments which are a cross between two or more traditional instruments. The most common example is the convertible loan, which starts life as a bond but probably turns into share capital at a later date.

IFA (*see* **Independent Financial Adviser**)

imputation tax system 51

IMRO (*see* **Investment Management Regulatory Organization**)

in arrears 88

in the money (of option) 300, 307

incentives (for directors) (*see* **directors' pay and perks**)

income 13

income gearing 57-59, 74

income shares 347

Income Tax (*see also* **tax shelters**) 2, 51, 207-208

income units 343

income yield (**running yield**) 204, 205 *et seq*

independent financial adviser (**IFA**) 33, 336

index-linked stocks 212 *et seq*

indexation. Adjusting in line with an index. Usually the index is the Retail Prices Index (RPI): the most commonly used measure of inflation. The UK government issues index-linked bonds and there are index-linked forms of National Savings (Granny Bonds). An indexed share portfolio (tracker fund) is one which seeks to match as closely as possible the composition and performance of a particular stockmarket index.

indexed portfolios, funds 73, 344

indices (currencies) 258-260

indices (property) 328

indices (stockmarket) (*see also* **FT**) 69 *et seq*

individual savings account (**ISA**) 33, 332, 333, 348 *et seq*

inducement (to sign a property lease)

330

industrial debentures (*see also* **corporate bonds**) 25, 202

industrial logic 174

industrial property 328

inflation (*see also* **indexation, RPI**) 7, 13, 16, 200, 261, 269-270

inflation accounting 54

inflation hedge 212

initial public offering, IPO. An international term for a stockmarket launch, now coming into more common UK use. 138-148

insider dealing, trading 172, 175, 356

insolvency. A business can go bust in two main ways: by running out of cash to pay its bills and other obligations or by having more liabilities than assets (owing more than it owns). 'Insolvent' is sometimes used to cover both cases. It is an offence for a company to trade while insolvent.

institutions (*see* **financial institutions**)

insurance (*see also* **Lloyd's of London**) 290, 310-319

insurance brokers 33, 336

insurance companies 30, 32, 165, 311, 320, 357

Insurance Companies Act 357

insurance company market 32, 311

insurance cycle 311

insurances (prices in *FT*) 340, 344

insured scheme (pensions) 32, 337

intangible assets 45, 81

Integrated Exchanges (**iX**) 8, 96-97

inter-bank deposits 252

inter-bank market 245, 248-249, 278

inter-bank rates 252

inter-dealer brokers 215

interest (in profit and loss account) 50

interest cover 58

interest rate differential 272

management advisory services 36

management buy-out, buy-in 35, 88, 176, 178 *et seq*

management of risk (*see also* **forward market, futures, forward rate agreements, options, caps, floors, swaps**) 31, 251, 272-273, 288 *et seq*, 301

managing agent (Lloyd's) 312

mandatory bid, offer 171 *et seq*

margin. In some markets, particularly futures markets, clients are only required to put up a proportion of the cost of what they buy: a form of deposit known as margin. But this margin will have to be topped up if it is eroded by adverse price movements. A **margin call** is the notice that the margin needs topping up, otherwise the investor will be **closed out**. 289, 294, 295

margin (interest rate). Margin in this sense is much the same as **spread**. If a **floating rate note** pays interest at 50 basis points over LIBOR, the 50 basis points is the **margin** over LIBOR.

margin trading. Buying shares or other securities without putting up the full price at the time; i.e. effectively speculating partly with borrowed money.

marginal. Frequently used in the sense 'marginal tax rate'. In the UK a high-earning individual would (in the 2000–01 financial year) have paid 10 per cent income tax on a very small first slice of his taxable income, 22 per cent on the next slice and 40 per cent on the top slice. Under the progressive tax system this means he will also pay the top 40 per cent rate on any margin of additional income he earns, and 40 per cent is therefore his marginal rate.

market (*see also* **stockmarket, futures market**, etc.) 15 *et seq*, 18-23, 26-28

market capitalization. Used of stockmarkets and of individual companies. The capitalization of the London equity market is the total market value of all the ordinary shares of all the companies listed on the market (usually excluding foreign-registered companies). The market capitalization (strictly, equity market capitalization) of Joe Bloggs Plc is the stockmarket value of all its ordinary shares: the number of shares in issue multiplied by the market price. If Bloggs has 10m share in issue and the price is 200p, Bloggs is capitalized at £20m. 68, 99

market price mechanism 19 *et seq*

market professionals 163

market purchases 169

market sentiment (*see* **sentiment**)

marketable 158, 243

marketable securities. Covers most forms of security that can be bought and sold in a market: bonds, shares, certificates of deposit, etc.

marketed (of securities) 36

marketmaker 20, 35, 97, 98, 103, 104, 122, 215, 233

matched bargain basis 101

maturity 198, 203

maxi ISA 348

Maxwell, Robert 359

medium- or long-term debt 47

medium-dated stocks 203 *et seq*

medium-term note (**MTN**) 250

mediums (gilt-edged) (*see* **medium-dated stocks**)

members' agent (Lloyd's) 312

members (of a company) (*see* **shareholders**)

Memorandum of Association (*see* **Articles of Association**)

merchant banks (*see also* **investment banks**) 34

merchant developer 326

closely modelled on it. NASDAQ also stands for the market that uses this system. It is now merged with the American Stock Exchange. 96, 97

natural gas 309

NatWest Bank (*see* **Blue Arrow affair**)

NAV (*see* **net asset value per share**)

nearby, nearest month, furthest month. If we are now in January and contracts in a futures market are actively traded for delivery dates in February, April, June, August and October, then the nearest month is February and the furthest is October.

negative (inverse) yield curve. Interest rates for deposits or securities of different maturity – three months, six months, a year, five years, ten years, etc. – can be plotted on a graph. When short-term interest rates are higher than longer-term ones, this line will start high and curve downwards. This is a negative or inverse yield curve. (*See also* **yield curve**.) 252

negative equity (*see also* **equity**). You have negative equity if the loans you took out to buy your home exceed the value of the home.

negotiated commissions. Have replaced the former fixed minimum commission structure for deals in securities on the stock exchange in Britain. Large institutional investors (or those who operate through brokers rather than buying at net prices) are free to negotiate the level of commission they will pay, which dropped sharply for large trades since Big Bang. Small private investors, however, have little bargaining power though have benefited from the emergence of **execution-only brokers** (q.v.). 103

net. Usually means 'after tax' or 'after expenses or other deductions' (*see also* **gross**).

net asset value (**NAV**) 48, 77-79, 93, 161, 326, 346

net borrowings 74

net cash inflow, outflow 63

net current assets (and **liabilities**) 47

net prices 106, 215

net profit, net profit available for ordinary shareholders 51, 52, 53, 60 *et seq*

net return 208

net tangible asset value 82, 93

new issues 138-148, 180, 213 *et seq*, 279

New York Stock Exchange (**NYSE**). The main stock exchange in the US, on which America's major corporations are listed. Also referred to as the 'Big Board', or 'Wall Street' where it is located. 96

nickel 307

NIF (*see* **note issuance facility**)

Nikkei 225 Average 73

nil paid 152

no par value 89

nominal value (face value, par value) 25, 26, 64, 89, 203

nominated adviser 141

nominee (name, company). Shares can be held for convenience (or, often, for secrecy) under the name of a nominee rather than that of the beneficial owner. Thus Fastbuck Nominees might hold shares on behalf of a number of the clients of Fastbuck Finance. UK companies have powers to require the identity of beneficial owners of shares held in nominee names, but the powers are of little use when the nominee is a secrecy-pledged Swiss bank. (*See also* **section 212**.) 109, 172, 356, 359

nominee account (in CREST) 109

non-bank private sector 244

non-equity capital An accounts heading for share capital that is not ordinary shares. In practice, covers

partnership finance (for property) 325

pass (a dividend) 62

pathfinder prospectus 145

pay and perks (*see* **directors' pay and perks**)

PE ratio (*see* **price-earnings ratio**)

peaks 116

penny stocks. Shares quoted in the market at prices of a few pence only – it used to be less than 10p, but the criteria have widened. The idea is that they should be a good speculation because they usually reflect companies that are down on their luck. The company could go bust, but if somebody gets a grip on it and improves its performance, the shares could rise many times in value. However, nowadays most penny stocks are ramped well above their likely worth in the hope of something of this kind happening. They may not be a bargain.

pension fund performance 36

pension funds (*see also* **occupational pension schemes**) 11, 30, 36, 51, 165, 320

pensions (for directors) (*see also* **directors' pay and perks**) 189

pensions. Pensions offered by employers (**occupational pension schemes**) are of two main types: those that offer a pension geared to final salary (**final salary schemes, defined contribution schemes**) and those where the pension is related solely to the amount of money that has been contributed (**money purchase** or **defined contribution** schemes). 332, 337-339

PEP (*see* **personal equity plan**)

percentages, percentage points. A fertile ground for confusion. If Payola Properties raises a loan at 10 per cent and Fastbuck Finance raises one at 12 per cent, Fastbuck is paying two **percentage points** more

for its money (the difference between 10 and 12). But Fastbuck is equally paying 20 **per cent** more for its money than Payola (because 12 is 20 per cent higher than 10). Writers often confuse the two measures. Usually the context makes the meaning clear, but one or two monumental misunderstandings have resulted. (*See also* **basis points**.) 27, 253

performance (of shares, etc.) 121, 345

performance criteria (for incentive schemes) (*see also* **directors' pay and perks**) 189, 191

performance funds. Funds which aim for above-average capital growth, usually at the expense of income and by accepting higher risks. The fund may also switch actively between investments.

permanent capital 44

permanent interest-bearing shares (**PIBS**). Effectively, a form of subordinated debt issued by building societies which they can count towards their capital for capital adequacy calculations. The need arises because mutual institutions do not have the option of raising equity finance in the stockmarket.

perpetual floating rate notes, perpetuals 281

Personal Equity Plan (**PEP**) 33, 333, 348

personal finance 332-350

personal guarantees 39

Personal Investment Authority (**PIA**) 353

personal loans 24

personal member (of CREST) 110

personal portable pensions (*see also* **mis-selling of personal pensions**) 338, 339

personal sector financial assets 333-334

prospectus forecast 142

prospectus, mini prospectus 36, 140, 142

provision (for bad debts, etc) 236

provisions (for liabilities and charges) 87, 165

proxy. A shareholder entitled to vote at the general meeting of a company may appoint a proxy to vote on his behalf. Directors of the company will act as proxies, or the shareholder could appoint a friend. Before the meeting the shareholder receives a **proxy card** which he may fill in and sign, nominating his proxy and indicating which way he wants his votes cast on the different resolutions.

prudential ratios (for banks) 232

PSBR (*see* **public sector borrowing requirement**)

PSDR (*see* **public sector debt repayment**)

public company. Public limited company, with 'plc' after its name. A company whose securities are (or may be) traded in a market or which invites the public to subscribe for its securities must be a plc. (*See also* **private company**.) 39–40

public offering of stock (gilt-edged) 214

public relations (*see* **financial public relations**)

public sector borrowing requirement (PSBR) 198

public sector debt repayment (PSDR). Describes the position when the government's income exceeds its expenditure, and it is able to repay existing debt rather than borrowing more. 198

public-to-private deal 175, 176, 179, 182

puff (a share). Over-promote the merits of a share, probably in a broker's circular or a press recommendation.

pull to redemption 208 *et seq*

purchasing power (*see* **inflation**)

purchasing power parity 260

pushing (of shares). Over-promoting a particular share to investors. (*See also* **ramp**, **puff** and **bucket shop**.)

put option 86, 281, 299

qualifications (auditors') 41

quarterlies. Quarterly results and dividend declarations produced by American listed companies. 40

quotation. Price quoted for a security, etc., comprising a bid and offer price.

quote (listing) 138

quote-driven 106

quoted, traded (company, share, etc.) 101

rack rent 323

ramp (a share). Over-promote a share to get the price up.

rank (for dividend) 89

ratchet 180

rating (in stockmarket) (*see also* **credit rating**) 67 *et seq*, 117 *et seq*, 142

rating agencies (*see* **credit rating**)

re-rated 117–118

re-rated downwards 117–118

readily saleable assets 79

real. The word 'real' in an investment context normally means 'adjusted for inflation'. If your money is earning 10 per cent interest in a year when prices rise by 4 per cent, your **real return** is around 6 per cent.

real estate (*see* **property**)

real rate of return (*see also* **indexation**, **real**) 200–201, 212–213, 242

real value 212

receiver. A receiver is put into a company to recover a specific debt or specific debts on which the company has defaulted (or sometimes comes in effectively at the request of the directors when they know the company is in trouble and likely to default). His job is to sell assets as necessary to recover the debt or debts. Occasionally he may be able to do this without its resulting in the company's closing down, in which case the company can revert to normal trading after his departure. But generally the appointment of a receiver is the beginning of the end and the company is eventually wound up.

resolutions covering the more routine matters require a simple majority to succeed. **Special resolutions**, required to alter a company's **articles of association** (q.v.), require 75 per cent of the votes cast to be in favour. This can be important in a takeover. If shareholders representing more than 25 per cent of the votes refuse to accept the offer, the bidder may gain control but will have difficulty in restructuring the victim company if non-accepting shareholders vote against proposals requiring a special resolution.

when the company being taken over will effectively be the dominant force in the combined group.

more politically sensitive fraud cases. 360

service (a debt). Meet the interest payments and capital repayment schedule of a loan. 86, 236

SETS (*see* **Stock Exchange Electronic Trading Service**)

settlement day 108

settlement. The process of clearing the paperwork that follows the purchase or sale of stocks and shares. In the past the client had to pay or be paid, had to deliver or receive share certificates, and purchases and sales had to be reconciled between the different marketmakers and brokers. These are **back office** operations and high share dealing volumes used to bring logjams. The introduction of the **CREST** (q.v.) electronic settlement system speeds up the settlement process and makes it cheaper. 8, 108 *et seq*, 215

SFO (*see* **Serious Fraud Office**)

shakeout 123

share (*see* **equity**, **ordinary shares**, **preference shares**, etc.)

share capital 88

share certificate 109

share exchange offer 168

share ownership, share-owning democracy 33, 102-103, 332-334

share premium account 92

share prices (in newspapers) 66 *et seq*

shareholders' funds 48, 74, 88, 157-158, 229

shareholders' interest (*see* **shareholders' funds**)

shareholders' rights 40-42, 90, 166-167, 194

shareholders 26, 39

shares (ownership of) (*see* **direct shareholdings**)

shelf registration. Process of registering and gaining approval for

the details of a security (a bond, say) in advance, so that issues may be made rapidly when later required.

shell company. A company, normally with a Stock Exchange quotation, which is now relatively inactive and has little by way of earnings or assets. Former plantation companies, whose estates in the Far East have now been nationalized, are a prime example. An entrepreneur with a vigorous private company will sometimes gain control of a shell company and inject his private business into it, thus gaining a ready-made stockmarket vehicle. This process is described as a **shell operation**.

shop property 328

short (of stocks, etc.) 111, 122

short end of the market (gilt-edged) 210

short sale, bear sale 111-112, 122-126

short sellers, selling 122

short-term borrowings 50

short-term interest rates 16

short-termism 165

shortage (in banking system) 246

shorts, short-dated (of gilt-edged) 203 *et seq*

SIB (*see* **Securities and Investments Board**)

side-by-side finance (for property) 325

simple interest (*see* **compound interest, simple interest**)

single asset property company (**SAPCO**) 327

single capacity 103

single property ownership trust (**SPOT**) 327

sinking fund. A form of reserve in a company's accounts, to which it allocates sums to cover the eventual repayment of a loan or the eventual expiry of a lease. (*See also* **wasting asset**.)

smaller companies fund 344

soft commissions. Commissions for financial services paid in kind rather than in cash. Before the Big Bang, brokers who derived large commissions from institutional clients under the fixed commission structure often gave part of the money back by providing customized research or paying for screen information systems for the use of the client. The competitive system following the Big Bang was meant to eliminate soft commissions.

soft commodities 303, 307

soft loan. A loan on terms more favourable than those applying to a normal commercial borrowing. Sometimes used to assist worthy projects – business start-ups in areas of high unemployment, etc.

sole trader 40

solicitors (*see also* **commercial lawyers**) 33

solvency ratio (of banks) 232

solvency. Being in a state to meet your obligations and pay your bills. (*see also* **insolvency**.)

sources of money, finance 44, 83

special dividend 162

Special Drawing Rights (SDRs). A form of artificial money created by the International Monetary Fund. Countries may hold part of their official reserves in the form of SDRs which can therefore be used for payments between countries – in this sense they can be a substitute for gold. 260

special resolution (*see* **resolution**)

special situation. Usually used to describe a company whose shares could rise sharply if a particular set of circumstances comes to fruition. Sometimes used of potential takeover stocks but more commonly of **recovery situations** – companies which have been in trouble but whose shares could rise sharply in value if management succeeds in turning the company round. Some funds specialize in investing in special situations.

specialist mortgage lenders. Mortgage providers for house purchase, who recoup the money they advance by floating **mortgage-backed securities** (q.v.) in the securities markets. 282

speculators. The old distinction between long-term investors and speculators has largely broken down. Many investors are speculators up to a point. Speculation normally implies taking above-average risk and often suggests short-term investment decisions. Though frequently maligned, speculators provide a useful service in most markets by taking advantage of any short-term anomalies in prices and thus preventing prices from getting out of line with each other. They may be less beneficial when they completely supplant genuine investors in a market. (*See also* **arbitrage**.) 288, 301

split (share split). If a share price becomes too **heavy**, the shares may be split. Instead of having one 20p share standing in the market at 900p, the investor ends up with, say, two 10p shares worth 450p each. The effect may be similar to that of a scrip issue, but the technicalities differ. In the case of a share split, the par value is reduced, and no capitalization of reserves is involved.

split-level trust 347

sponsors (to an issue) 141

SPOT (*see* **Single Property Ownership Trust**)

supervisory systems 8, 37, 313, 351-362

support (for currency) 255-256

support (for share price) 168, 173

surplus (pension fund) 338

surplus over book values 92

surrender values (insurance policies) 337

surveyors and estate agents (*see* **chartered surveyors**)

swap (interest rate or currency) (*see also* **equity-for-debt swap**) 77, 234, 251, 273, 285

switching 198

syndicate (at Lloyd's) 311 *et seq*

syndicated (venture capital finance) 180

syndicated loans 233, 278, 326

syndicates (of banks) 233, 278

systemic risk 228

take-out (for financier) 180

takeover 10, 126-127, 163-177

takeover activity 164 *et seq*

Takeover Code 169 *et seq*

Takeover Panel 169 *et seq*, 358

Talisman 109

tangible assets 45, 93-94

tap stock 214

TAURUS A vastly expensive attempt at an electronic settlement system by the London Stock Exchange. It never saw the light of day and was supplanted by the CREST system – which worked! (*See also* **CREST**, **settlement**.)

tax (*see also* **Capital Gains Tax**, **Corporation Tax**, **Income Tax**) 2, 36, 207-208, 333, 348-349

tax avoidance, evasion. Tax avoidance normally covers the lawful methods of minimizing tax liability. Tax evasion describes the unlawful methods.

tax credit 51, 62

Tax Exempt Special Savings Account (TESSA) 333, 348

tax haven. A country or area with low rates of tax where companies may register or individuals may hold their investments to minimize tax liabilities. The Bahamas, Cayman Islands and, up to a point, the Channel Islands are examples.

tax payable 47

tax shelter. A framework in which assets can be held to minimize tax liabilities. (*See also* **ISA**, **PEP**, **TESSA**). **Individual Savings Accounts** or **ISAs** provide a tax shelter for the investments held within them. 335

techMARK 7, 101, 138

technical correction 123

technical factors, analysis 120, 123, 201

technology stocks 344

telephone banking 233

tender (Treasury bills) 248

tender offer 141, 142 *et seq*, 214

tender panel 250

term insurance 336

term loan 44, 48

TESSA (*see* **Tax Exempt Special Savings Account**)

Third Market 101

Third World debt 235

tick (in financial futures) 304

tiger economies 4, 135

time value (of money) 18

time value (of option) 299

times earnings (*see also* **price-earnings ratio**) 66

tin 307

tip (a share) 5, 38, 120, 366

tip sheets 366

Tokyo Stock Exchange 96

tombstone advertisements 286

top slice (property income) 324

total assets less current liabilities 47

unrelieved ACT. The **advance corporation tax (ACT)** that companies used to pay to the Inland Revenue in respect of dividends was really a form of basic-rate income tax they deducted on behalf of the shareholder. It was called **advance corporation tax** because companies could offset the amount deducted against the corporation tax they were due to pay on their UK income. Companies with a high proportion of earnings from abroad might not have paid enough UK corporation tax to be able to offset the whole of the ACT against it. The amount that could not be offset was known as **unrelieved ACT**. Companies in this position were effectively being taxed twice on part of their income. ACT has now been abolished. (*See also* **foreign income dividend**.)

unsecured creditors 76

unsecured loan stock 83, 224

upside potential. Scope for rising in value. 'The shares have upside potential' means they stand a good chance of rising. Opposite of **downside potential** (q.v.).

upward re-rating 118

upwards only (rent review clause in property lease) 330

Urgent Issues Task Force (UITF) 192, 357

US GAAP. Generally accepted accounting principles in the United States. Some multi-national UK companies will produce abbreviated accounts prepared according to US principles in addition to their UK accounts.

USM (*see* **Unlisted Securities Market**)

valuations (of property) 36, 322-324

value of the pound 23, 24, 256, 259-260, 268-272

variable rate (*see also* **floating rate**) 25, 59

variable rate notes (**VRNs**). This term has come to describe a particular form of floating rate note where the interest rate will float in line with movements in LIBOR in the normal way, but also the margin over LIBOR paid on the notes will be reset at intervals.

vendor placing 150, 155

venture capital 35, 178-186

venture capital trust 184

venture capital funds 179 *et seq*

volatility (*see* **beta**)

volumes (share dealing) (*see* **turnover of shares**)

votes, voting structure 40, 166 *et seq*

voucher (tax) 51

Wall Street 96, 126, 128 *et seq*

wallpaper 168

War Loan 202

warehousing (of shares) 172

warrant 91, 99, 152, 281

wasting asset. Asset with a finite life whose value erodes with the passage of time. An option is a wasting asset in the sense that it becomes valueless on its expiry date if it is not exercised. Commonly used of short leases in the property world. The buyer of a five-year lease on a building needs to **amortize** (depreciate) the cost of his investment by setting aside each year enough money to have written off the cost of the lease by the end of the fifth year.

wealth of individuals 333-334

weight of money 125

white knight 167

whizz kid. Most frequently used of financially hyper-active entrepreneur who attempts to build a financial empire by frequent takeovers on the stock exchange. May also be used of particularly bright sparks in their chosen line of investment or business management.

whole life assurance 337

wholesale funds, deposits 31, 229, 233, 244